Punishing the Other

Punishing the Other draws on the work of Zygmunt Bauman to discuss contemporary discourses and practices of punishment and criminalization. Bringing together some of the most exciting international scholars, both established and emerging, this book engages with Bauman's thesis of the social production of immorality in the context of criminalization and social control, and addresses processes of 'othering' through a range of contemporary case studies situated in various cultural, political and social contexts.

Topics covered include the increasing bureaucratization of the business of punishment with the corresponding loss of moral and ethical reflection in the public sphere; punitive discourses around border control and immigration; and exclusionary discourses and their consequences concerning 'terrorists' and other socially and culturally defined outsiders.

Engaging with national and global issues that are more topical now than ever before, this book is essential reading for academics and students involved in the study of the sociology of punishment, punishment and modern society, the criminal justice system, philosophy and punishment, and comparative criminology and penology.

Anna Eriksson is a criminologist and penologist based at Monash University, Australia. In 2012, she received funding from the Australian Research Council for a three-year research fellowship on the topic of comparative penology, and this book is the first major publication to result from that project. She is also involved in other research projects, concerning children of prisoners, people with acquired brain injuries in the criminal justice system, preparation for release and parole, and restorative justice. Her latest book (with John Pratt), *Contrasts in Punishment: An Explanation of Anglophone Excess and Nordic Exceptionalism*, was published by Routledge in 2013. She has been a visiting academic at King's College London, UK; Örebro University, Sweden; and Oxford University, UK. Eriksson is a member of the advisory board of the Palgrave Studies in Prisons and Penology, and is the Director of the Imprisonment Observatory: http://art sonline.monash.edu.au/imprisonmentobservatory.

'Provocative and most thought-provoking, with Zygmunt Bauman as their point of departure, the concepts of morality and immorality are taken to task in this string of scholarly contributions by a wide array of international scholars. A must-read for everyone interested in and concerned about immorality of our time.'

Thomas Mathiesen, Professor Emeritus of Sociology of Law,
University of Oslo, Norway

'This important volume takes Zygmunt Bauman's classic *Modernity and the Holocaust* as its starting point, and innovatively applies it – by no means always uncritically – to the study of punishment and practices of exclusion. The authors, who include both established and emerging scholars, address a range of key topics such as imprisonment, immigration detention, the social control of sex offenders, Roma and indigenous populations. Anyone interested in the sociology of contemporary social control will learn much from this fine collection of essays.'

Anthony Bottoms, Emeritus Wolfson Professor of Criminology,
Cambridge University, UK

Punishing the Other

The social production of immorality revisited

Edited by
Anna Eriksson

LONDON AND NEW YORK

First published 2016
by Routledge
2 Park Square, Milton Park, Abingdon, Oxon OX14 4RN

and by Routledge
711 Third Avenue, New York, NY 10017

Routledge is an imprint of the Taylor & Francis Group, an informa business

© 2016 selection and editorial material, Anna Eriksson; individual chapters, the contributors

The right of Anna Eriksson to be identified as the editor of this work has been asserted by her in accordance with sections 77 and 78 of the Copyright, Designs and Patents Act 1988.

All rights reserved. No part of this book may be reprinted or reproduced or utilised in any form or by any electronic, mechanical, or other means, now known or hereafter invented, including photocopying and recording, or in any information storage or retrieval system, without permission in writing from the publishers.

Trademark notice: Product or corporate names may be trademarks or registered trademarks, and are used only for identification and explanation without intent to infringe.

British Library Cataloguing in Publication Data
A catalogue record for this book is available from the British Library

Library of Congress Cataloging in Publication Data
Punishing the other : the social production of immorality revisited / edited by Anna Eriksson.
pages cm. -- (Routledge frontiers of criminal justice ; 29)
1. Punishment--Moral and ethical aspects. 2. Criminology.
I. Eriksson, Anna.
HV8693.P825 2015
174'.93646--dc23
2015008569

ISBN: 978-1-138-77694-4 (hbk)
ISBN: 978-1-315-77291-2 (ebk)

Typeset in Times New Roman
by Taylor & Francis Books

To my father, who was so excited about this book.
Dad, I miss you every day and wish you could have seen it completed

Contents

List of figures	ix
List of contributors	x
Acknowledgements	xv
Abbreviations	xvi

	Introduction	1
	ANNA ERIKSSON	
1	Dehumanization, social contact and techniques of Othering: combining the lessons from Holocaust studies and prison research	11
	PETER SCHARFF SMITH	
2	The legal civilizing process: dignity and the protection of human rights in advanced bureaucratic democracies	30
	JONATHAN SIMON	
3	The rehumanization of the incarcerated Other: bureaucracy, distantiation and American mass incarceration	51
	DAVID A. GREEN	
4	Prisons and the social production of immorality	77
	ANNA ERIKSSON	
5	Swedish 'prison exceptionalism' in decline: trends towards distantiation and objectification of the Other	101
	ANDERS BRUHN, PER-ÅKE NYLANDER AND ODD LINDBERG	
6	Doing away with decency?: foreigners, punishment and the liberal state	124
	ANA ALIVERTI	

viii *Contents*

7 Immigration detention, ambivalence and the colonial Other   145
   MARY BOSWORTH

8 Controlling Roma in Norway: governing through the
   administration of social distance   165
   NICOLAY B. JOHANSEN

9 On Bauman's moral duty: population registries, REVA and
   eviction from the Nordic realm   184
   VANESSA BARKER

10 Immobilization in the age of mobility: sex offenders, security and
    the regulation of risk   208
    JOHN PRATT

11 From terra nullius to terra liquidus?: liquid modernity and the
    Indigenous Other   230
    HARRY BLAGG

12 Symbiotic Othering: terrorism, emotion and morality   247
    DEBRA A. SMITH

   Index   270

Figure

7.1 UK Immigration removal centres, June 2015   147

Contributors

Ana Aliverti is Assistant Professor at Warwick Law School, University of Warwick, UK. She holds a D.Phil. in Law (Oxford, 2011), an MSc in Criminology and Criminal Justice (Distinction, Oxford, 2008), an MA in Sociology of Law (IISL, 2005) and a BA in Law (Honours, Buenos Aires, 2002). Before joining Warwick, she was the Oxford Howard League Post-Doctoral Research Fellow (2012–2013) at the Centre for Criminology, University of Oxford, UK. Her work examines the intersections of immigration and criminal law regulation in Britain, in particular the functioning of criminal law in the policing of non-citizens. Her book *Crimes of Mobility* (Routledge, 2013), an empirical and theoretical examination of immigration crimes, was co-awarded the 2014 British Society of Criminology Book Prize. She is currently conducting a project on criminal courts, funded by the British Academy, with the aim of assessing the influence of citizenship and immigration status in criminal justice decision-making.

Vanessa Barker is Docent and Associate Professor of Sociology at Stockholm University, Sweden. She has published recent work on democracy and deportation, border control and ethnicity, and the welfare state and comparative penal sanctioning. In the US, she works on questions about the prison and the public sphere and is the author of *The Politics of Imprisonment* (Oxford University Press, 2009). In Europe, she is currently working on a comparative project on global mobility and penal order. She is a member of the editorial boards for *Theoretical Criminology* and the *Law & Society Review*, and is the European-based book review editor of *Punishment & Society*.

Harry Blagg is Professor of Criminology and Associate Dean (Research) in the Law School, University of Western Australia. He has worked both in the UK and Australia. His Australian work has mainly focused on issues related to the over-representation of Aboriginal people in the criminal justice system and the general problematic of postcolonial relations mediated through law, policing and criminal justice practices. Recent theoretical work has focused on the problem of inter-culturality and hybridity, in Europe as well as the antipodes, while recent research has included field work in outback Australia on conflict between the settler state and the Indigenous domain over issues of policing and governance (with Thalia Anthony, University of Technology, Sydney, Australia). Harry has published numerous articles in peer-reviewed journals and produced a steady stream of research reports from competitive grants, consultancies and commissions. His 2008 book, *Crime, Aboriginality and the Decolonisation of Justice* (Hawkins Press), has been described by a reviewer as 'a unique book that fills a yawning gap in Australian criminal justice literature'; another describes it as 'suffused with a depth of understanding and respect that should make it a landmark publication'.

Mary Bosworth is Professor of Criminology and Fellow of St. Cross College at the University of Oxford, UK and, concurrently, Professor of Criminology at Monash University, Australia. She has published widely on immigration detention and imprisonment, including, most recently *Inside Immigration Detention* (Oxford University Press, 2014). Mary is currently heading a five-year project on 'Subjectivity, Identity and Penal Power: Incarceration in a Global Age' funded by a Starter Grant from the European Research Council and a three-year International Leverhulme Network on External Border Control funded by the Leverhulme Trust. She is the Director of Border Criminologies (http://bordercriminologies.law.ox.ac.uk), the UK Editor-in-Chief of *Theoretical Criminology*, a co-editor of *Routledge Studies in Criminal Justice, Borders and Citizenship* and a member of the editorial board of the Clarendon Studies in Criminology.

Anders Bruhn is an Associate Professor in Sociology and Professor in Social Work at Örebro University, Sweden. Together with four colleagues, he forms the prison research group there, which is the leading prison research group in Sweden. His main field of research is work, organization and occupations in the public sector. He has published on various aspects of prison work, two recent examples of which, both co-authored with P.Å.Nylander and O. Lindberg, are 'The Prison Officer's Dilemma: Professional Representations among Swedish Prison Officers', in *Les Dossiers des Sciences de l'Education* (2010) and 'A Harsher Prison Climate and a Cultural Heritage Working against It: Sub-cultural Divisions among Swedish Prison Officers' in T. Ugelvik and J. Dullum (eds) *Penal Exceptionalism? Nordic Prison Policy and Practice* (Routledge, 2012).

Anna Eriksson is a criminologist and penologist based at Monash University, Australia. In 2012, she received funding from the Australian Research Council for a three-year research fellowship on the topic of comparative penology, and this book is the first major publication to result from that project. She is also involved in other research projects concerning children of prisoners, people with acquired brain injuries in the criminal justice system, preparation for release and parole, and restorative justice. Her latest book (with John Pratt), *Contrasts in Punishment: An Explanation of*

xii *List of contributors*

Anglophone Excess and Nordic Exceptionalism, was published by Routledge in 2013. She has been a visiting academic at King's College London, UK; Örebro University, Sweden; and Oxford University, UK. Dr. Eriksson is a member of the advisory board of the Palgrave Studies in Prisons and Penology, and is the Director of the Imprisonment Observatory: http://artsonline.monash.edu.au/imprisonmentobservatory.

David A. Green is Associate Professor and Deputy Chair of the Sociology Department at John Jay College of Criminal Justice, The City University of New York, USA. His research interests involve the interrelationship between crime, media, public opinion and politics in a comparative perspective. His first book, *When Children Kill Children: Penal Populism and Political Culture* (Oxford University Press, 2008), received the 2009 British Society of Criminology Book Prize. His work appears in *The British Journal of Criminology, Crime and Justice – A Review of Research, the European Journal of Criminology, Punishment & Society, Youth Justice* and *Crime, Media, Culture*. His contributions to edited books include 'Media, Crime and Nordic Exceptionalism: The Limits of Convergence' in T. Ugelvik and J. Dullum (eds) *Penal Exceptionalism? Nordic Prison Policy and Practice* (Routledge, 2012) and 'Political Culture and Incentives to Penal Populism' in H. Kury (ed.) *Fear of Crime – Punitivity: New Developments in Theory and Research* (Universitätsverlag Brockmeyer, 2008).

Nicolay B. Johansen is an Assistant Professor at the University of Alborg Faculty of Social Sciences, Denmark. He has published on social control from a range of perspectives, applied within various social spheres. His PhD discussed theoretical aspects of the concept, relating contemporary thinking about control to classical sociology. In his earlier work, Johansen has discussed social control of drug addicts, markets (anti-trust legislation), youth, crime, strangers (cities) and migrants. In a forthcoming book – *The Two Faces of Neoliberalism* – he addresses the changing control regimes in a well-functioning welfare state. In his present work he aims to provide a more profound understanding of the relation between the administration and politics of border controls in the neo-liberal era.

Odd Lindberg is Professor in Social Work at Örebro University, Sweden. He is a member of the prison research group at the university and his main field of research is bullying in school and prison research. He is now involved in a Nordic research project concerning drug treatment in Swedish prisons. He has published several articles on prison officers and drug treatment in prison, for example: Nylander, P.Å., Holm, C., Jukic, E. and Lindberg, O., 'Drug Treatment in Swedish Prisons – Moving towards Evidence-Based Interventions?', *Nordic Studies on Alcohol and Drugs* (2012); Kolind, T., Asmussen, V., Lindberg, O. and Touronen, J., 'Prison-based Drug Treatment in the Nordic Political Discourse: An Elastic Discursive Construct, *European Journal of Criminology* (2013); and Kolind, T., Frank, A.F., Lindberg, O.

List of contributors xiii

and Tourunen, J., 'Officers and Drug Counsellors: New Occupational Identities in Nordic Prisons, *British Journal of Criminology* (2014).

Per Åke Nylander is a Senior Lecturer in Social Work and in Criminology, at Örebro University in Sweden and a member of the prison research group there. He is also interested in research on drug abuse and treatment. Recent relevant publications include: Nylander, P.Å., Bruhn, A. and Lindberg, O., 'Emotional Labour and Emotional Strain among Swedish Prison Officers', *European Journal of Criminology* (2011) and Nylander, P. Å., Holm, C., Jukic, E. and Lindberg, O., 'Drug Treatment in Swedish Prisons – Moving towards Evidence-Based Interventions?', *Nordic Studies on Alcohol and Drugs* (2012).

John Pratt is Professor of Criminology at the Institute of Criminology, Victoria University of Wellington, New Zealand. From 2009 to 2012 he was James Cook Research Fellow and a Fellow of the Straus Institute for Advanced Studies of Law and Justice, New York University, USA. In 2012 he was elected to a Fellowship of the Royal Society of New Zealand. In 2013 he received the Mason Durie Medal from the Royal Society of New Zealand, awarded annually to the country's 'preeminent social scientist'. In 2014 he was awarded a Japanese Society for the Promotion of Science Fellowship. He has published extensively in the areas of the history and sociology of punishment and comparative penology. His two-part article, 'Scandinavian Exceptionalism in an Era of Penal Excess', published in the *British Journal of Criminology* in 2008, received the Radzinowicz Prize from the Editorial Board of that journal for the article that 'most advanced the discipline of criminology'. His latest book (with Anna Eriksson), *Contrasts in Punishment: An Explanation of Anglophone Excess and Nordic Exceptionalism*, was published by Routledge in 2013.

Peter Scharff Smith is Senior Researcher at the Danish Institute for Human Rights in Denmark. He has published books and articles in Danish, English and German on prisons, punishment and human rights, including works on prison history, prisoner's children and the use and effects of solitary confinement in prisons. He has also published books and articles on the history of the Waffen-SS and the Nazi war of extermination at the Eastern Front. His latest book is *When the Innocent are Punished: The Children of Imprisoned Parents* (Palgrave, 2014).

Jonathan Simon is the Adrian A. Kragen Professor of Law at University of California, Berkeley, USA. His work concerns the role of crime and fear of crime in the governance of late modern societies. His many publications include *Governing through Crime: How the War on Crime Transformed American Society and Created a Culture of Fear* (Oxford University Press, 2007) and, most recently, *The Sage Handbook of Punishment and Society* (2013, co-edited with Richard Sparks).

xiv *List of contributors*

Debra A. Smith is a Postdoctoral Research Fellow at the Centre for Cultural Diversity and Wellbeing, Victoria University, Australia. Her research focuses on the emotional dimension of radicalization, exploring both the personal and social environments in which decisions to engage in political violence are undertaken. Debra has conducted interviews with violent political extremists from a variety of different groups and worked on related projects ranging from the psychology of terrorism to how to measure and analyse the success of Countering Violent Extremism initiatives. She has published in the area of emotions and terrorism.

Acknowledgements

A heartfelt 'thank you' to all the contributing authors of this book, who embraced my idea and who gave generously of their knowledge and time throughout the process.

And to all the staff, prisoners and Corrections representatives who made my research possible.

I also want to thank Monash University and the Australian Research Council for providing funding and support; this book would not have been possible without it. Thanks also to SAGE, Polity Press, Cornell and the Justice Fellowship organization and its president Craig DeRoche for granting us permission to reproduce previously published material in this book. And to the Prato Centre staff who helped facilitate a fantastic symposium in the most beautiful surroundings. And finally to Rebecca Powell for timely, professional and enthusiastic research support, and to Julia Farrell, the best copy editor one could hope for.

Abbreviations

ADHD	Attention deficit hyperactivity disorder
ARC	Australian Research Council
CBT	Cognitive behavioural therapy
CPT	European Committee for the Prevention of Torture and Inhuman or Degrading Treatment or Punishment
DCM	Detention Custody Manager
DCO	Detention Custody Officer
DO	Discrimination Ombudsman
EEA	European Economic Area
EU	European Union
FVPLS	Aboriginal Family Violence Prevention and Legal Service
HMIP	Her Majesty's Inspectorate of Prisons
IRC	Immigration Removal Centre
JF	Justice Fellowship
NGO	Non-government organization
NPM	New Public Management
NRU	National Reception Unit
NSW	New South Wales
NT	New Territories
PIRA	Provisional Irish Republican Army
RCT	Randomized Control Techniques
REVA	*Rättssäkert och effektivt verkställighetsarbete*
SMT	Senior Management Team
SPPS	Swedish Prison and Probation Service
UK	United Kingdom
UKBA	UK Border Agency
US	United States
WA	Western Australia

Introduction[1]

Anna Eriksson

Zygmunt Bauman's concept of the social production of immorality (1989) has been used in examinations of the Holocaust, genocide and mass violations of human rights. However, it has rarely been applied to contemporary discourses and practices of exclusion, punishment and criminalization, and the aim of this book is to build upon and extend Bauman's thesis to focus on some of the contemporary challenges of our time. These include the increasing bureaucratization of the business of punishment taking place within a narrative of risk, with the corresponding loss of moral and ethical reflection in the public sphere; punitive discourses around border control and immigration; definitions of the Indigenous Other grounded in social and cultural understandings from the Global North, with devastating consequences; the tension between freedom of choice and high levels of anxiety and insecurity, resulting in the immobilization of certain groups and individuals; and moral panics concerning 'terrorists' as the constructed 'Other'. Following Bauman, then, this book asks: 'because we now respond this way, does that mean that this is the only way to respond?'. The simple answer to this question has to be 'no', and the contributions to this collection argue for scholarship that calls for a more morally informed decision-making process, a more ethical way, not only to respond to outsider groups, but also in the application of a critical analysis of their construction.

The topics of 'outsiders' and the construction of Otherness within criminology are not new of course, with seminal works by Stanley Cohen (1972, 1985, 1993, 2001), Howard Becker (1963) and the inspiration for this volume – the selected works by Zygmunt Bauman (1989, 1993, 2000, 2004, 2011; Bauman and Donskis 2013) – acting as a backdrop for the discussions presented in this book. However, the authors of this volume have been asked to apply their own research, from the United States (US), United Kingdom (UK), Sweden, Norway, Australia and New Zealand, to existing scholarship around ethics, morality and social control, and to extend this body of work by undertaking a comprehensive analysis of the underlying processes of Othering. Importantly, the chapters address contemporary challenges, as opposed to historical or purely theoretical ones.

2 *Anna Eriksson*

The chapters focus not so much on the fact that these groups are constructed as Others, but the *process* by which they become such. This includes a synthesis of the macro and micro processes of the techniques driving distantiation, as well as the obscured networks of power behind such conscious and unconscious strategies of exclusion, stigmatization and criminalization. In short, this book provides a critical analysis of social distancing in action and, when appropriate, a discussion of where *morality* is located within such processes and outcomes. We ask whether there is even space for moral considerations and, if not, what has pushed them out of the picture. And, crucially, are there ways to reintroduce morality into the decision-making process, or at least into the scholarship that sets out to critique it?

In 2012 I received funding from the Australian Research Council (ARC) under the then new scheme of Discovery Early Career Research Awards. This was a three-year research fellowship on the topic of 'Othering in penal policy and practice: a cross-national study'. The work by Bauman (1989), and in particular his thesis around the social production of immorality, made up the theoretical backdrop to a model of empirical research and normative considerations around contemporary practices of imprisonment. However, the processes of labelling, exclusion and punishment are of course not confined to prisoners, but apply to many other groups in our societies. I also experienced a strong sense of frustration and despair watching governments manipulating discourses around refugees in Australia, for example, where people fleeing for their lives across the sea and arriving (or not, as it may be, since many perish on the hazardous journey) on leaky boats to seek refuge in the 'lucky country' have been referred to as 'illegal immigrants' by a prime minister who doggedly ignored the fact that such a description was contrary to international human rights law. This conscious change in terminology laid the foundations for increasingly punitive strategies aimed at keeping these 'illegals' off our shores and placing them in detention camps on small pacific islands, with little chance of ever being allowed onto the mainland. These developments were exemplars of adiaphorization – a situation where actions and processes take place outside the realm of moral consideration (Bauman and Lyon 2012). Such a deliberate obfuscation of the language used to describe these refugees is also a clear example of what Cohen (1985), drawing on Orwell (1949), refers to as 'control talk' – 'the anaesthetic function of political language: how words might insulate their users and listeners from experiencing fully the meaning of what they are saying and doing' (273); or indeed Orwell's (1949) concept of 'doublethink', the insistence on believing that black is in fact white, despite overwhelming evidence.

So, in a time where the constructed division between 'us' and 'them' is frequently used as a tool of exclusion and demonization, I felt it pertinent to address this issue in a context larger than my own research on prisons. Hence, I asked a select list of academics whether they would be interested in taking up this challenge within their own areas of expertise. The result is this book, which brings together some of the most exciting international scholars, both established and emerging, to address processes of Othering through a range of contemporary case studies situated in various cultural, political and social contexts. I am immensely grateful for their generosity and willingness to engage with the ideas and challenges. Importantly, the writing of these chapters did not take place in a vacuum; instead, I was aiming for genuine debate and discussion of the key ideas behind this endeavour and of each chapter. This was achieved during a three-day workshop held in Prato, Italy, in late September 2014, to which all of the authors were invited and which was made possible thanks to generous funding provided by Monash University and the ARC. All authors had written full drafts of their chapters before we met, and, facilitated by our Tuscan surroundings, we worked through each chapter in turn. All authors then produced a final version based on feedback and further considerations. Hence, there is a strong theme running through the whole book, and each chapter builds on and adds nuance to the others. In addition, the contributors suggest alternative constructions, introducing a new moral and ethical dimension to the critique of criminalization and social control. None of the authors adopts a neutral position, but instead engages in arguments that politically and morally encapsulate the kind of scholarship that we all engage in too seldom.

The chapters essentially fall into three categories that can be loosely defined as: Othering in the penal sphere; Othering, immigration and the control of strangers; and the social process of Othering. However, I have resisted dividing the book into three distinct parts, instead allowing the chapters to flow naturally into each other. The titles will orient the reader as to what to expect.

Before outlining the structure of the book in more detail, there are some important points to be made about morality and its social production, and how we have approached this conundrum in this collection. Morality is not a straightforward concept, and philosophers, sociologists and psychologists all define it differently. Moreover, Bauman's work on the Holocaust is controversial and there are many who do not agree with his interpretation and explanation of events. But we have adopted Bauman's (1989) definition, that *immorality is conduct that forsakes the responsibility to others*. The social process underlying the production of morality and immorality can be summarized as follows: social *proximity* leads to feelings of *responsibility*, which in turn leads to moral behaviour; and, conversely, an *erosion of proximity* leads to a *diffusion of responsibility* and subsequent immoral behaviour. Morality, in this instance, is an *object* of social processes, not simply its *product*, as many individual-level theories argue. There are also so-called *techniques that erode proximity*, which can be physical things, personal strategies or social processes that serve to increase the social distance between 'us' and 'them'; and since responsibility diminishes with larger distances, such distantiation makes immoral behaviour towards the other more likely to occur. In the words of Bauman: 'Responsibility is silenced once proximity is eroded; it may eventually be replaced with resentment once the fellow human subject is transformed into the Other. The process of transformation is one of social

4 *Anna Eriksson*

separation' (1989: 184). It is crucial to note that *proximity in this instance is social, not necessarily physical.* Hence, it is, as history and indeed contemporary events clearly show, completely possible to stand face to face with the Other and kill him/her without remorse. This process of 'social Othering', coupled with techniques that dehumanize and devalue other individuals or groups (Kelman 1973; Kelman and Hamilton 1989), takes place in all spheres of social life, as the various contributions in this book attest.

Introducing the chapters

The book opens with a chapter by Peter Scharff Smith, a Danish human rights scholar and penologist who explores and questions Bauman's thesis on the Holocaust and what it means for a re-examination of genocide, and, importantly, for the discipline of criminology. In 'Dehumanization, social contact and techniques of Othering: combining the lessons from Holocaust studies and prison research', Scharff Smith draws out the key lessons relevant to prison research and argues that a focus on ideology and culture might be more useful than proximity when exploring dehumanization, social contact and techniques of Othering.

We then move more firmly into the penal sphere with the contribution by Jonathan Simon, who, in his chapter on 'The legal civilizing process: dignity and the protection of human rights in advanced bureaucratic democracies', argues that *Modernity and the Holocaust* (Bauman 1989) contains two invitations that he takes up. The first is to consider how human rights disasters short of the magnitude of the Holocaust develop out of the same 'civilized' conditions; and the second, having recognized the limits of modern institutions to protect fundamental human rights, is to consider what alternatives might exist, either recovered from 'pre-modern' practices or in the margins of modern ones. Taking up the first invitation, Chapter 2 considers mass incarceration in the US at the end of the twentieth century. Prisons may not be inherently places of inhumanity but, at some times and places, perhaps most times and places, they have unquestionably become so, and sometimes on the scale of atrocity or human rights disaster. Addressing the second invitation, Simon considers the potential for contemporary human rights law as a tool for resisting the intrinsic danger posed by modern democratic bureaucracies to the human rights of those who can be made to seem less worthy of them and removed from sight.

With the third chapter we remain in the US, where David Green examines 'The rehumanization of the incarcerated Other: bureaucracy, distantiation and American mass incarceration'. He argues that Bauman (1989) identifies two processes that together made the mass murders of the Holocaust thinkable and achievable. These were modernity's bureaucratic rationality, which deprived individuals of moral recognition and rendered them means to various evil ends, and the process of 'distantiation', which dehumanized those who would become victims of Nazi atrocities. Chapter 3 identifies 11 ways in which similar processes have worked to impede the moral recognition of incarcerated persons and the myriad harms wrought by American mass incarceration. It then considers Bauman's arguments in reverse, examining several evident currents in American penal thinking and practice that mollify the forces of Othering that Bauman identifies.

The penal scope is then narrowed with my own chapter, Chapter 4, on 'Prisons and the social production of immorality', which provides a comparative analysis of prisons in societies marked by inclusion and social cohesion, and prisons in societies where there are larger social distances between individuals and groups, and exclusion and stigmatization characterize responses to crime – in this instance, in Norway and Australia. The comparative perspective allows us to see things otherwise hidden by familiarity and routine, and as they could be or even ought to be, instead of for what they are. Based on 230 interviews conducted in 14 different prisons, I examine how both prisons as institutions and the people inside them have become Othered to different degrees in the two countries, and what this means for penal practice and individual experiences of imprisonment. The emphasis is on connecting practice inside and outside the prison walls, how they interact and what this says about the moral construction of people and institutions.

We then narrow the focus even further, as Chapter 5, 'Swedish "prison exceptionalism" in decline: trends towards distantiation and objectification of the Other', takes a closer look at staff and prisoner relations in that country. The authors, Anders Bruhn, Per-Åke Nylander and Odd Lindberg, note that the Nordic countries have a reputation for humane treatment of prisoners and a strong position on rehabilitative work in prisons – representing a kind of 'exceptionalism' in comparison with many other western countries. However, the Nordic countries are not a monolithic whole. There have always been some differences between them, not least when it comes to prison policy. And in the past decade these differences seem to have increased substantially. In this chapter, the changes in Swedish prison policy and organization are described and analysed, and the authors discern three important processes driving these changes. The first is an increasing emphasis on punishment as a means to protect society from criminals, leading to harsher prison regimes that prioritize security measures; the second is a focus on rehabilitation that rests on the primacy of individual psychological treatment models, with roots in so-called evidence-based medicine; and the third consists of the mechanisms used to manage the prison organization which emanates from neo-liberal economist models of public service organizational management – the breakthrough of the so-called New Public Management doctrine. Importantly, together these processes lead to a prison regime built on enhanced bureaucracy and technocratic engineering that engenders a growing objectification of the prisoner and a growing distance amongst management, staff and prisoners that counteracts positive relational work and seeing the Other as a subject. However, there are also a number of forces working against such developments, not least of which is a strong political and cultural tradition of humanity and

6   *Anna Eriksson*

good relational prison work at the societal level as well as amongst a great number of prison staff, and the potential impact of such resistance will be discussed

With Chapter 6, we move from the tangible perimeters that surround our prisons to the more permeable borders of the nation-state, with Ana Aliverti's chapter entitled 'Doing away with decency?: foreigners, punishment, and the liberal state'. In this chapter Aliverti examines the production and endurance of unjust practices of migration management in countries that pride themselves on upholding notions of equality, non-discrimination and legality. She argues that, rather than being part of an 'illiberal backlash', a counter-trend within liberalism, such practices are a manifestation of it. They are made possible and legitimized by the prevalent conception of justice as territorially bounded and limited to the citizens of the political community. Chapter 6 demonstrates that this bounded conception of justice is detrimental to those with weak claims of membership. Instead of being completely excluded from the realms of 'normal' justice, their legal status has served to legitimize a second-class justice system wherein certain protections of individual rights are attenuated and the resulting measures are rendered legally acceptable.

Mary Bosworth, in her chapter entitled 'Immigration detention, ambivalence and the colonial Other', examines the practical consequences of such policies in the UK, in an empirical piece which complements the theoretical and legal perspective highlighted by Aliverti. Bosworth draws on two years of fieldwork carried out in six British Immigration Removal Centres. She explores both how immigration detention constructs and relies on notions of Otherness and the ways in which staff and detainees deny and resist such constructions. Applying the idea of 'ambivalence', Bosworth reveals considerable disquiet and confusion amongst those residing and working in detention centres about the goals and execution of detention. Such disquiet, she suggests, raises the potential for other ways of thinking and acting in relation to migration control – a perspective that is also very useful when thinking about current policies and practices of immigration management in Australia.

Next, we shift countries as Nicolay B. Johansen, in Chapter 8, 'Controlling Roma in Norway: governing through the administration of social distance', takes a closer look at the ways in which Norway manages the current situation around the Roma, the presence of whom has placed the welfare state in a considerable moral dilemma. The philosophy of the Norwegian state itself is one of social inclusion, but the highly visible and unwanted presence of Roma begging on the streets has led to significant measures of exclusion. Importantly, these take place outside the sphere of criminal justice, and Johansen reveals how civil and administrative measures result in exclusion and expulsion, while allowing the state to maintain the moral high ground since these processes are not constructed as 'punishment' although their impact can be highly punitive.

Then we move geographically next door, where Vanessa Barker examines how deportation, as a public form of punishment, is inextricably linked to both older and contemporary forms of classification in Sweden: population registries. In Chapter 9, entitled 'On Bauman's moral duty: population registries, REVA and eviction from the Nordic realm', Barker examines ethnic classification schemes in Sweden and how they may warp the character of social relations, creating false binaries and false social facts that have built social distancing, and 'Othering', into the foundation of society. This makes contemporary deportation possible in a society nominally based on equality, openness and humanity. She argues that it is this moment of definition – the moment of social separation – that paves the way for the infliction of harm or violence on others, as those about to be deported, for example, have already been cast out of the realm of shared moral responsibility long before they have been taken to the border.

Leaving the borders of the nation-state behind, John Pratt examines 'Immobilization in the age of mobility: sex offenders, security and the regulation of risk' in Chapter 10. Here he notes that, in Bauman's *Modernity and the Holocaust* (1989), the very attributes of civilization that are associated with modernity and have brought about the suppression of irrational behaviour and the elimination of legitimate violence from everyday life by concentrating it in the authority of the state are also seen as having the means to produce conduct that is quite the opposite, based on fear and fantasies and leading to demands for the exclusion of those who are different or unacceptable in some way. The social production of immorality made the Holocaust possible by the authorization and routinization of state violence and the dehumanization of its victims. In his later work, particularly *Liquid Modernity*, Bauman speaks to the much more mobile and fluid social arrangements of the late twentieth and early twenty-first centuries. However, similar processes of immorality are still at work and can be seen in relation to penal measures targeted at sex offenders that have been introduced in most of the English-speaking societies in recent years. These include initiatives that allow prison sentences to be continued at their end and extensive restrictions to be imposed on the movements of sex offenders in public space. In effect, the age of mobility demands that those who are thought to pose the greatest risk to mobility are immobilized in such ways themselves.

This chapter then makes way for the discussions presented by Harry Blagg in Chapter 11 'From terra nullius to terra liquidus? Liquid modernity and the Indigenous Other'. Blagg argues that, disconcertingly, at a time when one of the most oppressed groups on earth – the world's Indigenous peoples – are struggling to hold on to their plots of earth, besieged by the exterminating angels of neo-liberal capitalism and globalization, some influential social theorists of the Global North have proclaimed the death of all that is solid, stressing the degree to which place has ceased to be the basis for belonging in a world of transience, fluidity and mobility. While Bauman's work remains indispensable to any critique of late modernity, it suffers from a weakness common to many social theorists of the Anglosphere, in that it universalizes the experience of the Global North. This chapter challenges a number of Anglospheric assumptions about the Indigenous Other and reinstates the ongoing

8   *Anna Eriksson*

importance of place as the locus for struggles between settler states and Indigenous peoples.

In the final chapter of the book, Debra Smith tackles the controversial topic of 'Symbiotic Othering: terrorism, emotion and morality' in Chapter 12. She argues that to be labelled a 'terrorist' has become synonymous with being morally reprehensible and therefore devoid of an essential aspect of humanness. Yet those labelled as terrorists commonly claim to be working from a position of high moral authority. In this chapter, the conflicting claims to moral authority that characterize terrorism are explored through an examination of the nexus between morality and the emotions. Morality has deep roots in the emotions, with feelings of anger, compassion, envy, grief and love providing knowledge and judgements about what is fair and just. By drawing on interviews conducted with members of the Provisional Irish Republican Army, Smith traces the social construction of Otherness by considering how being in the world with others generates emotional responses that contribute to the foundation of alternative moral positions.

In conclusion

What is moral can be highly disputed. It depends on many factors and is always relative to one's circumstances, which in turn are socially produced within different spheres of life. Hence, there is no *one* morality, but rather many, sometimes converging, sometimes conflicting. However, irrespective of definition, and the fact that one person's moral behaviour can be constructed and defined not only as immoral but also as illegal by others, as a group of authors we decided to adhere to Bauman's (1989) definition of morality as 'responsibility to others'.

In an ideal world, there could arguably exist an infinite number of different groups, all with their own ethical code, all providing their members with a sense of certainty, belonging and purpose. The boundaries marking the moral universe of such groups may be floating, transparent and malleable, allowing for entry and exit without causing disruption or anxiety for its members. However, this is rarely the case, partially due to the fact that most groups are constructed in opposition to something that they are *not*. Such opposition is not the only condition for a group's creation, but it is a necessary one. Only by defining ourselves against something or someone else does our own identity emerge and solidify. The inclusion of 'us' necessitates the exclusion of 'them'. And the more different the Other, the more of a threat they pose: to our identity, our moral stance, and our purpose of being. Moreover, the greater the threat posed by the Other, the more legitimatized are our increasingly punitive actions to keep them in their place, away from us, silenced and preferably hidden, so that their existence may no longer arouse feelings of anxiety in the age of liquid modernity (Bauman 2000).

And then there will always be those people with a combination of sufficient power and high levels of individual anxiety seeking certainty, who are not content with creating and supporting their own in-group; they also feel the need to actively debase those who might question the legitimacy of their particular moral construction, to expel, punish and silence all opposition – a process of distantiation and adiaphorization which several of the chapters in this book discuss. Zygmunt Bauman's work was certainly the key inspiration for this endeavour, challenging us to see that the common-sense view of the world may not be the truth we think it is. By engaging in a critical analysis of the techniques underlying the production of Others in our contemporary world, and by calling attention to the presence or absence of morality within such discourses, this book aims to lay bare the processes that lead to a division between 'us' and 'them' and also to suggest possible ways in which this can be addressed.

Dennis Smith (1998: 43), when writing about Bauman's scholarship, points out that one way to cope with the uncertainty of the postmodern human condition – a condition characterized by an unavoidable and often painful moral responsibility for our actions and the actions of those around us, without clear guidance – is to learn how to interpret and understand the choices and commitments that other people have made, so that we can communicate, share and argue with them. I hope that this book can achieve that and act as an impetus for similar debate amongst a much wider audience.

Note

1 Thanks to Polity Press and Cornell University Press for granting permission to reproduce previously published material in this chapter.

References

Bauman, Z. (1989) *Modernity and the Holocaust*, Ithaca, NY: Cornell University Press.
Bauman, Z. (1993) *Postmodern ethics*, Oxford: Blackwell Publishing.
Bauman, Z. (2000) *Liquid modernity*, Cambridge: Polity Press.
Bauman, Z. (2004) *Wasted lives: modernity and its outcasts*, Cambridge: Polity Press.
Bauman, Z. (2011) *Collateral damage: social inequalities in a global age*, Cambridge: Polity Press.
Bauman, Z. and Lyon, D. (2012) *Liquid surveillance: a conversation*, Oxford: Polity.
Bauman, Zygmunt and Donskis, Leonidas (2013) *Moral blindness: the loss of sensitivity in liquid modernity*, Cambridge: Polity Press.
Becker, H. (1963) *Outsiders: studied in the sociology of deviance*, New York: The Free Press.
Cohen, S. (1972) *Folk devils and moral panics*, London: MacGibbon and Kee.
Cohen, S. (1985) *Visions of social control: crime, punishment and classification*, Cambridge, UK: Polity Press.
Cohen, S. (1993) 'Human rights and crimes of the state: the culture of denial', *Australian and New Zealand Journal of Criminology*, 26(2): 97–115.
Cohen, S. (2001) *States of denial: knowing about atrocities and suffering*, Cambridge: Polity Press.

10 *Anna Eriksson*

Kelman, H. (1973) 'Violence without moral restraint: reflections on the dehumanization of victims and victimizers', *Journal of Social Issues*, 29(4): 25–61.

Kelman, H. and Hamilton, L. (1989) *Crimes of obedience: towards a social psychology of authority and responsibility*, New Haven, CT: Yale University Press.

Orwell, G. (1949) *Nineteen eighty-four*, London: Secker & Warburg.

Smith, D. (1998) 'Zygmunt Bauman: how to be a successful outsider', *Theory, Culture & Society*, 15: 39–45.

1 Dehumanization, social contact and techniques of Othering[1]

Combining the lessons from Holocaust studies and prison research

Peter Scharff Smith

In his famous book on *Modernity and the Holocaust* (1991), Bauman delivered a poignant critique of sociology and brilliantly described how modern bureaucratic decision-making can produce moral indifference, dehumanize victims and rationalize processes involving violence and atrocities on a massive scale. However, when drawing on Bauman's work to understand and describe techniques of Othering within the realm of criminology, the sociology of law and prison research, it is important to address a number of crucial misinterpretations. First, Bauman's analysis of the Holocaust and Nazi atrocities on the Eastern Front was partly wrong in that most of the killings happened in situations of face-to-face contact, which involved many thousands of perpetrators and was based on mechanisms very different from those that are described in *Modernity and the Holocaust*. Second, Bauman misjudged the role of physical distance in processes of violence and, for example, ignored that Stanley Milgram's experiment on obedience and authority showed how close proximity does not prevent most perpetrators from mistreating their victims. Research into the Holocaust and the Nazi war of extermination at the Eastern Front in recent decades has documented how the most important techniques of Othering at work were not primarily a product of bureaucratic decision-making but of other factors, not least Nazi ideology and what has been referred to as 'National Socialist morality'. In this contribution I describe some of these techniques of Othering, focusing on the role of ideology and social contact, and discuss some of the implications of this knowledge for criminology and current prison research.

The division of labour and the relationship between prison research and Holocaust studies

In 1893, Durkheim described the division of labour as one of the key features of modern society (Durkheim 1984). The result of this process is no more evident than in the academic disciplines available to students at universities all over the world. Long gone is the world of the renaissance university where law, medicine and theology were the main organizational pillars (Tamm *et al.* 2005: 8). Today, at the University of Copenhagen, for example, one can obtain a master's degree in more than 100 different subjects, which include disciplines such as 'Audiologopedics', 'EM Food of life', 'Eskimology' and 'Visual culture' (University of Copenhagen n.d., online). This has produced a huge and detailed bank of knowledge and expertise in very diverse fields and subjects. But it has also sometimes created branches of knowledge and academic disciplines that have lost touch with other disciplines and knowledge that are otherwise very relevant, and sometimes essential, to the subjects they study. The loss of knowledge that can follow such an anomic division of labour (to use Durkheim's terminology) is in my opinion one of the most important dangers of modern academic research. In a way, this was exactly the situation that Bauman encountered when he wrote *Modernity and the Holocaust*. He described how historians and academics from other disciplines had begun to grapple with the fact that the Holocaust was a product of our modern, rational and enlightened society and not a unique, freak incident, which could only be analysed as an example of how modernity and the civilizing process can on occasion derail and break down. Yet, according to Bauman, sociologists were at that time still trying to explain how a few bad people could trick all the good people and essentially understood the Holocaust as a 'failure' and as deviance from the norm (Bauman 1991: 3–5). Bauman instead chose to approach the Holocaust as a historical event that consisted of normal elements, all of which he found to be part of modern society (Bauman 1991: 8). He thereby helped bridge the gap between sociology and other disciplines, and worked towards avoiding an anomic division of labour in this very important area.

I remember encountering this type of problem as a young university student. I undertook my Master's degree at Roskilde University, south of Copenhagen, where an effort is made to teach students to work in a cross-disciplinary manner.[2] I chose social science and history as my major subjects and I remember being introduced to James G. March and Johan P. Olsen's *Rediscovering institutions: the organizational basis of politics* (1989) during a social science course about organizational theory. This was hot stuff at the time within the field of organizational theory. The main message in the book was that rational choice and planning theory had relied on the myth of a 'rational man' and forgotten about the powers of rules, institutions and culture. Hence, March and Olsen concluded that 'the individual personality and will of political actors is less important; historical traditions as they are recorded and interpreted within a complex of rules are more important' (March and Olsen 1989: 38). I was surprised but also uncertain. Was there something that I had misunderstood completely? I had just spent a year as a student in the history department and had read critical literature on the enlightenment, religion and modern society, from the hands of Max Weber and Anthony Giddens, among others. Hence I felt pretty certain that it was not exactly big news that people's actions are not always rational and that our decisions and habits tend to be formed not only by individual actors but also by our 'rules, norms and institutions' – as March and Olsen had rediscovered (1989: 171). What I had encountered was apparently an anomic division of labour within academia: a field of research which had developed on its own and seemingly forgotten important lessons from sociology and history, and much of the previous critique of enlightenment and modern society. It was of course valuable that March and Olsen had begun to address this problem with their 'new institutionalism', but, as they admitted towards the end of their book (and in a sense also in the title), their theory was in fact 'an old one' (March and Olsen 1989).

With the number of disciplines in existence today and the sheer amount of research available worldwide, there are undoubtedly many such cases of more or less anomic divisions of labour leaving their mark on many an academic discipline. As a scholar who began my career doing empirical research on the history of the Waffen-SS and the Nazi war of extermination at the Eastern Front, and for more than a decade has carried out prison research while working at a human rights institution, I see some challenges when it comes to the intersections between criminology and human rights as well as the intersections between criminology and studies of the Holocaust and other World War II atrocities. Regarding the first, I agree with Weber, Fishwick and Marmo, who recently concluded that, despite 'the clear relevance of human rights to crime and criminal justice, criminologists have been slow to apply human rights concepts in their work' (Weber *et al.* 2014: 72). I concentrate, however, on the second point here and argue that World War II and Holocaust studies can teach us invaluable lessons about how techniques of Othering can produce dehumanization and ill-treatment. This point has also been made by Maier-Katkin, Mears and Bernard, who talk about the 'historical inattention in criminology' when it comes to studying crimes against humanity, and attempts to analyse Nazi atrocities in this context (Maier-Katkin *et al.* 2014).

One example of how these two fields seem to have become detached is the otherwise very useful, broad and encompassing *Oxford history of the prison*, which attempts to trace the history of the prison from medieval times to the late twentieth century. But in this 425-page volume, the Nazi concentration camps, and the Soviet Gulag for that matter, are only mentioned very briefly in a few paragraphs as examples of how 'perverted' punishment and exploitation of convict labour can become (O'Brien 1998: 194). In reality, the ideology and the associated prison practice of the concentration camps and the Gulag are thereby more or less excluded from the history of the prison and from 'the practice of punishment in western society' (Morris and Rothman 1998).[3] Perhaps such research is part of a tendency to study criminological fields of research – prisons, punishment and crime – more or less detached from wartime and other events that are considered abnormal, which can be a comfortable way of simplifying and straightening out the histories of these practices, thereby avoiding fully analysing the breaks, upsets, distortions and novel practices that appear in periods of upheaval and sudden change. As explained by Ruth Jamieson, the event of war in such cases becomes 'a kind of temporary parenthesis around normalcy' (Jamieson 2014: xiii).[4] Bauman did not make that mistake – on the contrary, he argued that the Holocaust consisted of normal elements that can tell us something about our own societies.

The social production of immorality: explaining the Holocaust according to Bauman

Although the division of labour has exploded within academia, there are even today scholars who master countless disciplines and seem to jump completely effortlessly from one school of thought and knowledge to another. These individuals, the Webers and Durkheimians of our time, certainly include people like Zygmunt Bauman. Bauman clearly made an important contribution to closing the gap between Holocaust studies and criminology/sociology with *Modernity and the Holocaust*, in which he described how modern bureaucratic decision-making can dehumanize victims and rationalize processes involving violence and atrocities on a massive scale.

According to Bauman, moral indifference can be produced through bureaucratic procedures which rely on the ethics of the civil servant, who substitutes 'moral responsibility' with 'discipline' and 'self-denial' (Bauman 1991: 22). In Bauman's version of history, this was essentially what happened in the Third Reich and made the Holocaust possible. By maintaining discipline, obeying orders and seeking rational solutions through routine procedures the 'animal pity' otherwise experienced in the face of human suffering was, according to Bauman, overcome and ordinary people were turned into murderers and conscious collaborators (Bauman 1991: 18–23). Bauman describes mediation of action as an important element in this process – and of modern society in general – which allows 'a great distance between intentions and practical accomplishments' (Bauman 1991: 24). According to Bauman, the resulting 'physical and/or psychic distance' between acts and their consequences 'quashes the moral significance of the act and thereby pre-empts all conflict between personal standards of moral decency and immorality of the social consequences of the act' (Bauman 1991: 25).

The archetypical example of Bauman's thesis is probably the former German bureaucrat, Walter Stier, who was head of the 33rd State Railways office and was interviewed many years later by Claude Lanzman as part of his famous documentary *Shoah*. Walter Stier's 33rd office was responsible for the 'special trains'. Stier explains that these 'so-called resettlement trains' were ordered by the Ministry of Transport of the Reich and that he later learned, when fleeing from Warsaw, that those being resettled 'could have been Jews, or criminals, and others'. But Stier knew that the trains were going to Treblinka and Auschwitz and he openly admit that his office was responsible for assuring that they reached their destination. Lanzman, in his interview, asks Stier if he knew that Treblinka meant extermination for the passengers of these special trains, and Stier answers:

> Of course not!
> *You didn't know?*
> Good God, no! How could we know? I never went to Treblinka. I stayed in Krakow, in Warsaw, glued to my desk.

You were a ...
I was strictly a bureaucrat!

(Shoah-Part 1 n.d: Interview with Walter Stier)

This conversation could almost have been written as a script by someone wanting to illustrate Bauman's thesis. It is, however, obvious that Walter Stier's replies were made after the war and the question is, therefore: to what degree can they be used to explain how he thought and acted during the war? It was, for example, a normal part of the defence of several high-ranking SS men to portray themselves as innocent bureaucrats, as I discuss below in the more famous cases of Otto Ohlendorf and Adolf Eichmann.

Yet there is no doubt in my mind that Bauman was right in locating the Holocaust as something that was part of modern society and based on 'normal' elements, and that bureaucracy and modern technology helped speed up the process of annihilation. But Bauman went too far by claiming that the 'choice of physical extermination ... was a product of routine bureaucratic procedures', that the Holocaust was 'generated by bureaucracy' and that it never came into conflict with 'the principles of rationality' (Bauman 1991: 17).[5] Empirical historical research has proven this to be incorrect, and there are many examples to that effect (Heer and Naumann 1995; Cüppers 2011; Bauer 2001; Cesarani 2005). One of the main drivers behind the Holocaust was Nazi ideology, which to a large degree was modern, but clearly also contained anti-modern elements and a longing for a rural society based on the alleged relationship between 'blood and land' ('*Blut und Boden*') (Burleigh and Wippermann 1994: 11, 16ff, 304ff).[6] This ideology and the way it developed produced many decisions and actions, which were not rational in a traditional Weberian sense – or rather, they were 'value-rational' more than they were 'instrumentally rational' (Weber 1978: 24). Diverting resources towards killing Jews while slave labour was badly needed is but one example of this (Cesarani 2005: 7). Treating civilians at the Eastern Front as 'subhumans' and killing them by the millions, instead of utilizing their animosity towards Soviet communism, is another. Furthermore, as shown in several studies, the Third Reich was not truly a bureaucracy according to Weber's definition but developed into a *polycratic state* (Burleigh and Wippermann 1994: 16; Cesarani 2005: 11). This was not least apparent in the machinery of destruction and the Holocaust, whereby numerous competing agencies and organizations, without clear and often overlapping mandates, worked with great zeal and ideological enthusiasm towards 'the final solution' and genocide (Longerich 2008; Cesarani 2005).

Another important lesson of the Third Reich, which to Bauman's defence was only fully revealed by new empirical studies published during the 1990s, was that not only did *Einsatzgruppen*, concentration camp guards and Waffen-SS extermination units commit mass atrocities, but ordinary German Wehrmacht units were deeply involved as well (Heer and Naumann 1995). In short, being one of the millions of soldiers and police officers on the German pay role at the Eastern Front during World War II was almost certain to bring you into

16   *Peter Scharff Smith*

contact with the war of extermination, and hundreds of thousands became
directly involved as perpetrators themselves.

Perpetrators and face-to-face atrocities: re-reading Milgram's study

In the words of Yehuda Bauer, 'structures do not explain why bureaucrats
sent people to their deaths' (Bauer 2001: 30). As mentioned above, and as
I demonstrate in greater detail below, bureaucracy was not a necessary pre-
condition for the Holocaust and, although bureaucrats and bureaucratic
decision-making did speed up the process of annihilation during the short
reign of the Third Reich, this was not the most important factor in explaining
either *how* or *why* it was done. As many an empirical study has revealed, the
vast majority of Nazi atrocities involved face-to-face contact between perpetrators and victims, and the techniques of Othering at play during these
encounters were therefore not bureaucratic in nature and could not rely on the
production of moral indifference through physical distance (Browning 1998;
Welzer 2006; Heer and Naumann 1995).[7] The most effective techniques of
Othering had to help facilitate and produce extreme violence in close proximity with the victims, which often included many children. Interestingly, this
is not only clear from many empirical historical studies (the lessons of which I
return to below), but is also evident in Stanley Milgram's famous experiment
on obedience and authority, which Bauman devotes an entire chapter to in his
famous book, but in my opinion partly misread.[8]

In Milgram's study, the subjects were instructed to act as teachers and give
the 'learner' an electric shock when they gave a wrong answer and to turn
the voltage up one level each time. The whole experiment was led by a stern-
looking 'experimenter' wearing a grey technician's coat. Both the experimenter
and the victim (learner) were actors and no real shocks were administered to
the latter, who, however, acted as if they did receive shocks. Through a
number of different experimental set-ups different variables were tested,
including distance to the victim, gender and institutional context. The overall
finding was that the subjects were surprisingly obedient and a shockingly high
percentage were willing to go all the way and administer the highest level of
shock – allegedly 450 volts – although the victim at 300 volts yelled that he
was no longer participating in the experiment, shrieked in agony already at
315 volts and later became completely silent (the control panel read 'Danger
severe shock' from 375 volts and upward, and simply 'XXX' from 435 volts and
up). In this set-up, where the subject could hear but not see the victim, 65 per cent
of all subjects proceeded to give the victims the full 450 volts. In a different
set-up with touch proximity between subjects and learners, 30 per cent of the
former proceeded to give the victims the full 450 volts (Milgram 1975: 35).

Bauman cites Milgram in explaining that 'only' 30 per cent administered
all shock levels in the touch-proximity set-up, which he uses to support his
theory concerning bureaucratic decision-making, distance and moral indifference (Bauman 1991: 155). But, while it is certainly true that being removed

far away from their subjects/victims undoubtedly makes moral indifference easier for bureaucrats, the primary lesson of Milgram's experiment seems to be another. To put it differently, saying 'only' 30 per cent is a misunderstanding. The interesting and depressing fact is that *as many as* 30 per cent kept giving the victims electric shocks even in a situation of close proximity. Furthermore, an additional 27.5 per cent continued to give their victim shocks between two and 12 times after he had clearly stated that he wanted no further participation in the experiment (Milgram 1975: 35).

One of the most important lessons of Milgram's study is therefore that people are capable of mistreating each other *despite* close proximity. The fact is that none of the four experimental set-ups in Milgram's study (remote, voice feedback, proximity and touch proximity) bears any resemblance to a bureaucrat's working conditions. In all set-ups, the subject receives answers and reactions from the victim with varied intensity; and in the 'voice feedback' set-up screams and protests (later followed by complete silence) were clearly heard, yet despite this 62.5 per cent continued to administer the highest level of shock on the command of the experimenter. Such a situation has nothing in common with coordinating train transportation from an office in Berlin.

As we shall see in the following section, the reality at the Eastern Front and in the concentration camps during World War II sadly confirms this particular part of Milgram's findings in the sense that ordinary people willingly committed large-scale atrocities in close proximity with their victims. Therefore, the techniques of Othering at work under such conditions did not have much to do with bureaucratic decision-making and moral indifference through distance. But, through different methods, moral indifference can be produced, even in such extreme situations.

Techniques of Othering and the Holocaust

In August 1941, as the front moved quickly eastwards during the initial phase of Operation Barbarossa, Waffen-SS units began operations in the occupied Pripet Marshes, a gigantic area covering parts of Poland, Belorussia and Ukraine. In the events that followed, the SS Cavalry Regiments and the 2. SS brigade began killing and executing Jewish civilians by the thousands. During one week, for example, one single SS Cavalry Regiment reported having killed 13,788 'raiders', which was a euphemism for Jews and other civilians. During these operations the losses of the SS soldiers amounted to two dead and 15 wounded. The report detailed how the SS soldiers had been challenged by the terrain. The 'women and children' had been 'driven into the marshes', but, as the report explained, 'the marshes were not so deep that drowning could be achieved. After a depth of one meter you often reached solid ground (probably sand), so sinking was not possible' (The military history archive in Prague 1941; Christensen *et al.* forthcoming). The preferred method of killing, therefore, became shooting – as in most other similar cases all over the Eastern Front. However, many victims were also burned or beaten to death,

18   *Peter Scharff Smith*

collapsed while being used as slave labour or in the later death marches, or were gassed in the mobile gas vans or death camps.

One of the most well-known descriptions of how extermination by shooting could proceed is provided in Christopher Browning's detailed analysis of Police Battalion 101's massacre at Józefów, in Poland. In July 1942, the battalion was tasked with rounding up 1,800 Jews, sending the fit males to work camps and then killing the women, children and elderly. These last three groups were to be assembled at the marketplace in Józefów, loaded onto trucks and driven to the forest where the firing squads waited. The Germans in the forest were instructed by the battalion doctor and a sergeant on how and where to shoot the victims. When the trucks with the women, children and elderly started to arrive in the forest, these civilians were individually paired with an equal number of German policemen who began to march them down the forest path. The victims were then ordered to lie down and the policemen stepped up behind them, 'placed their bayonets on the backbone above the shoulder blades as earlier instructed' and fired in unison, as ordered. Two firing squads were assembled and they took turns picking up new groups of Jewish civilians, walking them down the forest path and executing them at point blank range. A number of German policemen were relieved of this duty as they could not handle it, but they were quickly replaced with others. As the shootings were proceeding too slowly according to the German plans, more firing squads were assembled, fewer policemen were used to escort the Jews, and the process was thereby speeded up. The men of the second company, however, were not instructed in how to shoot the victims, and some of the Jews were only wounded at first. As one of the executioners later explained, 'At first we shot freehand. When one aimed too high, the entire skull exploded. As a consequence brains and bones flew everywhere'. As explained by another witness, even when killing as instructed, 'often the entire skull or at least the entire rear skullcap was torn off, and blood, bone splinters, and brains sprayed everywhere and besmirched the shooters'. Yet the shootings continued regardless, and in the evening there were so many dead bodies in the forest that it was difficult to find places where the new Jews arriving could lie down. Around 17 hours after the police battalion had arrived in the area its work was finished and it returned to Józefów where alcohol was distributed and many of the German policemen began drinking heavily (Browning 1998: 55).

An empirically informed view on how the killings and shootings were actually carried out reveals that we could hardly be further removed from the bureaucrat's office; therefore, whatever techniques of Othering were present had to take effect within a completely different context with completely different factors at play. Even in the death camps, where the killings were partly industrialized (in what Bauman sees as the technologically most advanced and most modern form of extermination – Bauman 1991: 26), thousands of perpetrators came into close proximity with their victims and witnessed unbelievable scenes as part of the process of extermination. This even included the camp commanders and the many high-ranking SS visitors. As described by

Rudolf Höss, the commander of the Auschwitz camp, he and his staff experienced and dealt brutally with small children who had to be lured into the gas chambers and adults who suddenly screamed on the way to the gassing and were dragged behind a building and shot in the neck. 'I remember, too', Höss calmly explains in his memoirs, 'a woman who tried to throw her children out of the gas chamber, just as the door was closing. Weeping she called out, "At least let my precious children live." There were many such shattering scenes, which affected all who witnessed them' (Höss 1994: 75).

It is argued here that the techniques of Othering at work in the concentration camps were primarily based on dehumanizing situational factors and, as I discuss below, Nazi ideology. The former began as soon as the victims arrived in the camps, where they were kicked, beaten, undressed and had their hair cut, among other degradations (Levi 2003: 24). Such acts obviously involved close physical contact with the victims, who included women and children. The same was true when it came to the common mode of extermination by the Nazi *Einsatzgruppen* as well as for numerous police and military units: shooting was conducted face to face. There could be hundreds or even thousands of victims at a time and they were typically shot in the neck in front of mass graves. In addition, hundreds of thousands of civilians were killed as part of the '*Bandenbekämpfung*' (the alleged anti-partisan warfare) and millions were exterminated in the death camps, which, as demonstrated above, also involved close proximity with the victims (Cüppers 2011; Longerich 2008; Heer and Naumann 1995; Smith *et al.* 1999: 92).

In other words, the 'moral sleeping pills' that helped the perpetrators carry out such atrocities were not primarily provided 'by modern bureaucracy and modern technology', as Bauman argues, but must have come from somewhere else. The social production of moral indifference had to help overcome physical proximity and could not build on bureaucratic or technological distance. Different techniques of Othering could, however, work under such conditions and make 'invisible' the 'humanity of the victims' and 'evict them from the universe of obligation' (Bauman 1991: 26).

Some of the techniques of Othering that may have helped facilitate the exterminations are related to ideology, obedience to authority, peer pressure, de-individuation, unity in primary groups and even career-based motives (Browning 1998; Bartov 1992; Milgram 1975; Zimbardo 2007: 259, 297).[9] There is specialized literature on several of these social and psychological mechanisms, and they have to a greater or lesser extent all been discussed with regard to the Holocaust. On a very general note, it is not surprising that obedience to authority, peer pressure and de-individuation often play important psychological roles in military formations and can sometimes help explain the group behaviour of soldiers committing atrocities. The theory of unity in primary groups is perhaps less discussed in the sociological/criminological literature but is also relevant since it attempts to explain group cohesion in military units through the existence of primary groups of individuals who stay together, feel a special kind of bond, rely on each other and bolster the

20 *Peter Scharff Smith*

group's morale. It has been argued with regard to warfare at the Eastern Front during World War II that such primary units originally formed the backbone of the German army but were destroyed by the Nazis' extremely heavy losses, while others argue that cohesion was actually maintained through these primary units.[10]

Regardless of whether these various techniques worked together or alone, they (or at least some of them) could influence the actions of soldiers, bureaucrats and others during World War II, to a degree where the psychology of the individual perpetrator clearly mattered less than the situational (and societal) norms that surrounded these actions. In line with this, it is also widely agreed today that the Nazi perpetrators were generally 'ordinary men' and it has been argued in a number of studies that even in the SS only a few men were deviants or psychopaths (Welzer 2006; Browning 1998; Zimbardo 2007; Krenn and Rappaport 1994: 82). In a sense, this was indirectly discovered by a few criminologists very soon after the war, although it seems that these findings never made much of a mark in international sociology and criminology – at least not until several decades later. Criminologist Karl O. Christiansen, for example, studied collaborators in Denmark and found that they were not pathological and were not like 'ordinary criminals' in that they were more similar to the average Danish citizen in terms of social class and education (Christiansen 1950, 1955, 1970). In the case of the Danish volunteers in the Waffen-SS, whom Christiansen also studied, most did, however, have one thing in common, apart from being 'normal': their ideological conviction and support for Nazism (Christensen *et al.* 1998).

Harald Welzer argues that atrocity-producing situations can be understood and analysed at three levels: first, in relation to society's norms; then in relation to the relevant situational norms; and third, on an individual level involving the personality of the perpetrator (Welzer 2006). In the Third Reich all three levels were to varying degrees influenced, often very significantly, by Nazi ideology. More than being a modern bureaucratic state, a totalitarian state or a fascist state, the Third Reich was a racial state 'organised increasingly upon racial rather than class lines' (Burleigh and Wippermann 1994: 305).

Ideological Othering in theory and practice at the Eastern Front

If we attempt to take an overall look at all of the available research and empirical evidence on mass killings, the Holocaust and Nazi atrocities committed at the Eastern Front and in the Balkans during World War II, there is no doubt that ideology played a central role – not always and not in all processes of Othering, but very often so. It is perhaps Bauman's biggest mistake that he refused to credit ideology with an important role in the making of the Holocaust. In stark contradiction to all the available evidence, Bauman even claimed that over-ideological individuals were weeded out of the *Einsatzgruppen* and that the SS did not rely on ideology (Bauman 1991: 20). Here Bauman could not be more wrong. The SS embodied Nazi ideology and attempted to create political

Dehumanization, social contact and Othering   21

soldiers in the Waffen-SS who, time and time again, were taught to kill for ideological reasons and to a very large extent did exactly that. Interestingly, Bauman makes the mistake of ignoring ideology by deviating from his own principle of analysing the Holocaust as consisting of 'normal' elements. Ideological convictions are not foreign to modern society and 'normal' people can become ideologically convinced – regardless of whether or not the contents of these convictions are normal, abnormal, modern or reactionary, or appear identical with pre-modern sentiments. Anti-Semitism and other forms of xenophobia or racism are not necessarily specifically modern or pre-modern, but history has certainly taught us that they are normal.[11]

Several scholars have analysed how Nazi ideology from the early 1930s to the end of the war gradually helped produce an increasingly brutal practice. The key ideological concept was race, and the Nazi enemy was the '*Untermenschen*' (subhumans). The ideological dehumanization of large sections of the world population thus proved especially effective because, as pointed out by the German historian Bernd Wegner, Nazism lacked any of the humanistic and moral boundaries that other competing ideologies possessed (Wegner 1990: 47). Hence, not only the exclusion but also the elimination of unworthy 'subhumans' became standard practice in the Third Reich, and such atrocities were considered both necessary and honourable acts within the ideological universe of Nazism.

As Himmler explained to a group of Waffen-SS soldiers on 13 July 1941 in Stettin, the war against the Union of Soviet Socialist Republics was, in Nazi terminology, 'an ideological battle between races'.[12] Around a year later, the *Reichsführer-SS* complained to a group of officers from SS division Das Reich that many German soldiers had entered the war at the Eastern Front with a mentality formed by the culture prevalent at the Western Front, which had led some to believe that 'also Jews were human beings'. But Himmler found that such sentiments had not troubled the SS and reiterated that the war was not between nations or political systems, but between two races, which would lead to the obliteration of one of these (The German National Archive in Berlin 1942: 2–3). The lower-level troops were also often supplied with similar instructions, which required that they showed no mercy and did not express 'false' humanity when they faced the allegedly racially inferior enemy (The military history archive in Prague 1943; The military history archive in Freiburg 1943; Christensen *et al.* forthcoming).

Bauman claims that the SS administration turned everything into 'strictly disciplinary rules … freed from moral judgement' and cites former *Einsatzgruppen* leader Otto Ohlendorf, from his Nuremberg defence, where he claimed that he merely performed his duty as ordered, just as Eichmann later argued in Jerusalem (Bauman 1991: 22). But, like many others, Bauman was tricked by the legal defence of Ohlendorf, Eichmann and others. As careful empirical analysis has since uncovered, these men, and many others, were ardent Nazis and for ideological reasons they believed that it was their job to kill Jews and other alleged 'subhumans'. Ohlendorf, for example, was in reality 'the quintessential

22   Peter Scharff Smith

ideological soldier' and by no means a self-denying civil servant who did not pass moral judgement on himself (Earl 2009: 145). As described by Hillary Earl:

> Ohlendorf did not blindly carry out orders; his actions, as always, were motivated by conviction. In the final analysis, any attempt to portray Ohlendorf as an 'obedient soldier' fails. He was an independent player who carried out orders, in essence, for essentially ideological reasons.
>
> (Earl 2009: 150)

Similarly, Adolf Eichmann was by no means the typical value-free, self-denying bureaucrat that Hannah Arendt described in her book on the 'banality of evil'. On the contrary, as later research has shown, Eichmann became an ardent, creative and ruthless ideologist who believed that 'the Jews were a powerful enemy who had to be combated relentlessly' (Cesarani 2005: 16).

It is equally wrong to claim that the SS administration relied on discipline without morals. Rather, all discipline in the SS was structured according to ideology, and hence morals, perhaps to a degree unseen in any other Nazi organization. SS law was based on ideology and stipulated countless punishments for purely ideological reasons (for example, against homosexuality, sex with 'other races' or for marrying a racially 'unfit' partner). Clear proof of how the SS did not simply seek to employ rational, modern and effective methods of mass killing is found in the way that cases of the impulsive execution of Jews, carried out without order from above ('*Judenerschiessungen ohne Befehl und Befugnis*'), were handled by the SS courts. The dilemma of how these cases were to be handled was solved ideologically and not according to military logic. Himmler ordered that the motive behind the shootings was to be the deciding factor, meaning that if the SS men had been ideologically motivated when carrying out unauthorized killings of Jews, then they were not to be punished. If the motive, on the other hand, was 'sadistic' or 'sexual', then the perpetrator should be punished (Wegner 1990: 326). The SS system was not primarily a modern, rational bureaucracy; it was an ideological organization.

As described by Harald Welzer, 'National Socialist morale' considered it 'good and useful' to help solve the 'Jewish question', and to do this in such a radical manner that future historians would never have seen but only heard of Jews (Welzer 2006: 48). Any act that could help realize this vision was both good and necessary, according to National Socialist ideology and culture as it developed and was practiced from 1939, especially after 1941. As explained by Zimbardo, dehumanization of victims can arise through their 'exclusion from the moral order of being a human person' and in the Third Reich this process of exclusion was based on ideology and what Welzer calls 'National Socialist morale' (Zimbardo 2007: 307). And when ideological dehumanization took place and functioned as a technique of Othering at the Eastern Front, in the death camps, and so on, in situations where power had been transferred exclusively to one side, an atrocity-producing situation was created. The involved parties on the German side even thought that they were doing a good deed by killing Jews and other alleged 'subhumans' – based on the ideological premise that they were in fact helping the future of humankind. This was all the 'moral sleeping pills' that they needed.

It was through the practice of this ideological doctrine that the 'animal pity' of the victims was overcome. Not least in the SS was this vision realized. As several SS publications and educational orders demanded, the SS soldiers should not simply learn Nazi ideology, they should 'live it' (Smith *et al.* 1999). What this meant in the face of the victims – even defenceless women and children in concentration camps – and how Nazi ethics was to be practised in such situations, was clearly spelled out many times, for example, by Himmler in his infamous Posen speech held for a gathering of SS officers. Here, Himmler openly addressed 'the extermination of the Jewish race'. He described how difficult it was to take part in all the killings (that is, to overcome the 'animal pity') but, according to him, the SS had achieved this in a morally correct way:

> Most of you know what it means when one hundred corpses are lying side by side or five hundred or one thousand. To have stuck it out and at the same time – apart from exceptions caused by human weakness – to have remained decent fellows, that is what has made us hard.
>
> (Quoted in Cohen 2002: 80)

The consequence of such a way of thinking is also explained by a Danish Waffen-SS volunteer in his diary:

> A Jew in a greasy kaftan walks up to beg some bread, a couple of comrades get a hold of him and drag him behind a building and a moment later he comes to an end. There isn't any room for Jews in the new Europe, they've brought too much misery to the European people.
>
> (Smith *et al.* 1999)

As historian Wendy Lower has shown, many of the hundreds of thousands of German women who went east during the war and were employed in roles such as Red Cross nurses, school teachers and administrative staff also participated in atrocities of their own free will, although such activities bore no direct relation to their work. But many of these women were fuelled by ideological and anti-Semitic beliefs, and became 'revolutionaries who were conditioned to accept violence, to incite it, and to commit it, in defence of or as an assertion of Germany's superiority' (Lower 2014: 166).

Ideology was, in other words, the most effective mechanism of Othering present in the production of Nazi atrocities. By killing Jews one would live according to National Socialist morale and therefore not only be a 'decent' fellow, in the words of Himmler, but also someone who had contributed actively to the solution of 'the Jewish question' and thereby to the greater good. An act – in this case, mass killings – that would normally be conceived as inhuman and immoral thereby became decent, necessary and heroic within the context of the Nazi ethical framework. And the mechanism through which this transformation took place was primarily (but by no means exclusively) ideology.

Prison research and the lessons of the Holocaust

For criminologists, and prison researchers from other disciplines who have an interest in techniques of Othering, the most fundamental lesson of the atrocities committed at the Eastern Front and as part of the Holocaust during World War II is perhaps that we need to keep studying what goes on inside prisons – the social interactions, culture and situational factors at play – and analyse how these affect and influence the actions of prisoners, staff and others who come into contact with these institutions. This does not mean that we should leave the politics of imprisonment and the broader societal effects of incarceration unexamined. As I have argued elsewhere, prisons should preferably be studied as part of – rather than detached from – the surrounding society, as such analysis will likely make it easier to understand and perhaps change their wider societal meaning and function (Smith 2014). It nevertheless means that our analysis of the general trends in penal policy should also be informed by empirical research into what goes on inside prisons. Without such knowledge, our theoretical work risks losing contact with empirical realities, which is essentially what happened for Bauman in his attempt to explain the Holocaust.

The classical sociological study of prisons established long ago that they are social systems that, to varying degrees, involve intimate social contact between those who live and work in these institutions, and we therefore still need to keep the role of the 'prison community' in mind when we study these facilities (Sykes 1974; Crewe 2012). Focusing primarily on bureaucratic culture and political decision-making based on social distance can obscure how prisons actually work and operate. So, while Bauman's theory on the social production of moral indifference can clearly be used to explain some of the ways in which punishment is planned and carried out in the modern or late-modern western world, one has to be careful when applying it in an attempt to understand what goes on inside prisons because these institutions are sites of social contact and social interaction – although this interaction is regulated, limited and sometimes distorted compared to that of the outside world. When the mistreatment and misuse of force occur in prison, for example, different techniques of Othering will often be involved which can help overcome the 'animal pity' of the prisoners *despite* their close proximity, rather than through increased social distance.

One could perhaps argue that one specific prison environment is different in that regard – namely, supermax prisons and other facilities that utilize large-scale, long-term solitary confinement. Perhaps this is *the* prison environment where it makes the most sense to apply Bauman's concept of the social production of moral indifference through distance and mediation of action.[13] As Bauman has himself argued, the Pelican Bay supermax prison in California, with its 'entirely automated' design and 'virtually no face-to-face contact' between guards and inmates, appears to aim at creating a form of almost total isolation that can 'reduce the Other to a pure incarnation of the punishing force of law' (Bauman 2000: 209). The creation of supermax prisons is likely to be, at least partly, the result of policies and bureaucratic decision-making based on distance from victims – in this case, prisoners. That more than 80,000 prisoners are currently subjected to such regimes in the United States (US) certainly looks like the social production of moral indifference and prison pain on a grand scale.[14] We should, however, not forget that the large-scale use of solitary confinement also exists in other jurisdictions where these practices are based on very different penal policies. The case of Swedish remand imprisonment is a striking example. According to statistics from the Swedish prosecution service, almost 70 per cent of all remand prisoners were subjected to 'restrictions' in 2013, which means that in most cases they were imprisoned in solitary confinement (Åklagarmyndigheten 2014: 91). In effect, these incredible figures mean that at any time significantly more than one-eighth of the entire Swedish prison population is in solitary confinement or very similar conditions. The point here is that the Swedish use of solitary confinement is produced by a very different policy compared to supermax imprisonment in the US and therefore requires a different analysis for us to understand it.[15] But there may still be room for Bauman's theories in both cases.

In any case, that supermax prisons and other administrative uses of solitary confinement have created spaces of confinement with almost no social contact also raises the question of whether or not social action inside these prisons produces moral indifference based on distance. It is not possible to fully address this interesting question within the scope of this chapter but, inspired by the lessons from empirical studies of Nazi atrocities, I would like to make one observation. The history of supermax prisons shows us that social contact exists even in these institutions and that mistreatment, which has little to do with bureaucratic cultures and decision-making, can take place in such facilities. The *Madrid v. Gomez* case brought against Pelican Bay and the state of California in the 1990s clearly confirms this. Incidents of guard brutality in Pelican Bay included beatings and physical violence under various circumstances, 'confinement of naked or partially dressed inmates in outdoor holding cages during inclement weather', and excessive use of the so-called foetal restraint, among other abuses.[16] In one particularly horrible incident, a mentally ill inmate was forced into a tub with scalding water and suffered second- and third-degree burns. A nurse at the Special Housing Unit infirmary where the incident took place testified that the inmate 'was in the bathtub with his hands cuffed behind his back, with an officer pushing down on his shoulder and holding his arms in place'. The nurse overheard the prison officer saying about the prisoner, who was African-American, that it 'looks like we're going

26   Peter Scharff Smith

to have a white boy before this is through, that his skin is so dirty and so rotten, it's all fallen off' (*Madrid v. Gomez* 1995; Smith 2007).

Once again techniques of Othering are at work here, which are not part of a culture of discipline, routine and the division of labour (bureaucracy), but have much more in common with the dynamics uncovered in, for example, the Stanford prison experiment, and at the Eastern Front during World War II for that matter. Prison staff started to mistreat prisoners because the institutional context dehumanized them and released a violent potential. Prison staff did *not* mistreat prisoners because they were ordered to, because it was part of the official prison routine or because they were civil servants and bureaucrats who were employed to do such work. Perhaps this is also a reminder that we should not be *too* focused on locating social action in the form of instrumental rationality in the context of imprisonment. If we acknowledge both the situational factors at work and the possible presence of ideologies – currently, for example, that of penal populism – then perhaps we should also be looking for value-rational social action when we look into what goes on inside places of punishment. In *Economy and society* Weber clearly stated that he did not believe in 'the actual predominance of rational elements in human life' and he warned that there is always 'a danger of rationalistic interpretations where they are out of place'. As Weber drily concluded, 'all experience unfortunately confirms the existence of this danger' (Weber 1978: 7).

Notes

1   Thanks to Polity Press for granting permission to reproduce previously published material in this chapter.
2   Normally at Roskilde University you start with two years of basic multi-disciplinary training, whereafter you can major in two disciplines over the next three years. On the negative side, you come out with less in-depth knowledge of your major, compared to many other universities, while, on the plus side, you will learn to work in two or more disciplines.
3   This phrase is the subtitle of the book.
4   However, according to Jamieson that tendency is changing, and criminologists are now more 'conscious of the need to consider how good a fit there is between war and their explanatory frameworks' (Jamieson 2014: xiv).
5   Bauman admits that the Holocaust was not 'determined' by bureaucracy or that bureaucracy 'must' result in Holocaust, but continues to argue that a 'bureaucratic culture ... was the very atmosphere in which the idea of the Holocaust could be conceived' (Bauman 1991: 18).
6   Bauman acknowledges the presence of anti-modern elements in the process that led to the Holocaust, but according to him these did not structure the process or provide it with any of its mechanisms but merely supplied it with a sort of primitive fuel: 'The irony of history would allow the anti-modernist phobias to be unloaded through channels and forms only modernity could develop', (Bauman 1991: 46).
7   In contrast to all these studies, Bauman wrongly argues that the extermination process became technologized in a way that separated the perpetrators and their victims (Bauman 1991: 26).
8   Milgram's experiment has since been the target of much discussion and controversy. Some historians rightly criticize the way in which Milgram's results have

been uncritically exported to a completely different time and place – World War II and the Holocaust. While this criticism is certainly valid, it has apparently also led to the misconception among some historians that Milgram's research is completely useless. See, for example, Cesarani (2005: 352 ff.). From a social-psychological point of view, Milgram's experiment tells us something about how people are capable of mistreating other people in certain situations and sheds light on *some* of the relevant factors in that regard.

9 See also Maier-Katkin *et al.*, who, in their theory of crimes against humanity, make six 'propositions' which include variations on the above-mentioned and also address the question of 'societal strain' and 'aggression' (Maier-Katin et al. 2014: 239 ff.).

10 For a discussion see, for example, Bartov (1992).

11 Here Bauman disagrees as he defines racism as 'strictly a modern product' made possible only by modernity (see Bauman 1991: 61). Bauman focuses on the structural and scientific elements of modern racism and downplays the role of ideology (see Bauman 1991: 73 ff.).

12 'Ein Weltanschauungskampf und ein Kampf der Rassen.' Quoted from Jürgen Förster (2003) 'Die weltanschauliche Erziehung in der Waffen-SS', Matthäus, Kwiet, Förster and Breitman (eds), *Ausbildungsziel Judenmord?*, Frankfurt, Fischer, p. 103. See also George H. Stein (1984), *The Waffen SS: Hitler's elite guard at war, 1939–1945*, Ithaca, NY, Cornell University Press, p. 126.

13 There are perhaps even more extreme examples and those are the cases of Black site imprisonment and other secret forms of incarceration.

14 I await Keramet Reiters's historical analysis of how supermax prisons have actually evolved, which should help us answer this question. For an analysis of supermax imprisonment, see Shalev (2009).

15 There is a common Scandinavian history when it comes to the use of solitary confinement during pre-trial. See Peter Scharff Smith (2006), 'The effects of solitary confinement on prison inmates: a brief history and review of the literature', in M. Tonry (ed.), *Crime and justice*, Vol. 34, Chicago, IL, Chicago University Press.

16 *Madrid v. Gomez*, 889 F. Supp. 1146 (N.D. Cal. 1995). A foetal restraint (hogtying) 'involves handcuffing an inmate's hands at the front of his body, placing him in leg irons, and then drawing a chain between the handcuffs and legs until only a few inches separate the bound wrists and ankles'. The massive number of incidents reported in this case took place in different parts of the Pelican Bay prison, which is made up of three different units, only one being (a very large) supermax, while one of the other units is a maximum security prison.

References

Åklagarmyndigheten (2014) *Häktningstider och restriktioner*, Report, January. Online. Available: www.aklagare.se/PageFiles/12915/rapport_haktningstider.pdf (accessed 10 December 2014).

Bartov, O. (1992) *Hitler's army: soldiers, Nazis, and war in the Third Reich*, Oxford: Oxford University Press.

Bauer, Y. (2001) *Rethinking the Holocaust*, New Haven, CT: Yale University Press.

Bauman, Z. (1991) *Modernity and the Holocaust*, Oxford: Polity Press.

Bauman, Z. (2000) 'Social issues of law and order', *British Journal of Criminology*, 40: 205–221.

Browning, C. (1998) *Ordinary men: Reserve Police Battalion 101 and the Final Solution in Poland*, New York, NY: Harper Perennia.

Burleigh, M. and Wippermann, W. (1994) *The racial state*, Cambridge: Cambridge University Press.

28 Peter Scharff Smith

Cesarani, D. (2005) *Eichmann: his life and crimes*, London: Vintage.

Christensen, C.B., Poulsen, N.B. and Smith, P.S. (1998) *Under hagekors og Dannebrog. Danskere i Waffen SS 1940–45*, Copenhagen: Aschehoug.

Christensen, C.B., Poulsen, N.B. and Smith, P.S. (forthcoming) *Waffen-SS: Europas nazistiske soldater*, Copenhagen: Gyldendal.

Christiansen, K.O. (1950) *Mandlige landssvigere I Danmark under besættelsen*, Copenhagen: Direktoratet for Kriminalforsorgen.

Christiansen, K.O. (1955) *Landssvigerkriminaliteten i sociologisk belysning*, Copenhagen: GAD.

Christiansen, K.O. (1970) 'Recidivet blandt danske landssvigere', *Kriminalvidenskab*, 58: 302–313.

Cohen, S. (2002) *States of denial*, Cambridge: Polity.

Crewe, B. (2012) *The prisoner society: power, adaptation, and social life in an English prison*, Oxford: Oxford University Press.

Cüppers, M. (2011) *Wegbereiter der Shoah*, Darmstadt: Primus Verlag.

Durkheim, E. (1984) *The division of labour in Society*, London: Macmillan.

Earl, H. (2009) *The Nuremberg SS-Einsatzgruppen Trial, 1945–1958*, Cambridge: Cambridge University Press.

Förster, J. (2003) 'Die weltanschauliche Erziehung in der Waffen-SS', in J. Matthäus, K. Kwiet and J. Förster (eds), *Ausbildungsziel Judenmord?*, Frankfurt: Fischer.

Heer, H. and Naumann, K. (eds) (1995) *Vernichtungskrieg: Verbrechen der Wehrmacht 1941 bis 1944*, Hamburg: Hamburger Edition HIS.

Höss, R. (1994) 'Autobiography of Rudolf Höss', in *KL Auschwitz seen by the SS*, Óswiecim: The Auschwitz-Birkenau State Museum.

Jamieson, R. (ed.) (2014) *The criminology of war*, Burlington: Ashgate.

Krenn, G.M. and Rappaport, L. (1994) *The Holocaust and the crisis of human behavior*, New York: Holmes and Meier.

Levi, P. (2003) *The drowned and the saved*, London: Abacus.

Longerich, P. (2008) *Heinrich Himmler: Biographie*, München: Siedler Verlag.

Lower, W. (2014) *Hitler's furies: German women in the Nazi killing fields*, London: Vintage Books.

Maier-Katkin, D., Mears, D.P. and Bernard, T.J. (2014) 'Towards a criminology of crimes against humanity', in R. Jamieson (ed.), *The criminology of war*, Burlington: Ashgate.

March, J.G. and Olsen, J.P. (1989) *Rediscovering institutions: the organizational basis of politics*, New York: The Free Press.

Milgram, S. (1975), *Obedience to authority*, New York: Harper Torchbooks.

Morris, N. and Rothman, D.J. (eds) (1998) *The Oxford history of the prison: the practice of punishment in western society*, Oxford: Oxford University Press.

O'Brien, P. (1998) 'The prison on the continent', in N. Morris and D.J. Rothman (eds), *The Oxford history of the prison: the practice of punishment in western society*, Oxford: Oxford University Press.

Shalev, S. (2009) *Supermax: controlling risk through solitary confinement*, Devon: Willan Publishing.

Lanzman, C. 'Shoah-Part 1: Interview with Walter Stier', YouTube, uploaded July 2009. Online. Available: www.youtube.com/watch?v=c2I9Ccb520A (accessed 10 December 2014).

Smith, P.S. (2006) 'The effects of solitary confinement on prison inmates: a brief history and review of the literature', in M. Tonry (ed.), *Crime and justice*, Vol. 34, Chicago, IL: Chicago University Press.

Smith, P.S. (2007) 'Prisons and human rights: the rise of solitary confinement in Denmark and the US from the 1820s until today', in S. Lagoutte, H.O. Sano and P.S. Smith (eds), *Human rights in turmoil*, Leiden: Martinus Nijhoff Publishers.

Smith, P.S. (2014) *When the innocent are punished: the children of imprisoned parents*, New York: Palgrave Macmillan.

Smith, P.S., Christensen, C.B. and Poulsen, N.B. (1999) 'The Danish volunteers in the Waffen SS and German warfare at the Eastern Front', *Contemporary European History*, 8: 73–96.

Stein, G.H. (1984) *The Waffen SS: Hitler's elite guard at war – 1939–1945*, Ithaca, NY: Cornell University Press.

Sykes, G.M. (1974) *The society of captives*, Princeton, NJ: Princeton University Press.

Tamm, D., Dübeck, I. and Slottved, E. (2005) *Juraen på Københavns Universitet 1479–2005*, Copenhagen: Copenhagen University.

The German National Archive in Berlin: NS19/4009, Rede des Reichsführers-SS am 19.6.1942 vor dem Führerkorps der Division [Das Reich].

The military history archive in Freiburg: RS 2–2/14, Ic. Sonderbefehl 2.5.1943.

The military history archive in Prague: RFSS KDOS, box no. 24, SS-Kavallerie-Regiment 2, Bericht über den Einsatz Pripjetsümpfe, d.12.8.1941.

The military history archive in Prague: N SS DR ks. 8, Ic Nachrichtenblatt Nr.3, 14.9.1943.

University of Copenhagen, *Kandidatuddannelser*, Denmark, online. Available: http://studier.ku.dk/kandidat/a-z/ (accessed 4 September 2014).

Weber, L., Fishwick, E. and Marmo, M. (2014) *Crime, justice and human rights*, Basingstoke: Palgrave Macmillan.

Weber, M. (1978) *Economy and society*, Vol. 1, Berkeley, LA: University of California Press.

Wegner, B. (1990) *Hitlers politische Soldaten*, Paderborn: Schöningh.

Welzer, H. (2006) *Täter: wie aus ganz normalen Menschen Massenmörder werden*, Frankfurt: Fischer.

Zimbardo, P. (2007) *The Lucifer effect: understanding how good people turn evil*, London: Random House.

Cases

Madrid v. Gomez, 889 F. Supp. 1146 (N.D. Cal. 1995).

2 The legal civilizing process[1]

Dignity and the protection of human rights in advanced bureaucratic democracies

Jonathan Simon

Introduction: two civilizing processes or one?

Twenty-five years ago Zygmunt Bauman, in *Modernity and the Holocaust* (Bauman 1989), urged social scientists to consider the implications of the Holocaust for the conventional assumptions about the social foundations of morality. Based on this common narrative, the rise of rational self-interest and modern bureaucratic forms of collective organization are seen to align with a historic reduction in both actual violence and the tolerance of individual members of society for cruelty. Yet, when we look at what is now known about the making of the Holocaust, according to Bauman we find that rationality, self-interest and social organization are not obstacles to genocide, but necessary elements. Bauman did not reject the insights of sociology about the civilizing process (Elias 1978), nor question the benefit of having a central state suppress local violence in favour of centrally organized state power, bound by the rule of law (conditions that in many instances create a sense of security and freedom for citizens), but he recognized their dual edge. The same forces, aligned with a determined social goal (such as a classless, Aryan or perhaps drug-free society), could lead to unprecedented violence and cruelty. At the book's end, Bauman (1989: 198) suggested that independent sources of morality not tied to contemporary social values, something more abundant before the completion of modernization, could be necessary to guard against the worst tendencies of modern social organization (although he admittedly did not say much about where these might come from, except the pre-social existential conditions of humans).

This chapter takes up two invitations presented in *Modernity and the Holocaust* (1989). First, to consider how human rights disasters that fall short of the magnitude of the Holocaust may develop out of the same 'civilized' conditions. The chapter considers mass incarceration in the United States (US) at the end of the twentieth century (Simon 2014a) as an example of a sub-Holocaust human rights catastrophe. Prisons are not inevitably places of abuse and inhumanity but, at times and places, perhaps most times and places, they have unquestionably become so and sometimes on the scale of atrocity (or human rights disaster). One such was the 'convict lease system' that prevailed in a number of Southern states of the US from the end of the Civil War until at least World War I, in which Black citizens convicted of minor property crimes were often sentenced to years of labour for private contractors who had little incentive not to work them to death (Lichtenstein 1996; Oshinsky 1997). More recently, the quadrupling of the national imprisonment rate between the late 1970s and late 1990s, what punishment and society experts call 'mass' or 'hyper' incarceration, resulted in another widespread human rights disaster, the scope of which is only now emerging. The warehousing of prisoners, a large portion of them burdened by chronic illness, under conditions of medical and mental health deprivation exacerbated by extreme overcrowding, has led to uncounted premature deaths in the thousands and the experience of degradation by tens of thousands nationwide (Fleury-Steiner 2008; Simon 2014a).

Mass incarceration was not planned as a form of genocide, but it bears many of the traits that Bauman associated with the capacity of modern bureaucratic societies to create such events, including highly insulated state agencies capable of cutting off routine contact between members of the public and members of the excluded population. Like the Holocaust, mass incarceration was perpetrated by some of the wealthiest and most advanced states in the US: not where one might expect, at the periphery of the US penal state in places like our now notorious 'War on Terror' prisons like Guantanamo Bay Naval Station in Cuba, or Abu Ghraib prison in Iraq, but in the centre of the domestic legal system, under the eyes (sometimes blinded) of courts and in places like California that have mass media, liberal values and highly educated citizens (Gilmore 2008; Alexander 2010).

Second, I want to consider the potential for contemporary constitutional law, infused with human rights law, as a 'new and improved' shield for resisting the intrinsic danger posed by modern democratic bureaucracies to the human rights of those who can be made to seem less worthy and removed from sight. Admittedly, the past 40 years of mass incarceration have not been encouraging ones for the proposition that the rule of law imposes a permanent restraint on modern sovereignty. Likewise, modern international human rights law, including the *Universal Declaration of Human Rights* and the *International Covenant on Civil and Political Rights*, has proven more effective at providing a foundation for condemning human rights catastrophes after the fact than preventing them. This chapter argues that the influence of modern human rights law on national constitutional law is a more promising candidate that has emerged since (and in response to) the Holocaust. The best examples are the German Constitution and the *European Convention on Human Rights*, both of which have been credited with limiting the move towards US-style mass incarceration (Whitman 2003; van Zyl Smit and Snacken 2009). In the US, which thus far is not subject to any binding body of treaty based on human rights law, there is an emerging body of law finding enhanced protection for human dignity in existing constitutional provisions, such as the Eighth Amendment's prohibition on 'cruel and unusual punishment' and the

32 *Jonathan Simon*

Fourth Amendment against 'unreasonable searches and seizure' (Henry 2010; Bowers 2013; Simon 2014a).

In modern post-World War II US constitutional jurisprudence, a key term for this human rights value is 'civilization', or more precisely a 'civilized society'. For example, in the critical recent decision requiring California to reduce its prison population by the sum of more than 40,000 prisoners in order that longstanding court orders requiring dramatic improvements in prison medical and mental health care could be implemented, Justice Anthony Kennedy wrote for a narrow 5:4 majority: 'A prison that deprives prisoners of basic sustenance, including adequate medical care, is incompatible with the concept of human dignity and has no place in civilized society' (*Brown v Plata* 2011, 1928).

I will return to other aspects of *Brown* in the final section of this chapter, but for now will consider the phrase 'civilized society' – a 'place' defined for our purposes by institutions and practices that respect 'human dignity'. The US Supreme Court, albeit only a handful of quite different times, has evoked the nation's 'evolving standards of decency' as a 'civilized society' to hold certain punishments to be 'cruel and unusual', though not the equivalent of torture. What might this idea, of a 'civilized society' with 'evolving standards of decency' (what I will call for present purposes the 'legal civilizing process'), add, if anything, to the existing sociological notion of the 'civilizing process' (Elias 1978)? Does a legal civilizing process offer us any protections against turns towards mass human rights disasters that sociological civilization did or does not? The precedents are not at first blush promising. Talk about 'civilization' and 'decency' might seem to be an invitation to judicial subjectivity (the worry of conservatives like Justice Scalia) or, perhaps worse, the regulatory strategies that have so often followed from the sympathetic response of elites to the suffering of certain groups among the poor, such as children of immigrants, people with psychiatric disabilities and female sex workers, among others. A more optimistic scenario suggests that modern human rights law, once embodied in capable legal centres of power, can counter-balance the inherently degrading tendencies of bureaucracies that take totalizing control over populations excluded from general public knowledge.

Today the best-case scenario for that is Europe (van Zyl Smit and Snacken 2009), where, despite populist strains in penal policy, the worst excesses of American-style mass incarceration have not gained a significant footing, including widespread, prolonged solitary confinement as a prison management tool and life sentences with no meaningful release mechanism (common in the US, rare in Europe and recently condemned by the European Court of Human Rights).[2] An optimistic reading of the US situation (Simon 2014a) is that, spurred on by the excesses of mass incarceration, US courts are moving to upgrade the very thin form of dignity jurisprudence adopted in the period 1950 through 1980. Dignity-based constitutional rules are not a gainsay or talisman that can freeze degrading tendencies in the penal or immigration systems of advanced bureaucratic democracies, but they are a form of counter-power – a legal civilizing process that can check those tendencies.

Mass incarceration as a human rights disaster

Bauman's reading of the Holocaust gives any student of penal power pause at the potential of incarceration to promote mass human rights violations. Following conviction for felony (in the US or a similar offence in other countries), legal prisoners face the likelihood of physical distancing, exclusive bureaucratic management and the self-enclosing power of expert technical knowledge. These techniques are not themselves the methods of genocide, but they played a crucial role in enabling the Nazi genocide by removing its potential victims from the everyday sphere of encounter and imagination, conditions which seem to be crucial sources for moral responsibility in individuals.

From this perspective, the modern prison poses a dilemma. Invented in the eighteenth century to replace practices that enlightened opinion deemed inhumane, such as torture on the scaffold, prison has had a long career seeking to reinvent itself from regular scandals that have belied its humanity. Since the Holocaust, the prison has faced the additional challenge, not only of avoiding reversion to torture, but also of being an inherent threat to the human rights of prisoners by removing them physically from the everyday experience of citizens and subjecting them to direct rule by a correctional bureaucracy. On the other hand, if the modern prison does not always lead to the mass dehumanization and degradation of its prisoners, it is precisely because some of these same elements, including bureaucracy and expert technical knowledge, operate to hold prison regimes accountable to human rights norms and observers.

Mass incarceration in the US marked a significant departure from the nation's post-World War II record of seeking to improve protection for human rights in prisons.[3] Beginning in the 1940s, the federal government and several of the leading industrialized states set out to reframe corrections along the lines of the modern mental health establishment, with a focus on diagnosis, individualized treatment and normalizing deviant behaviour. From the 1960s through the 1980s, civil rights lawyers, acting on behalf of state prison inmates (many in the South), relied in part on this new correctional penology to convince federal judges that racist and abusive informal prison regimes and antiquated prisons that lacked access to decent medical care violated the Eighth Amendment's ban on 'cruel and unusual' punishment (Feeley and Rubin 1998).

At virtually the same time, state governments began to commit themselves to a policy of expanding imprisonment as a response to ordinary non-violent property and drug crimes in an effort to repress violent crime through general incapacitation. Beginning in the 1980s, this state effort received growing federal support, and both state and federal prison systems began to grow rapidly, reaching a national average of more than four times the rate of imprisonment in the 1970s. Concentrated on urban communities of colour, where violent crime rates were far higher than metropolitan averages, this campaign greatly increased the racial disproportionality of the prison population (which had been marked from the beginning of statistics in the 1920s) to shocking highs. At its peak in

34 *Jonathan Simon*

the 1990s, this combined state and federal effort produced a flow of prisoners in which African-American men were nine times more likely to be present than white men, given each group's relative proportion of the overall population (that is down to six to one in the 2012 data) (Carson and Golinelli 2013: 25).

Much has been written about this carceral wave (Garland 2001; Wacquant 2009; Alexander 2010) but, for our purposes, only one feature is salient: it has produced human rights violations on a scale far in excess of the correctional past. While mass incarceration is no Holocaust, it can fairly be described as a human rights disaster, or in the more measured words of Supreme Court Justice Stephen Breyer, 'a big Human Rights problem' (quoted in Simon 2014a: 149). By widening the net of people convicted of crimes sent to prison, and increasing the length of time required for many traditional imprisonment crimes, mass incarceration took hold of a population different in kind than the traditional prison population, one with a heavy burden of chronic illness problems associated with poverty, substance abuse and repeatedly disrupted lives. This manifests itself in psychiatric illnesses like schizophrenia and in physical illness like diabetes, Hepatitis C and HIV. Intended to incapacitate prisoners, not rehabilitate them, mass incarceration prisons were built without adequate facilities or routines to cope with these problems. These problems deepened as fiscal crises following the internet bust of 2000, the 2001 recession that was worsened by 9/11, and the Great Recession of 2008–2009 largely ended new prison construction by states, while mass imprisonment policies continued to operate. As a result, at the start of this decade, half the states had chronic overcrowding, some experiencing more than twice the design capacity for entire systems.

Thus, within the history of the US prison, mass incarceration reflected a significant shift towards inhumanity on a broad scale. Tellingly, many features detailed in Bauman's study can be observed in this shift. Particularly important was the role of the penal bureaucracy. This included both frontline correctional workers and administrators in correctional agencies, who during this period became increasingly cut off from the influences of a global correctional profession with important ties to science and social relief efforts and became increasingly tied to state politics and self-referential in its normative demands (Page 2011). Other professions, including medicine and psychology, which had long been involved in supervising prisoners, were largely excluded during the era of mass incarceration. Always distanced from the general population, prisoners were increasingly at the mercy of mostly public and sometimes private bureaucracies lacking any oversight by authorities with a general community role, other than the courts.[4]

California became a national example of mass incarceration as inhuman punishment when the Supreme Court issued its 2011 *Brown v. Plata* decision, which upheld a sweeping judicial order capping California's prison population as a percentage of design capacity (137.2 per cent), ordering the state to achieve that goal in two years (since extended), presumably through the diversion of felons to local jails and non-incarcerative sentences. Central to the decision – the first in decades that had strongly affirmed prisoners' rights – was a record of tremendous suffering due to the state's 'deliberate indifference' towards the medical and mental health needs of the prison population. As noted above, the Court's majority invoked 'civilized society' in rejecting the state's clear democratic preference for addressing crime with incarceration. The dissenters, in contrast, would have given the state more time to reduce overcrowding and address unmet medical and mental health needs in the name of keeping California citizens safe from the risk of crime posed by any prisoner release or diversion.

As a result of *Brown v. Plata*, California lawmakers reversed several decades of prison sentence expansion to exclude a large swathe of felony convictions for non-violent, non-serious, non-sexual felonies, reducing its prison admissions by a startling 65 per cent in 2012 and leading a nationwide decline in both prison population and imprisonment rates for the first time in nearly four decades (Carson and Golinelli 2013: 20). Coming at a time when politicians and the media had already begun to sour on mass incarceration, *Plata* added a human rights dimension missing in most other debates on incarceration. It is far too early to declare mass incarceration over. Indeed, recent data suggests that the prison population is growing again after several years of decline (Eckholm 2014). However, given that most of the downward trend in US prison populations has come from one case condemning California's form of mass incarceration, it is surely worth exploring how strengthening the legal civilizing process might check the human rights-abusing potentialities of its sociological cousin. The remainder of this chapter draws lessons from three key moments in the US Supreme Court's treatment of the legal civilizing process since it was first observed in the aftermath of the Holocaust.

Evolving standards of decency?

The first appearance of modern human rights dignity talk in a US Supreme Court decision came a decade after the *Universal Declaration of Human Rights* and in a most curious case. In *Trop v. Dulles* (1958), the Court overturned the decision of a court martial stripping Trop of his US citizenship as punishment for his wartime desertion of his post when in the armed forces. Writing for only four of the five justices who voted to strike down the sentence as 'cruel and unusual', Chief Justice Earl Warren observed that, although the penalty 'involved no physical mistreatment, no primitive torture', it actually was a more significant harm, threatening 'the total destruction of the individual's status in organized society', the very 'right to have rights'. *Trop* was an unusual case in every respect, but in the 1970s the Supreme Court applied the same doctrine to strike down a life sentence without parole for a small-time (but persistent) property offender, suggesting that conventional state penal policies might also be subject to this kind of 'decency'.

Two decades later, in *Harmelin v. Michigan* (1991), at the height of the 'War on Crime' and mass incarceration, the Supreme Court upheld a life

36   Jonathan Simon

sentence without the possibility of parole for the crime of possessing 650 or more grams of crack cocaine. Writing for another plurality, Justice Anthony Kennedy suggested that the broad range of utilitarian purposes served by prisons, and the deference that courts owe to democratic policy-making choices, means that prison sentences should almost never violate the Eighth Amendment. Along with a 1994 case instructing the lower courts to defer to the expertise of state prison officials (*Farmer v. Brennan*), the Supreme Court had largely withdrawn the Eighth Amendment from any role in checking mass imprisonment. It would be capital punishment alone, and that only to a very limited degree, in relation to which the Constitution would set limits on substantive penal choices.

In several decisions since 2010, the Supreme Court has signalled that it may be revitalizing the 'evolving standards of decency doctrine'. In *Graham v. Florida* (2010), the Supreme Court rejected life without parole sentences imposed on juveniles for non-homicide crimes (a position later extended to all life without parole sentences for crimes committed as juveniles). In *Brown v. Plata* (2011), the Supreme Court let stand a lower court order requiring California to reduce its prison population by nearly 40,000 inmates, despite the *Prison Litigation Reform Act 1996*, which requires federal courts seeking to reform unconstitutional conditions in state prisons to balance the need to remedy the constitutional violations with the effect on public safety.

The 'evolving standards of decency' doctrine under the Eighth Amendment, and the concept of human dignity said to underlie it, offers no talisman that can prevent advanced bureaucratic democracies from engaging in systematic cruelty, but it can provide a legal basis for individual justices to learn lessons from wartime failures of the rule of law (Chief Justice Earl Warren and Justice Kennedy). An even more promising approach is that taken by the European Council, where a strong dignity-based charter (the *European Convention on Human Rights*) has been strengthened further by the creation of bureaucratic governmental agencies (the European Committee for the Prevention of Torture and the Committee of Ministers of the Council) with a mission of enforcing the Convention by inspecting places of detention and producing guiding norms for problematic areas of state coercion (such as prisons and psychiatric hospitals).

Trop v. Dulles

The rule of law, including the US domestic Constitution, has a long history of fading during national emergencies. During the Civil War and World War I, executive authority (some with, some without, Congressional affirmation) was used to repress individuals engaged in ordinary democratic dissent. In both instances, courts generally declined to intervene. Most infamously, during World War II, the US engaged in one of the largest scale human rights violations in its history – the forced removal of all persons of Japanese ancestry from the West Coast of the US. When this action was formally reviewed by the Supreme Court, in *Korematsu v. United States* (1944: 219), the Court upheld the classification and imposition of a terrible burden on the basis of nationality, the first time ever an explicit racial classification had been approved, on the grounds that dire necessity made it permissible: 'When under conditions of modern warfare our shores are threatened by hostile forces, the power to protect must be commensurate with the threatened danger.'

After World War II, the adoption of the *Universal Declaration of Human Rights* in 1948 signalled the beginning of a new effort to deepen the human rights protections in both domestic and international law. In the US, the Supreme Court under Chief Justice Earl Warren, whose term began in 1954, began a process of reforming criminal justice institutions through enforcement of the Fourth, Fifth, Sixth and Eighth Amendments of the US Constitution.

Trop v. Dulles (1958), decided four years into Warren's transformative Chief Justiceship, represented the most significant early effort to discern the implications of the new focus on human dignity for the state's power to punish.[5] Trop was a soldier who deserted in French West Africa during World War II when he briefly escaped from the Casablanca jail before turning himself over to a US military vehicle. He was convicted by a court martial and dishonourably discharged from the army. Under a statute dating to the Civil War but renewed in 1940, Congress made loss of citizenship a consequence of wartime desertion, but only if the soldier were discharged from the military and not given a chance to complete his service, which is what happened to Trop and apparently thousands of other servicemen during the war. Trop claimed that the loss of citizenship for wartime desertion violated the Eighth Amendment's prohibition on 'cruel and unusual punishment', but the Court had previously upheld capital punishment, presumably a more severe penalty, for the very same crime:

> Since wartime desertion is punishable by death, there can be no argument that the penalty of denationalization is excessive in relation to the gravity of the crime. The question is whether this penalty subjects the individual to a fate forbidden by the principle of civilized treatment guaranteed by the Eighth Amendment. ... While the State has the power to punish, the Amendment stands to assure that this power be exercised within the limits of civilized standards.
>
> (Trop v. Dulles 1958: 99)

In conventional terms of comparing crimes and penalties, denaturalization might not seem 'cruel and unusual', but Chief Justice Warren, on behalf of a plurality of four[6] (thus not a majority), argued that the Eighth Amendment's meaning should not remain static but instead be changed over time as society 'matured': 'The Amendment must draw its meaning from the evolving standards of decency that mark the progress of a maturing society' (*Trop v. Dulles* 1958: 101). This was the beginning of the 'evolving standards of decency doctrine' – what we are calling the legal civilizing process.

38   *Jonathan Simon*

Thus far, Chief Justice Warren's opinion makes the legal civilizing process sound a lot like its sociological cousin (Elias 1978). In the crucial sections of his concurring opinion, the Chief Justice gave more substantive shape to his reasons for viewing forfeiture of citizenship as beyond the limits of decency (*Trop v. Dulles* 1958: 102):

> There may be involved no physical mistreatment, no primitive torture. There is instead the total destruction of the individual's status in organized society. It is a form of punishment more primitive than torture, for it destroys for the individual the political existence that was centuries in the development. The punishment strips the citizen of his status in the national and international political community. His very existence is at the sufferance of the country in which he happens to find himself. ... In short, the expatriate has lost the right to have rights.

This evocative phrase, seemingly lifted without attribution from Hannah Arendt (1951), may not have been intended to set a threshold for conditions that would be indecent but instead to place human dignity at the centre of power, symbolized here by the sovereign power of the nation to punish a soldier/ citizen. Not only would Trop have lost his US nationality but, lacking an alternative passport, he also faced the possibility of being unwanted in any state and thus a refugee subject to the whim or mercy of states and individuals.

Trop v. Dulles was clearly a limited precedent for the purposes of the penal state. It did not involve a prison sentence, the routine punishment for US felonies, and thus had seemingly little implication for routine punishment. Trop escaped the stigma of felony crime, being associated with the shame but not danger posed by desertion. In any event, Chief Justice Warren served more than a decade more without revisiting this promising doctrine. Warren, a former prosecutor and governor, probably believed that fixing police and prosecutorial abuses would be more efficacious in limiting the repressive power of the state than attacking prison sentences at a time when the dominant ideology supported rehabilitative penology and most states were moving towards shorter prison sentences.

Harmelin v. Michigan

Trop v. Dulles was decided in 1958 at a time when prison populations in the US remained near their traditional rate of about 100 prisoners per 100,000 in the population as a whole. In the early 1980s, a more conservative Court struck down a sentence of life in prison without parole imposed on a person with a long record of petty property crime, again citing the evolving standards of decency (*Solem v. Helm* 1983). But, as the prison population began to rise sharply in the 1980s and 1990s, the Supreme Court signalled that its analysis of imprisonment under the 'evolving standards of decency' would be dramatically narrowed. The key shift came in a case involving a sentence of 'life without parole' for possession of more than 650 grams of cocaine. Harmelin argued that such a severe sentence, for what amounted to a non-violent drug possession crime, was so disproportionate as to offend the Eighth Amendment on the civilized law ground that we have been discussing. The majority rejected the claim but disagreed on why. The Court's most conservative justices rejected the Eighth Amendment claim on the grounds that the Constitution does not include any proportionality doctrine, at least not when it comes to prison sentences (as opposed to capital punishment). On this theory, states may sentence residents to prison sentences of any length, assuming they have been properly tried and convicted, and the sentence is for a rational purpose. Justice Kennedy's concurrence, joined by several other centrists on the Court, argued that the Eighth Amendment did include a proportionality principle, as part of the evolving standards of decency of a maturing society, but that the pursuit of objectivity necessary to discern these standards makes them very narrow indeed:

> The Court therefore has recognized that a punishment may violate the Eighth Amendment if it is contrary to the 'evolving standards of decency that mark the progress of a maturing society'. ... In evaluating a punishment under this test, 'we have looked not to our own conceptions of decency, but to those of modern American society as a whole' in determining what standards have 'evolved', ... and thus have focused not on 'the subjective views of individual Justices', but on 'objective factors to the maximum possible extent'.
>
> (*Harmelin* 1991: 1014)

Justice Kennedy emphasized this quest for objectivity in setting out four principles that tremendously limit the scope of proportionality review by courts:

> The first of these principles is that the fixing of prison terms for specific crimes involves a substantive penological judgment that, as a general matter, is 'properly within the province of legislatures, not courts'. ... Determinations about the nature and purposes of punishment for criminal acts implicate difficult and enduring questions respecting the sanctity of the individual, the nature of law, and the relation between law and the social order. ... The efficacy of any sentencing system cannot be assessed absent agreement on the purposes and objectives of the penal system. And the responsibility for making these fundamental choices and implementing them lies with the legislature .... The second principle is that the Eighth Amendment does not mandate adoption of any one penological theory. ... Third, marked divergences both in underlying theories of sentencing and in the length of prescribed prison terms are the inevitable, often beneficial, result of the federal structure. ... The fourth principle at work in our cases is that proportionality review by federal courts should be informed by 'objective factors to the maximum possible extent'. ... The

40   *Jonathan Simon*

Eighth Amendment does not require strict proportionality between crime and sentence. Rather, it forbids only extreme sentences that are 'grossly disproportionate' to the crime.

(*Harmelin* 1991: 1000–1001)

Based on these four factors, all of which place deference to state power to imprison in a higher and higher priority, Justice Kennedy reasoned that the scope of analysis previously entertained by the Court (in which Harmelin's sentence would have been considered in comparison with those of similar offenders in other states and offenders with the same kind of sentence in his state) should only be considered if the Court's own assessment of the gravity of the offence and the severity of the crime are 'grossly disproportionate'.[7] Although Harmelin's sentence was the harshest prison sentence possible, and second only to capital punishment among possible punishments, Justice Kennedy had no problem finding that possession of cocaine in such a large quantity was in fact a crime of violence equivalent or close enough to actual murder (the crime for which life without parole is most typically given):

Petitioner's suggestion that his crime was nonviolent and victimless, echoed by the dissent ... is false to the point of absurdity. To the contrary, petitioner's crime threatened to cause grave harm to society. ... Quite apart from the pernicious effects on the individual who consumes illegal drugs, such drugs relate to crime in at least three ways: (1) A drug user may commit crime because of drug-induced changes in physiological functions, cognitive ability, and mood; (2) A drug user may commit crime in order to obtain money to buy drugs; and (3) A violent crime may occur as part of the drug business or culture. ... Studies bear out these possibilities and demonstrate a direct nexus between illegal drugs and crimes of violence. See generally *id.*, at 16–48. To mention but a few examples, 57 percent of a national sample of males arrested in 1989 for homicide tested positive for illegal drugs. ... The comparable statistics for assault, robbery, and weapons arrests were 55, 73, and 63 percent, respectively. ... In Detroit, Michigan, in 1988, 68 percent of a sample of male arrestees and 81 percent of a sample of female arrestees tested positive for illegal drugs. Fifty-one percent of males and seventy-one percent of females tested positive for cocaine. ... And last year an estimated 60 percent of the homicides in Detroit were drug related, primarily cocaine related.

(*Harmelin* 1991, citations omitted)

Kennedy and the other centrist justices also dismissed the potential for unfairness in such an extremely harsh sentence for what was, formally speaking, a possession offence on the grounds that Harmelin (and others like him) had a clear choice not to engage in conduct that was becoming a major focus of social concern and governmental response. Indeed, mandatory sentences, then very much in fashion, were deemed by many to be fairer because

The legal civilizing process 41

they were more transparent than mid-twentieth-century indeterminate sentencing systems that allowed parole release:

> This system is not an ancient one revived in a sudden or surprising way; it is, rather, a recent enactment calibrated with care, clarity, and much deliberation to address a most serious contemporary social problem. The scheme provides clear notice of the severe consequences that attach to possession of drugs in wholesale amounts, thereby giving force to one of the first purposes of criminal law – deterrence. In this sense, the Michigan scheme may be as fair, if not more so, than other sentencing systems in which the sentencer's discretion or the complexity of the scheme obscures the possible sanction for a crime, resulting in a shock to the offender who learns the severity of his sentence only after he commits the crime.
>
> (*Harmelin* 1991: 1007–1008)

Justice Kennedy's concurring opinion in *Harmelin* came to define the scope of what we have called legal civilization for the purposes of the Eighth Amendment.[8] Many of the features that Bauman identified as critical to enabling human rights abuses under conditions of sociological civilization apply here as well. First, ignoring the point of having a legal civilization test, Justice Kennedy's *Harmelin* analysis tied the standard closely to the organized governing bureaucracy itself (precisely that part of society that can cause human rights disasters). Faced with multiple reasons to defer to state penal choices, the promise that 'evolving standards of decency' might restrain populist penal measures, aimed at pleasing voters at the expense of demonized criminal threats, became an illusion. This deference infected the Eighth Amendment overall. Three years after *Harmelin*, in *Farmer v. Brennan* (1994: 845) the Court rejected an Eighth Amendment claim from a transsexual (male to female) prisoner who had been raped and brutalized by other prisoners after being housed in the general population despite asking for protective treatment. The Court noted that courts should be reluctant to second-guess management decisions of prison officials because they 'face the unenviable task of keeping dangerous men secure in humane conditions', despite the fact that Farmer, guilty of property crimes, posed little danger to anyone, and the prison in which he was held was neither secure nor humane.

Second, the association of crime with violence is featured, and violence with an emergency that necessitates risky decisions that may require overriding a particular individual's right to hope for a future as an individual. If the state can define carrying crack cocaine as a threat akin to homicide, there is little to stop it from doing that with those who possess far smaller weights, those who use drugs, or those loitering in drug-infested areas. Here it is worth noting that 1991, the year in which *Harmelin* was decided, was at or near the peak of a wave of homicides that most criminologists at the time associated with crack cocaine sales and which pushed the homicide rate to its highest level in the twentieth century.

42 *Jonathan Simon*

Third, respect for human dignity, unnamed here except in its prior core association with the 'evolving standards of decency' doctrine, receives acknowledgement only in terms of choice, and whether *Harmelin* had a clear chance to avoid exposing himself to this very severe penalty. This is fully consistent with the prevailing legal and philosophical views of dignity that closely associate that word – so central to post-World War II human rights treaties – with the Kantian conception of rationality (Waldron 2013). Under this prevailing conception, individuals who choose to commit crimes subject to extreme penalties, aimed at deterring conduct deemed highly dangerous to the social order, place their rationality and dignity on the side of their law-breaking. Thus it was seen that imposing harsh punishment in such cases is precisely the way to honour their human dignity. Based on this view, a system of mercy, predicated on executive or judicial discretion, would arguably demean that very dignity.

Brown v. Plata

In the second decade of the twenty-first century there is evidence that the idea of legal civilization as a restraint on the state's penal power is being revived. Its strongest articulation came in a 2011 decision, *Brown v. Plata*, where the Court upheld a cap on California's mammoth prison population after years of chronic overcrowding that had prevented previous court orders from fixing a broken system of health care delivery in prison. The case was a consolidation of two distinct Eighth Amendment cases involving challenges to treatment in the entire California prison system (then the largest in terms of prison population in the US). *Coleman v. Wilson* (1995) found that the state had been 'deliberately indifferent' to the fate of thousands of prisoners with serious mental illness in failing to provide adequate professional staff or treatment space at its massive new prison complexes and failing to develop procedures to screen for prisoners suffering from mental illness or suicidal conditions, or to respond to those conditions. Judge Lawrence Karlton of the US District Court for the Central District of California ordered the state to create a constitutionally adequate mental health care system and appointed a 'special master' to oversee the implementation of his order across a system that included thirty or more facilities. *Plata v. Davis* (2002) found a similar systemic failure to provide adequate staff or infrastructure to deliver medical care to prisoners who increasingly suffered from complex chronic illnesses requiring careful monitoring of individual prisoners. The state initially entered a negotiated 'stipulation' in which it agreed that the problem was a constitutional violation and agreed to remedy it within three years. Instead, finding a lack of progress in 2005, Judge Thelton Henderson of the US District Court for the Northern District of California placed the entire prison medical system under a court-appointed 'Receiver' (a role best known in bankruptcy law) to oversee the operation of the system and to implement the remedy.

The two cases became linked in 2009 when both judges joined in convening a special three-judge court to consider whether a population cap was

The legal civilizing process 43

necessary to complete the long-frustrated remedial orders in the two cases (14 years and seven years, respectively). Since the late 1990s, California prisons had been operating at two to three times their design capacity. With every available space crammed with extra bedding (often in the form of triple bunks), delivery of health care services to prisoners with chronic conditions faltered, and efforts to implement remedies in both of these gigantic litigations over prison condition reform proved futile. The special vehicle of the three-judge court and the demanding standard required before a population cap could be imposed on a state prison system were both products of the *Prison Litigation Reform Act 1996*, a historically unprecedented federal law limiting the jurisdiction of the federal courts to protect the civil rights of state prisoners and signed by President Bill Clinton at the height of the War on Crime. Before it can order a population cap, the court must find that overcrowding is the main cause of the unconstitutional conditions and that no remedy short of limiting the state's power to increase the prison population will provide relief. Even then the court must determine that a population cap would not significantly endanger public safety.

In August 2009, the three-judge court ordered the State of California to reduce its level of overcrowding to 137.2 per cent of design capacity (from near 200 per cent systemwide) within a two-year period. The order did not, formally speaking, require that the state turn away prisoners. California might have met the population cap through a massive programme of prison construction or by sending those with felony convictions to private prisons. But, as a practical matter, given the state's weak financial position during the Great Recession, and because of the strong resistance to privatization from California's powerful union of prison officers, both the court and the state recognized that only the diversion of potential prisoners to other sentences could possibly achieve the target set by the court in the time permitted. With political leaders dead set against any 'early release' of existing prisoners (many of whom suffered from the greatest medical and mental health problems), the state had to consider ways to keep people from becoming prisoners in the first place by diverting some portion of the people newly sentenced to prison terms by courts or formerly incarcerated people who violated the conditions of their community release and would normally be sent back to a state prison. Ultimately the state would do both.

In the meantime, the State of California appealed on the grounds that the population cap was not necessary to remedy the existing unconstitutional conditions and that it would endanger public safety. The US Supreme Court upheld that cap with a vote of 5:4. Directly invoking Chief Justice Warren's appeal in *Trop v. Dulles* for 'civilized' treatment and the parallel claim that the protection of human dignity forms a central purpose of the Eighth Amendment, but this time for a majority of the Supreme Court, Justice Kennedy wrote:

> Just as a prisoner may starve if not fed, he or she may suffer or die if not provided adequate medical care. A prison that deprives prisoners of basic sustenance, including adequate medical care, is incompatible with the

44 Jonathan Simon

concept of human dignity and has no place in civilized society. Respect for that dignity animates the Eighth Amendment prohibition against cruel and unusual punishment.

(*Brown v. Plata* 2011: 1928)

Whether or not *Brown v. Plata* will mark a turning point remains to be seen. It is already responsible for the largest prison population reduction in modern history (although the latest figures show the California prison population growing despite the caps, which apply only to prisoners housed in California prisons and not private prisons or jails contracted to hold them). It clearly marks the return of the idea of civilized treatment or society, and the related ideas of evolving standards of decency and protection of human dignity. Nor is it a singular decision. In other recent Eighth Amendment decisions of the same majority coalition (traditional progressives plus Justice Kennedy), the Supreme Court has signalled a growing concern with the excesses of populist penality. These include decisions to abolish capital punishment as a penalty for raping a child (where there is no homicide), or for homicides committed by juveniles, and to abolish life without parole sentences for juveniles.

There is a long history of constitutional rights fading during wartime emergencies, only to be revitalized in the aftermath, sometimes with enhanced protections against the next wave of emergencies. All in all, this pattern is more compatible with Bauman's thesis about sociological civilization than it is an exception to it. Nonetheless, there are a number of features of the recent revival of the legal idea of 'civilized society', what we have called the legal civilizing process, that recommend it as a framework to resist the ready deployment of conventional criminal justice bureaucracies to exclude and degrade minority populations.

The concept of dignity underlying the concepts of civilization and evolving standards of decency has shifted in recent decades from a focus on rationality and choice to one on the life course and the existential features of the human condition (and the suffering inherent in that condition). For the first several decades after World War II, the emphasis on human dignity in human rights law was read to emphasize values of equality and liberty, centred in the idea of autonomy and human agency. In such a framework, extreme deprivations of rights can be readily justified if seen as a response to the threat of violence to others. According to this view, like Harmelin, who presumably chose to earn the economic premiums rewarded for those willing to run the risks of criminal trafficking, those who violate laws sincerely enacted to protect public safety have made a rational choice, and harsh punishment may be considered completely consistent with human dignity. Since the 1990s, dignity has been increasingly associated with the human condition in a more embodied and social sense. From this perspective, the requirements of sustaining a human life, and human forms of suffering anchored in the life course (adolescence, childbirth, ageing and dying), require limits on punishment quite apart from the rational choices of the person who has violated the law.

The legal civilizing process   45

This case is also noteworthy because the federal statute that formed the major ground for the state's appeal, the *Prison Litigation Reform Act*, is an example of a law intended to insulate state institutions from the potential checking power of the courts (steps that signal a movement towards a greater human rights catastrophe, on the Bauman model). The explicit purpose of the law was to make it harder for state prisoners to bring constitutional issues into federal court, which it does through multiple means (requiring a three-judge rather than one-judge decision, allowing permissive joinder for law enforcement agencies and setting high standards for remedies). The law drew a particularly strong line against judicial remedies that interfere with the ability of states to imprison as many people as they choose to, requiring the court to reject a population cap if it proves a significant risk to public safety even when it is necessary to remedy a constitutional violation. The fact that the three-judge court in *Plata* ordered a massive reduction in prison population, even under that standard, is a demonstration of the resilience of federal courts as shields against state penal power. The *Plata* court created a powerful factual record that demonstrated that the characterization of the broad prison population as a danger to the community requiring penal incapacitation, central to mass incarceration, was inaccurate in many cases. The tens of thousands of prisoners who were part of the *Coleman* class action,[9] all of whom suffered from a major mental illness, and the even larger number of prisoners with serious chronic illnesses or injuries requiring sustained medical treatment and monitoring, of which the *Plata* case found the state incapable, are far more at risk of premature death at the hands of the state than they are a risk of danger to others. Indeed, Justice Kennedy references the concept of 'evolving standards of decency' in a footnote in which he indicates just how broad was the harm of California's human rights abuses:

> Plaintiffs rely on systemwide deficiencies in the provision of medical and mental health care that, taken as a whole, subject sick and mentally ill prisoners in California to 'substantial risk of serious harm' and cause the delivery of care in the prisons to fall below the evolving standards of decency that mark the progress of a maturing society.
>
> (*Brown v. Plata* 2011: 1926, note 4)

The fact that a very conservative US Supreme Court upheld this decision is likely to be a major signal to other lower courts that overriding state penal preferences is sometimes necessary. Indeed, after decades of instructing federal courts to defer to state penal policies and administrative expertise, the *Brown* (2011: 1928) majority laid a clear rationale for intervention: 'A prison that deprives prisoners of basic sustenance, including adequate medical care, is incompatible with the concept of human dignity and has no place in civilized society.' Further, efforts to compel courts to balance constitutional violations with other considerations, such as the *Prison Litigation Reform Act*, must ultimately be subordinated to obligation to remedy constitutional violations:

46   *Jonathan Simon*

> If government fails to fulfill this obligation, the courts have a responsibility to remedy the resulting Eighth Amendment violation. ... Courts must be sensitive to the State's interest in punishment, deterrence, and rehabilitation, as well as the need for deference to experienced and expert prison administrators faced with the difficult and dangerous task of housing large numbers of convicted criminals. ... Courts nevertheless must not shrink from their obligation to 'enforce the constitutional rights of all "persons," including prisoners'. ... Courts may not allow constitutional violations to continue simply because a remedy would involve intrusion into the realm of prison administration.
>
> (*Brown v. Plata* 2011: 1928–1929)

During the growth era of mass incarceration, deference to state penal choices and expertise, intensified by popular expressions of frustration over violent crime, left courts largely absent in setting limits to bureaucratic power in the penal setting. Given the degree to which this setting is one that is already distanced from the public and normal political processes, courts play a singular role against this particularly risky pathway to mass human rights abuses in advanced democratic societies. As a precedent, *Brown v. Plata* is likely to launch challenges to prison and jail conditions all over the country. While the component cases in *Brown v. Plata*, and the crisis in medical and mental health care exposed therein, took decades to hold the state's mass incarceration policies accountable, challenges in other states would be likely to move faster – although perhaps not fast enough to unwind degrading conditions that exist all over the country where overcrowding and chronic illness-burdened prison populations are more the rule than the exception. Courts can play a checking role but cannot ultimately carry the full burden of policing the human rights of people caught in our distended penal and policing systems.

Conclusion

Is there a legal civilizing process? Here Europe offers an intriguing counter-example. Following World War II and through the early 1970s, the US and Western Europe had similar approaches to the relationship between human rights and the authority of national (or, in the US federal system, state) penal and police authorities. In both cases limited protections of individual rights were anchored primarily in national constitutions or criminal procedure codes. Incarceration rates were higher in the US but not dramatically so, and capital punishment was in use in both Europe and the US. Today, as everyone knows, the two are quite different (Whitman 2003). Despite not insignificant increases in the scale of incarceration in many European Union member states, and a high concentration of racial and nationality or immigration status minorities among the incarcerated (De Giorgi 2006; Wacquant 2009), there is no clear analogue to American-style mass incarceration in any European state. Likewise, a transnational set of values and institutions is now recognized as necessary to the security of human rights in Europe, and the end of capital punishment across the world is now a continental purpose. While there are many differences in political institutions, culture and history that may explain this, the fact that European penal systems are subject to a body of human rights law informed by the concept of human dignity that has no current correlative in the US is extremely promising (van Zyl Smit and Snacken 2009). In the European Union, it is importantly not just the courts as instruments of human rights, but also agencies with expertise, budgets and transnational political clout, like the European Committee for the Prevention of Torture and the Committee of Ministers of the Council of Europe, which promulgate the European Prison Rules (2006).

From the 1960s through the 1980s, US federal judges played a celebrated role in civilizing brutal state prison practices, many of which dated back to the nineteenth century (Feeley and Rubin 1998). Then, during the last decade of the twentieth century through the first decade of this century, mass incarceration introduced a new kind of degradation into American corrections, one based on late-twentieth-century technologies and a commitment to an extreme version of penal incapacitation as a primary societal justification for imprisonment (Simon 2014a). Courts by and large failed to check these tendencies, approving supermax prisons and irreducible life sentences for adults as compatible with the evolving standards of decency. We can see at play many of the forces that Bauman's analysis indicates, especially the perception of a national emergency around violent crime, which enabled the judiciary to avoid a confrontation with mass incarceration. But, arguably we also see the consequences of an underdeveloped legal civilizing process, one too weak to bolster restraints on inhumane treatment or seed counter-centres of power. In this respect, a gulf opened up between the US and legal systems, like those of Europe, with fully formed, 'postmodern' constitutions anchored in human rights and human dignity.[10]

Today we are at the end of that cycle, and we appear to be at the start of another period in which the meaning of human rights within the US Constitution is being enhanced – a process that began in the US after World War II, but was left incomplete after the 1960s. This does not mean that mass incarceration is going to disappear anytime soon. The better wager is that it will shrink a little and morph into something superficially more legitimate, such as a focus on violent and repeat offenders, but which is likely to be just as racialized and even more degrading (Simon 2014b).[11] What is needed is not legal guarantees of respect for human rights – those are a liberal fantasy – but legal sources of counter-power and resistance to degradation that take the form of litigation, public investigation and shaming, and norm shaping within the penal and police bureaucracies. In the case of the US, the sociological civilizing process is quite advanced (even if not complete by European standards), but the legal civilizing process has just begun.

48 Jonathan Simon

Notes

1 Thanks to Polity Press and Cornell University Press for granting permission to reproduce previously published material in this chapter.
2 A closer inspection suggests that Europe has far from a perfect record on the treatment of prisoners, even in 'core' European societies like France (Kimmelman 2009).
3 Historians would rightly point out that American correctionalism has delivered failure far more commonly than the promise of rehabilitation-oriented treatment (McClennon 2008; Spillane 2014). What distinguished mass incarceration after the 1970s, however, was the decision to pursue widespread incapacitation with little pretence of protecting human dignity.
4 In contrast, the European Community, subject to the *European Convention on Human Rights*, specifically requires member states to integrate prison services with the institutions that deliver those services generally (see van Zyl Smit and Snacken 2009).
5 His first landmark, *Brown v. Board of Education* (1954), did not directly reference dignity but seems deeply informed by it.
6 Ironically the fifth vote in the judgement was none other than William Brennan (*Trop v. Dulles* 1948: 107), who would later write a powerful concurrence of his own on dignity and capital punishment, once again for a plurality in *Furman v. Georgia* (1972). Here he saw little room for judicial limitations on public policy choices: 'And where Congress has determined that considerations of the highest national importance indicate a course of action for which an adequate substitute might rationally appear lacking, I cannot say that this means lies beyond Congress' power to choose' [citing to *Korematsu*].
7 Notice that this puts the subjective views of the justices ahead of the more objective comparison of the sentence with the empirical record, while claiming to be serving 'objectivity'.
8 In the 2003 case of *Ewing v. California*, Justice O'Connor's majority opinion for the court relied on Kennedy's *Harmelin* concurrence to uphold California's notorious three-strikes law, which imposed a life sentence with no realistic chance of parole on a person convicted of a property crime (predicated on past serious or violent felonies on his record).
9 US law permits similarly situated parties to join in a 'class' that becomes a single legal party for the purposes of the case.
10 I first heard this use of 'postmodern' in a recent discussion here at Berkeley Law on comparative constitutional law with Justice Anthony Kennedy of the US Supreme Court and Justice Rosie Abella of the Supreme Court of Canada. Justice Abella used this to describe charters like those in Canada and South Africa that took a human rights perspective and internalized it into the national legal system.
11 Half of California prisoners are now under a life, death or extended prison sentence under the three-strikes law (Carson 2014: 13).

References

Alexander, M. (2010, 2nd edition 2012) *The New Jim Crow: Mass Incarceration in an Age of Colorblindness*, New York: New Press.
Arendt, Hannah (1951) *The Origins of Totalitarianism*, New York: Shocken Books.
Bauman, Zygmunt (1989) *Modernity and the Holocaust*, Ithaca, NY: Cornell University Press.
Bowers, J. (2013). 'Probable Cause, Constitutional Reasonableness, and the Unrecognized Point of a "Pointless Indignity"', *Stanford Law Review* 66: 987–1054.

The legal civilizing process 49

Carson, A. and Golinelli, D. (2013) *Prisoners in 2012: Trends in Admissions and Releases 1991–2011*, Washington, DC: US Department of Justice, Bureau of Justice Statistics.

Carson, A. (2014) *Prisoners in 2013*, Washington, DC: US Department of Justice, Bureau of Justice Statistics.

De Giorgi, A. (2006) *Rethinking the Political Economy of Punishment: Perspectives on Post-Fordism and Penal Politics*, London: Ashgate Publishers.

Eckholm, E. (2014) 'Number of Prisoners in US Grew Slightly in 2013, Report Finds', *The New York Times*, September 16, A12. Online. Available: www.nytimes.com/2014/09/17/us/number-of-prisoners-in-us-grew-slightly-in-2013-report-finds.html?_r=0 (accessed February 2, 2015) .

Elias, N. (1978) *The Civilizing Process*, New York: John Wiley & Sons.

Feeley, M. and Rubin, E. (1998) *Judicial Policy Making and the Modern State: How the Courts Reformed America's Prisons*, New York: Oxford University Press.

Fleury-Steiner, B. (2008) *Dying Inside: The HIV/AIDS Ward at Limestone Prison*, University of Michigan Press.

Garland, D. (2001) *The Culture of Control: Crime and Social Order in Late Modern Society*, Chicago: University of Chicago Press.

Gilmore, R. (2008) *Golden Gulags: Prisons, Surplus, Crisis, and Resistance in Globalizing California*, Berkeley, CA: University of California Press.

Henry, L. (2010) 'The Jurisprudence of Dignity', *U. Penn. L. Rev.* 160: 169–233.

Kimmelman, M. (2009) 'Abroad: A New Film Focuses France on its Overcrowded Prisons', *New York Times*, October 7, C1. Online. Available: www.nytimes.com/2009/10/08/movies/08abroad.html?_r=0 (accessed February 2, 2015).

Lichtenstein, A. (1996) *Twice the Work of Free Labor: The Political Economy of Convict Labor in the South*, London: Verso.

McClennon, R. (2008) *The Crisis of Mass Imprisonment: Protest, Politics, and the Making of the American Penal State 1776–1941*, Cambridge: Cambridge University Press.

Oshinsky, D. (1997) *Worse than Slavery: Parchman Farm and the Ordeal of Jim Crow Justice*, New York: Free Press.

Page, J. (2011) *The Toughest Beat: Politics, Punishment and the Prisoners Officers' Union in California*, Berkeley, CA: University of California Press.

Simon, J. (2014a) *Mass Incarceration on Trial: A Remarkable Court Decision and the Future of American Prisons*, New York: New Press)

Simon, J. (2014b) 'Law's Violence, the Strong State, and the Crisis of Mass Imprisonment (for Stuart Hall)', *Wake Forest Law Review* 49: 649–676.

Spillane, Joseph F. (2014) *Coxsackie: The Life and Death of Prison Reform*, Baltimore, MD: Johns Hopkins University Press.

van Zyl Smit, D. and Snacken, S. (2009) *Principles of European Prison Law & Policy: Penology and Human Rights*, Oxford: Oxford University Press.

Wacquant, L. (2009) *Punishing the Poor: The Neoliberal Government of Insecurity*, Durham, NC: Duke University Press.

Waldron, J. (2013) 'Citizenship and Dignity' New York University Public Law and Legal Theory Working Papers. Paper 378. Online. Available http://lsr.nellco.org/nyu_plltwp/378 (accessed February 2, 2015).

Whitman, J. 2003. *Harsh Justice: Criminal Punishment and the Widening Divide Between Europe and the United States*, New York: Oxford University Press.

50 *Jonathan Simon*

Cases

Brown v. Board of Education, 347 United States Reports (U.S.) 483 (1954) (Brown I)
Brown v. Plata, 131 Supreme Court Reporter (Sct) 1910 (2011)
Ewing v. California, 538 US 11 (2003)
Farmer v. Brennan, 511 US 825 (1994)
Furman v. Georgia, 408 US 238 (1972)
Graham v. Florida, 130 SCt 2011 (2010)
Harmelin v. Michigan, 501 US 957 (1991)
Korematsu v. United States, 323 US 214 (1944)
Solem v. Helm, 263 US 277 (1983)
Trop v. Dulles, 356 U.S. 88 (1958)

US=United States Reports (the official but much delayed publication of the Supreme Court of the US).
SCt=private but reliably published edition of Supreme Court decisions, unofficial but usually available in libraries and online.

3 The rehumanization of the incarcerated Other[1]

Bureaucracy, distantiation and American mass incarceration

David A. Green

Introduction

Some may find it at first incongruous, disrespectful, even perverse, to apply Bauman's theory in *Modernity and the Holocaust* (1989) to account for Americans' persistent tolerance of, and enthusiasm for, the punitive (mis)treatment of American criminal offenders. After all, barring those awaiting trial and the small number of wrongly convicted, nearly all of the 2.2 million inhabitants of American prisons and jails arguably deserve punishment for some felonious wrongdoing, however mild. And this distinction alone places them as a group quite apart from the 6 million Jews, 6 million Poles, 3 million Slavs and 3 million Ukrainians who, without any comparable distinction or taint of criminal culpability, were summarily exterminated by the Nazis between 1933 and 1945. Yet, the same social processes that enabled the horrors of the Holocaust serve to perpetuate American mass incarceration. Bauman's work on the Holocaust might, in fact, be especially apt in a discussion of American mass incarceration, particularly the catastrophic damages wrought on low-income, urban, minority neighbourhoods by its chief feeder in recent decades – the 'War on Drugs' – which former journalist and moral agitator David Simon has called a 'holocaust in slow motion' (The house I live in 2012).

This chapter, beginning with the first of five sections, summarizes Bauman's main arguments by explaining how bureaucratic rationality and social distantiation enable collective human mistreatment. The second section considers 11 cases that exemplify the mechanisms by which these twin forces operate in the context of American mass incarceration. While Bauman's twin forces continue to work in and on American society, they have also been challenged recently by several counter-discourses and counter-movements, the aims of which function to mollify the two forces that enable 'Othering'. Thus, the third section examines the rehumanizing effects of increasing proximity with the Other, while the fourth identifies four socio-penal counter-movements, discourses and practices that achieve these effects. The first of these is a reconfigured offender ideal type, constructed primarily by conservative Christian reformers and advocates for prisoner re-entry programmes, which rehumanizes offenders as needful and sympathetic rather than wholly volitional and

52   David A. Green

cunning, by recognizing both their redemptive potential and society's responsibilities towards them. The remaining three developments include restorative, community and participatory justice models, all of which in different ways rehumanize offenders by debureaucratizing justice processes, treating offenders as members of a shared moral community and closing the social distance between offenders, victims and the rest of us.

Bauman's twin enablers: bureaucratic rationality and social distantiation

Bauman (1989) identifies two processes that together made the mass murders of the Holocaust both thinkable and achievable. These were modernity's rationalization and bureaucracy, which produced amoral spaces and worked to reduce individuals to means to various evil ends; and the process of 'distantiation' (p. 100), which functioned to dehumanize those who would become victims of Nazi atrocities. His central arguments in *Modernity and the Holocaust* can be summed up as follows:

> Being inextricably tied to human proximity, morality seems to conform to the law of optical perspective. It looms large and thick close to the eye. With the growth of distance, responsibility for the other shrivels, moral dimensions of the object blur, till both reach the vanishing point and disappear from view. ... The alternative to proximity is social distance. The moral attribute of proximity is responsibility; the moral attribute of social distance is lack of moral relationship, or heterophobia. *Responsibility is silenced once proximity is eroded; it may eventually be replaced with resentment once the fellow human subset is transformed into an Other.* The process of transformation is one of social separation. It was such a separation which made it possible for thousands to kill, and for millions to watch the murder without protesting. It was the technological and bureaucratic achievement of modern rational society which made such a separation possible.
>
> (Bauman 1989: 192, 184, emphasis in original)

Here Bauman connects the role of social proximity to one's sense of moral responsibility to and for others, responsibility that is broken down by the social distancing characteristic of bureaucratic systems. Bureaucracies render their own activities beyond the reach of moral interrogation, removing compassion from human relationships and enabling moral indifference to suffering.

Bauman's work helps not only to explain the means of expansion of American mass incarceration – the policing of powerless communities, the criminalization of particular kinds of conduct, the prosecution of some and not others, the harsh sentencing of some and not others, and so on – it also helps account for the quiet indifference[2] of the American people in the face of their country's dubious rise as the world's champion incarcerator. American mass incarceration and the myriad practices that support it institutionalize social distance and inhibit human emotional proximity, thereby leading to what Bauman calls 'adiaphorization', the method by which 'systems and processes become split off from any consideration of morality' (Bauman and Lyon 2012: 7). It is 'the socio-political process of expunging ethical considerations from managerial regimes' (Nellis 2013b: 46) by 'making certain actions, or certain objects of action, morally neutral or irrelevant – exempt from the categories of phenomena suitable for moral evaluation' (Bauman, 1995: 149). Adiaphorization explains the relegation of some individuals to the amoral space beyond what Susan Opotow calls 'our scope of justice'.

> For social categories inside our scope of justice, concerns about deserving and fair treatment are salient. We perceive harm that befalls them as lamentable or outrageous. For social categories outside the scope of justice, the concepts of deserving and fair treatment do not apply and can seem irrelevant.
>
> (Opotow 1995: 347)

American penality appears especially susceptible to Bauman's two agents of holocaust. The next section identifies ten factors associated with bureaucratic rationality and/or social distantiation that work against the moral recognition of the criminal Other. These inhibit the establishment of empathy for the incarcerated and compassion for their travails in and outside prison.

Mechanisms in American penality that permit harsh treatment and indifference to suffering

First, the heterophobia that Bauman describes is especially salient in the United States (US), an exceptionally diverse nation of immigrants with a citizenry that has grown more polarized along ideological lines over the past 20 years (Pew Research Center 2014). The emotional proximity that Bauman believes is necessary for compassion and the moral consideration of others continues to erode in American life. Media outlets, for commercial reasons, increasingly cater directly to the distinct tastes and ideological dispositions of their audiences (Manjoo 2008), while increasing numbers of Americans cluster together geographically, in ideological enclaves, ensuring that few encounter citizens with differing ideological views in the course of their normal daily routines (Bishop and Cushing 2008). This polarization and increasing social distancing is evident as well in both houses of Congress, where partisan gridlock has become normalized and bipartisan compromise has become anathema to a growing number of legislators. All this suggests that Bauman's warning of the dangers of heterophobia is especially pertinent for Americans.

Second, according to Whitman (2003), Americans also maintain a high tolerance for punitive degradation, defined as treatment that makes the individual feel 'inferior, lessened, lowered' (p. 20), and the:

54   David A. Green

intoxication that comes with treating people as inferiors ... [means] it is very hard to control ourselves when we act the part of a superior chastising an inferior, especially to the extent that we tend to think of criminals ... as somehow polluted.

(p. 23)[3]

European legal systems, in contrast, appear to be built on a sober recognition of these risks and thus provide far more protections from the intoxications of derogation and do much more to ensure respect for human dignity than American systems do. For instance, van Zyl Smit and Snacken (2009: 86–125) identify the following guiding principles of European prison law and policy, which aim to ensure:

1   the restriction of imprisonment as a last resort;
2   respect for basic human rights in prison;
3   normalization of prison regimes (life in prison should resemble normal life outside);
4   facilitation of social reintegration upon release as the ultimate goal of incarceration;
5   participation in civil society while incarcerated (to encourage normalization and to increase visibility and transparency of prison life for those outside);
6   the importance of prison staff training and staff–prisoner relationships;
7   the independent inspection and monitoring of staff and management; and
8   the prevention of discrimination.[4]

Together these principles minimize the risks of social distantiation, by humanizing inmates, and of mindlessly punitive bureaucratic inertia, by fostering some measure of emotional proximity between guards and inmates. The American punished generally lack most if not all of these institutional protections (Ferguson 2014).

Third, penal principles and practices have knock-on effects for public perceptions of both punishment and the punished. As Whitman argues:

European efforts to guarantee respectful treatment are ... inevitably exercises in a kind of psychological engineering, directed, in prison law for example, at both inmates and guards. In a larger sense, they are exercises in psychological engineering directed at the public at large – efforts to discourage ordinary folk from treating offenders as status inferiors.

(Whitman, 2003: 25)

The comparative dearth of such protections in American prison law enacts a very different kind of psychological engineering upon inmates, guards and ordinary citizens: the kind that normalizes, even rejoices in, status degradation. And 'cruelty in punishment, born of cruelty in the mores of society, makes those mores yet more brutal in turn' (Tissot 1875, quoted in Whitman 1998: 176).

For instance, the proliferation of American mass-cultural images of prisons as brutal containment blocks for monsters coexists with conflicting images of prisoners with free cable TV receiving undeserved educational opportunities unavailable to the law-abiding working class. Public ignorance of mass incarceration's real effects on individuals, families and communities also coexists alongside the public's prurient nonchalance about prison's most brutalizing and dehumanizing practices. A commonplace in American entertainment culture is the blithe, cruel, often blackly comic acceptance of prison rape as a given rite of passage for a new inmate. Admonitions against 'dropping the soap' routinely appear – a dehumanizing 'cold joke' that humiliates and mocks victims (Glover 2001: 36). The debasing principle of less eligibility also appears readily accepted by mainstream American culture, perhaps in part because it is so seldom challenged by the kinds of counter-narratives that the European guiding principles establish.

Fourth, according to Bauman, the consensus view among historians is that 'the perpetration of the Holocaust required the neutralization of ordinary German attitudes toward the Jew, not their mobilization' (1989: 185). A similar neutralization of moral concern for the staggering numbers of Americans affected by mass incarceration is achieved in part by the sheer incomprehensibility of the numbers. With just 5 per cent of the world's population, the US holds nearly 25 per cent of its prisoners (Travis *et al.* 2014). One in three black men will serve time in prison, and a black man is more likely to go to prison than to marry, go to college or join the military (Simon 2007). About 2.2 million Americans are incarcerated in jails and prisons (The Sentencing Project 2014), and the number of minor children with an incarcerated parent stands at around 2.7 million (The Pew Charitable Trusts 2010). Yet these figures are difficult if not impossible to apprehend in the form of individual human beings.

Nicholas Kristof has used his column in *The New York Times* to rail against a range of global injustices over the years, learning in the process that even the most appalling experiences of human suffering must be personalized in order to move a large audience emotionally. In one tellingly titled column, 'Save the Darfur puppy', he writes, 'the human conscience just isn't pricked by mass suffering, while an individual child (or puppy) in distress causes our hearts to flutter' (Kristoff 2007). He cites in support a body of social-psychological research. For example, 'psychic numbing' (Lifton 1967) occurs 'in many, if not all, episodes of mass-murder neglect', which dampens one's 'capacity to experience *affect*, the positive and negative feelings that combine with reasoned analysis to guide our judgments, decisions, and actions' (Slovic 2007: 80, emphasis in original). Compassion for the plight of the beleaguered paradoxically recedes as the numbers affected grow.

In her highly influential best-selling book *The new Jim Crow*, Michelle Alexander utilizes a similar humanizing device in her opening paragraph, in the person of Jarvious Cotton, a disenfranchised African-American prison inmate from Mississippi. Cotton's story is intended to humanize the anonymous, often black faces of the incarcerated:

56   *David A. Green*

> Cotton's great-great grandfather could not vote as a slave. His great-grandfather was beaten to death by the Ku Klux Klan for attempting to vote. His grandfather was prevented from voting by Klan intimidation. His father was barred from voting by poll taxes and literacy tests. Today, Jarvious Cotton cannot vote because he, like many black men in the United States, has been labeled a felon and is currently on parole.
>
> (Alexander 2010: 1)

The difficulty with Alexander's device in this case is that Jarvious Cotton was convicted of a murder he committed when he was 27 years old, a detail that Alexander excludes from her account. His conviction for this crime, not his race *per se*, is the reason he is denied the franchise similarly denied to his forebears for no fault of their own (Forman 2012).

Fifth, the faceless but highly racialized anonymity of such a massive collective, especially rendered so often in official and everyday discourse as categories – such as offenders, felons, criminals, blacks, Latinos, immigrants, illegals, which so easily embody stereotypes – works against establishing emotional proximity, no matter how unfairly treated or sympathetic such a population might be. 'What would stir their moral conscience if focused on persons they knew, aroused hardly any feelings when targeted on an abstract and stereotyped category' (Bauman 1989: 190). The power of stereotypes in the perpetuation of 'racial indifference' (Alexander 2010) and 'malign neglect' (Tonry 1995) is further evidenced by at least five social science literatures that confirm a strong, stubbornly persistent degree of racial bias towards African-Americans, consistent with the nation's history (Tonry 2011b: 80). Especially striking among these is the distantiation that occurs when Americans – often but not always unconsciously – associate a black face with a threat (Eberhardt 2005; Eberhardt *et al.* 2004). Moreover, the categories themselves are often created through official acts of legislation, which, in turn, legitimate the distantiation that permits others' suffering to continue and suppresses uncomfortable moral questions (Bauman 1989).

Sixth, distantiation is not always simply absorbed unwittingly via one's immersion in the cultural soak of everyday Othering cues and the common out-group narratives propagated by news and entertainment media and by folk wisdom. Sometimes it is explicitly taught as requisite knowledge to qualify as a functionary in the penal bureaucracy. Ferguson's (2014) account of the training of American prison guards is illustrative. First, in contrast to the European standard training regime of two years, during which time officers come to internalize the overriding, universal correctional goal of inmate social reintegration (Jacobson 2014), '[m]ost [US] states require [only] a high-school education and six weeks of training' (Ferguson 2014: 129). Second, in the US '[t]he distance claimed [between guard and inmate] even before the experience [of prison work begins] is telling. Correctional officer training emphasizes preparation to meet an enemy more than rehabilitation techniques' (Ferguson 2014: 130); according to the Bureau of Labor Statistics, of the list of six duties required of guards, five involve discipline, control and surveillance, and only one mentions rehabilitative goals (Bureau of Labor Statistics, as presented in Ferguson 2014: 129–130). Thus, American prison guards are trained to understand their role as maintaining a frontline defence to protect an innocent and frightened public from a collective enemy with the face and character of a stereotype – the sort that every first-year criminology student is taught to question.[5]

Seventh, the bureaucratic compartmentalization of the systems of criminal justice ensures that no single individual or group holds any sufficient responsibility for their often iatrogenic effects. The bureaucracy of criminal justice ensures that the various players remain cogs in a great machine (Weber 1968) whose divisions of labour insulate individual 'functionaries from the dark side of punishment. … Legislatures create criminal statutes, police use them to arrest, prosecutors charge, juries decide, judges pronounce sentence, and prison officials carry out the sentence' (Ferguson 2014: 13). In such a bureaucracy, 'everyone and no one' is responsible (Dzur 2012: 18). 'The separations in the function of punishment mean that no single official ever has to look directly into the abyss. No one punisher need feel the full burden of creating suffering' (Ferguson 2014: 13). Bauman also tells us that, in bureaucracies,

> '[p]roblems' call for better, more rational designs, not for soul-searching. The actors occupy themselves with the rational task of finding better means for the given – and partial – end, not with the moral task of the evaluation of the ultimate objective (of which they have but a vague idea, or for which they do not feel responsible).
>
> (Bauman 1989: 195)

And, unlike European prison systems, where guiding principles and extensive staff training ensure the internalization of offender reintegration as the 'ultimate objective', the American prison system (comprising the systems of its federal and constituent state organs) lacks a widely shared, clearly articulated penological purpose, save that of secure confinement.

Eighth, even the best of penological intentions cannot fully insulate inmates from moral relegation and mistreatment. German Field Marshall 'Moltke the Elder' famously observed that no battle plan survives first contact with the enemy. Similarly, penological 'aspiration, the necessary spark in creating a legal framework, must give way to the maintaining power of an enforcer' (Ferguson 2014: 62). Punishment regimes exist in:

> an atmosphere that is part animus, part evasion, part entrenched habit, part bureaucratic indifference, part an insensitivity that some would call stoicism, and every part surveillance at levels tolerated nowhere else in the course of social human behavior. … No matter how enlightened punishment becomes, no matter what aspirations theorists use to justify

58 David A. Green

what should be done, the institutional infliction of suffering will deteriorate into something worse than it was.

(Ferguson 2014: 21–22, 96)

This echoes Rothman's (1980) distinction between 'conscience and convenience': the conscience dictates the principles of offender treatment, while the convenience demanded by day-to-day bureaucratic routines, and the countless discrete acts by countless discrete practitioners, tend to undermine the noble goal to which the conscience aspires. And, again, generally speaking, over the past few decades, American penality has virtually failed even to indulge the conscience with any optimism in its penal aspirations.

Ninth, Kant's (2011/1798) dictum barring the distantiating treatment of moral agents as means to someone else's ends is routinely violated by American law-makers and criminal justice practitioners, and not because they reject desert-based rationales in favour of consequentialist punishments. In the structurally politicized American criminal justice arena – where risk-averse legislators determine much of sentencing policy and similarly risk-averse prosecutors, sheriffs and many judges are elected – penal policy and prison management practices and the powers to prosecute and sentence have been increasingly used since the 1980s as means to achieve a very different set of non-penological ends, 'such as winning elections, fighting cultural wars, and resisting acceptance of the reality that the United States had become a multi-ethnic and multi-racial country' (Tonry 2014: 504).

Tenth, distantiation has also increased since the early 1970s with the decline of the rehabilitative ideal (Allen 1981) and its replacement by an offence- rather than offender-based system (Mauer 2001). Criminological positivism no longer animates the thinking of officials to the extent that it did formerly and has since been dismissed by some as a morally bankrupt excuse-making exercise. James Q. Wilson – whose well-documented influence on crime and punishment policy during the 1970s and 1980s in particular was probably unmatched – summarizes the view when he rejects as 'hopelessly romantic' Rousseau's optimistic view of human nature, which, 'naturally, assigns great importance to motives in judging an offender, and so is sympathetic to … *excuses* based on human need and social stress' (Wilson and Herrnstein 1985: 519–520, emphasis added). Among conservatives in particular, Rousseauian optimism has, at least until recently (as discussed below), been replaced by a conception of the criminal as a predatory, rational calculator. Following Christie (1986: 25), such a stiff characterization allows for the caricature and categorization of both 'ideal victims', as 'weak, respectable, and blameless', and 'ideal offenders', as 'overpoweringly strong, morally bankrupt, and remorseless' (Dzur 2012: 16).[6]

Eleventh, and finally, the American criminal justice system itself seems premised on just such a pessimistic perception of human nature, and it thus provides the structural and cultural supports to institutionalize and reinforce this pessimism. Wilson argues that, in the name of moral persuasion, 'the very process by which we learn to avoid crime requires that the courts *act as if crime were wholly the result of free choice'* (Wilson and Herrnstein 1985: 529, emphasis added). His influential contention neutralizes and nullifies any criminological theory or philosophy of punishment that assumes the best about people, replacing it with one that assumes the worst. It is likely no coincidence that the ascent of this notion as the new penological common-sense corresponded with a five-fold increase in the American imprisonment rate between 1972 and 2010 (Travis *et al.* 2014).

Assumptions about human nature operate unconsciously and usually remain unexamined, but they nonetheless exist among the cognitive tools that we use when we make decisions about how to treat others, and when, and if we register our moral outrage at their mistreatment. Their relevance to this discussion is rooted in their influence on the regularity with which, and the likelihood that, individuals in a culture can recognize criminal Others as members of the same moral community and that they will develop the emotional proximity that fosters fair treatment and compassion. Particularly negative conceptions of human nature would appear to accelerate and engender Othering because, if we believe humankind to be naturally fallen and polluted, one's culpability increases and we are more able to countenance the mistreatment of one who has wounded us. In turn, these conceptions animate bureaucratic routines and practices, establishing an inertial flow of mistreatment which demands even more institutional controls on its powers than would punishment systems (like Europe's) that are premised on a more hopeful view of human nature, one holding that inmates should, and thus *can*, be successfully reintegrated. Conservative, pessimistic views of human nature would, therefore, seem to render one especially susceptible to the effects of distantiation, and, in turn, to both of Bauman's 'two extremes' when responding to injustice and the suffering of strangers: 'the threat of neglect [and denial,[7] on the one hand,] and callousness and the temptation to oppress', on the other (Bauman 1998: 18).

Together these eleven forces, practices and ideational constraints – most of which are peculiarly American – increase social distance between the criminal Other and those of us outside prison walls, while also regularly violating the Paterson principle (Ruck 1951) well established in Europe (van Zyl Smit and Snacken 2009: 100) that offenders are sent to prison *as* punishment, not *for* additional punishment. However, these examples do not tell the whole story.

Rehumanization and proximity with the incarcerated Other

The preceding sections clearly indicate that many policies, dominant cultural practices and bureaucratic exigencies establish, ensure and reproduce distantiation between unconvicted and convicted Americans, which, in turn, feeds moral indifference and callousness towards the plight of incarcerated Others and facilitates their mistreatment. Many of these policies and practices remain so deeply embedded in American cultural attitudes and sensibilities that reformers may despair at the prospects of meaningful change. However, this chapter has an additional aim: to chart several rising currents in American

60   David A. Green

culture which are slowing, altering, maybe even reversing, the course of some of the bureaucratizing and distantiating forces that Bauman identifies as necessary preconditions for the collective mistreatment of other human beings.

Just as the absence of emotional proximity enables mistreatment of the Other, its presence can enable altruism. 'An act is altruistic if it benefits some individual, but at a cost to the altruist who willingly performs the act' (Tuschman 2013, 329). Monroe (1991) studied the characteristics of selflessly heroic rescuers, those 'extreme altruists' who had endangered themselves to help others with no expectation of reciprocal treatment. The one trait 'shared by heroic rescuers concerned how they viewed themselves in relation to other people ... [T]hese selfless individuals perceived themselves as "strongly linked to others through a shared community"' (Monroe, quoted in Tuschman 2013: 399). Emotional proximity with others made the difference. Rescuers saw themselves reflected in other people and they felt part of a greater whole.

The ongoing moral debates about gay marriage and the War on Drugs provide two examples that are illustrative of the shifts possible in moral optics as the emotional proximity with those formerly deemed Others increases. In 2013, the Supreme Court[8] struck down a key provision in the US *Defense of Marriage Act 1996* which defines marriage as a union between a man and a woman. The decision made same-sex couples eligible for the first time for federal marriage benefits in those states where such marriages are legal. The movement for 'marriage equality' has since made great advances and enjoyed endorsements from surprising corners.

As Bauman explains, '[r]esponsibility, this building block of all moral behaviour, arises out of the proximity of the other. Proximity means responsibility, and responsibility *is* proximity' (Bauman 1989: 184, emphasis in original). *The Onion* (2013), a satirical newspaper and website, published a column written by God in which He pledged His newfound support for marriage equality because His own son is gay. The comic absurdity of the piece mimics the evident reasoning behind a string of similarly justified professions of support for gay marriage and, more importantly for our purposes, it demonstrates the power of proximity to rehumanize the Other. Senator Rob Portman, an Ohio Republican, changed his stance on gay marriage after his own son came out. Portman said, 'It allowed me to think of this issue from a new perspective, and that's of a Dad who loves his son a lot and wants him to have the same opportunities that his brother and sister would have – to have a relationship like Jane and I have had for over 26 years' (quoted in McDonough 2013). Archconservative former Vice-President Dick Cheney, whose daughter married her long-term same-sex partner in 2012, also bucked his party by endorsing marriage equality.

Of course, the sting in *The Onion*'s satire is found in the implication that one can only feel compassion and empathy for those with whom one has close personal proximity and connection, no matter the injustices they suffer. A recent study, for example, found that judges with daughters, especially conservative judges, were more likely to decide cases in favour of feminist

Rehumanization of the incarcerated Other 61

agendas than those who only had sons (Glynn and Sen 2014). This empathy-in-proximity phenomenon also brings to mind those high-profile conservative public servants – like Jeffrey Archer, the English novelist and former Tory MP – who became outspoken activists for prison reform only after they themselves had been incarcerated. The late Chuck Colson (President Nixon's so-called hatchet man and founder of Prison Fellowship), Pat Nolan (former Californian Republican State Assemblyman enlisted by Colson to join Prison Fellowship and now promoting prison reform at the Conservative Union) and Bernard Kerik (former New York City Corrections Commissioner and Police Commissioner in Mayor Rudy Giuliani's administration) were all well positioned to know about, and do something about, the harms of harsh sentencing policy or the poor state of American prisons before their experiences as inmates, yet none did. They are named here not to condemn them for their crimes, denigrate their subsequent reform work or implicate them as hypocrites. Instead, the good, altruistic works that Colson and Nolan in particular have performed since their release are illustrative of the power of proximity and personal experience – as well as, conversely, the power of inertial cultural disregard and indifference for, and ignorance of, the extent and myriad impacts of mass incarceration in the US.

In interviews conducted for an ongoing study on the evolution and significance of the 2007 *Second Chance Act* (about which more below), several informants employed in American government agencies suggested to me that some white southern law-makers in Congress are now reconsidering their former support for draconian drug sentencing, in part because these laws increasingly impact their own rural white constituencies. Drug abuse is, for them, no longer associated merely with the urban ghettoes so distant from their own experience, and those caught up in the prosecution of the War on Drugs do not conform to racial stereotypes, but instead are folks that look much like themselves – 'people whom one knows and has charted into one's map of the world as persons, rather than anonymous specimens of a type' (Bauman 1989: 186). In short, the social distance between them and the prescription drug and methamphetamine abusers in their constituencies has diminished. Consequently, these offenders now fall within their 'scope of justice' (Opotow 1995) and are thus deserving of more than harsh punishment.

From one perspective, and for reasons that Bauman's work helps to explain, the 'success' of American mass incarceration as a strategy could thus hold the key to its own undoing. Proximity is the reason. The social distance between gay and straight people in American society has closed dramatically in my lifetime. Sixty-five per cent of Americans report that they know a gay person, support for gay marriage is high and marriage equality has become a prominent civil rights issue on the national stage. In contrast, only 20 per cent of Americans report that they know a victim of gun violence, which might help explain why, in spite of a spate of high-profile mass shootings that spurred President Obama to demand the reform of gun laws, there is still little meaningful political movement in support of stricter gun controls (Lawrence 2013). Yet, as with gay marriage, fewer ordinary Americans remain untouched by

62   *David A. Green*

mass incarceration due to the vast numbers it has netted. Personal proximity to an addicted or convicted person – whether a family member, friend, colleague or neighbour – could cast in an unfavourable light a punishment system that, had it maintained the stability in numbers incarcerated that it had till the early 1970s, might not have attracted as much public interest. Now its tentacles reach into every community, though far more deeply and pervasively in minority – especially poor, black – neighbourhoods and communities. The damages wrought on individuals, families and communities by the system's overreach are now much harder to overlook and they appear ripe for both pragmatic and moral re-evaluation.

Four American agents of offender rehumanization

Nellis (2013b: 34) laments the retreat of humanism in criminal justice discourse, which he defines as:

> a belief system predicated on the absolute moral worth of all human beings, regardless of race, class, creed, colour or culture. It presents human beings, collectively and individually, as capable of great good, while acknowledging that under certain circumstances they are, collectively and individually, easily rendered capable of great evil.

Yet, these are fascinating, even encouraging, times for the close, humanist observer of American punishment. Imprisonment rates in most states have stabilized or declined, nearly half the states and the federal government have rolled back a range of punitive sentencing policies (Travis *et al.* 2014) and sentencing reform has become a high-profile and bipartisan national issue, indicated most recently by the *Smarter Sentencing Act*,[9] which, at the time of writing, is moving its way through Congress. The executive branch has also announced a range of progressive reforms. These include clemency for federal prisoners serving unduly harsh drug sentences and the My Brother's Keeper initiative, launched 'to address persistent opportunity gaps faced by boys and young men of color and ensure that all young people can reach their full potential' (The White House 2014).

The cynic may understandably dismiss the latter as empty rhetoric, but the initiative's name is unusual for a couple of reasons. First, nowhere in the 30-minute roll-out speech did President Obama cite the biblical origin of the phrase, but he did emphasize moral themes by referencing each citizen's social proximity to and moral responsibility for others. He invoked a traditional Tanzanian adage, 'my neighbor's child is my child', and called on those Americans who have achieved success in a culture and economy rife with disparities of opportunity to recognize that 'each of us has an obligation to give every child the same chance this country gave so many of us' (Obama 2014).[10] Second, it is not apparent from its title what the initiative aims to accomplish. Government-sponsored initiatives tend towards technocratic language, with titles clearly

Rehumanization of the incarcerated Other 63

articulating the desired outcome: the Open Government Initiative aims to increase government transparency; the Justice Reinvestment Initiative aims to reinvest money formerly spent on corrections and criminal justice in needy communities; and the Safe Kids/Safe Streets programme has readily recognizable aims. My Brother's Keeper is anything but a technocratic name and betrays little about what it seeks in terms of concrete aims. Instead, it interpellates or hails citizens as subjects (Althusser 1971), calling on them to recognize their 'social proximity [to] and moral responsibility' for the Other (Bauman 1989: 184). It constitutes a moral call to serve others.

In similar ways, four additional criminal justice movements – the first more surprising and also much less well documented than the other three – also endorse humanist values and reintroduce morality into the works in various ways. All four appear to serve roughly parallel interests with roughly parallel effects. The first is a new, increasingly common, rehumanized reconceptualization of the criminal offender. The other three movements – restorative, community and participatory justice – are sometimes conflated, but there are important distinctions between them. Together these developments provide a means to understand the dehumanizing processes that Bauman describes, but in reverse. They demonstrate how the brutalizing processes of bureaucratization and distantiation may be successfully challenged, conceptually and practically, to reduce the human costs of criminal punishment and to mollify its attendant after-effects.

The reconstructed offender ideal type

The first movement can be characterized as an ongoing reconceptualization of the character and potential of the convicted offender – a reidealized offender, one deserving of empathy, with deeply rooted but addressable social needs. This reconstruction is happening along two fronts simultaneously and in ways quite separate from the similar reconstructive effects accomplished by restorative, community and participatory justice models. These latter models do their de-Othering and rehumanizing work primarily by making justice processes less bureaucratic and thereby increasing proximity with offenders. In contrast, these two additional means work directly to reverse the effects of distantiation and facilitate greater offender proximity with others in a community, both emotionally and spatially.

The first of these is the American prison re-entry movement, which officially began in 1999 when Jeremy Travis popularized the term while heading the National Institute of Justice. Travis intended to focus public and policy attention on the 'iron law of corrections' – the inescapable fact that nearly all incarcerated offenders (95 per cent) will some day be released (Travis 2005). This reframed offenders not as permanently discarded Others with whom society need no longer interact, but as temporarily detained citizens who, in time, will return to our communities, as 708,677 did in 2010 (Guerino *et al.* 2011). The concept and goal of successful prisoner re-entry inevitably demands that attention be paid to reducing the prospect of reoffending in order to preserve public safety, which, in turn, necessitates the consideration of offenders' needs and deficits. This logic recasts the offender as a real individual with concrete needs that must be addressed, not because we are soft on crime, but, more practically, because we value a safe society in which released offenders no longer offend. The very concept of prisoner re-entry, then, has humanizing effects on the offender. S/he becomes a human being with a unique set of addressable needs and social deficits, which we as a society are responsible to fulfil and to remedy.

The same logic might also extend to the project of justice reinvestment (Clear 2011). Though not typically justified in moral terms (Tonry 2011a), justice reinvestment nonetheless rests on the recognition that incarceration does great damage to already disadvantaged communities. It aims to divert and reinvest monies formerly spent on incarceration to rebuild 'the human resources and physical infrastructure – the schools, healthcare facilities, parks, and public spaces – of neighborhoods devastated by high levels of incarceration' (Tucker and Cadora 2003: 3). The very recognition of this damage and devastation implies moral responsibility by casting light on the collateral economic, political and familial consequences of punishment for those left behind in disadvantaged communities when, for instance, large numbers of marriageable men are incarcerated (Lynch and Sabol 2004).

The second means by which offenders are being reconstructed is evidenced by a growing number of high-profile conservative leaders, many of whom share deeply held Christian and evangelical worldviews that serve, as well, to inoculate them against 'soft-on-crime' accusations. They invoke a reconstructed offender ideal type, one who is a child of God, redeemable, both in need of and worthy of others' help and for whom all have a moral responsibility to assist. 'It is the weakness of the Other which makes me responsible. It is the strength of the Other that makes me obliged. One is obliged towards the strong. One is responsible for the weak' (Bauman 1998: 19, original emphasis). It follows that an ideal-typical offender reconstructed as needful, weak and feckless rather than fearsome and powerful, elicits greater empathy and feelings of responsibility from others. This reconstruction reduces social distance between 'us' and 'them', invites offenders to participate in the moral community and places them within our scope of justice.

The conservative advocacy group Right on Crime[11] held its first 'leadership summit' in Washington, DC in May 2014. Republican Newt Gingrich, former Speaker of the House during the Clinton administration years and former candidate for the Republican presidential nomination in 2012, spoke there and 'articulated his hopes that new technologies and leadership in conservative states would allow more criminal offenders to be *educated and effectively rehabilitated*' (Right on Crime 2014, emphasis added). According to the email summary of the event:

> Former Oklahoma Congressman J.C. Watts closed the day with a compelling story about just [sic] as a twenty dollar bill doesn't lose its value if

it's crumpled up or dropped in dirt, people don't lose their *value as human beings and as Americans* just because they commit crimes, renewing his support for continued efforts to find effective *rehabilitation* methods.

(Right on Crime 2014: emphasis added)

On this note, Nellis (2013b: 34) reminds us that rehabilitation is a 'secular ideal distilled from an essentially religious idea of a person's intrinsic worth and latent moral capacity'.

This surprising rhetorical shift provides audiences with a set of cognitive raw materials to think compassionately about offenders and their treatment, and even to reject the traditional conservative pessimism about human nature. Sam Brownback, the Republican Governor of Kansas, said in a Judiciary Committee Hearing in 2007 that Americans must recognize 'that every person is a beautiful, unique soul, a child of a living God, regardless of whether they are in prison or not' (US Senate Joint Economic Committee 2007: 5). New Jersey Governor and Republican presidential hopeful Chris Christie recently said of drug offenders: 'We need to be there even for those who stumble and fall. We need to be there to lift them up' (Ball 2014). Former Republican State Senator and Attorney-General of Virginia, Mark Earley, who from 2002–11 led Prison Fellowship, claims for religious reasons to regret his previous support for harsh penal policies: 'If Moses [who murdered a man] or Paul [who oversaw the stoning of Saint Stephen] had lived in Virginia or any state in the United States today, they would be serving, had they been caught, a multiple-decade prison sentence' (quoted in Suellentrop 2006). President George W. Bush said the following at the signing ceremony for the 2007 *Second Chance Act*, a law that provides seed funding for prisoner re-entry programmes:

> It's through the acts of mercy that compassionate Americans are making the Nation a more hopeful place. ... We believe that even those who have struggled with a dark past can find brighter days ahead. ... The work of redemption reflects our values ... [and] will build on work to help prisoners reclaim their lives. ... It will help our armies of compassion use their healing touch so lost souls can rediscover their dignity and sense of purpose. ... [W]e're standing with you, not against you ... the least shall be first.

(Bush 2008)

These are just a few examples of prominent conservative Republicans espousing views that eliminate the distantiation with which conservatives in particular have formerly been associated, by rhetorically establishing emotional proximity with criminal offenders as members of their own moral communities.

66   David A. Green

Restorative justice and the return of stolen conflicts

In a similar way, restorative justice is reworking previously rigid cultural fabrications of ideal victims and ideal offenders (Christie 1986) by increasing proximity with real victims and offenders. Restorative justice, like community and participatory justice models, provides 'institutional practices that challenge men and women to strain against their fixed ideas by presenting competing narratives and offering proximity to three-dimensional human beings capable of suffering' (Dzur 2012: 16). It closes the social distance dividing offenders, victims and legal authorities, and impedes the bureaucratic inertia that enables and perpetuates unjust and oppressive penal consequences. Braithwaite further argues, 'We invite to a criminal trial those who can inflict most damage on the other side. With a [restorative justice] conference we invite those who might offer most support to their own side' (Braithwaite 2003: 61).

He insists as well that one aim of restorative justice is 'to institutionalize *restoration of dignity* for offenders' (Braithwaite 2003: 57, emphasis in original). It should be of little surprise, then, that some of the most forthright advocates of the movement are outspoken and deeply religious (Hannem 2013; Nellis 2013a). Justice Fellowship (JF), the policy arm of the Christian-based advocacy organization Prison Fellowship, launched a new campaign in the spring of 2014 to promote restorative justice as the preferred alternative to traditional criminal justice processes. In its email announcement, JF's president, Craig DeRoche writes:

> Restorative Justice is a set of principles that recognizes and advances the *dignity and value of human life* in the criminal justice system. It prioritizes victim participation, promotes offender responsibility, and cultivates community engagement. … The political debates on the right and left have forgotten *the role of values* in healing victims, holding offenders accountable, and engaging communities. We intend to return the discussion back to what really matters – restoration.
>
> (DeRoche 2014, emphasis added)

Moreover, '[c]ourts produce distance' (Dzur 2012: 17). Legalese and due process considerations reduce emotional proximity, even when, as in the courtroom, rare spatial proximity with an offender occurs. Restorative justice instead not only seeks to debureaucratize and retrieve 'stolen conflicts' (Christie 1977: 4), but also employs rehumanizing processes that must attend to the particularities of the offender, the victims and the offence. It thus reduces distantiation and increases proximity, reintroducing morality into the cold administration of justice[12] and rendering offenders more than mere means to technologically judicious ends. As Smith puts it:

> Restorative justice tends to address offenders as moral interlocutors capable of transformation rather than as animals shuttled through a bureaucratic

process. ... [T]his counters the dehumanizing aspects of justice systems that treat offenders as abstract numbers to be processed according to governing penal metrics.

(Smith 2014: 107)

Community justice

The third rehumanizing movement, community justice, also reduces distantiation by increasing proximity and debureaucratizing justice work. Bauman (1989: 192, emphasis in original) explains the bureaucratic process by which moral consideration for the Other is progressively attenuated:

> *The further away the sequence moved from the original act of Definition, the more it was guided by purely rational–technical considerations, and the less did it have to reckon with moral inhibitions.* Indeed, it all but ceased to necessitate moral choices.

Similar can be said of policing and the routine processing of criminal cases by the traditional courts – morality is displaced. Community justice programmes instead break down bureaucratic barriers and return 'a semblance of ownership to a local community as to how criminal justice is done' (Nellis 2013b: 39).

Community justice is embedded in part in Etzioni's communitarianism, which privileges informal social control and the role of rights and responsibilities (Nellis 2013b: 38). Examples of community justice include the Liverpool Community Justice Centre, modelled on a similar centre in Red Hook, Brooklyn, which engages a range of community members to develop ways to solve local problems and prevent crime. These models pull the practitioner out of her typical role as a criminal justice system drone with no view of the forest for the trees, ensuring that both remain in focus.

To clarify the distinction between the two approaches, 'Restorative justice is about cases, community justice is about places' (Crawford and Clear 2003: 216). The former is also reactive while the latter is most concerned with proactively enabling greater collective efficacy to improve life in local communities and reduce crime. 'A restorative justice program "works" when key constituents experience a restorative process and end up feeling restored by it. Community justice programs "work" when the quality of life in a given place improves' (Crawford and Clear 2003: 216).

A degree of 'anti-statism' most often animates restorative justice and community justice models. 'It is no coincidence that the rise of restorative justice and the ascendancy of neo-liberal ideology have unfolded simultaneously. They both proclaim an end to universality and state monopoly and imply a privatization of disputes and justice by prioritizing private and parochial forms of control' (Crawford and Clear 2003: 224). Both models 'seek to curtail and limit the role of criminal justice professionals' (Crawford and Clear 2003: 217), relying heavily on deliberation and dialogue among the public rather than state 'stakeholders'. They are thus, by definition, anti-bureaucratic, inhospitable to

68   *David A. Green*

the sorts of practices and routines that dehumanize offenders and victims. Of course, should restorative and/or community justice programmes succeed and become dominant paradigms to challenge traditional criminal justice, the professionalization of their own practitioners will surely require some degree of bureaucratization.

Participatory justice

The term participatory justice here refers to the sorts of values and structures outlined by the likes of Bibas (2012) and Dzur (2012), among others. These aim to reconfigure criminal justice and penal processes by enlisting greater lay participation to exercise legitimate and consequential powers to shape policies and justice outcomes. It relies heavily on the principles and practices of deliberative democracy and thus has much broader applications that extend beyond the realm of criminal justice. It challenges the mistaken notion that lay publics are always monolithically punitive towards criminal offenders and it enlists them to participate meaningfully in criminal justice decision-making, as through expanding traditional jury service in trials,[13] and in the shaping of criminal justice and penal policy-making, as through the utilization of deliberative forums like Citizens' Juries and Deliberative Polls (see Green 2006). These instruments allow for the generation of informed 'public judgment' (Yankelovich 1991) about key issues in ways that remove the mediating influence of mass media cues, folk wisdom and simple ignorance.

The institutionalization of greater public deliberation would enable governments not only to better inform citizens and better assess their sentiments and the limits of their tolerances, but also to help rebuild public trust and confidence in the political process. It is the erosion of this trust and confidence that has made the tactic of penal populism so attractive to politicians in the first place, and addressing it directly, rather than rhetorically pandering to the worst fears of select groups, seems more advisable, both pragmatically and democratically (Green 2014). So participatory justice appears particularly well suited to bolstering the legitimacy of political institutions, but its strengths extend further.

Ferguson (2014: 17) tries to solve the 'puzzle of communal apathy' towards the rising human costs of harsh American punishment by pointing to 'an unplumbed cultural configuration of ignorance, confusion, anger, and misunderstanding'. Increasing participatory justice through 'jury-like procedures and quasi-formal participatory mechanisms' (Dzur 2012: 106) could, in effect, militate against communal apathy by improving public knowledge and prevent Bauman's heterophobia by ensuring that the Other is morally recognized by facilitating greater and regular proximity among diverse citizens. As Dzur explains:

> The separation from a reality of suffering human beings, the inability to
> see or feel what is happening to them, is a problem of public morality. ...

> Lay participation in criminal justice is needed because it brings otherwise attenuated people into contact with suffering human beings, draws attention to the ways laws and policies and institutional structures prolong that suffering, and makes possible – though does not guarantee – greater awareness among participants of their own responsibility for laws and policies and structures that treat people humanely ... [T]he evasion of concern for others, the dismissal of some as fully human beings ... is the first barrier to be overcome on the way to justice. ... Lay participation within institutional settings, especially when it makes non-futile, load-bearing contributions to decisions, offers the attunement to others as fellow citizens that triggers responsibility for them.
>
> (Dzur 2012: 19, 14)

Participatory justice removes distantiation by insisting on proximity, and increases the chances that bureaucracies will remain responsive to, and responsible for, the humanity of those processed.

Conclusion

All four of the movements discussed in the previous section – the reconceptualization, particularly among conservatives, of the needful offender entitled to help and empathy; the restorative and community justice movements; and the more fledgling push for greater participatory justice – are relatively new arrivals on the landscape of American punishment. Though restorative justice certainly has a longer history than the others – Braithwaite (2002: 12–13) reminds us that it 'has been the dominant model of criminal justice throughout human history for perhaps all of the world's peoples' – it appears to have made fewer inroads in American criminal justice than it has in the other Anglophone countries with which the US is often compared, including England and Wales, Canada, Australia and New Zealand. While the sympathetic reconceptualization of the needful offender calls on citizens to consider the morality of the treatment of offenders, the remaining three models recast the focal participants of the crime-and-punishment drama, disrupting traditional bureaucratic criminal justice processes and rendering them less faceless and routinized, and more attuned to human weakness, individual differences and civic responsibility. Together these militate against Bauman's dehumanizing forces of distantiation and bureaucratic rationality.

Whatever the merits and weaknesses of these four new developments, they all serve an important purpose beyond their more instrumental goals of, for instance, achieving more just outcomes: *they each cast the offender in an altogether different light than traditional criminal justice processes do*, and this light is illuminative for all citizens, even those who are barely paying attention. The ensuing counter-narratives that follow in the wake of these four models provide citizens with new cognitive frameworks and enable alternate ways of thinking and the creation of new norms.[14] These cultural consequences – the

70 David A. Green

reshaping of the public attitudes, sensibilities and cognitive schemas that facilitate new habits of mind – are perhaps just as important as any other identifiable restorative, community or participatory justice outcome, like victim satisfaction, recidivism reduction, crime prevention or enhanced legitimacy. For, according to Merton's (1948) 'self-fulfilling prophecy' and the Thomas theorem that 'If men define situations as real, they are real in their consequences' (Thomas and Thomas 1928: 572), our attitudes and sensibilities are shaped powerfully by the range of cognitive schemas and 'ideational resources' made available to us, and these raw materials constitute our problem definitions and the narratives that we use to explain criminality and to justify and regulate its punishment (Green 2009).

For 30 years or more, the rhetoric of American punishment has been decidedly harsh towards, condemnatory of and distantiating to offenders. This penal harshening has been thoroughly documented ad nauseam by many scholars of the causes and consequences of American mass incarceration. Yet it would be a mistake to characterize American postmodern punishment as exclusively punitive. Ongoing shifts in the American penal landscape indicate that the hegemony of the punitive consensus is under assault, and only some of these indicators are discussed here (see Green 2015, forthcoming, for more penal reform drivers and catalysts). Reformers currently enjoy a window of opportunity to facilitate real and lasting change in the direction that Bauman's work leads. To justify mass incarceration on the grounds that public attitudes and sensibilities support it is wrong – not only on factual grounds (because it overlooks massive public ignorance of its realities) but morally, too:

> because we know, looking backward, that the prevailing sensibilities of an era often are deeply regretted later. Mainstream American sensibilities in the past have supported policies – slavery, the near-extermination of indigenous North American peoples, the internment of Japanese-Americans, sterilization of the mentally ill, ostracism of homosexuals – that we now believe to be wrong in some timeless sense. Sensibilities of particular times and places may have supported such attitudes and practices, but few people today believe that justifies them. And so it is with crime and punishment. ... Capital punishment, indiscriminate private possession of handguns, and mass imprisonment of black men in early twenty-first century America will someday be widely deplored and deeply regretted.
>
> (Tonry 2004: viii, 63)

Evidence of a significant degree of collective regret for mass incarceration now accrues.

The lesson of humanizing rhetorical devices like the Darfur puppy – or, more appropriately for our purposes, the prison inmate's baby – helps chart the course for effective strategies to increase Americans' emotional proximity with the incarcerated Other.[15] Without it, the damages wrought by American penal policies and mass incarceration are much less likely to secure the

Rehumanization of the incarcerated Other   71

collective moral scrutiny required for change. Anecdotes that put a human face to suffering trigger emotional responses that even the most staggering statistics cannot. A run of documentary films released in the past few years make good on this strategy. These include two by HBO (*Prison terminal* [2013 chronicles the death of an elderly, terminally ill inmate in an Ohio prison, while *The university of Sing Sing* [2011] tells the stories of a handful of students graduating from an in-prison degree programme at New York's infamous Sing Sing prison); a five-part CNN series, *Death row stories* (2014), on the experiences of death row inmates; two PBS FRONTLINE episodes comprising a series entitled 'Locked Up in America' (*Solitary nation* [2014] examines the brutalizing effects of solitary confinement; while *Prison state* [2014] looks at 'the cycle of mass incarceration in America', specifically in Kentucky); and the Sundance Grand Jury Prize-winning film on the collateral consequences of the War on Drugs, *The house I live in* (2012). American mass incarceration 'effaces the human face of the Other' (Bauman 1989: 222). These recent films not only serve to inform mass audiences about the scale and human costs of mass incarceration, but also convey its effects on individual human beings with human faces, with whom audiences can readily empathize. These films trouble traditional cognitive categories that define the dehumanized criminal, rendering the Other a morally recognizable human being.

Notes

1 Thanks to Polity Press and Cornell University Press for granting permission to reproduce previously published material in this chapter.
2 This characterization refers to the American public at large and should by no means be read to discount the years of relentless grassroots advocacy of groups like The Sentencing Project and Families Against Mandatory Minimums, as well as the work of newer players like The Pew Research Center and the Marshall Project.
3 Nietzsche's (1961: 124) admonition to 'mistrust all in whom the impulse to punish is powerful' is echoed by Ferguson (2014: 30), who advises, 'No one who likes to punish should be allowed to inflict it'.
4 Of course, as other chapters in this volume attest, the degree to which these principles actually affect and shape day-to-day conduct and practices will differ widely among prisons and jurisdictions. The key point here is that the principles exist.
5 Ferguson (2014: 99) bracingly reminds us that 'those who use direct coercion in a punishment regime, police and correctional officers, possess the least education, training and oversight in the system [though prosecutors probably enjoy even greater autonomy]; [and] controls on their ability to use physical force are minimal'.
6 Similarly simplistic, essentialist rhetoric is found in a new National Rifle Association slogan which captures the organization's plan to counter the threat of mass shootings: 'The only thing that stops a bad guy with a gun is a good guy with a gun' (Lichtblau and Motoko 2012).
7 By recasting the roles of his 'victims' and 'perpetrators', Cohen's (2001) 'atrocity triangle' in *States of denial* offers another useful framework with which to analyse American indifference to mass incarceration. Here the victims become the incarcerated and their families, the perpetrators are those operatives within the penal

72   *David A. Green*

bureaucracy whose actions perpetuate continued suffering and the 'observers' are 'those who see and know what is happening' (p. 14), comprising, then, practitioners, citizens and politicians who know better but who, by permitting the system to operate unchanged, preserve the status quo.

8 See *Hollingsworth v. Perry* and *Windsor v. United States*.
9 The *Smarter Sentencing Act* would reduce sentences by disregarding mandatory minima for drug offenders in federal prisons, where they constitute half of all inmates (Federal Bureau of Prisons 2014).
10 Obama's rhetoric here includes clear Christian overtones, often associated with the Right, but it also reflects typically liberal views of human nature. Liberals tend to believe in a cooperative human nature, value compassion and sympathy, and show a 'strong antipathy to self-interested behavior' (Tuschman 2013: 307). Conservatives tend, instead, to embrace a view of human nature as naturally competitive, and conservative politicians 'tend to make more appeals to the public based on the assumption of a self-interested audience' (Tuschman 2013: 307).
11 The group aims to reposition 'criminal justice reform as a central element of the conservative movement' (Right on Crime 2014).
12 Of course, it must be remembered that the coldness of due process has a moral justification: namely, and ostensibly, to ensure fairness and to protect the rights of the accused.
13 Currently, 95 per cent of federal criminal cases in the US result in plea bargains, not jury trials. Figures for the states are estimated at 90 to 95 per cent (Devers 2011). Though caseloads at the state level doubled between 1976 and 2002, jury trials declined sharply from 3.4 per cent of criminal cases to only 1.3 per cent over the same period (Dzur 2012: 120).
14 A norm 'limits the range of tolerable behavioural patterns and privileges certain kinds of conduct as normal, while casting all other sorts as abnormal' (Bauman 1989: 24).
15 Some humanist readers – those who do not need what they might ridicule as marketing gimmicks like these to feel empathy for others – might regard these strategies as crass and manipulative. However, I am less concerned with offending their moral intelligence than with identifying practical strategies to change the ways in which rationally ignorant Americans talk about, think about and act towards the mass incarcerated.

References

Alexander, M. (2010) *The new Jim Crow: mass incarceration in the age of colorblindness*, New York: The New Press.

Allen, F.A. (1981) *The decline of the rehabilitative ideal: penal policy and social purpose*, New Haven, CT: Yale University Press.

Althusser, L. (1971) *Lenin and philosophy, and other essays*, trans. B. Brewster, London: Monthly Review Press.

Ball, M. (2014) 'Chris Christie's new compassionate conservatism', *The Atlantic Monthly*, 22 June, online, available: www.theatlantic.com/politics/archive/2014/06/chris-chris ties-new-compassionate-conservatism/373186 (accessed 15 December 2014).

Bauman, Z. (1989) *Modernity and the Holocaust*, Ithaca, NY: Cornell University Press.

Bauman, Z. (1995) *Life in fragments: essays in postmodern modernity*, Oxford: Blackwell.

Bauman, Z. (1998) 'What prospects of morality in times of uncertainty?', *Theory, Culture & Society*, 15: 11–22.

Bauman, Z. and Lyon, D. (2012) *Liquid surveillance: a conversation*, Oxford: Polity.

Rehumanization of the incarcerated Other 73

Bibas, S. (2012) *The machinery of criminal justice*, Oxford: Oxford University Press.

Bishop, B. and Cushing, R. G. (2008) *The big sort: why the clustering of like-minded America is tearing us apart*, Boston, MA: Houghton Mifflin.

Braithwaite, J. (2002) *Restorative justice and responsive regulation*, New York: Oxford University Press.

Braithwaite, J. (2003) 'Restorative justice and a better future', in E. McLaughlin, R. Fergusson, G. Hughes, and L. Westmarland (eds), *Restorative justice: critical issues*, London: Sage.

Bush, G. W. (2008) *Remarks on signing the Second Chance Act of 2007*, US Government Printing Office, online, available: http://findarticles.com/p/articles/mi_m2889/is_14_44/ai_n25401702/ (accessed 15 December 2014).

Christie, N. (1977) 'Conflicts as property', *British Journal of Criminology*, 17, 1–15.

Christie, N. (1986), 'The ideal victim', in E. A. Fattah (ed.), *From crime policy to victim policy: reorienting the justice system*, Basingstoke: Macmillan.

Clear, T. R. (2011) 'A private-sector, incentives-based model for justice reinvestment', *Criminology and Public Policy*, 10: 585–608.

Cohen, S. (2001) *States of denial: knowing about atrocities and suffering*, Oxford: Polity.

Crawford, A. and Clear, T. R. (2003) 'Community justice: transforming communities through restorative justice?', in E. Mclaughlin and G. Hughes (eds), *Restorative justice: critical issues*, London: Sage.

Death row stories (2014) film, dirs A. Gibney and R. Redford, US: CNN Original Series.

DeRoche, C. (2014) 'A really big first for us!', email, 4 June, justicefellowship@pfm.org.

Devers, L. (2011) *Plea and charge bargaining: research summary*, Washington, DC: Bureau of Justice Assistance, US Department of Justice.

Dzur, A. W. (2012) *Punishment, participatory democracy, and the jury*, New York: Oxford University Press.

Eberhardt, J. L. (2005) 'Imaging race', *American Psychologist*, 60: 181–190.

Eberhardt, J. L., Goff, P. A., Purdie, V. J. and Davies, P. G. (2004) 'Seeing black: race, crime, and visual processing', *Journal of Personality and Social Psychology*, 87: 876–893.

Federal Bureau of Prisons (2014) *Inmate statistics*, Washington DC, online, available: www.bop.gov/about/statistics/statistics_inmate_offenses.jsp (accessed 15 December 2014).

Ferguson, R. A. (2014) *Inferno: an anatomy of American punishment*, Boston, MA: Harvard University Press.

Forman, J. (2012) 'Racial critiques of mass incarceration: beyond the new Jim Crow', *New York University Law Review*, 87: 101–146.

Glover, J. (2001) *Humanity: a moral history of the twentieth century*, London: Pimlico.

Glynn, A. N. and Sen, M. (2014) 'Identifying judicial empathy: does having daughters cause judges to rule for women's issues?', *American Journal of Political Science*, published online 9 May, DOI: 10.1111/ajps.12118.

Green, D. A. (2006) 'Public opinion versus public judgment about crime: correcting the "comedy of errors"', *British Journal of Criminology*, 46: 131–154.

Green, D. A. (2009) 'Feeding wolves: punitiveness and culture', *European Journal of Criminology*, 6: 517–536.

Green, D. A. (2014) 'Penal populism and the folly of "doing good by stealth"', *The Good Society*, 23(1): 73–86.

Green, D. A. (2015, forthcoming) 'American penal reform catalysts and prospects', *Punishment & Society*.

Guerino, P. M., Harrison, P. M. and Sabol, W. (2011) *Prisoners in 2010*, Washington, DC: US Department of Justice, Bureau of Justice Statistics.

Hannem, S. (2013) 'Experiences in reconciling risk management and restorative justice: how circles of support and accountability work restoratively in the risk society', *International Journal of Offender Therapy and Comparative Criminology*, 57: 269–288.

Jacobson, M. (2014) 'Comparing American/European penal policies and prisons: policy implications of touring with US prison officials', paper presented at the Graduate Center, City University of New York, New York, 10 April.

Kant, I. (2011/1798) 'The penal law and the law of pardon', in M. Tonry (ed.), *Why punish? How much?*, New York: Oxford University Press.

Kristoff, N. D. (2007) 'Save the Darfur puppy', *The New York Times*, 10 May, online, available: www.nytimes.com/2007/05/10/opinion/10kristof.html (accessed 15 December 2014).

Lawrence, J. (2013) 'Why gay marriage is getting political traction (and why gun control isn't)', *The National Journal*, 8 April, online, available: www.nationaljournal.com/politics/why-gay-marriage-is-getting-political-traction-and-why-gun-control-isn-t-20130408 (accessed 15 December 2014).

Lichtblau, E. and Motoko, R. (2012) 'N.R.A. envisions "a good guy with a gun" in every school', *The New York Times*, 21 December, online, available: www.nytimes.com/2012/12/22/us/nra-calls-for-armed-guards-at-schools.html? (accessed 14 December 2015).

Lifton, R. J. (1967) *Death in life: survivors of Hiroshima*, New York: Random House.

Lynch, J. P. and Sabol, W. J. (2004) 'Assessing the effects of mass incarceration on informal social control in communities', *Criminology and Public Policy*, 3: 267–294.

McDonough, K. (2013) 'GOP Sen. Rob Portman endorses marriage equality', *Salon*, 15 March, online, available: www.salon.com2013/03/15gop_senator_rob_portman_endorses_marriage_equality/ (accessed 14 December 2014).

Manjoo, F. (2008) *True enough: learning to live in a post-fact society*, Hoboken, NJ: Wiley.

Mauer, M. (2001) 'The causes and consequences of prison growth in the United States', *Punishment & Society*, 3: 9–20.

Merton, R. K. (1948) 'The self-fulfilling prophecy', *The Antioch Review*, 8: 193–210.

Monroe, K. R. (1991) 'John Donne's people: explaining differences between rational actors and altruists through cognitive frameworks', *Journal of Politics*, 53: 394–433.

Nellis, M. (2013a) 'Analysing penal innovation', *International Journal of Offender Therapy and Comparative Criminology*, 57: 267–268.

Nellis, M. (2013b) 'Dim prospects: humanistic values and the fate of community justice', in J. Winstone and F. Pakes (eds), *Community justice: issues for probation and criminal justice*, Collumpton, Devon: Willan.

Nietzsche, F. (1961) *Thus spoke Zarathustra: a book for everyone and no one*, trans. R. J. Hollingdale,New York: Penguin Classics.

Obama, B. (2014) 'Remarks by the President on 'My Brother's Keeper' Initiative', online, available: www.whitehouse.gov/the-press-office/2014/02/27/remarks-president-my-brothers-keeper-initiative (accessed 15 December 2014).

Opotow, S. (1995) 'Drawing the line: social categorization and social exclusion', in B. B. Bunker and J.Z. Rubin (eds), *Conflict, cooperation, and justice: essays inspired by the work of Morton Deutsch*, San Francisco, LA: Jossey-Bass.

Rehumanization of the incarcerated Other   75

Pew Research Center (2014) *Political polarization in the American public*, online, available: www.pewresearch.org (accessed 15 December 2014).

Prison state (2014) film, dir. D. Edge, US: PBS FRONTLINE.

Prison terminal (2013) film, dir. E. Barens, US: HBO Documentary Films.

Right on Crime (2014) 'Right on Crime leadership summit 2014', email, 4 June, update@texaspolicy.com.

Rothman, D. J. (1980), *Conscience and convenience: the asylum and its alternatives in progressive America*, Boston, MA: Little, Brown and Company.

Ruck, S. K. (ed.) (1951) *Paterson on prisons: being the collected papers of Sir Alexander Paterson*, London: Frederick Muller Ltd.

Simon, J. (2007) *Governing through crime: how the war on crime transformed American democracy and created a culture of fear*, New York: Oxford University Press.

Slovic, P. (2007) '"If I look at the mass I will never act": psychic numbing and genocide', *Judgment and Decision Making*, 2: 79–95.

Smith, N. (2014) *Justice through apologies: remorse, reform, and punishment*, Cambridge: Cambridge University Press.

Solitary nation (2014) film, dir. D. Edge, US: PBS FRONTLINE.

Suellentrop, C. (2006) 'The right has a jailhouse conversion', *The New York Times*, 24 December, online, available: www.nytimes.com/2006/12/24/magazine/24GOP.t.html (accessed 15 December 2014).

The house I live in (2012) film, dir. Eugene Jarecki, US: Charlotte Street Films.

The Onion (2013) 'I feel very strongly about the issue of same sex marriage because I have a gay son', *The Onion*, 23 March, online, available: www.theonion.com/articles/i-feel-very-strongly-about-the-issue-of-same-sex-m,31820/ (accessed 15 December 2014).

The Pew Charitable Trusts (2010) *Collateral costs: incarceration's effect on economic mobility*, Washington, DC: The Pew Charitable Trusts.

The Sentencing Project (2014) 'Fact sheet: trends in U.S. corrections', online, available: http://sentencingproject.org/doc/publications/inc_Trends_in_Corrections_Fact_sheet. pdf (accessed 14 December 2014).

The university of Sing Sing (2011) film, dir. T. Skousen, US: Moxie Pictures.

The White House (2014) *My brother's keeper*, Washington DC, online, available: www. whitehouse.gov/my-brothers-keeper (accessed 15 December 2014).

Thomas, W. I. and Thomas, D. S. (1928) *The child in America: behavior problems and programs*, New York: Knopf.

Tonry, M. (1995) *Malign neglect: race, crime, and punishment in America*, New York: Oxford University Press.

Tonry, M. (2004) *Thinking about crime: sense and sensibility in American penal culture*, New York: Oxford University Press.

Tonry, M. (2011a) 'Making peace, not a desert: penal reform should be about values not justice reinvestment', *Criminology & Public Policy*, 10: 637–649.

Tonry, M. (2011b) *Punishing race: a continuing American dilemma*, New York: Oxford University Press.

Tonry, M. (2014) 'Remodeling American sentencing: a ten-step blueprint for moving past mass incarceration', *Criminology & Public Policy*, 13(4): 503–533.

Travis, J. (2005) *But they all come back: facing the challenges of prisoner reentry*, Baltimore, MD: Urban Institute Press.

Travis, J., Western, B. and Redburn, S. (2014) *The growth of incarceration in the United States: exploring causes and consequences*, Washington, DC: The National Academies Press.

Tucker, S. and Cadora, E. (2003) 'Justice reinvestment: to invest in public safety by reallocating justice dollars to refinance education, housing, healthcare, and jobs', *Ideas for an Open Society*, 3(3).

Tuschman, A. (2013) *Our political nature*, Amherst, NY: Prometheus Books.

US Senate Joint Economic Committee (2007) *Hearing. Mass incarceration in the United States: at what cost?*, Government Printing Office Hearing, 4 October.

van Zyl Smit, D. and Snacken, S. (2009) *Principles of European prison law and policy: penology and human rights*, Oxford: Oxford University Press.

Weber, M. (1968) *Economy and society*, New York: Bedminster Press.

WhitmanJ. Q. (1998) 'What is wrong with inflicting shame sanctions?', *The Yale Law Journal*, 107: 1055–1092.

WhitmanJ. Q. (2003) *Harsh justice: criminal punishment and the widening divide between America and Europe*, New York: Oxford University Press.

Wilson, J. Q. and Herrnstein, R. J. (1985) *Crime and human nature: the definitive study of the causes of crime*, New York: Simon & Schuster.

Yankelovich, D. (1991) *Coming to public judgment: making democracy work in a complex world*, Syracuse, NY: Syracuse University Press.

4 Prisons and the social production of immorality[1]

Anna Eriksson

Introduction

Prisons can be unforgiving places, filled with hard people, hard attitudes and hard times. They are places where retribution and punishment dictate the daily order, while hope and redemption cower in the corner. Prisons can also be conceived of as frightening places, filled with people deemed too dangerous to walk among us, people who are intrinsically different from us, and who are given too much, cost too much and whose exclusion from most human rights is only correct and proper. But prisons are also full of people who are poor and often lacking in education; who are addicted to alcohol, drugs or gambling; who are sometimes violent, but most often not. Prisons are places that increasingly warehouse the mentally ill and those with intellectual and neurological impairments. They are places where people are stripped of their identity and sometimes their humanity, and where they are given very little to maintain a sense of self and dignity.

However, prisons can also be places where humanity, mutual respect, and a sense of hope and meaning characterize daily life. They can be places where the people who work there are filled with a sense of duty, of doing an important vocation, of wishing they could do more if they only had the resources and support. Prisons are often quiet places, characterized by order, routine and boredom, with only the occasional outburst of excitement and action. Many of the people who live and work in prisons also have a wicked sense of humour and are guided by values of camaraderie, loyalty and respect.

Thus, the above descriptions depict two distinct pictures of prison life. For some reason, the former 'common-sense' version seems easier to accept, the latter more confronting and complex. Of course, most people do not have access to the information that would allow them to construct a more accurate picture of prison life; hence, it is on unsubstantiated knowledge that we base our opinions and consequent moral judgement of the people who reside therein and seem so different from us. The common view certainly supports such a construction, validated by news reporting keen to point to the evilness of prisoners and the plight of those who guard them. Populist politicians also favour such narratives, facilitating as they do a tough stance on law and order, situating the elected leader as someone who is capable of protecting the vulnerable public against these easily identified undesirables of society. Prisoners – as opposed to people who are yet to commit an offence or who have not yet been apprehended or successfully prosecuted – are convenient political cannon fodder. They are all too readily labelled, excluded, demonized and dehumanized. Through such processes of distantiation, a clear division between 'us' (the good) and 'them' (the bad) is created. The constructed 'Other' – the prisoner – now rapidly falls outside the universe of obligation (Fein 1979), effectively evicted from moral consideration. The plight of the Other, then, is no longer our concern, and we cover ourselves in the comfortable shroud of indifference.

In my research on prisons, I have become increasingly interested in the underlying process of such constructions of difference and where morality is situated in such constructions. So I seek to question not just why, but *how*, some prisoners are constructed by wider society as different in ways that suggest they are of less moral worth than others. I have observed how they are labelled, excluded and often punished beyond their sentence with few avenues of return. However, the comparative nature of my research has also given me the opportunity to observe prisons that minimize or largely avoid this kind of stigmatization and exclusion. This led me to further question how this process of Othering took place and what, if any, difference it made for individual prisoners and staff members behind the walls, and, finally, what the operation of such institutions says about the wider society within which they exist. To try to answer these questions I conducted face-to-face interviews with 230 staff and prisoners in 14 different prisons, seven of them across two Australian states, and seven in Norway, during a ten-month period in 2013–2014. The argument in the overall research project is located at two levels: the micro-social environment within the prison ('behind the walls'), and the macro-social level of wider society ('outside the walls'). These were studied in their own right, but, importantly, the focus was also on the extent to which they interact: for example, the impact of events in prison on outside policy and practice, and the impact of policy and other macro-level variables on day-to-day practice behind the walls.

Prisons do not exist in a vacuum; they are, as we know, a reflection of the society that contains them. Some regimes are characterized by a more inclusive approach, aimed at rehabilitation and integration as opposed to exclusion and continuous labelling. In *Contrasts in punishment: explaining Anglophone excess and Nordic exceptionalism* (Pratt and Eriksson 2013), written together with John Pratt, we discussed this dichotomy. We put forward that the Nordic countries have been identified as a region with more humane prison conditions, higher work satisfaction among prison staff, less violence and disorder in prison, a stronger emphasis on treatment and a less pronounced 'public punitiveness' – in short, as an 'exception' in penal policy and practice (Cavadino and Dignan 2006; Green 2008; Lacey 2008; Pratt 2008a, 2008b; Pratt and Eriksson

2013). This thesis has not been without its opponents, however, with the main critique emanating from scholars within the Nordic countries themselves (Mathiesen 2012; Scharff Smith 2012; Ugelvik 2012; Barker 2013). At the core of the critique is the argument that we conducted a historical and cultural analysis without in-depth empirical research conducted *inside* the prisons, hence missing important nuances in all countries. Consequently, the overall aim of the new research discussed in this chapter was to more fully understand three inter-related topics: first, the interaction among staff, inmates and the physical prison environment in different penal settings (maximum, medium and minimum security), to try to gauge what broadly makes prisons better or worse for those on the inside; second, how the nature and quality of different styles of interaction between the groups mediate proximity in different prison *and* national contexts; and third, the extent to which variables inside and outside the walls interact and the result of such interactions. This research builds on and adds important nuance to the Nordic exceptionalism thesis, but I also wanted to take that argument one step further and introduce the issue of morality in this context. Specifically, I sought to explore how prisons, as institutions, and prisoners, as people, have been placed outside the moral obligations (Fein 1979) of the broader community, with the hope of generating a discussion that can be generalized and translated into different penal settings, whether in other jurisdictions or other types of penal institution.

Theoretical framework: constructions of morality and total institutions

Zygmunt Bauman describes the process of distantiation, of Othering, in his seminal book *Modernity and the Holocaust* (1989), in which he refers to such processes as 'the social production of immorality', outlined in the Introduction to this book. I found his writings around morality and responsibility for the Other particularly compelling and in many ways applicable to institutions of punishment in our modern times. In particular, he provides a framework for thinking about the micro- and macro-processes that drive, perpetuate or indeed counteract the identification, exclusion and punishment of certain groups in our societies. This approach allowed me to identify practical variables within different prison environments that can erode proximity, such as physical barriers between people, the use of technology, task-oriented approaches to security, language use and dress code, to mention but a few. Focus on such variables can be used to argue for real change behind the walls, as well as lending a framework for normative theory production.

Notably, this chapter explicitly recognizes that prisons are *total institutions*, and I would argue that this particular phenomenon can be equally important when understanding processes of Othering and erosion of proximity in relation to both prisons as institutions and prisoners and staff as groups and individuals existing inside such institutions. A total institution, in the words of Erving Goffman, is a place where:

80   *Anna Eriksson*

First, all aspects of life are conducted in the same place and under the same single authority. Second, each phase of the member's daily activity is carried on in the immediate company of a large batch of others, all of whom are treated alike and required to do the same thing together. Third, all phases of the day's activities are tightly scheduled, with one activity leading at a prearranged time into the next, the whole sequence of activities being imposed from above by a system of explicit formal rulings and a body of officials. Finally, the various enforced activities are brought together into a single rational plan purportedly designed to fulfil the official aims of the institution. ... The handling of many human needs by the bureaucratic organization of whole blocks of people ... is the key fact of total institutions.

(Goffman 1961: 6)

Inherent to the concept of the total institution (Goffman 1961) – in this case the prison – is a particular set of social arrangements that can amplify the speed at which the erosion of proximity takes place, while simultaneously and effectively hiding the potentially devastating consequences from the public gaze and moral scrutiny. This set of social arrangements includes a pre-existing division between staff and prisoner groups (for example, the identification, naming and placing in groups before prisoners enter prison for the first time), which in turn takes place within a hierarchical and bureaucratic organization, further obscuring prison practice from moral evaluation (Bauman 1989). Indeed, 'one of the main accomplishments of total institutions is staging a difference between two constructed categories of persons – a difference in social quality and moral character, a difference in perception of self and other' (Goffman 1961: 111).

Goffman (1961: 4) also notes about total institutions that

their encompassing or total character is symbolized by the barrier to social intercourse with the outside and to departure that is often built right into the physical plant, such as locked doors, high walls, barbed wire, cliffs, water, forests, or moors.

This is an important point, particularly for the comparative perspective. The prison as a total institution does not have to be a high-security prison; it can be an island or a farm. From the outside, the latter seems open and relaxed enough, but prisoners in my research often spoke about these places in the same terms as they did about high-security prisons. The pains of imprisonment (Sykes 1958/2007), such as being deprived of family and friends, having to spend time with a group of people whose only common denominator is the prison in which they exist and the deprivation of freedom, are experienced as tangible losses irrespective of security level and prison design. Moreover, a total institution (Goffman 1961) is a place where the physical barriers that divide our lives into places – such as work, sleep and play – have been torn down. In

Prison and social production of immorality 81

many prisons, all these tasks are performed in the same space, while in the company of people one might rather avoid. But even though these physical divisions more or less cease to exist in prison, other barriers and divisions are erected in their place: between us and them, between those with power and those without, between the more or less worthy and indeed between the more or less human.

Significantly, the environment of a total institution sends powerful social and physical cues as to what is deemed appropriate behaviour, or indeed 'appropriate' ways to think; and it can be astounding how rapidly people adjust to such an environment, before too long seeing it as 'normal' and 'just the way things are'. Prisoners talked about this in the interviews, saying that it takes between one day and one week to adjust to the prison environment and the expectations that it conveys. However, this does not mean that prisoners settle, that they are comfortable in such an environment, but rather that you have no choice but to adjust to a foreign and unnatural environment. This was a distinction many of the interviewees made very clear. As one prisoner in high security mentioned, 'you don't have a choice; you have to assimilate or break' (P6HPuQ).

Staff are also subject to the forces of the total institution. The induction starts during training, but where Australia and Norway differ sharply is in the level of Otherness assigned to prisoners during this time. In Australia, prisoners are constructed, to an extent, as the enemy, as dangerous people who will take every opportunity to manipulate and use you, and who need to be closely guarded due to their inherent capacity for violence. In Norway, by contrast, prisoners are constructed as clients of the welfare state, whose rehabilitation is the main priority, and as people who have made some bad choices and who can make better ones with the aid of professional and genuine staff members. This distinction emerged as a strong theme in all of the interviews with staff; and it is interesting, although discouraging, to note how early the Othering of prisoners occurs in Australia – long before staff have even had a chance to meet any prisoners. What the Australian training does achieve is to convey a set of preconstructed views of prisoners as dangerous, as different, as people with whom staff have nothing in common, existing in a different universe of obligation (Fein 1979, 2000) – in short, as Others. This does *not* mean that staff and prisoners in Australia are any less moral, but rather that the forces that can negate personal responsibility and moral relationships are all the more powerful, placing prisons in Australia at a distinct disadvantage when it comes to positive change. Hence, the negative forces of the total institution work in conjunction with the social production of immorality, inherently intertwined within the penal environment, which can result in a dehumanization of prisoners and staff alike.

Together, these frameworks (the total institution and the social production of immorality) can help explain how it is possible to be engaged in face-to-face interaction with little moral reflections, in an environment in which feelings of responsibility towards the constructed Other have become diffused to the point where abuse and violence not only become possible, but may be inevitable. So, if immorality is highly correlated to an erosion of proximity, the question becomes: how can proximity be *increased* within a prison milieu? This question is straightforward; yet the answer is not. Prison environments differ, between high, medium and low security regimes, between different jurisdictions in the same country (as in Australia's eight states and territories) and between different countries. They differ because of the size of the prison, its aims, who runs it, and who owns it. They differ because they are born of diverse historical, social, cultural and political environments. They also differ due to the extent that outside environs penetrate and affect day-to-day practices on the inside. So what works in one prison may not work in another, for reasons that are often obscured behind daily prison routines.

In what follows, I first examine how prisons as institutions have become 'Othered' to different degrees in Australia and Norway, and the possible consequences of this process behind the walls. I then argue that the aims of imprisonment impact on the models of practice that are employed, such as task-focused versus people-focused practice, and how that in turn relates to proximity in the different prison environments. The final section of the chapter examines formal and informal interactions between staff and prisoners in the two countries. Importantly, many of the issues discussed in this chapter are multifaceted. For example, the level and form of informal interactions within a prison can be indicators of pre-existing distance (driven by variables outside the walls and distinct 'prison culture' variables), as well as drivers of further erosion of proximity between individuals and groups. And, finally, the nature of informal interactions can be a driver for reduced distance, for the responsibilization of social relationships which can result in increased trust and decreased hostility and violence between groups and individuals – in short, a more humane, less harmful prison environment for both prisoners and staff. Hence, each factor is a site of several opposing and competing forces. The comparative nature of the research assists in laying bare such dynamics and hopefully adds nuance to existing studies of prison life.

The Othering of prisons as institutions

That prisons in Australia exist outside feelings of responsibility for many is arguably evident in the high levels of punitiveness, reflected in news reporting, public opinion calling for harsher and longer punishment, and law and order posturing by the state and territory governments (Kornhauser 2013, Pratt et al. 2005). As in all other countries, public opinion about prisons is generally uninformed (Roberts and Hough 2002), and there is a significant lack of accurate reporting when it comes to prison conditions and the people inside these institutions, staff and prisoners alike. Public understandings of what prison is like are largely based on American TV shows and films. The public, in this instance, includes those people who are yet to enter the prison as either inmates or staff. This became evident when I asked about their expectations of prisons, either

Prison and social production of immorality 83

when they were first sentenced or when they applied for the job. The vast majority said that they thought it would be a horrible, frightening and dangerous place, and they based this on what they had seen on TV shows from America. Those with a different, more accurate view of Australian prisons either had a father or older relative who had served time before, or, among staff, had someone in the family or friendship circle who had worked or was currently working in a prison.

But even though staff and prisoners quickly learned of the reality of Australian prisons, the Othering of prisons as institutions with the resulting minimization of responsibility (Bauman 1989) by those outside the walls had tangible and continuing effects inside the walls. For example, in medium- and minimum-security prisons, where prisoners lived in self-catering, cottage-style accommodation (as part of the strategy to increase freedom and responsibility with the aim of release), prisoners were allowed to buy whatever food they wanted as long as they had money in their account (and they were only allowed to spend $140 per week, which had to cover food, extra clothes, cigarettes, coffee, soft drinks, and so on). However, because of a concern about public opinion, management would cross out certain items that might be seen as 'luxury' items, such as prawns and beef fillet (keeping in mind that these are not necessarily expensive in Australia). There was also a distinct reluctance among prison governors to report 'good news stories', such as prisoners having access to a swimming pool (which during a week-long 40-degree heatwave, not uncommon in Australia, can help cool some rather hot tempers), or prisoners doing an incredible job planting gardens and growing vegetables for the prison, and so on, all because prisons in Australia are supposed to be harsh to match public opinion and not embarrass hard-line politicians. So good news became bad news for the prison. And this concern about public opinion among policy-makers and politicians when making their decisions about prison practice can be completely counterproductive. The following two examples illustrate this.

While I was conducting my fieldwork in one of the Australian states, two prisoners escaped from (or rather, walked out of) an open prison in the state's north. They were caught within a few days and immediately sent to high security, their chance of ever being allowed back into low security reduced to zero. However, by that time, the media had reported on the incident, noting that one of the prisoners had been sentenced for murder, the other for armed robbery. No further violent offences were committed while the pair were on the loose (they did buy a beer at a local tavern and later stole a car to travel away from the area) and nor was it acknowledged that the two prisoners were due for release before too long and that time in an open prison was an important part of their pre-release preparation (news.com.au 14 April 2014; ABC News 15 April 2014a; ABC News 17 April 2014b). The week after this incident, I was conducting interviews at another open prison in the same state, 1,500 km away from where the escapes had taken place, and was told by staff and prisoners that the nine long-termers who had been staying at this

84   *Anna Eriksson*

prison had now been moved back, or 'tipped', to high security, purely to prevent an adverse public reaction. Both staff and prisoners were angry about this and, as one of the staff members mentioned, 'Sending nine long-termers back to high security was a crazy, knee-jerk reaction to [the] escapes. ... Long-termers provide a stabilizing influence on the camp; it is the short-termers who are the problem here' (S8LA1). The nine who were tipped had done nothing wrong, were due for release within between one and three years and, with them now being sent back, not only was all the progress they had made negated, but they were also punished for something someone else had done wrong. Bizarrely, despite this move being made to reassure the public, there was no media reporting about this in the following weeks and months. How can the public have an opinion on something if it does not even know about it? And then what does it matter? The prisoners, being of little moral worth to the decision-makers in the city, were pawns to be moved in a game of public acceptance and government legitimacy. Staff who raised concerns based on prisoner welfare were ignored. Indeed, reflecting the nature of the total institution, staff in Australia are banned from publicly commenting on their work. Therefore, their views could safely be disregarded – safely, that is, for political purposes, not for prison practice.

The ripple effects of the walk-offs did not stop there. Two months later I was conducting interviews in a high-security prison in the same state. There I was told that the official message coming from 'town' (Corrections Head Office) was that no more long-term prisoners with a history of violent offending were allowed to be sent to the low-security prison until further notice. Staff commented on this as being an 'arse-covering exercise, just in case something happened', and that it was completely counterproductive since these men, some of whom had spent up to 30 years in prison, would now be released into the community straight from high security instead of progressing incrementally through a system designed to gradually socialize them towards release. Arguably this significantly reduces their chances of post-release success.

The second example comes from the other state where I conducted interviews. On 22 September 2012, 29-year-old Jill Meagher started out on the 10-minute walk home from a pub in an inner-city suburb of Melbourne. She never reached home and six days later her body was found dumped north of the city. She had been brutally raped and murdered, and the police soon arrested Adrian Bayley, who confessed to the crime. He was subsequently sentenced to life in prison, with a minimum term of 35 years. What made this case particularly newsworthy was the fact that Jill Meagher had only had a few drinks at the pub with her work colleagues from the ABC (the major Australian public broadcaster). She was newly married, very pretty and pictures of her and her husband on their wedding day were repeatedly aired on the television news. She was 'one of us'. Indeed, she was the 'ideal victim' (Christie 1986). The challenge for Corrections was that Bayley had been on parole at the time of the offence and had a long history of violent offending. The Parole Board subsequently became the subject of considerable scrutiny

(Callinan 2013) and, as a consequence, law changes were quickly introduced – the Corrections Amendment (Parole Reform) Bill 2013 and the Corrections Amendment (Further Parole Reform) Bill 2014 – by a government that had come to power on a strong 'law and order' platform, keen to be seen to protect the public against these 'monsters'. The legislative change made applying for and being granted parole incredibly difficult, not only for prisoners with an offending history that included violent and sexual crimes, but for *all* prisoners, irrespective of their offending history. The legislation was passed with little opposition; after all, it only affected people who had already been excluded from the universe of obligation (Fein 1979, 2000) of most people. As such, their suffering was deemed to be of little consequence.

During the interviews conducted in 2014, when the new legislation had come into effect, it became clear that there were now compulsory courses to be undertaken by prisoners before they could be considered for parole. These courses addressed violent offending and drug and alcohol addiction. However, they were not available at all prisons, meaning that prisoners had to be transferred to partake in the course, and if they were refused transfer for security reasons, they could not undertake a course and therefore could not be considered for parole. Prisoners who had been sentenced for drink-driving and tax fraud were all required to undertake the violence course, regardless of the fact that violence was not a relevant factor in their offending. Furthermore, prisoners who had a history of violent offending but no previous involvement with drugs and alcohol had to participate in the addiction course to be considered for release. Needless to say, these changes caused considerable stress, anger and uncertainty among the prisoners, and all those interviewed were aware of the reason for this change. As a result, Bayley is being kept in isolation in the maximum-security unit within one of the high-security prisons in the state, since the other prisoners blame him for these changes which have adversely affected every prisoner in the jurisdiction.

Moreover, the consequent slow-down in release – it is now more difficult to get a parole hearing and to be granted parole should you get a hearing – has led to all prisons across the state bursting at the seams, with double-bunking all too common, shipping containers being brought in to deal with the overcrowding, difficulties gaining access to limited release preparation programmes and exacerbated mental health concerns (Victorian Ombudsman 2014; Cook 2014; Lee 2014; Mills 2014). The government seized on the climate of public outrage directed at Bayley, in particular, but all criminals more generally, to introduce new legislation that abolished suspended sentences. Convicted people should now either be sentenced to community corrections or go straight to prison, and this move, the public was told, was intended to direct more people into community-based sentences. However, as a recent report from the Sentencing Advisory Council (2013) demonstrates, the prison population in this state was on the rise anyway, and after the new legislative changes the result has been, unsurprisingly, that more people are being sent to prison while fewer are leaving. Corrections in this state is now facing a considerable challenge, not necessarily because of something it did wrong (the blame was placed on the Parole Board), but because of factors beyond its control. This suggests that prison practice can change rapidly in Australia, influenced by outside-the-wall factors. And due to an existing erosion of proximity between prisons and the society in which they exist, such effects are tangible and swift behind the prison walls. The result is, unfortunately, not a safer society, but a society into which frustrated and angry people will be released with a confirmed and deepening distrust and disrespect for authority, and without adequate preparation for life on the outside.[2]

The situation in Norway is starkly different. As part of the welfare state, prisons have not become Othered to the same extent (Pratt and Eriksson 2013) – a situation that resonates behind the walls. The most obvious and recent example of this is the aftermath of the atrocity committed by Anders Behring Breivik on 22 July 2011, when he first bombed the Department of Justice building in central Oslo, killing eight people, and then went out to the island of Utøya where the Social Democratic youth group had their summer camp. Here he hunted down, shot and killed a further 69 people. And another 42 people were injured that day. This event shook Norway to the core and the details have been covered extensively elsewhere (see, for example, *En av oss: en berättelse om Norge* [*One of us: a story about Norway*] by Åsne Seierstad 2013). The point here, however, is that no laws were changed in the aftermath, and staff in the prisons where Breivik spends his time have gone out of their way to ensure that this 'exceptional' prisoner, this 'alien', does not affect the way in which other prisoners are treated. The most tangible change is a second fence that has been added around one of the high-security prisons where Breivik is incarcerated, but whether this is intended as a strategy to keep him in or keep other people out (who would like to get their hands on him) is unclear.

Importantly, when prisons as institutions become Othered, excluded from the moral responsibility of the community, it is not only prisoners who are labelled and excluded – it is also prison staff. They, too, are affected by the forces that work to include or exclude the prison, and this can have a ripple effect behind the prison walls. As mentioned by one prison officer in Australia, 'You feel like no one is on your side – prisoners are against you, management is against you, the town on the outside is against you' (S9RA1). This disregard for the work prison that officers do, by the public and by Corrections leadership, was frequently commented upon in the interviews. For example, 'Being a prison officer, it is a very unsupported profession, by the government and by society' (S8HA1); 'It is seen as low-status, but this is one of the most important jobs in society' (S6MA2); 'The forgotten profession … until something goes wrong' (S4HA2). Indeed, even though there are a large number of professional prison officers who genuinely care about prisoners' welfare and simulta-neously manage to provide the necessary measures of security and safety, they are, by working in the prison, tainted by association. Many prison officers are reluctant to tell people they meet on the outside about the type of work they do, often having a story ready about working as a public servant, knowing that working as a prison officer is not a respected profession.

In Norway, again, the situation is rather different, lending support to the argument that not only have prisons not been Othered to the same extent, but also that this is linked to tangible effects behind the walls. As a rule, the prison staff I interviewed in Norway felt that they were doing an important job and that they were valued by their colleagues, managers and many of the prisoners. They also felt that the wider society appreciated the difficult task that they had to undertake. As one of the uniformed officers in a high-security prison said, 'This is the best and the most difficult job in the world' (S2HIN). The same staff member later expanded on the topic of the working environment:

> I have been very fortunate with the boss on the first wing where I worked, where he was very particular about seeing everything within a bigger context, and that we should work according to two principles, which are that we should do our best to prevent further criminality, and prepare the inmates as much as possible so that they can function in society one day in the future. ... And when you work within such broad guidelines, well I find it very difficult to *not* become motivated by that, because when we have a success story with one of our prisoners, then there is a very positive response from outside [wider society]. So that is almost enough to keep the motivation up in this job.
>
> (S2HIN).

Moreover, it is not seen as a low-status profession, in the way that it can be in many Anglophone countries. This is arguably evident by the educational background of the staff I interviewed, which often included a university degree within the social sciences, a teaching degree with subsequent work within schools, degrees and work within psychology and psychiatry, and so on. This also clearly signifies that prisoners are part of the welfare state in Norway, requiring skilled workers who are provided with adequate support to undertake a challenging profession. Importantly, prisoners are seen as people, not Others; and 95 per cent of the staff interviewed answered the question 'Why did you choose this job?' along the lines of: 'I wanted to work with people'. In Australia, the answer to that question ranged from 'I was made redundant from my old job', to 'I live locally and the prison was advertising at a time when I was looking for work' or 'this is my retirement plan. [I] doubt they'll run out of prisoners any time soon'. Quite a few staff also said that they wanted to work with people, but these were always staff who did not wear a uniform during work, but rather civilian or work clothes (teaching or programme staff, and industry or gardening staff, for example). The extent to which prisons in the two countries have been moved outside or retained within the moral universe of 'us' is also, I argue, reflected in the level of training provided for staff, which in turn reflects the level of importance placed on the job by the state and the tasks staff are expected to undertake. In

88   *Anna Eriksson*

Australia, training ranges from eight to 12 weeks, recently cut to four to six weeks in several places due to staff shortages at a time of rapidly increasing prison populations. In Norway, the training is two years, half of which is spent at the training college, with the rest spent in the various prisons under the oversight of teachers and mentors. And there is no staff shortage in Norway. In 2014, there were 2,000 applicants for the 300 places at the training college.

What are prisons for? Aims, practice and proximity

That the overarching aims of imprisonment dictate practice may sound self-evident, but this has some rather significant effects that became particularly obvious in carrying out the comparison between Norway and Australia for this research. The official aims of most prisons are 'to protect the community', to 'punish', to 'deter' and to 'rehabilitate'. Yet it is only the first aim that is subject to any real evaluation, measured as it usually is by prisoners not escaping while in custody. However, with the aim of rehabilitation comes an added question: for how long should the community be protected? If it is only for the term of imprisonment, then prisons do not have to do much more than safely contain humans. If, however, that protection is extended into the post-release period, then a whole other set of arrangements needs to be in place for this to occur. In Australia, the aim to rehabilitate is present in all prisons, but is often modified and trumped by security concerns. As mentioned by one prisoner in a high-security prison, 'The system is not designed to rehabilitate; just to lock up' (P1HA2). Another prisoner in the same institution said that 'Punitiveness trumps rehabilitation any day of the week' (P3HA2).

Moreover, the aims of practice, in true bureaucratic fashion, are measured against key performance indicators that tend to be quantitative in nature as opposed to the more difficult to measure qualitative aims that can encapsulate human nature and personal change. The key word in Australian prison practice is 'compliance', whereby a certain set of goals has to be met every year for the prison to be allowed to continue its practice. To have high standards of practice is of course a good thing. But in the same way in which official crime rates are collected, it is only those things that are actually reported that are measured. Three less positive consequences flow from this. First, prison work in Australia today consists of a significant amount of paperwork. A task-focused prison has to search a certain number of cells every day. Contraband is looked for and hopefully not found, altercations between inmates noted, use of illegal drugs prevented, and so on. All of this is recorded multiple times. Often there is a second checklist to check the first, and then a third checklist to check the second one. Second, and more worryingly, this amount of paperwork has replaced human interaction, since there is not enough time for both tasks, effectively eroding proximity and increasing the distance between the prisoners and staff. As several staff members, working at all levels of security, commented:

Prison and social production of immorality 89

Our job consists of a hell of a lot of paperwork now.

(S2HA2)

Prison work now is 70 per cent paperwork and 30 per cent prisoner work. It has been a doubling and tripling of paperwork in the last few years. But it is only so we are compliant so if something happens they can blame someone for it.

(S4MA2)

There is a form for everything here ... this bureaucracy that you have to go through. ... Paperwork has replaced human conversations, and means staff don't have to do anything, just file the paper.

(P1LA2)

A focus on compliance makes prison work into a paper job instead of people job.

(S5HA2)

And third, what is not reported has not (officially) happened. In several prisons this had been the view held by former governors, meaning that abuse towards staff, abuse within the prisoner groups, drug use and self-harm sometimes went unreported, or at least unrecorded. This made staff feel significantly unsupported by their own boss, resulting not only in low job satisfaction, but also in a dangerous prison culture for everyone. So, as a general rule, *prisons in Australia are task oriented*, whereas *prisons in Norway are people oriented* – a distinction reflected in aims and resulting practice.

Prisons in Norway use checklists as well. But the focus on people places the prisoners' needs at the centre of practice. Staff, as the professional people who are supposed to deliver on the targets on a day-to-day basis, are also central. As mentioned earlier, staff in Norwegian prisons in general feel valued, like they are doing a challenging and important job, and are supported by the leadership. Notably, they have a common sense of purpose: *to release people who can be your neighbour*. In the interviews, staff at all security levels in Norway clearly conveyed this experience of prison work. Such aims have led to a practice in which dynamic security – face-to-face interaction – has become central. And this approach to practice has also led to different 'categories' of prisoner, such as violent offenders and sex offenders, sharing the same wing. In Australia, sex offenders are quickly segregated into so-called protection units. In Norway, the philosophy is that prisoners need to be resocialized, to become people who can coexist with other people whom they do not necessarily like, so that they can return as functioning members of society and not resort to violence when confronted by people whom they would consider to be of lesser moral worth. In some prisons, men and women are mixed (in different units in high and medium security, and in the same units in low

90 *Anna Eriksson*

security), with the same aim. I described this practice to some of my Australian interviewees and asked both staff and prisoners whether they thought such a practice would be successful in Australia. The response was a mix of amusement and disbelief. But it is worth reminding the reader here that I am not suggesting that staff in Australia are more punitive or have a less sophisticated ethical orientation and nor am I suggesting that prisoners in Australia are any better or worse than those in Norway. Instead, I am arguing that they are the product of the social, physical and cultural environment in which they work and live, and that their individual morality is the object of such bureaucratized and total institutions.

Proximity and interactions across the divide

So far I have discussed how outside variables can affect inside practice. I will now move on to look at how inside practice, on its own, can affect social distance between staff and prisoners and how proximity can be bridged or further eroded by different approaches to interaction and communication. As mentioned earlier, interaction style is a multifaceted variable. Hence, it can be an indicator of pre-existing distance driven by outside-the-walls variables discussed above; it can be a distinct 'prison culture' variable that leads to further erosion of proximity between individuals and groups within the prison; and, finally, it can be the catalyst for increased proximity and responsibilization of social relationships within the prison.

Formal interactions

All prisons are places of routine and tightly controlled schedules. As Goffman (1961: 6) notes,

> all phases of the day's activities are tightly scheduled, with one activity leading at a pre-arranged time into the next, the whole sequence of activities being imposed from above by a system of explicit formal rulings and a body of officials ... the various enforced activities are brought together into a single rational plan purportedly designed to fulfil the official aims of the institution.

Not only do these interactions structure the day, but their form and content also send powerful messages as to the social structure, status and moral worth of the groups inside. In essence, prisoners are, in more ways than one, 'foreigners inside' (Bauman 1989: 36) – a concept that Bauman applied when discussing the Jewish population in relation to the Holocaust. But I find this conceptualization applicable to the modern prison, where an impressive amount of rules and regulations, aimed at controlling and confining prisoners, dictate the daily order and coexistence of staff and prisoners, but also support the daily order in important ways:

An important point to remember is that all such apparently antagonistic measures were at the same time vehicles of social integration. Between them, they defused the danger that a 'foreigner inside' cannot but present to the self-identity and self-production of the host group. They set up conditions under which cohabitation without friction was conceivable. They spelled out behavioural rules which, if closely observed, could guarantee peaceful coexistence in a potentially conflict-ridden and explosive situation.

(Bauman 1989: 36)

One such routine interaction is the practice of giving and taking orders. As Collins (1988: 211–12) argues,

The experience of giving orders makes people self-assured, proud, or even arrogant, and they identify themselves with the official ideas in whose name they give orders. Conversely, the experience of taking orders from other people makes people fatalistic, externally conforming but privately alienated from authority and the official ideas in whose name they are given orders.

This reflects a modern prison culture, as well as capturing Bauman's (1989) argument that such forms of hierarchical and institutionalized praxis can effectively work to silence concerns about the moral consequences of the orders given, as well as serving to alienate and dehumanize the recipient of that order.

However, based on the data collected during my fieldwork, such an uncompromising standpoint does not necessarily ring true in prison practice in either country. Instead, I argue, the inevitable presence of the Other (Levinas 1981, 1982), of seeing and interacting with the Other every day, leads to a situation where feelings of responsibility towards the Other arise, unbidden or encouraged as they may be. As a consequence, formal interactions are often modified by mutual exchanges that contain a certain level of respect. In Australian prisons, at least, this was highlighted by staff and prisoners alike as something that made life on the inside significantly more bearable, as well as safer for everyone (in Norwegian prisons, this aspect was so taken for granted that it was rarely commented upon).

As one prisoner in a low-security prison in Australia mentioned, 'The best way to keep a prison safe is for staff to be more approachable; they always win in the end, but can prevent a lot of stuff by treating prisoners with respect. … But for some staff, power gets to their heads' (P9LA2). And another prisoner observed, 'If you speak with respect, you get that back' (P5HPuA1), echoing comments from the majority of interviewees, who identified respect as one of the key aspects of a well-functioning prison. When I asked prisoners in Australia about the qualities of a good prison officer, one of them, echoing many of the others, said,

They have to treat you humanely – you did something wrong, but you don't encourage a person to be good and reintegrate if you are just a fucking arsehole – and that is why there is such a separation between the two groups. ... They have to be sympathetic that this is the most traumatic experience of our lives.

(P3LA1)

The giving and taking of orders is an inevitable reality in a total institution; but the *way* in which the orders are given matters a great deal, an importance resting within both substance and procedure, which became obvious during the fieldwork. In short, when orders given are experienced as reasonable, within the legitimate requirements of the prison, and when they are given in a calm, authoritative and respectful manner, prisoners tend to comply and, importantly, do so with their integrity and humanity respected and intact. However, when orders are given that are experienced as petty, intrusive and demeaning, compliance might still occur, but an immediate erosion of proximity takes place, diffusing feelings of responsibility towards the staff member and, indeed, towards the entire authority that the staff member represents.

Custodial staff vary in their willingness and ability to give orders in a respectful manner. This difference exists between individuals, not necessarily between institutions or countries. When staff members treat prisoners in a way that clearly signals the prisoners' lack of moral worth, answering the question, 'Why?' with a 'just because I say so', it signals an oppositional and disrespectful stance. The reaction tends to be one of defiance, anger, frustration and reciprocated disrespect. In an example from Norway, when a staff member says, 'I am in charge here, that is just the way it is' (S9HHN), that is the beginning of the end of that working relationship. As mentioned by a custodial officer in a medium-security prison in Australia, 'Being civil and respectful decreases the distance and makes the job more manageable. Inconsistency increases the distance' (S7MA2).

Aside from the direct giving of orders – a reality of prison life that staff and prisoners alike accept as necessary – a perhaps more important situation related to communication is when prisoners are given information about a particular decision related to them. This could be a decision about a request made by prisoners, regarding, for example, extra time on the phone, visits, changing of one's cell to avoid a particular cell mate, changing of wing or prison, access to courses and education, different food, the keeping of books or arts materials in the cell, access to work or to change work, access to medical care or a psychologist, and so on. Prisoners who highlighted the importance of humane interaction frequently commented on this aspect of staff–prisoner interaction. Apart from being away from family and the overall deprivation of freedom, this was seen by prisoners as the biggest challenge of being inside. The following two quotes illustrate what many said in Australia: 'Staff do not have to justify decisions, their attitude is that "we [the staff] are right, you are wrong"' (P6HA2); and 'The biggest challenge here, that is being

Prison and social production of immorality   93

told what to do instead of being *asked*; they strip you of your human rights. If they treated you like a human, that would change a lot' (P10HA2). When I asked prisoners and staff in Norway if such decisions were explained and justified, the answer was almost always 'yes', and it was seen by staff as an important aspect of the rehabilitation work that prisoners need to learn to receive bad news without acting up but that such news had to be delivered in a way that provides an opportunity for reflection and understanding. Norwegian prisoners, too, reported that staff always explained decisions when they could, and when they could not it was usually because the decision was taken elsewhere – to be made by the prison manager or parole board, for example – and the individual staff member did not have access to the necessary information. However, if parole is denied in Norway, the prisoner is given a reason for this and then the prisoner and his or her caseworker will sit down together and work out a plan that allows the prisoner to meet the requirements imposed upon them.

The key issue here revolves around substantial and procedural justice (Jackson et al. 2010; Tyler 1990). When decisions are explained, when prisoners feel that the process by which they are treated is fair, even if it leads to an outcome with which they might disagree, a more respectful, more humane and more secure prison environment is created for everyone. This was recognized by the Australian and Norwegian custodial staff interviewed in my research. As one staff member at a low-security prison in Australia said, 'It is important to justify/motivate/explain decisions to prisoners, within reason, as long as it is not a security risk' (S2LA1). Similarly, a prisoner in a different Australian state observed that 'treatment by staff is very important – they don't have to be nice and friendly all the time, but fair, consistent and respectful' (P7MA2).

However, it is one thing to recognize the importance of such communication and another to implement it in routine practice. There was significantly more evidence of procedural justice practices in Norwegian prisons than in Australian ones across the security-level spectrum. Prisoners and staff in Australia are accustomed to larger social distances and more formal means of communication. Because this is the norm in many prisons it is usually unquestioned. In this regard, the key factor here then becomes *consistency*. As long as a staff member always responds in the same fashion, their approach comes to be recognized and can be more easily negotiated. Furthermore, this provides certainty in an environment where uncertainty is a significant stress factor. One prisoner in a high-security prison in Australia succinctly summarized this when he stated, 'In [prison x], staff would reply to your question with "yes, no, or fuck off" – but at least you knew where you had them' (P2HA2). This arguably reflects the earlier discussion about the position of prisons in relation to the moral responsibility of the broader society towards those inside, which filters through the walls, affecting the people inside, including the moral worth they afford each other. It also means that certainty and consistency often trump procedural justice concerns when it comes to a 'better' environment as far as

94 *Anna Eriksson*

prisoners are concerned, particularly in an environment where the diffusion of responsibility between the two groups has become entrenched.

There is little dispute over the fact that there are much larger social distances between prisoners and staff in Anglophone prisons than there are in the Nordic ones (Pratt and Eriksson 2013). The research presented here set out to explain how such distances materialize and how they can be bridged. Within the research question existed a personal assumption of mine: that smaller distances between the two groups would always be a good thing. However, after my first round of interviews in Australia it became obvious that this was a mistaken and even naïve assumption. The absolute majority of prisoners and custodial staff in Australian prisons saw smaller social distances as a distinctly negative occurrence. For example, 'Greater staff–prisoner interaction is not desired by prisoners here, just that the interaction that takes place happens in a respectful and humane manner' (P3HA2), said a prisoner in high security. Thus, according to many interviewees, the distance is there for a reason and should be kept. As mentioned by another prisoner in low security, 'There is a line, that is the first thing you learn in prison. Staff will use you, they don't care. And staff who encourage information-sharing are putting prisoners at risk' (P2LA2). Similarly, a custodial officer in high security stated that

> It is the prisoners who are creating that [distance] – prisoner attitude, who they are, and how they live their lives. Staff are here to help them, that is what we are paid to do. It doesn't matter if we are nice to these guys. Firstly, they see blue versus green,[3] and if they *do* want to talk or be closer, then other prisoners will "police" that – dogs. It is the criminal mentality, the bullies lead, and the weaker follow' (S10HA1). Not everyone shared this view, however, and as a prisoner in the same institution said, 'To me it is not "them versus us"; I am here for what I have done, they are here to work.
>
> (P3HA1)

These views were arguably based on ingrained cultures within each of the two groups such that the distance, the difference, is perceived to be an important part of the identity, agency and reluctant coexistence of the individuals inside prison. This culture provides a framework, a guide for action and interaction. It provides a choice and a personal stance, backed up by powerful group dynamics, within an environment where the choices made in everyday life on the outside have been effectively removed. However, a clear and often large distance does not have to lead to dehumanization and conflict. What is central here is the way in which communication is performed over the divide. Staff and prisoners all agreed that 'A respectful and professional relationship makes everyone safe' (S1HA2). Hence, the *mode of communication* seems more important than the actual and large social distance in Australian prisons, in the same way that such communication is equally important to prison practice in Norway, where the social distance is significantly smaller.

Informal interactions

In all my interviews I asked prisoners and staff whether they ever engaged in any informal activities with the other group, such as cooking and eating food together, playing board games or sport, and a range of other activities. In Norway, the answer was 'yes, of course' from both groups. For example, as one staff member who worked in the high-security prison in Norway that houses the 'worst of the worst', including Anders Breivik,[4] commented,

> On the secure wings we tend to play bingo together, it is easy to organize and appreciated by the inmates. I also exercise together with them, prepare food and so on. ... It is something quite special about sitting around the table having dinner with them, and realize that "this is really quite normal!"
>
> (S2HIN)

A female officer in the same high-security prison said,

> Well, of course we play board games and cook food together out on the wing, but I have also been fortunate enough to have accompanied them out on day trips and such, when we head out to the forest for the day. It is really rewarding, for them and us, to see each other in a different environment. ... And they tend to take much more responsibility when we are out, and they also relax more, are in a better mood, simple things like that.
>
> (S2HIN)

In another high-security prison, it was mentioned that

> Yes, we are with them during the day, with work, programmes and education activities, but also in the exercise hall where we sometimes train with them and play soccer, land hockey and such things. On the wing, we eat dinner, play cards, and chat in the exercise yard. The inmates have small teams that organize the evening meal for the whole wing, and we are often invited by them to share dinner. So I think we spend a fair bit of time with them, and that is something we learn from day one that, that our job is to spend time with them.
>
> (S4HHN)

Such informal interactions make up an important part of the operational model in Norway, which is centred on dynamic security and milieu therapy. In Australia, however, the answer to the same question was 'no, never', at least in relation to uniformed staff. Some quotes will illustrate the social distance that exists between the two groups in Australian prisons and the reluctance to increase proximity by such means. One medium-security prison had originally been designed with such informal interactions in mind but, during the interviews with staff in early 2014, the comments on this issue included: 'No, no and no. Simply would not happen.' When asked whether he would play soccer with the inmates, this staff member said: 'I would rather pull out my own fingernails' (S6MA2). However, he also made the point that he would not play sport any day of the week, with anyone. Another officer observed that 'the prison was designed for staff and inmates to eat together out in the common areas of the units, but as far as I know, that has never happened' (S1MA2). In addition, staff commented that it 'never really happened, I just wouldn't feel comfortable about that sort of thing' (S4MA2), and [I'm] 'not sure why it is gone, but now it would be pretty much unthinkable' (S2MA2). In a couple of high-security prisons, staff mentioned that management prohibited such informal interactions and 'we can't even play pool with them, management thinks it blurs the line' (S1HA2). Prisoners felt equally strongly about such interactions, knowing that to be seen to spend time with staff in this way would give them the name 'screw lover' and place them in danger, quickly ostracized by the other prisoners. As one high-security prisoner who had been in and out of prison for 30 years stated, 'the trade instructor, I even shook his hand at Christmas. In the old days, I would have punched *myself* for doing that!'

Prisoners were indeed very clear about what makes a prison better or worse: people and the way they interact. As mentioned by an Australian prisoner in high security: 'People matter. The physical environment is less important' (P8HA1). This social environment to which this prisoner and others referred related not only to the prisoner–staff divide but also to the social world of the prisoner groups themselves, which is of utmost importance to the quality of their day-to-day existence. As another prisoner, this time in low security, commented, 'Doing jail in itself is easy; it is the other people dragging you down. … People make the prison … and the physical environment doesn't really matter' (P3LA2). This was echoed by an officer from a high-security prison, who said, 'environment is less important – it is mainly due to how the officers relate to prisoners and also how prisoners relate to officers' (S6HA1). Staff recognized this very clearly, and many of them felt, 'You get what you give' (S3LA1) and 'I treat prisoners the way I want to be treated – with respect' (S4HPA1). The point is that under the hegemonic influence of the total institution such sentiments may not always play out in practice. For example, in low-security prisons in Australia, wheres the perimeter might consist of a low fence, or no fence at all, static security is minimal. Here, dynamic security becomes more important but the interactions are still very much formal – a high-security mentality is tangible. Therefore, it is not merely interactions *per se* that are important. Indeed, if custodial staff spend most of their working day behind glass walls supervising prisoners from afar, only to emerge into the prisoners' social world at muster times, then the 'people factor' is a negative contributor to the social order. It is the *quality* of human interaction that matters, not the quantity. It became obvious during this research that a stark, high-security environment can be made to feel better, more humane, if

Prison and social production of immorality 97

characterized by such interactions, in the same way in which an open prison can feel cold and punitive due to a lack of such interactions. Hence, a large social distance is not necessarily negative. Rather, it depends on the *type and form of interaction* that takes place across the divide. Prisoners and staff in both Australia and Norway were very clear about what such interaction looked like: it was characterized by respect, clear boundaries, consistency, trust and certainty.

Conclusion

Particular cultural, social, historical and political variables lend support to different *approaches* to punishment in Norway and Australia (Lacey 2008; Pratt and Eriksson 2013). However, when it comes to prison *practice* they only represent one set of variables that influences a particular security arrangement. Factors outside the prison walls cannot, by themselves, effect proximity and its erosion on the inside. Instead, uniquely on-the-inside variables need to be examined, several of which have been discussed in this chapter. In particular, the *quality* of human interaction inside prisons is crucial for establishing and maintaining an appropriate distance.

A prison that is 'good',[5] then, is one where the individual human rights of prisoners and staff alike are respected, and those released after their sentence are deemed fit to be anyone's next door neighbour. It is clear that some prisons have a higher success rate than others in this endeavour. In my small sample of 14, most of those 'good' prisons are to be found in Norway, but there are also important exceptions to the rule in that country. In Australia, the 1,000-bed high-security institutions may fail in many of the areas that signify a 'good' prison, but for reasons that are often beyond the control of staff. There are also wings or areas in individual Australian prisons where the practice aligns with what is happening in Norway. Therefore, a complex picture emerges that defies simple classification and simple solutions.

What, then, are the 'better' prisons doing differently? 'Good' prisons are people oriented as opposed to task oriented. They emphasize dynamic security. They are characterized by a high level of informal interaction. Prisoners wear their own clothes, even in high security. They are smaller (between 60 and 400 prisoners), with smaller units (a maximum of 12 prisoners per unit), single cells and high staff to prisoner ratios. They provide meaningful work, vocational training, education and leisure time, including sports, arts and music. They provide opportunities for prisoners to take responsibility and not be passive vessels in their own punishment. They have staff who are highly trained, who have integrity and good management of personal boundaries, and whose motivation for working in a prison is the desire to work with people. They are also forward-looking, in that their focus from day one is on preparing prisoners for release. Importantly, this can take place on all security levels, from high, to medium, to low and to so-called transition prisons. They are characterized by active efforts to prevent social distance from becoming too large and by counteracting the negative impacts of the total institution

98 *Anna Eriksson*

that otherwise automatically erode proximity. 'Good' prisons also consciously avoid practices that dehumanize, instead encouraging both staff and prisoners to see the individual person behind the role and/or uniform.

Clearly, prison practice in Australia and Norway takes place within rather different societal, cultural and political contexts, and these contexts affect practice on the inside in different ways. Therefore, it is important to recognize that prisons are indeed a reflection of the society in which they exist and that there is an ongoing conversation between events inside and outside the prison walls, both influencing the other in various ways.

The extent to which prisons as institutions have become Othered in Australia places them at a disadvantage. It is more difficult to implement and sustain positive change in a total institution that is largely unsupported and subject to moral silencing by the society that requires it. However, I firmly believe that such change is not impossible, even though the total institution, as its own peculiar beast, in combination with the eviction of the prison from public moral responsibility, poses a particular challenge. There seems to be ways in which the erosion of proximity, which often takes place routinely due to the two above-mentioned challenges, can be ameliorated. These ways can be physical, manifest in the design of prisons and individual units, but above all they can be personal, creating opportunities for face-to-face interaction between 'us' and 'them', never eradicating the difference between the groups completely, but equalling out their moral worth and forcing mutual recognition of the persons involved. This, in turn, can counteract a diffusion of responsibility by not allowing the erosion of proximity to go too far and, as a consequence, establishing a practice that can release a person fit to be your next door neighbour as opposed to a 'risky ex-prisoner' from whom you need protection.

But why does it matter whether there is less opposition and hostility between staff and prisoners? Why does it matter whether prisons are characterized by humane treatment and deprivation of liberty as the main punishment, as opposed to stripping away a long list of rights? It matters because we want people who have served time to return to the community and not commit further offences. It is as simple as that. On a normative level, it also matters because we want to live in a society where everyone's rights are respected: yours, mine and the rights of those who are not like us. And it matters because the lines that demarcate 'us' from 'them' can shift rapidly and unpredictably – it is not a line set in stone, but rather on a sandy beach awaiting the next high tide.

Notes

1 Thanks to Polity Press and Cornell University Press for granting permission to reproduce previously published material in this chapter.
2 It is important to note here that Corrections in this state is currently engaged in a significant change of its practices in terms of pre-release preparation and post-release support, recognizing the urgent need for this. A recent state election has also seen a change from Liberal to Labour, the latter of which has a somewhat less

Prison and social production of immorality   99

punitive stance on prisons and punishment, so there is hope of this untenable situation being addressed.

3 The colour of their respective uniforms, which is not such an issue in Norway since prisoners at all levels of security wear their own clothes, is an important subject for future publications from this research.

4 It is important to note, though, that Breivik is not serving his time on a wing shared with other prisoners due to the risks that this would pose for his safety. Breivik, along with prisoners who are suffering from acute mental distress or have proven themselves to be a direct danger to other prisoners and staff, is held in a different part of the prison where prisoners are isolated from the mainstream. However, on the mainstream wings that are referred to in the quotes, prisoners who have been sentenced for murder and other violent offences are mixed with those sentenced for sex offences against adults and/or children – a practice unheard of in Australia.

5 I am placing this word in quotation marks, since many would argue that prisons as institutions are illegitimate and hence 'good prison practice' is an oxymoron. However, as long as we have prisons – and I suspect that they will be around for a while longer – it is worth making this distinction in theory and research, because the people who live and work inside these institutions certainly do.

References

ABC News (2014a) *Convicted murderer on the run after Queensland prison escape*, 15 April.

ABC News (2014b) *Prisoners Tony Morgan, Bradley Kuhl caught after high-speed chase near Rockhampton*, 17 April.

Barker, V. (2013) 'Nordic exceptionalism revisited: explaining the paradox of a Janus-faced penal regime', *Theoretical Criminology*, 17(1): 3–23.

Bauman, Z. (1989) *Modernity and the Holocaust*, Ithaca, NY: Cornell University Press.

Callinan, I. (2013) *Review of the parole system in Victoria*, Victoria, Australia: Department of Justice.

Cavadino, M. and Dignan, J. (2006) *Penal systems: a comparative approach*, London: Sage.

Christie, N. (1986) 'The ideal victim', in E. Fattah (ed.), *From crime policy to victim policy*, New York: St Martin's Press.

Collins, R. (1988) *Theoretical sociology*, San Diego, CA: Harcourt, Brace, Jovanovich Publishing.

Cook, H. (2014) 'Crowded prisons add to mental health crisis', *The Age*, 26 February.

Fein, H. (1979) *Accounting for genocide: national responses and Jewish victimization during the Holocaust*, New York: Free Press.

Fein, H. (2000) 'Civil wars and genocide: paths and circles', *Human Rights Review*, 1(3): 49–61.

Goffman, E. (1961) *Asylums: essays on the social situation of mental patients and other inmates*, New York: Anchor Books/Random House.

Green, D.A. (2008) *When children kill children: penal populism and political culture*, Oxford: Oxford University Press.

Jackson, J., Tyler, T.R., Bradford, B., Taylor, D. and Shiner, M. (2010) 'Legitimacy and procedural justice in prisons', *Prison Service Journal*, 191: 4–10.

Kornhauser, R. (2013) 'Reconsidering predictors of punitiveness in Australia: a test of four theories', *Australia and New Zealand Journal of Criminology*, 46: 221–240.

100 *Anna Eriksson*

Lacey, N. (2008) *The prisoners' dilemma: political economy and punishment in contemporary democracies*, Cambridge: Cambridge University Press.

Lee, J. (2014) 'Prisoners moved into shipping containers', *The Age*, 6 January.

Levinas, M. (1981) *Otherwise than being or beyond essence*, Pennsylvania: Duquesne University Press.

Levinas, M. (1982) *Ethics and infinity*, Pennsylvania: Duquesne University Press.

Mathiesen, T. (2012) 'Scandinavian exceptionalism in penal matters: reality or wishful thinking?' in T. Ugelvik and J. Dullum (eds), *Penal exceptionalism? Nordic prison policy and practice* (pp. 13–37), London and New York: Routledge.

Mills, T. (2014) 'Rehabilitation shortfall in Victoria's prisons', *The Age*, 4 September.

News.com.au (2014) 'Escaped murderer was "low security threat"', 14 April.

Pratt, J. (2008a) 'Scandinavian exceptionalism in an era of penal excess: part I – the nature and origins of Scandinavian exceptionalism', *British Journal of Criminology*, 48(2): 119–137.

Pratt, J. (2008b) 'Scandinavian exceptionalism in an era of penal excess: part II – does Scandinavian exceptionalism have a future?' *British Journal of Criminology*, 48(2): 275–292.

Pratt, J. and Eriksson, A. (2013) *Contrasts in punishment: an explanation of Anglophone excess and Nordic exceptionalism*, London and New York: Routledge.

Pratt, J., Brown, D., Brown, M., Hallsworth, S. and Morrison, W. (2005) *The new punitiveness: trends, theories, perspectives*, Cullompton: Willan Publishing.

Roberts, J. and Hough, M. (eds) (2002) *Changing attitudes to punishment: public opinion, crime and justice*, Cullompton: Willan Publishing.

Scharff Smith, P. (2012) 'A critical look at Scandinavian exceptionalism: welfare state theories, penal populism and prison conditions in Denmark and Scandinavia', in T. Ugelvik and J. Dullum (eds), *Penal exceptionalism? Nordic prison policy and practice* (pp. 38–57), London and New York: Routledge.

Seierstad, Åsne (2013) *En av oss: en berättelse om Norge* [One of us: a story about Norway], translated from Norwegian to Swedish by Jan Stolpe, Falun, Sweden: Albert Bonniers Förlag.

Sentencing Advisory Council (2013) *Victoria's prison population 2002–2012*, State of Victoria: Sentencing Advisory Council.

Sykes, G. (1958/2007) *The society of captives: a study of a maximum security prison*, Princeton, NJ and Oxford: Princeton University Press.

Tyler, T. (1990) *Why people obey the law: procedural justice, legitimacy and compliance*, New Haven, CT: Yale University Press.

Ugelvik, T. (2012) 'The dark side of a culture of equality: reimagining communities in a Norwegian remand prison', in T. Ugelvik and J. Dullum (eds), *Penal exceptionalism? Nordic prison policy and practice* (pp. 121–138), London and New York: Routledge.

Victorian Ombudsman (2014) *Investigation into the rehabilitation and reintegration of prisoners in Victoria: discussion paper*, Melbourne, Australia: Victorian Ombudsman.

Legislation

Corrections Amendment (Parole Reform) Bill 2013.
Corrections Amendment (Further Parole Reform) Bill 2014.

5 Swedish 'prison exceptionalism' in decline[1]

Trends towards distantiation and objectification of the Other

Anders Bruhn, Per-Åke Nylander and Odd Lindberg

Introduction

In the aftermath of World War II, the Nordic countries have become quite famous for having a comparatively humane prison policy with a clear aim of rehabilitating prisoners to lead a normal life after their sentence has been served. This prison policy is sometimes called Scandinavian or Nordic exceptionalism (Pratt 2008). Researchers have observed the arguably more humane prison treatment in these countries compared to the more excessive prison regimes in other western jurisdictions (Pratt and Eriksson 2013). The existence of such differences has gained further attention in contemporary debates on prison regimes – not least because of an existing general trend towards increasingly harsh punitive regimes in the Global North, related to the successive shift from socio-liberal to neo-liberal or even neo-conservative political regimes (Garland 2001; Wacquant 2004). However, the existence of Nordic exceptionalism has been questioned by Nordic researchers, who argue that it is easy to be persuaded of such by the small size of prisons, low numbers of prisoners in relation to space and high standard of facilities, among other aspects of the prison system in these countries. Oppression may be practised in a more concealed way, hidden under a glossy surface (see Dullum and Ugelvik 2012).[2] Further, researchers have stressed several important differences among the Nordic countries. Some of these differences are explored in this chapter and in the chapter by Eriksson in this volume. In fact, it seems that Nordic countries are developing along quite different routes today.

This chapter examines current changes in Swedish prison policy and organization. It is based on some recent interviews and a re-reading of data from several prison research projects (Lindberg 2005; Nylander *et al.* 2008, 2011, 2012; Bruhn *et al.* 2010, 2012; Holm and Jukic 2013; Kolind *et al.* 2013). This re-reading is done through the lens of different theories concerning social change in late modernity. A theoretical point of departure is Bauman's theory of the instrumental rationality of modern bureaucratic regimes and how these trigger a distantiation of the 'Other' (Bauman 1989).

Among the Nordic countries, Sweden today probably provides the most advanced example of an ongoing process of transformation from a socio-democratic welfare state[3] to a neo-liberal one. In relation to the prison system, we contend that this neo-liberal trend has engendered a technocratic change that profoundly reifies and dehumanizes the Other – in this context, the prisoner. However, the situation in Swedish prisons is still very different from prisons in many Anglophone countries (see the chapters by Green, Simon and Eriksson). What is interesting here, though, is the progression of change, and how it relates to Swedish culture and the history of its welfare state. A number of developmental processes at the political and organizational levels are converging at the present time, effectively replacing a well-established policy based on a belief in the need for rehabilitative work built on constructive relations between staff and prisoners, and in moral responsibility based on social and emotional proximity. We discern three particularly important processes that are effecting such change. Two of these emanate at the prison policy level and are in conflict – the profound dilemma inherent in prison work of the need to find a balance between punishing offenders and keeping them in safe custody, and rehabilitating prisoners to lead a normal life after their sentenced has been served. The first process entails an increasing emphasis on punishment and protecting society from criminals, leading to harsher prison regimes and priorities placed on security measures. The second concerns rehabilitation and rests on the primacy of individual psychological treatment models, with roots in so-called evidence-based medicine. The third mechanism, the so-called New Public Management doctrine, emanates from neo-liberal economic models of governance of public sector organizations. Below we will discuss all three processes. However, first we consider some significant developments in Swedish penal and prison policy in earlier periods. This is necessary to gain a richer picture of the magnitude of current changes, but also for understanding forces working against these changes. These forces, anchored in a strong tradition of humanitarianism in treating prisoners, may explain the somewhat more fragmented picture of prison policy in Sweden compared to other western countries.

Changes in prison policy under the impact of political macro-level changes

Framing the context

We hold that the above-mentioned developmental processes to be scrutinized in this chapter are expressions of two parallel but intimately intertwined trends in western society. The first can be characterized as a backlash to late modernity – to risk society, fragmentation and the break-up of older, stable societal structures (Castells 1997; Bauman 2001; Beck 1992). A sense of diminished safety, rootlessness and inequality have all engendered greater fear and a receptiveness towards simplified doctrines. This is fertile soil for authoritarian and oppressive prison regimes, placing concerns with protecting society from criminals at the forefront of public debate. The other trend relates to bureaucracy and principles of prison governance based on neo-liberal ideology about the 'small state' and the primacy of the economy (Hood 1991, 1995; Power 1997). Within this context, the deviant, the criminal, is seen as either an *economic man* choosing criminal acts on the basis of calculations about risks and benefits, or as someone suffering from some kind of psychological or psychiatric disease that requires special treatment.

As Bauman (1989) demonstrates, the bureaucratic machine is amoral; it is a means to an end, whatever the end. The affinity between technocratic and bureaucratic ideas about governance and certain ideologies about societal ends cannot be taken for granted and is no coincidence. How they relate to each other depends on the macro-social context. By referring to the distinction between the means and ends of prison policy, we can discern three distinct eras of Swedish prison policy since World War II, albeit with some crossover among them. The pathway on which a certain paradigm develops is initially curved and fragmented, long before it reaches hegemony. The first era, between World War II and the end of the 1960s, may be characterized as one of paternalistic social engineering. The second – the radical era – is one of enhanced individualization, beginning with the left-wing radicalization of the 1970s and 1980s. The present era may be characterized as one of technocratic social engineering in conjunction with neo-liberal ideas of the economic man and rational choice. During these eras, the prison policy dilemma between punishment, safe custody and rehabilitation has been handled in rather different ways.

The history of the Swedish welfare state and prison policy

The era of paternalistic social engineering: leave it to the experts

From the mid-nineteenth century, the Swedish prison system was dominated by Philadelphia model cell prisons, yet complemented by a few penal labour prisons and small local jails (Nilsson 1999). These cell prisons were replaced by new prisons with common wings and industry workshops in the first half of the twentieth century. However, it was when the Social Democratic Party took office in the 1930s that a new era in criminal and prison policy emerged. This era, based on a new welfare state ideology, came to prominence during the three decades following World War II. Sweden was a prosperous country at the time, and a state with extensive resources for societal reforms. State policy was centred around values of equality, yet was also quite paternalistic. Thus, the state was seen as the kind gardener with a positive ontology of human nature, and humankind was perceived as possessing abilities that would flourish under the right circumstances. The task of preventing crime and criminality was seen as achievable through all-embracing programmes for societal change away from poverty and towards equality and social integration. Crime and other forms of deviance were expected to decrease as an effect of welfare policy. Rehabilitation of those who, in spite of such policies and programmes, committed crimes was seen as a task for the experts. Such deviance was often seen as an expression of individual illness that could be cured with appropriate treatment. Paradoxically, and in contrast with the positive ontology of human growth, individual treatment methods were rooted in medical science, and a rather pessimistic view of an unchangeable human nature underpinned these 'illness cases' (Andersson and Nilsson 2009: 67–103).

Trust in bureaucratic measures and medical expertise led to increased differentiation of both the forms of punishment and the types of prisons for sorting prisoners according to the most suitable type of prison stay. However, these categorizations did not fully translate into day-to-day prison practice, which stayed much the same irrespective of institution type and prisoner categories. All in all, teaching prisoners normal behaviour via learning to labour was the main tool for rehabilitation (Andersson and Nilsson 2009: 95). One important reason behind this may be the inertia of the prison organization. Even though the 'bureaucracy-ideal' was a dominating principle in the system (Weber 1922/1983; Bauman 1989), the hierarchical control line downwards was weak, local prison governors had a significant amount of autonomy, and the belief that the role of prison officers was only to guard had strong cultural roots. Two elements of this era are important to consider when discussing today's situation: the paternalistic belief in expertise and social engineering, and the strong position of medical science in treating the 'ill ones'.

The radical era: collective unity for equal opportunities

The year 1968 and subsequent years are often treated as marking a period of qualitative change in the progression of modernity (Boltanski and Chiapello 2007; Wagner 1996). Several authors have captured important elements of this change, such as individualization, a belief in the value of deliberation, a weakened belief in science and mistrust towards all forms of authority and the break-down of traditional social collectives (see Bauman 2001; Melucci 1989; Beck 1992). The result was a political awakening, especially among the younger generations. In the beginning this was captured by different Third World solidarity movements, in particular the Vietnam movement. Soon it spilled over into a more general interest in societal problems channelled by new left-wing forces, fuelling collective struggles for societal change. One area that soon came into focus was that of exclusion and those living outside the bounds of mainstream society, such as criminal offenders. The concept of 'social heritage' was launched, and ideas about rehabilitation increasingly became based on sociological insights at the expense of the psychiatric paradigm. There was a rise in the influence of social movements pushing for better conditions in prisons and for empowering prisoners to take collective action against oppression. One such movement was the National Association for Humanizing the Correctional Service, formed in 1966.[4] It consisted of social workers, social scientists, lawyers, ex-prisoners and other people engaged in the prison debate. The association was dissolved in 1984 and has never resurfaced.[5]

The predominant organizational trends during this time favoured decentralization. The already existing regional and local autonomy in the prison system became even stronger. Several prison governors in those years were policy-makers with strong convictions about humane prison treatment. To see the subject, the individual prisoner, and his/her social situation was a point of departure for rehabilitative efforts. Under the influence of a generalized movement for greater democratization of working life, prisons were developed in a deliberative way, involving cooperative councils for staff and prisoners. Prisoners were also allowed to form their own union. In response to criticisms of poor prison conditions, local treatment efforts, opportunities for education and possibilities for short-term leave increased for prisoners. Traces of this radical period lived on, albeit severely weakened, in the 1980s and 1990s. This decline was related to a strong ideological counter-campaign against the political left that began in the 1980s, the main architect of which was the Swedish Employers Association (Eskilsson 2005; Bresky et al. 1981). Its aim was to fight collectivism and 're-establish' the ego.[6] In prison policy, a slow process return to the belief in individual factors and illness as causes of criminality began.

The doctrine that nothing works in prisoner rehabilitation, which influenced many prison systems in the mid-1970s, has never had much impact in Sweden (Martinson 1974). Forces in favour of humanistic prison treatment were strong. Another piece in the puzzle was the heated debate about blue-collar working conditions. A major research project on prison officers in Sweden revealed alarming results, such as stress, poor health and impoverished working conditions (Härenstam 1989). What has become known as the Personal Officer reform of 1991 was the main result of these developments.[7] Its aim was twofold: to develop job content and motivational work. The reform rested on the belief that good relations between prison officers and prisoners are a prerequisite for rehabilitation. Through personal dialogue with the prisoner in planning time in prison, helping with visits, furlough, motivating for treatment and so forth, officers were able to build constructive relations with prisoners. Further, this approach was seen as a central element in 'dynamic' (as opposed to static) security. By being committed to the prisoner's specific situation and needs, the officer was expected to create relational proximity and mutual trust, ideas strongly anchored in social psychological theories about treatment (cf. Bronfenbrenner 1979; Scheff 1997; Bowlby 1997). Most prison officers who were appointed as Personal Officers had special responsibility for between four and ten prisoners. This reform was prioritized during the coming decade.

Neo-liberalism in the driver's seat: a new era of social engineering?

General prison policy

Sweden has 47 prisons divided into three security categories (2014). Category 1 denotes the highest security level, and category 3 open prisons. Six prisons are for women (about 6 per cent of the prison population). In mid-2014, the total prisoner population was about 4,300, a decrease on previous years (around 5,000 in the years 2006–2010). There may be several reasons for this decline. First, prisoners with sentences shorter than two months today serve this by wearing an electronic tag or doing community service. These groups never enter a prison. Second, a growing inefficiency within both the judicial system and the police due to ongoing processes of organizational change, alongside changed court policies with regard to sentencing, such as a reduced sentence length for drug-related crimes, seem to have contributed to a reduced prison population.

The context of penal and prison policy development in the late 1980s and onwards is one of a right-wing turn in Swedish society as a whole, a growing influence of the neo-liberal paradigm and a far-reaching critique of the social-democratic welfare state (Nilsson 2013). After the millennium shift, in particular, we may speak about a renaissance of moral engineering, with individual choice at its centre. In the 2000s, those with an illness or psychiatric/psychological defect are now handed over to the medical sciences, as in the first era discussed previously. All in all, citizens are moulded to live according to the 'right' moral by the law. This means a renaissance of ideas about general prevention and deterrence via longer sentences. The individual is seen as driven by instrumental rationality. Therefore, crime prevention is about avoiding risks in different societal contexts. The opportunity structure must be reduced and 'criminogenic' situations prevented. Preventing crime becomes a question of deterrence and control. And there is less emphasis on inequality and bad social conditions as causes of crime. Even voluntary work mirrors this fad for individual over collective responsibility. A new type of organization for prisoner support was formed in 1997, Criminals Return into Society.[8] Its work involved ex-prisoners helping released convicts to re-establish their lives in society. The message is that every individual has a choice about what kind of life they want to live.

Two aspects of criminal policy have significant effects on the prison system. First, a great number of policy changes are legitimized via appeal to the somewhat ambiguous concept of public legal consciousness, that is, general and established norms and values about right and wrong.[9] And research and accumulated knowledge in the field is de-emphasized. Together with the heated media debate about prison and punishment, this becomes an arena for political profiling and recurrent changes in priorities. Criminal policy thus becomes contradictory, unstable and unpredictable (Nilsson 2013: 150), leading to repeated changes in prisoners' living conditions as well as staff working conditions. Second, criminal policy basically discerns two types of crime – heinous and regular – equating to a division between 'hopeless cases' and those prisoners who can be rehabilitated. On this account, regular criminals may be motivated to undertake treatment via soft measures; while the others – gang members, professional criminals and the insane – have to be kept in safe custody for the sake of society (Nilsson 2013: 190). In relation to the regular category of criminal, in particular, the engineers from the first era (discussed above) – the experts in individual therapy, such as psychiatrics and psychologists – are back on the scene. This time, however, they occupy an even stronger position, having cognitive behavioural therapy and the evidence movement to lean on. This is reflected not least in the internal research organization of the Swedish Prison and Probation Service (SPPS), to which a professor in psychiatry was recruited as its director in 2005. Its scientific board includes 15 professors from different universities, the vast majority of whom are from clinical psychology, psychiatry and medicine. Furthermore, ready-made, manual-based treatment programmes are taking over at the expense of efforts towards developing daily relational and motivational work based on the skill and practical experience of Personal Officers.

In the following, we describe the three processes mentioned in the introduction in more detail: the security turn, which gives priority to safe custody; the medicalization of treatment; and the shift towards an audit society. These are the driving forces for a new form of social engineering built on neo-liberal ideology and a rationalistic bureaucracy, resulting in objectification of the prisoner.

Keeping prisoners in safe custody

A number of spectacular events in 2004 led to a 'security turn'. Four prison escapes were conducted, using different strategies. Two of them were preceded by a break-in by persons outside the prison, while the other two included weapons being smuggled inside and hostage-taking of staff. This led to a great deal of turbulence in the political arena. The Ministry of Justice was questioned. The General Director of the SPPS was replaced by a former senior manager in the area of security policing. In a way, this security turn was the catalyst that gave added momentum to an already existing trend towards greater securitization. However, the events of 2004 should not be reduced to a mere confirmation of this trend. An official committee report released in its aftermath (SOU 2005) led to a long line of changes in the prison system. New electric fences that were impossible to break through were installed around all closed prisons. Three segregated high-security units were created within category 1 prisons. Staffing, routines and rules were changed in all prisons. The number of specialized security officers was increased, and their status was raised. In our own survey conducted in 2008, for 38 per cent of all prison officers the majority of tasks assigned to them were related to security, while the Personal Officer group had decreased to around 50 per cent. And this shift in staffing has probably continued in subsequent years.

Today, risk assessment and different control tasks are guiding all activities in prisons. Heavy investment has been made into electronic control devices such as cameras, remote-controlled locks and metal detectors. Further, the SPPS intelligence department has grown rapidly. It is now a large, secluded department based at the SPPS headquarters working with data collection of all kinds in cooperation with local intelligence prison staff and the police. On

108 *Anders Bruhn, Per-Åke Nylander, Odd Lindberg*

a policy level, it is worth noting here two measures introduced in the aftermath of 2004. First, a new vision for the SPPS: 'No escapes – no drugs'. Second, *'lag om kriminalvård i anstalt'* (roughly translated as 'law about criminal care in prison') is now being replaced by 'the prison law'. Both initiatives are of great symbolic value, reflecting the difference in attitude between the view that 'prisoners are dangerous and we have to keep them away from us' and the belief from previous eras that 'prisoners are victims of an unjust society'. Below we discuss five examples of security measures. All of them facilitate distance between prisoners and prison staff. Together they add to the stigmatization of prisoners, drawing a sharp line against the Other. These measures are the establishment of National Reception Units (NRUs), the introduction of security experts within prisons, the instalment of shell protection and new super-security units, and greater everyday control of prisoners.

National Reception Units

An NRU for all male prisoners sentenced to four years or more was established in Kumla Prison (category 1) in the mid-1990s. A similar unit for women sentenced to more than two years was opened in a women's prison some years later (category 2 – Ekbom *et al.* 2011). Management and organization of these reception units were further developed after 2004. Prisoners begin their prison stay at these units for a six-week risk and needs assessment period performed by psychological experts, involving a number of psychological tests and constant observation of the prisoners' behaviour. After this period, decisions are made about which prison category and wing-type the prisoner will be assigned to. The NRUs are interesting in several ways in relation to our theme here. They represent a technocratic approach aimed at categorizing and sorting prisoners in terms of risk behaviour and susceptibility to treatment. Of course observation allows for the consideration of unique factors in individual cases. However, the approach rests heavily on 'objectivity', using standardized, ready-made schemas. According to some, risk assessment undertaken and decisions made by staff from a distance, without the decision-maker coming into close contact with or getting to know the prisoner, guarantees objectivity and best results (Holm and Jukic 2013: 74–75).

Categorization of prisoners on a scale of dangerousness also means that there is a risk of the prisoner being stigmatized once transferred to prison. A six-week incarceration in a high-security prison (NRU) and a four-year prison sentence signals dangerousness to staff and prisoners in receiving units, and the level of risk or danger they are seen to pose may be a cause of prejudice when it comes to positive relation-building between prisoners and staff. It may engender distance and hostility between them, counteracting prisoners' ability to develop trust and expectations of 'fair' treatment from the prison system. Moreover, staff sometimes define prisoners on the basis of their placement: 'He is in this wing; in other words he is dangerous' (Holm and Jukic

2013: 109).[10] Risk classification might also restrict prisoners' opportunities to change their placement and/or develop new activities and possessions, while incarcerated (see, for example, Ekbom *et al.* 2011; Hörnqvist 2010).

Special security staff

As stated above, an important aspect of prison officers' professional skills is to be able to strike a balance between security and rehabilitation in relation to individual prisoners in the context of unique circumstances (see also Nylander *et al.* 2008; Bruhn *et al.* 2010). However, the new organizational structure implemented in many prisons in Sweden in several ways deflates the value of and need for these skills among ordinary staff. First, the number of special security officers has increased. Further, a position of security specialist and manager of security work has been introduced in every prison, under the title commander-in-control.[11] This semi-military position has been given extraordinary power. In most prisons they have the jurisdiction to act in every issue that they assess as being important in relation to security. Second, security staff carry with them equipment normally used by police, such as army-style boots, capsicum spray, a baton and handcuffs. Emergency forces have also been set up – groups trained to handle fights and riots in prison. This specialization, this new division of labour, has important consequences for prisoner–staff relations. One is that the presence of security staff signals distance and readiness to fight; it is not part of their role to foster personal relations with prisoners. Another consequence is that, programmatically but also in the minds of regular officers, the concept of 'dynamic security' has taken a strong foothold in prison work. This concept, originally coined by management, advocates a view of security as handled by a comprehensive view balancing a range of aspects and security measures. Of centrality here is the need for good personal relations between prisoners and prison staff. Such relations are seen as the most effective tool for preventing violence. Today, peacekeeping via relational work is de-emphasized by management, almost regarded as unimportant. This downplaying of relational work also leads to conflict between groups of officers (Nylander *et al.* 2008). Such conflicts, together with the impact of external signs of status and the enhanced powers of security staff, were clearly at play when we visited one of the open prisons. Many of the experienced officers at this prison were working with prisoner re-entry planning, and the atmosphere was quite relaxed. The new commander-in-control – walking around in military boots and acting with great inflexibility towards prisoners – did not seem to understand this prison culture. This caused tension among the staff and suspicion among the prisoners. In the staff room, the commander was heavily ridiculed. However, the irony here was that the regular staff and prisoners found common ground in their dissociation from the commander.

Finally, heightened security measures means more pressure on staff because they have to manage the frustration and conflicts that follow. This in turn may force regular officers to distance themselves from prisoners. Several prison officers in different prisons that we visited expressed this. In a survey free-text comment, one prison officer stated: 'The security measures to prevent escapes is paid for by prisoners' welfare and by general staff security in the prison' (Prison Officer, category 2 prison).

As a consequence, the introduction of security staff, and the greater priority given to their work, has caused greater distance between staff and prisoners and conflicts among staff, and has damaged the prison climate, according to the interviewees in this research.

Shell protection

The most visible consequence of the 2004 events was the new physical external security measures such as gates, walls and fences, in essence the 'shell' around the prison. Additional and electrified fences were quickly built around closed prisons. Gates were reconstructed to make them impossible to break through with motor vehicles. Metal detectors and the presence of sniffer dogs were also increased. No electronic equipment except what belongs to the prison is allowed among prisoners. All visitors and prison staff are rigorously controlled via observation from the central gate house. And electronic monitoring of prison areas has increased. The consequences are clear. First, increasing use of CCTV and scanning techniques for controlling prisoners' daily life leads to less face-to-face contact between prisoners and staff. This in turn facilitates more distance and less relational work; for example, staff sit in the office looking at a camera screen instead of being out among the prisoners. Second, the measures related to preventing access to the outside world are symbolic of deterrence. They signal distance and inaccessibility to the rest of society. Visiting a prison is no longer a reality for ordinary people. Even visiting relatives may be deterred by the increased control measures. Gate staff at one prison said that it was common for visitors to cancel their visit when faced with the heightened security control measures to which they are subjected. Third, the measures increase distance between groups of staff insofar as one group of prison officers is authorized to control another. A Personal Officer in a closed prison expressed the antagonism between subgroups of officers:

> It's those little kinds of things. The security group work on their own a lot .... And they treat us Personal Officers as if we aren't worth as much as them. They have a way of putting us down and giving orders, and maybe criticizing too, instead of approaching us. They can sneak around in the bushes and monitor the staff. And, well, you don't really know what they're doing.
>
> (Nylander *et al.* 2008)

The precedence given to security staff in decision-making on the ground and the downplaying of positive relational building crucial for dynamic security have impacted several levels of prison work. Mistrust among staff has become more entrenched within prison culture – both towards prisoners and between staff. This, together with regular officers being subjected more often to security regulation and assessments by security staff, counteracts relational and motivational work.

Super-security units

The Minister of Justice survived the political turbulence of 2004, partly by promising to build three new super-security, escape-proof units for high-risk prisoners. This decision was almost immediately implemented. These segregated and isolated units, with their own specially trained staff, have been installed within three category 1 prisons. They have room for 20 prisoners each. The need for 60 such places in a small country like Sweden was soon questioned publicly.[12] However, the political need to take action was clearly prioritized. The units have never been filled up since their inception, probably because they are oversized for Swedish needs. Units like these have several consequences for in-prison relations. Security routines for staff–prisoner contact are extreme, and there is a considerable distance between staff in these units and other prison staff. No other staff and no visitors are allowed in the units. There is no communication between the prisoners here and prisoners in other wings. If and when a prisoner is transferred from such a unit to a regular wing, that prisoner is at risk of being stigmatized by other prisoners and staff, although this is also influenced by the prisoner's status and previous social networks. These units contain only about 1 per cent of the total prisoner population in Sweden. However, the symbolic effect, especially given the backdrop of the media hype surrounding them, is much broader. It signals the need to keep the 'Other', the criminal, far away not only from ordinary, law-abiding citizens, but also from 'ordinary' prisoners.

Ordinary day control

One of the 'pains of imprisonment' described by Sykes more than 50 years ago is the lack of autonomy of the prisoner, no longer able to decide what to do and when to do it (Sykes 1958). Such restrictions have been further detailed and refined today. All prisoner movements are planned, escorted, communicated and monitored by staff via the electronically equipped panopticon of today. All escorts of prisoners are synchronized by radio communication. The control measures have also been increased in relation to prisoners' daily walks outdoors:

> Earlier we could walk beside the girls and talk to them about things they wanted to talk about, things that perhaps made them feel bad. In this way we could build relations with the girls. Now we have to stand on the steps outside the building and monitor the girls walking 20 metres below us.
>
> (Prison officer, women's prison)

112 *Anders Bruhn, Per-Åke Nylander, Odd Lindberg*

This is an example of what Bauman (1989) calls adiaphorization: a set of practices that silence moral consideration, instead focusing on task completion and ignoring the human consequences of actions. Such measures explicitly send a signal to the officers to keep a distance and not to develop social proximity with prisoners.

Another example is the prohibition on smoking in all Swedish prisons, introduced in 2006. Smoking is only allowed outside the prison buildings, normally during the prisoner walks in the yard two times a day. The physical health of prisoners and staff may well benefit from the prohibition. However, the already utterly limited autonomy and the psychological well-being may suffer severely. The prisoners' own cigarettes, tobacco and lighters are kept in the office, and, once outdoors, each prisoner is handed a cigarette from his own packet. No smoking also means one less activity for restless, frustrated prisoners. Not being able to have a talk over a cigarette together also means fewer opportunities for staff to communicate with prisoners:

> Let's say we have a new prisoner who is a drug addict and feels bad. He calls on us during the night and wants to have a cigarette to calm down. The officer who goes to the cell and tells this prisoner that there is a smoking ban in the prison will probably have a problem with that prisoner during his whole imprisonment. If we, on the other hand, could say, 'Of course come out and we'll have a cigarette and talk this over', this would be very positive for the relation and the prisoner's view of the system. The ban is so daft.
>
> (Prison Officer, category 1 prison)

Thus, the smoking ban may counteract relational work perhaps especially at times when prisoners feel bad and need to talk and be heard. Moreover, the searching of prisoners' cells has substantially increased over the past decade (Krantz and Elmby 2007). Now visitations are accompanied by a search for cigarettes and lighters. An obvious result is an increasing number of conflicts and prisoner feelings of oppression, and visitation routines become more about a performance emphasizing the difference between us and them.

Rehabilitation of prisoners

Rehabilitation work is now first and foremost based on psychiatric assessment and treatment that has at its core standardized, manual-based programmes and/or psychopharmacologic drugs. The Other is categorized and treated on the basis of diagnosis. This means treatment based on 'evidence-based' measures developed on general criteria, rather than in-depth knowledge about unique individuals with unique life histories. Thus, these programmes are built on a technological approach that produces distance between the programme staff and the clients. This means a 'paradigm shift' away from the Personal Officer approach that was dominant during the 1990s. The latter was, as mentioned above, aimed at developing the prison officer role towards skill in relational work, having responsibility for counselling and motivational work with a small group of prisoners. This work demands proximity and in-depth knowledge of unique individuals, including their strengths and weaknesses. In the 1990s, the prison authority therefore invested in developing officer competence in methods like Motivational Interviewing. Yet the Personal Officer institution is now in decline, and management is making no effort to develop it in the current climate. The development of skills in motivational work among ordinary prison officers is not prioritized. However, because this position of Personal Officer still formally exists, individual officers still have some discretion to develop such motivational skills themselves.

Treatment programmes: what kind and to what extent?

In mid-2014, Swedish prisons had in total 728 places for individual treatment: 113 in category 1, 567 in category 2 and 48 in category 3 prisons (the category 3 places are mainly focused on preparing for release). Treatment programmes in Swedish prisons have in total about 5,000 participants per year. Yet this does not mean that 5,000 individuals attend each year, as each prisoner may attend multiple programmes. Since the mid-1990s, the SPPS has substantially increased its investment in such programmes (see Nylander *et al.* 2012). Today (late 2014), there are 13 different accredited programmes concerning sex offenders, violent crime, drug abuse and general criminality. As a rule, the minority of non-Swedish-speaking prisoners are excluded from these programmes, particularly since the latter are all structured around oral communication.

Treatment efforts are thus normally either based on a psychiatric diagnosis (such as ADHD – attention deficit hyperactivity disorder) to be treated by pharmacological drugs and/or take the form of special treatment programmes for motivated prisoners. Most programmes are based on cognitive behavioural therapy (CBT), looking to achieve individual behavioural change using different techniques aimed at increasing self-knowledge (Holm *et al.* 2014; Nilsson 2013). Even if the cause of the crime committed is seen as emanating from personality factors, this does not mean an adjustment to unique personalities. They are based strictly on schematic steps to be followed in a certain order. Through these techniques, prisoners are supposed to learn and act according to the 'right' manner in situations where, for example, drugs are available or possibilities to commit crime occur, by internalizing better strategies for coping with difficult situations (Nilsson 2013). The programmes stem from the 'evidence movement', with its focus on accreditation of 'evidence-based' programmes. New departments have been created whose aim is to develop comprehensive databases of prisoners, detailing their levels of success in the programmes.

The effects of programmes are evaluated, preferably via research based on so-called RCT (Randomized Control Techniques). Here, an experimental design with control groups used for comparison proves efficacy. Because such evidence is drawn from a highly controlled experiment situation, the application of programmes in real life must follow exactly the same routines. Otherwise the evidence is undermined. Thus, there is no room left for adjusting to the life histories and current social context of individuals. The result is distance and routinized relations between treatment staff and prisoners. Moreover, CBT programmes do not encourage relation-building approaches. On the contrary, they may work in the opposite direction (Ackerman and Hilsenroth [2001] cited in Duncan *et al.* 2010: 131):

> By inflexibly and excessively structuring treatment, the therapist risks empathic failures and inattentiveness to clients' experience. Such a therapist is then likely to overlook a breach in the relationship and mistakenly assume she has not contributed to that breach. Dogmatic reliance on particular relational or therapy methods, incompatible with the client, imperils treatment.

This clearly carries the danger of objectifying the prisoner, seeing him/her as a person to be 'fixed', void of individual characteristics and life stories.

The impact of specialization in rehabilitative work

The alleged scientific treatment strategy has important implications for all rehabilitative work in Swedish prisons. To an increased extent, treatment is handed over to specially trained officers, who have a more distanced role in relation to prisoners and everyday prison life than ordinary officers. This is especially noticeable in the larger prisons. At the same time, as mentioned above, the role of relational work in the mundane activities of day-to-day prison life is downplayed. The former managerial strategy to develop the ordinary prison officer role (the Personal Officer reform) has been replaced by one that runs the risk of impoverishing this group. When the Personal Officer approach first gained influence on a broad scale in the 1990s, prison officers stationed in treatment wings normally also functioned as programme leaders. They were expected to run programmes parallel to their ordinary work in the wing. Thus, they were involved in daily interactions with prisoners, including outside programme time. The theoretical point of departure was that solid and substantial relations, key to rehabilitative work, have to be developed on an ongoing basis. Yet it seems that these ideas have been discarded. Particularly in large prisons, programme leaders are now specially trained and certified to work only with programmes. Interview findings from a research project about drug treatment that two of us have been involved in confirm this (see Holm *et al.* 2014). In a large category 1 prison, the programme team was not involved in any daily interactions and activities with prisoners. They did not even have their office in the same building as the treatment wing. They met prisoners only during programme sessions. The prison governor told us that the programme leader role in this way had become more professional (Holm *et al.* 2014). The same view was expressed by the programme leader:

I have worked in both systems and it is much better now. We only run programmes and do not work on the wing. All in the group of programme leaders agree that this is the best way to organize the treatment. We are more professional now.

(Programme Leader, category 1 prison)

This trend is also confirmed in an interview we conducted with a former senior manager in the SPPS research department. The provision of treatment by specialized groups is increasingly common in big prisons with adequate resources. The result is not only a loss of contact and daily interaction with prisoners in their day-to-day activities, but also limited contact between programme leaders and regular staff about what is happening in the different organizational arenas. This obviously erodes proximity with prisoners. Interactions between programme leaders and prisoners are limited to group sessions. Opportunity for deeper dialogue on subjects with individual prisoners is limited, framed as it is by the manual and other group attendants. And possibilities for deeper relation-building outside, as well as in, the group sessions are reduced. The lack of room for involving significant wing staff in the treatment process is also obvious. Keeping them away from the therapeutic process in programmes counteracts constructive relation-building and the shaping of a good therapeutic environment.

Much research has demonstrated the importance of a positive therapeutic alliance based on a partnership in which the prisoner is treated as a subject and unique individual (see Duncan *et al.* 2010). In our interviews, both the governor and the programme officers seemed to support an approach that involves not taking part in prisoner life outside programme sessions under the flag of professionalism. Yet what was meant by 'professional' here is unclear. One thing that is clear, though, is that programme officers develop a common occupational identity as programme leaders. This sense of community is also expressed in common values and language derived from the CBT manuals. This distanced professionalism may lead to objectification and a dehumanization of the Other. Consequently, the individual prisoner vanishes into a reified category independent of individual background, needs and motivation (cf. Lipsky 2010).

A de-skilling of regular officers?

Clearly there is a division of labour within the key group in prison work – the prison officers. Besides the large number of regular officers, some become security specialists and others become programme experts. Both security and programme specialists are developing occupational roles on the basis of a special kind of technical skill: the security staff for using special equipment and security measures; the programme leaders for mediating fixed programmes based on standardized manuals. Because they are officers specifically trained for this mission in a quite narrow and superficial way, the latter lack the degree of competence required to be on solid ground in the theoretical context of these programmes. They develop just enough skill to fulfill the task they are assigned to do by the organization – a professionalism following an organizational logic only rudimentarily linked to real professional knowledge (Evetts 2013).[13]

This new division of labour also affects the ordinary prison officer role. Where previously they were explicitly expected to be involved in prisoner treatment, they are now becoming distanced from this kind of work. Some officers may experience this as an impoverishment of their occupational role, especially those in treatment wings who have applied for their jobs because of a special interest in rehabilitative work. The findings from both the interviews and surveys conducted in our different projects revealed that a great many officers from treatment, as well as regular, wings value relational and motivational work as the most stimulating aspect of their job (Bruhn 2013). The route now taken by management means deprivation and a risk of deskilling ordinary officers. Another consequence is that it is creating status hierarchies among the officers. Ordinary prison officers are also at risk of becoming more distanced from prisoners, even meeting increasing hostility from prisoners because of not being expected to do anything but simply guard: 'We ordinary prison officers [prison officers working on the wing] are becoming the bad guys and the programme leaders are the good guys' (Prison Officer, category 1 prison).

A reduction in motivational work for ordinary prison officers means a return to the period prior to the Personal Officer reform. Rehabilitative efforts are increasingly directed towards already motivated prisoners. Ordinary officers become guards once again, in practice not expected to undertake motivational work and thereby try to influence prisoners to change their lifestyle. One of the prison governors in a study of ours made a statement that is a clear illustration of today's sorting of prisoners into 'possible' and 'hopeless cases':

> I am not sure that we should have a treatment wing in this prison. Very few prisoners ... there are some but they are very few who are very motivated to attend programmes for their own sake, to really change their behaviour, there are some but not many.
>
> (Prison Governor, category 1 prison)

Running prisons in an audit society

The last piece in the puzzle is related to the managerial methods used in today's audit society (Power 1997). New Public Management (NPM) is the generic term for the prevailing administrative trend of recent decades. NPM basically rests on the logic surrounding two key components in the management of public service: the market and bureaucracy. The latter is the most prominent in the SPPS, which is managed according to a tight system of quality control that prioritizes cost efficiency measurements. Public officials are governed via detailed management directives, budget control and standardized, quantitative indicators. The SPPS is highly influenced by NPM. These management methods are well suited in relation to both the new security policy and the above-discussed evidence-based programmes. The former era of decentralization has now definitely come to an end. Power and control over organizational performance have become highly centralized.

An initial step towards centralization was taken in 2007 when the SPPS was reorganized into a single authority. Former local authorities became regional offices responsible for the implementation and coordination of central prison policy. The autonomy and discretion to take initiatives and develop local prison policy that previously characterized the system became severely restricted – and this impacted the management of local prisons and ordinary prison staff. As in the public sector as a whole, we see a revival of the traditional, rationalistic machine-bureaucracy model with top-down decision lines and centralized power (Weber 1922/1983). However, now the system rests on the use of new information and communication techniques – ensuring performance control at every level of the organization. Additionally, a growing number of managers at different organizational levels lack experience in prison work, as they are managerial technocrats. Nevertheless, in comparison with other countries such as the UK, though, Sweden still seems to have some local managers with a background in the prison organization (cf. Liebling 2010; Liebling and Crewe 2012).

Today, the SPPS is permeated by systems of performance control. These include the already described sorting out and treatment of prisoners in different units and locations on the basis of instrumental rationality and objectifying standardized criteria such as risk and type of crime committed, diagnosis and expected motivation. The different organizational units are given clearly defined assignments with instructions on expected outcomes and allocated resources. Budget allocations with performance targets based on quantitative indicators are implemented and tightly followed at every level and unit of the organization (for example, number of risk assessments to be completed or number of prisoners expected to complete a programme). Evaluations and quality control are normally based on such quantitative measures. Qualitative evaluations are of less interest because they are difficult to relate to cost efficiency on an aggregate level.

Forces working against distance, reification and Otherness

The developments described in the previous sections have not taken place without opposition. On the contrary, changes have been met with criticism and resistance from different organizational levels as well as in the political and societal spheres. Here it is important to understand the historical roots and the inertia of the formal structures, culture and institutionalized thought of the former social democratic welfare state. Convictions about humane prison policy and the importance of reintegrating prisoners in society still have a strong foothold in Swedish culture – among different political parties as well as the general public. Politicians in different camps (even on the Right) and a vast majority of ordinary citizens seem quite supportive of a more humanistic approach. This is also evident in media debates. Yet, at the same time, there is ambivalence. The media often presents a (in many ways false) picture of rising crime rates. This creates fear and a perceived lack of safety, triggering strong opinions in favour of repressive measures towards crime. This fear is exploited by different political forces. Since 2004, and especially after 2006 when a new right-wing government took power, not only is an enhanced security policy apparent, but demands for longer sentences for many types of crimes have also been made, and the number of life sentences handed down has increased markedly.

Inside the prison organization, on an institutional and local management level, values about a humanistic prison policy remain strong. This may often work towards creating space for improved motivational work on a day-to-day basis, undermining the worst expressions of objectification and distancing of prisoners. The Personal Officer institution is still programmatically stated to be a tool for rehabilitative work. Prison officers are effectively 'street-level bureaucrats', and as such they must translate and apply formal rules and regulations to unique situations and individual prisoners (Lipsky 2010). This process requires a certain level of discretion in undertaking assessment and acting accordingly. Especially in category 2 and 3 prisons, the Personal Officer role offers some potential to develop motivational work inside the organizational context. Of special interest here may be that the state of the Swedish labour market has made it easy for the SPPS to recruit often quite highly educated people to prison officer positions. Today, about 30–40 per cent of officers have some sort of academic degree. Especially women who apply for officer positions often have degrees in social and behavioural sciences (see Bruhn 2013). These highly educated prison officers often expect to be able to work according to a conviction that social work with clients means motivational and rehabilitative work. It seems natural to expect them to try to use their discretion in undertaking such work in prison. Not least in prison wings where individuals with such views function as informal leaders, we might expect staff subcultures to develop that are very much in favour of motivational work (see Nylander *et al.* 2008; Bruhn *et al.* 2012). Thus, in practice actions that counteract the forces of social distance and objectification discussed above, and adjustments to unique situations and individual prisoners, are probably happening all the time in ordinary prison life. These adjustments are largely built on proximity, based on insights about the Other as a human being of flesh and blood.

Conclusion

In comparison with many other countries in the Global North, Swedish prison (and penal) policy may still be characterized as relatively humane. To understand why, one has to be aware of its strong roots in a welfare regime dominated by a social democratic party that held office for several decades.

What have been described above, though, are three interacting processes of change that are fast assuming predominance. These have to be related to a wider context of successive orientation and change towards a neo-liberal welfare regime, even though vital parts of the system and politics of the old welfare regime remain. Today we may say that Sweden has a neo-liberal welfare regime but a somewhat muddled one – that is, with strong elements of the former welfare policy. The same can be said of the country's prison policy.

We have described what we see as a palpable trend in Swedish prison policy. Strongly anchored understandings about the importance of relational work built on proximity, and seeing the Other as a unique individual, are now being replaced by a policy of distance and objectification of the Other. Thoughts and convictions that underpin the Personal Officer institution – to develop personal (but not private) relations characterized by mutual trust as fundamental aspects of rehabilitative work – are now fading away. Three ongoing processes are working as mechanisms of change. Two relate to the goals of penal policy and are synthesized in an ideological conviction about the reasons for crime: crime is seen either as a result of either the wrong choice (the neo-liberal axiom of the rational man) or a mental disease (in accordance with psychiatric diagnosis). In the first case, questions about deterrence and security become vital – ordinary people shall be protected and crime shall be made utterly unattractive. Some of these 'wrong choices', however, are made on the basis of misinformation. Based on this view, these are people who have mistakenly taken the wrong path. With adequate treatment they can get back on track, equipped with better tools to stay on the right side of the law. Others are viewed as ill – suffering from a diagnosed mental illness and in need of individual therapy and medication. The latter also goes for those suffering from severe drug addictions. This is the way to treat the prison dilemma of security/punishment versus rehabilitation in Swedish prisons today: by deterrence and increased security, on the one hand, and psychiatric (evidence-based) treatment programmes, on the other. This new approach means a revival of a kind of technocratic social engineering built on sorting prisoners into different treatment categories based on simplified quantitative measures, and a specialization of certain groups of staff at the risk of degrading the ordinary officer who works daily in close proximity to prisoners to the role of an emotionally detached guard. These policy developments marry tightly with neo-liberal ideology about the small state and the primacy of economism for running public service authorities, resulting in today's management models – the merger of traditional bureaucratic thinking built on detailed regulation, categorization, performance measures and documentation with the conquests of new information and communication technologies.

The combined result of these developments has been the creation of distance from the Other, the reification of prisoners, who are treated as objects instead of unique individuals. Bauman's (1989) adiaphorization concept captures this – the systematic establishment of work practices that detach staff from moral considerations. These bureaucratic and technocratic approaches do not necessarily mean seeing the Other as bad or threatening. Rather, they entail work practices that create *indifference* towards the Other as a person, removing moral considerations in favour of instrumental task completion. However, although the bureaucratic organization may 'only' create indifference, at the same time the strong ideological messages emanating from the neo-liberal turn in general penal and prison policy trigger moral dissociation from the Other, an active although often unintended dehumanization. As a result, slowly and successively feelings of condemnation and fear towards the prisoner – now outside the sphere of moral consideration – take root among otherwise well-meaning staff.

Notes

1 Thanks to Polity Press for granting permission to reproduce previously published material in this chapter.
2 One example, albeit very 'concealed', is the case of remand prisons. Sweden has been criticized by the European Committee for the Prevention of Torture and Inhuman or Degrading Treatment or Punishment (CPT 2009) (the UN Committee against Torture has also criticized Sweden in this respect) for the frequent use of restrictions in remand units, making the time in remand similar to solitary confinement for people waiting for trial. There is also a risk that the time spent in isolation may be very long because of significant turnaround times in Swedish courts.
3 Even though the Social Democratic Party was responsible for the development of the welfare state, we would like to argue that the policies during this era would be better characterized as socio-liberal, rather than as a purely social-democratic welfare regime. However, we keep the terminology that better reflects international understandings of the Swedish situation.
4 Swedish: Riksförbundet för kriminalvårdens humanisering KRUM.
5 In Norway a similar type of organization – KROM – is still active.
6 The first big public campaign run by the employers' organization was titled 'Invest in yourself'.
7 This model seems to have had some influence on prison organizations in other countries such as Australia and the UK. In these countries it is often referred to as case work.
8 Kriminellas revansch i samhället, KRIS.
9 Swedish: 'Det allmänna rättsmedvetandet'.
10 Thanks to Claes Holm for important contributions in this section.
11 Sw. Vakthavande befäl.
12 Among others by the Director of the International Centre for Prison Studies in London, Andrew Coyle, in a Swedish TV news magazine.
13 Some programme leaders, though, are external professionals with academic degrees in the social and behavioural sciences.

References

Andersson, A. and Nilsson, R. (2009) *Svensk kriminalvårdspolitik* [Swedish penal policy], Malmö: Liber.
Bauman, Z. (1989) *Modernity and the Holocaust*, Cambridge: Polity Press.

Swedish 'prison exceptionalism' in decline 121

Bauman, Z. (2001) *The individualized society*, Cambridge: Polity Press.

Beck, U. (1992) *Risk society: towards a new modernity*, London: Sage.

Boltanski, L. and Chiapello, E. (2007) *The new spirit of capitalism*, London: Verso.

Bowlby, J. (1997) *Attachment and loss*, London: Pimlico.

Bresky, T., Schmid, I. and Scherman, J. (1981) *Med SAF vid rodret: granskning av en kamporganisation* [With SAF at the helm: examination of a battle organization], Stockholm: Liber.

Bronfenbrenner, U. (1979) *The ecology of human development*, Cambridge, MA: Harvard University Press.

Bruhn, A. (2013) 'Gender relations and division of labour among prison officers in Swedish male prisons', *Journal of Scandinavian Studies in Criminology and Crime Prevention*, 14: 2.

Bruhn, A., Lindberg, O. and Nylander, P.Å. (2010) 'The prison officer's dilemma: professional representations among Swedish prison officers', *Les dossiers des sciences de l'education*, 23: 77–95.

Bruhn, A., Lindberg, O. and Nylander, P.Å. (2012) 'A harsher prison climate and a cultural heritage working against it: subbcultural division among Swedish prison officers', in B. L. Dullum and T. Ugelvik (eds), *Penal exeptionalism? Nordic prison policy and practice*, Routledge: London.

Castells, M. (1997) *The power of identity*, Oxford: Blackwell Publishers.

Dullum, B.L. and Ugelvik, T. (2012) *Penal exeptionalism? Nordic prison policy and practice*, Routledge: London.

Duncan, B.L., Miller, S. D., Wampold, B.E., and Hubble, M.A. (2010) *The heart and soul of change: delivering what works in therapy*, Washington, DC: American Psychology Association.

Ekbom, T., Engström, G. and Göransson, B. (2011) *Människan, brottet, följderna. Kriminalitet och kriminalvård i Sverige* [Man, crime, consequences. crime and criminal care in Sweden], Stockholm: Natur & Kultur.

Eskilsson, S. (2005) *Från folkhem till nytt klassamhälle: ett högerspöke berättar* [From the Swedish welfare state to a new class society: tales from a right-wing ghost], Rimbo: Fisher & Co.

European Committee for the Prevention of Torture and Inhuman or Degrading Treatment or Punishment (CPT) (2009) *Report to the Swedish Government on the visit to Sweden carried out by the European Committee for the Prevention of Torture and Inhuman or Degrading Treatment or Punishment (CPT) from 9 to 18 June 2009*, CPT/Inf (2009) 34.

Evetts, J. (2013) 'Professionalism: value and ideology', *Current sociology/Current Sociology Review*, 61: 778–796.

Garland, D. (2001) *The culture of control*, Oxford: Oxford University Press.

Härenstam, A. (1989) *Prison personnel: working conditions, stress and health – a study of 2000 prison employees in Sweden*, Stockholm: National Institute of Psychosocial Factors and Health, Department of Stress Research, Karolinska Institute.

Holm, C. and Jukic, E. (2013) *ORIKA: Operativ riskbedömning i kriminalvårdsanstalt.* [ORIKA: Operative risk-assesment in prisons], Örebro: Örebro University Working Papers and Reports Social Work, online, available: www.oru.se/PageFiles/62926/ORIKA%20Working%20Papers%20and%20Reports.pdf (accessed 14 November 2014).

Holm, C., Lindberg, O., Jukic, E. and Nylander, P.Å. (2014) 'Flera nyanser av blått. Kriminalvårdare på behandlingsavdelningar – deras beskrivningar av yrkesroller, drogbehandling och de intagna', *Nordisk Kriminalvidenskaplig tidskrift*, 101: 183–204.

Hood, C. (1991) 'A public management for all seasons?', *Public Administration*, 69: 3–19.

Hood, C. (1995) 'The "new public management" in the 1980s: variations on a theme', *Accounting, Organizations and Society*, 20(2–3): 93–110, retrieved from http://search.proquest.com/docview/38661267?accountid=8028.

Hörnqvist, M. (2010) *Risk, power and the state: after Foucault*, New York: Routledge.

Kolind, T., Asmussen, V., Lindberg, O. and Touronen, J. (2013) 'Prison-based drug treatment in the Nordic political discourse: an elastic discursive construct', *European Journal of Criminology*, 10: 659–674.

Krantz, L., and Elmby, J. (2007) *Kriminalvårdens redovisning om drogsituationen 2005–2006* [The SPPS Account on the Drug Situation 2005–2006], Norrköping: Kriminalvården.

Liebling, A. (2010) '"Governmentality" and governing corrections: do senior managers resist?', in Leonidas K. Cheliotis (ed.), *Roots, rites and sites of resistance: the banality of good*, Basingstoke: Palgrave Macmillan.

Liebling, A. and Crewe, B. (2012) 'Are liberal-humanitarian penal values and practices exceptional?', in T. Ugelvik and B. L. Durum (eds), *Penal exceptionalism? Nordic prison policy and practice*, New York: Routledge.

Lindberg, O. (2005) 'Prison cultures and social representations: the case of Hinseberg, a women's prison in Sweden', *International Journal of Prisoner Health*, 1: 143–161.

Lipsky, M. (2010) *Street level bureaucracy: dilemmas of the individual in public services*, New York: Russell Sage Foundation.

Martinson, R. (1974) 'What works? Questions and answers about prison reform', *The Public Interest*, Spring: 22–54.

Melucci, A. (1989) *Nomads of the present: social movements and individual needs in contemporary society*, London: Raduis.

Nilsson, R. (1999) *En välbyggd maskin, en mardröm för själen: Det svenska fängelsesystemet under 1800-talet* [A well-built machine, a nightmare for the soul: the Swedish prison system during the 19th century], dissertation, Lund:Lund University Press.

Nilsson, R. (2013) 'From learning to labour to learning to self-control: the paradigmatic change in Swedish prison policy', *Journal of Scandinavian Studies in Criminology and Crime Prevention*, 14(S1): 24–45.

Nylander, P.Å., Bruhn, A. and Lindberg, O. (2008) 'Säkerhet eller rehabilitering. Om subkulturell differentiering bland kriminalvårdare' [Security or rehabilitation. On sub-cultural differentiation among prison officers], *Arbetsmarkand & Arbetsliv*, 14(3).

Nylander, P.Å., Lindberg, O., and Bruhn, A. (2011) 'Emotional labour and emotional strain among Swedish prison officers', *European Journal of Criminology*, 8: 469–483.

Nylander, P.Å., Holm, C., Jukic, E. and Lindberg, O. (2012) 'Drug treatment in Swedish prisons: moving towards evidence-based interventions?', *Nordic Studies on Alcohol and Drugs*, 29: 561–574.

Power, M. (1997) *The audit society: rituals of verification*, Oxford: Oxford University Press.

Pratt, J. (2008) 'Scandinavian exceptionalism in an era of penal excess: Part I – the nature of roots of Scandinavian exceptionalism', *British Journal of Criminology*, 48: 119–137.

Pratt, J. and Eriksson, A. (2013) *Contrasts in punishment: an explanation of Anglophone excess and Nordic exceptionalism*, London and New York: Routledge.

Scheff, T.J. (1997) *Emotions, the social bond and human reality: part/whole analysis,* Cambridge: Cambridge University Press.

SOU (2005) (Swedish Government Official Reports Series), *Säkert inlåst? En granskning av rymningarna från Kumla, Hall, Norrtälje och Mariefred 2004.* [Safely locked up], Betänkande av rymningsutredningen, SOU: 6.

Sykes, G.M. (1958) *The society of captives: a study of a maximum security prison,* Princeton, NJ: Princeton University Press.

Wacquant, L. (2004) *Fattigdomens fängelser* [The Prisons of Poverty], Eslöv: Symposion.

Wagner, P. (1996) 'Crises of modernity: political sociology in historical contexts', in S.P. Turner (ed.), *Social theory and sociology,* London: Blackwell.

Weber, M. (1922/1983) *Ekonomi och samhälle* [Economy and society], Lund: Argos.

6 Doing away with decency?[1]
Foreigners, punishment and the liberal state

Ana Aliverti[2]

Some years ago, Barbara Hudson concluded her paper on 'Justice at the borders of community' thus:

> The ideal of equality based on qualities humans have in common served well to underpin the move of western societies from absolutism to constitutionalism, but in confronting the move from the inviolable sovereignty of the nation-state to the challenges of a globalised, suspicious, fragmented world, where we must constantly travel to the borders of our overlapping communities, borders where encounters with aliens are inescapable, new ideas are needed.
>
> (Hudson 2006: 245)

This chapter takes this conclusion as a starting point to analyse the challenges posed by mass human mobility for the ideas and practices of justice. Liberal theories of justice are premised on a particular conception of society as fairly bounded in the most literal sense (Duff 2001: 40; Zedner 2010: 400, 2013: 46). Under this view, societies are communities of citizens, who have been 'born from the soil', grow within them and exit them at death. While modern western states stubbornly portray their societies as unified by a common identity and tradition which often have strong ethno-cultural and religious connotations (Anderson 2013; Barker 2013; Aas 2013), this romantic resurrection of the autochthonous and the parochial is in stark contrast with the cultural, ethnic, religious hyper-diversity and pluralism of these national communities. This hermetically sealed view of a national community is unrealistic from a historical point of view, yet it is even more untenable in contemporary societies, given the unprecedented levels of human mobility brought about by globalization (Bosniak 2008: 6).[3]

Nancy Fraser has claimed that existing theories of justice are strongly wedded to a Westphalian frame which regards justice as territorialized, whereby its scope is limited to the 'citizenry of a bounded political community' (Fraser 2008: 400). Under this view, justice is conceived of as 'a domestic relationship between fellow citizens' (Fraser 2010: 282). As a consequence, she posits, prevailing conceptions of justice exclude 'binding obligations of justice that cut across borders'. Fraser's project is to shed light and theorize on the emergence of potentially emancipatory forms of justice that challenge and expand the limited frame of reference of the Westphalian model. Instead, my concern here is to examine the production of novel, oppressive control strategies within the purview of modern liberal states that are obstinately clinging to that traditional frame while shielding it from scrutiny.

This chapter demonstrates that this bounded conception of justice is detrimental to those with weak claims of membership, specifically undocumented and documented foreigners, and permanent residents. Instead of being completely excluded from the realms of 'normal' justice, their legal status, I argue, has served to legitimize a second-class justice system in which certain protections of individual rights are attenuated. In this vein, legal and bureaucratic classifications – namely, immigration status and nationality – stemming from this bounded conception of justice are reified and naturalized, rendering the differential treatment applied to non-nationals morally acceptable. This chapter focuses on the role of these legal and bureaucratic classifications – and their operationalization through penal and quasi-penal practices of exclusion – in the erosion of the sense of responsibility towards certain non-citizens, which in turn makes the differential, more intensive application of coercive powers against this group acceptable without seemingly offending standards of decency held dear in western societies. Indeed, these standards of decency are often deployed to justify such differential treatment. Paraphrasing Zygmunt Bauman, to exclude 'unwelcome migrants' is defended in public discourse and policy statements as an act of good sense and justice (Bauman 2000: 207). Following Bauman, I argue that the rationalization of difference based on formal membership is crucial to understanding the production, endurance and legitimization of unfair, harmful and inhumane border control policies and practices in 'civilized' societies.

Focusing on specific measures and practices that either directly or indirectly target this group, I illustrate the ways in which the creeping of nationality into 'mainstream' criminal justice institutions attenuates the standing of certain foreigners as subjects of justice. Indeed, citizenship can be conceived as one of the last legal categories that allow legally sanctioned differential treatment (Dembour 2003). The legal and discursive construction of citizenship status as a social sorting device to select the 'best and brightest' and dispose of unwanted non-citizens or non-full citizens has served as a legitimizing force to justify their precarious standing. Further, nationality as a legitimate sorting device to attribute rights has supplanted other, now prohibited grounds for social sorting – particularly race and class. Yet, as an acceptable, taken-for-granted and pervasive criterion for discriminatory treatment, citizenship still serves to conveniently conceal ethno-cultural and classist categories. Hence, issues of race, ethnicity and class are acutely pertinent to an understanding of present border regimes (Bowling 2013). Although the manifestations of the exclusionary vent of formal membership are not new, they have become increasingly apparent in recent times as the integrity of national boundaries

126 *Ana Aliverti*

and the security of national communities are constantly in need of being reasserted and reassured.

Theories of exclusion: foreigners as subjects of justice

The promise of Enlightenment-liberal traditions is emancipatory in nature: to restrict the prerogatives of the sovereign by establishing strong political, legal and procedural limits on the exercise of its political power. Yet, as critical and feminist writers have shown, historically such an emancipatory and liberating potential mainly benefited a particular social group – middle-class, white men – while excluding the poor, non-whites and women. This marginalization was made possible through the normalization and universalization of the perspective of the privileged group and the concomitant denial of difference and heterogeneity (Young 1990). As Seyla Benhabib (1992: 152) puts it, 'by identifying the experience of a specific group of subjects as the paradigmatic case of the human as such' – the white, male, propertied or professional adult – the universalism upon which the liberal tradition is based implicitly or explicitly presents those who fail to meet those standards as abnormal, denying their standing as full subjects of rights and responsibilities.

Poststructuralists point to this inescapable weakness of liberalism – in order to delineate and define the group to be included, 'Others' must be excluded. This Other thus plays an essential definitional boundary-drawing function (Bauman 1993: 24). This 'negative imperative' is not a mere accidental oversight but a constitutional necessity of liberalism (Hudson 2003: 184; Bauman 2004: 31). The subject of justice is constructed by contrast to who he is not, *his* opposite. Such dichotomies serve to justify the application of dissimilar standards of justice against different Others. As a consequence, the tenets of rights-respecting democratic governance do not apply to them. In turn, by presenting the characteristics of the legal subject as universal and the norm, the law creates normative expectations about the 'ideal citizen'. Iris Young takes issue with the point of departure of dominant theories of justice premised on a 'normative ideal of community' which glosses over existing inequalities and idealizes a homogenized community. Such a basic premise necessarily conceals existing inequalities and consequently prevents us from remedying them. Instead, Young proposes to build theories of justice based on the 'general historical and social conditions in which we exist' and 'on the assumption that there are group differences and that some groups are actually or potentially oppressed or disadvantaged' so we can avoid the perpetuation of injustices (Young 1989: 261).

From this viewpoint, the denial to certain groups of their standing as full subjects of rights and responsibilities in contemporary societies is not conceived as part of an 'illiberal backlash', or a counter trend within liberalism, but rather as an inherent manifestation of it (Anderson 2013; Gibney 2013). Bauman claims that modernity as a cultural project spanning from the Enlightenment facilitates, instead of inhibits, immoral behaviour. Racism is not a negation of modernity but precisely its product because it is based on processes of rationalization that legitimize differential treatment of human beings and ultimately the elimination of the Other (Bauman 1991: 61). Intolerance to everything that cannot be assimilated is 'the natural inclination of modern practice'. The pursuit of order, and the purging of ambivalence, he asserts, 'sets the limits to incorporation and admission. It calls for the denial of rights ... of everything that cannot be assimilated – for the de-legitimation of the other' (Bauman 1993: 8). Bauman claims that modernity and civilization have not eliminated irrationality, barbarism and violence; instead, under modern conditions '[v]iolence has been taken out of sight, rather than forced out of existence' (Bauman 1991: 97). It has been centralized, monopolized, instrumentalized and 'turned into a technique' (Bauman 1991) and as such is immune from any moral evaluation of its ends. Society is not the social factory of morality, Bauman maintains, but the opposite: certain societies create the conditions in which immoral behaviour becomes not merely possible but even acceptable (Bauman 1991: 174). In modern societies, the 'social production of immorality' is enabled through the strong emphasis on the bureaucratic pursuit of efficiency to the detriment of morality (Bauman 1991: 24). Instrumental effectiveness, Bauman says, has become the paramount standard by which practices and policies are judged, while foreclosing the moral evaluation of the ends to be pursued. The products of modernity – bureaucracy, science and technological advancement – have emptied human action of ethical evaluation and freed human beings from innate moral constraints.

This body of work is relevant for understanding contemporary border control regimes in liberal states. More precisely, a critical reading of liberal institutions, ideas and practices can shed light on the apparent paradox of the production and endurance of unjust practices of migration management in countries that pride themselves on notions of equality, non-discrimination and legality (Bowling 2013: 301; see also Simon, this volume). Legal and bureaucratic classifications, I argue, play a crucial role in legitimizing the differential treatment of certain foreign nationals by eroding the sense of moral responsibility towards them and making the differential, more intensive application of coercive powers against this group acceptable and compatible with the standards of decency upheld in these societies.

While critical legal theory has been instrumental in challenging injustices within the polis so as to expand the promise of equal citizenship to groups hitherto marginalized because of race, class, gender, sexual orientation or disability, formal (non-)membership rarely appears as a category in need of deconstruction and scrutiny. On the whole, there has been an indifference or outright reluctance to engage with citizenship in its negative, exclusionary connotations. This blind spot in critical theory can partly be explained by the enduring notion of the nation-state as an analytical point of departure of legal, political and social thought (Fraser 2010). As Linda Bosniak (2008: 11) suggests, the difference that membership makes is generally perceived by 'antisubordination' theorists as necessary to preserve 'the community within which the struggle against social subordination takes place'. Exclusion is necessary to maintain the territorial and symbolic battlefield where the fight for equal citizenship takes place.

And yet perhaps more than ever the exclusionary edge of membership is crucial to understanding contemporary forms of subordination and oppression inside affluent western liberal states. Further, citizenship as a key mechanism for determining rights and prerogatives subsumes and conceals older 'vectors of subordination', such as race and class, while recreating and reinforcing hierarchies of citizenship in a deeply divided and unequal world (Aas 2013). The distinction that emerges is not clear-cut, between citizens and foreigners, members and non-members. While historically British nationality and immigration laws were formally raceless and classless, they have been instrumental in keeping the black and the poor from the former colonies out of the British Isles (Dummett and Nicol 1990; Gilroy 1982). Similarly, more contemporary policies that seek to cherry pick the best and brightest uphold standards of individual worthiness, which in turn subtly connect to social class and ethno-cultural dimensions. In other words, not all foreigners are outsiders; equally, not all citizens are insiders.

In the same way that in liberal states the idea of citizenship as a universal, neutral and abstract category has enforced a 'homogeneity of citizens' and concomitantly created a group of 'second class citizens' who formally enjoy citizenship rights but are in practice socially and politically marginalized (Young 1989), the abstraction of citizenship has also contributed to the disavowal of global inequalities and the role of citizenship as a social control tool in reinforcing these inequalities. Understood thus, citizenship is relational and assumes strong ethno-cultural and geopolitical dimensions as a social sorting device. It matters which state does the sorting and against whom. The global hierarchy of citizenship is embedded in the unequal global distribution of resources, so that matters of nationality and belonging are strongly associated with race and poverty (Anderson 2013: 41; see also Barker, this volume). Further, as Stephen Castles (2005: 691) observes, the existing global hierarchies do not replace those at the national level but rather interact with them, making starkly apparent the contrast between the legal principle of equality of nation-states and citizens, on the one hand, and the reality of hierarchy and exclusion, on the other.

To say that citizenship has become a crucial social sorting device inside the community, and not only at the port of entry, does not mean that non-members as a group are new pariahs within liberal states. Far from being strangers stripped of basic rights and liberties, in contemporary liberal democracies such as Britain, legal residents enjoy a range of rights almost on a par with citizens – from education and healthcare, to access to justice and employment. Even though immigrants outside the law, without legal status, are increasingly driven to live under clandestine conditions by stricter internal immigration enforcement, it is inaccurate to describe those conditions as beyond the pale of the law. More precisely, as subjects of justice, at least in Britain, non-citizen defendants formally enjoy the same procedural rights as do their citizen counterparts. Even in terms of sentencing there is no single specific provision that authorizes the consideration of immigration status as relevant for deciding the type and amount of punishment upon a criminal conviction.

From this perspective, critical accounts that draw a line between, on the one hand, the liberal inside populated by equal and free citizens and, on the other, the outside policed by illiberal principles and practices are untenable as a descriptive and normative statement of the 'liberal project' (see, for example, Cole 2000; Bauman 2004). This is not least because, to paraphrase Bosniak (2008: 4), the border follows foreigners wherever they go, and national boundaries are therefore not decisive for delineating the boundaries of citizenship. But it is also because the impact of immigration status on the standing of foreigners as subjects of justice is more complex and elusive than the straightforward application of the 'bare life' thesis suggests (Aas and Bosworth 2013). Indeed, while certain instances of 'penal exceptionalism' based on membership status are undeniable – in Britain, recent counter-terrorism measures spring to mind as obvious examples (of which more are discussed below) – most of the everyday punitive management of foreigners is less ostensibly illiberal and controversial, though equally troubling. The creeping of citizenship into mainstream (criminal) justice contributes to the forging of a distinctive system of justice.

In the face of the real or perceived erosion of state sovereign powers, the persistent embracing of an outmoded Westphalian conception of justice has served to legitimize the attenuation of the standing of non-citizens as subjects of justice in an era of universality of rights and equality before the law. I argue that this attenuated standing, and the concomitant relevance of citizenship and immigration status to criminal justice decision-making, is manifest in three main spheres: first, the expansive, substantive criminalization of non-citizens through offences that are directly or indirectly associated with their status as non-members; second, the application of facially neutral procedural and sentencing standards which have a detrimental, harsher effect on non-members; and finally, the almost inexorable operation of status-based measures stemming from immigration law in lieu of criminal intervention or as collateral sanctions, in particular administrative removal. Collectively, the resulting intensified operation of penal and quasi-penal norms is instrumental for the territorial exclusion of undesirable non-citizens.

In the next section, I sketch a typology of measures that serves to illustrate the different manifestations of the embryonic system of 'abnormal' or 'precarious' justice (Aas 2014). While this catalogue is not exhaustive and is focused on Britain, it is representative of trends elsewhere.

Contours of 'abnormal' justice

Much has been written about the intertwining of immigration and criminal laws, institutions and practices – dubbed in the literature 'crimmigration'

(Stumpf 2007; Eagly 2010; Chacón 2012; Aliverti 2013a). This literature suggests that the dovetailing of these distinctive regulatory spheres has been detrimental to foreigners caught up in the resulting net of controls which have enlarged the discretion of law enforcement agencies, increased (formal) criminalization alongside limited procedural and substantive protections of non-citizen defendants and led to tougher sanctions upon conviction. This merger also means that the sites of control are no longer confined to the walls of criminal courts, police stations and prison cells (see also Johansen and Bosworth, this volume). Rather, the resulting measures inhabit fluid institutional and legal spaces, which in turn demand new research techniques to account for their specific qualitative and quantitative dimensions (Bosworth 2014: ch. 2).

The fluidity of these spaces also militates against their visibility and accountability. Ingrid Eagly echoes others when she points to this pervasive aspect of 'non-citizen justice': 'the criminal–immigration merger is an area that is based on policies and practices that are often hidden from view. The intersection of criminal prosecution and immigration enforcement is also highly unregulated' (Eagly 2013: 165; see also Aas 2014). Indeed, statistics on foreign national prisoners are remarkably patchy: they are rarely disaggregated on country of origin (such as European Union (EU)/non-EU), ethnic group, immigration status, type of crime, or length or type of sentence, for example. The picture is even less clear when it comes to non-citizens being dealt with through non-criminal institutions in terms of the frequency of immigration-related arrests, number of immigration detainees in specific centres and prisons, figures on deportation orders based on criminal convictions, and the like. These data deficiencies thwart any attempt to reach meaningful conclusions at the national level, draw comparisons across countries or estimate the real extent of the criminalization of foreign nationals. It has been argued that the pervasive weakness of data is linked to the identity of the subjects to be counted and arguably reveals more than it conceals. Indeed, the strategic reluctance of unwelcome migrants to be traceable and the zeal with which the host states endeavour to block their way in and dispose of them once found militate against the visibility and practical worth of the resulting data. In other words, the fact that these people are bound to be pushed out renders detailed classification redundant and unworthy.

Bearing in mind these limitations, in what follows I provide a brief – albeit necessarily incomplete – account of the different ways in which formal citizenship status permeates mainstream criminal justice institutions and stretches its boundaries. In so doing, I build on the 'crimmigration' literature while expanding its purview to cover less discernible sites of 'non-citizen justice' without claiming to exhaust these avenues. I outline three main families of measures. The first group comprises criminal law measures, which are not specifically directed at non-citizens but are overwhelmingly enforced against them. The second segment groups together criminal law–type measures that are specifically directed at non-citizens. The third and final category is populated by non-criminal measures. For this third category, even if they are regulatory in

Foreigners, punishment and the liberal state   131

nature these measures are predominantly justified by the same rationale underpinning punishment: deterrence, incapacitation and retribution.

'Citizen' criminal law

The criminalization of non-citizens is neither dominated by nor limited to status-based crimes. Indeed, at least in England and Wales and other European countries, non-citizens are more likely to be caught by the criminal justice system through the operation of 'ordinary' offences, rather than immigration-related crimes. Convictions for drug offences are behind a significant proportion of the population of foreign inmates in English and Welsh prisons. In 2009, almost one-third of foreign prisoners were convicted for drug-related crimes, compared to 14 per cent of British national prisoners (Bank 2011: 187). Women are even more likely to be imprisoned for drug offences: almost half of the foreign female population in 2010 (46 per cent) were behind bars for drug supply – more precisely, importation of Class A drugs – compared to 21 per cent of the native female population[4] (Prison Reform Trust 2012: 3). The vast majority of them (81 per cent) were from black and other ethnic minority backgrounds (HMIP 2009: 8). Because drug offences are deemed to be serious, people convicted of them are highly likely to receive lengthy custodial sentences and be eligible for deportation. Drug offences were by far the largest crime category that triggered automatic deportation of foreigners from 2008 to 2012, followed by possession and/or use of false documents.[5]

Other countries in Europe report high conviction rates among foreigners for drug-related offences. Almost half of the foreigners housed in Italian prisons are charged with drug-related crimes (Istat 2012: 9). The same holds true for the US, where the compounded effect of the 'War on Drugs' and the 'War on Immigration' has contributed to swamped federal prisons and forced demographic changes in their population (Bosworth and Kaufman 2011: 439; McLeod 2012: 167). In 2014, 50 per cent of the federal prison population comprised drug-related offenders as the single-largest category of inmate, followed by immigration offenders (which made up 11 per cent of the federal prison population). Yolanda Vázquez (2011: 665) noted that in 1991 60 per cent of Latinos convicted in federal courts were convicted for drug offences and that drug-related offences are one of the main crimes leading to administrative removal.

Fraud and counterfeiting constitutes the second-largest criminal category behind the incarceration of foreign nationals in England and Wales (Bank 2011). Convictions for 'fraud and forgery' among foreign national prisoners accounted for 8 per cent in 2009 and 6 per cent in 2012 (Ministry of Justice [MoJ] 2010, 2013a). Foreigners are more likely to be incarcerated for fraud-based offences than their British counterparts, as only 1.5 per cent of the latter were in prison for these crimes (MoJ 2013a: Table A1.21). Foreign national women are more likely than foreign males to be in prison for document fraud: in 2009, 16 per cent were jailed for these offences, in contrast to 7 per cent of

132   *Ana Aliverti*

their male counterparts; and in 2012, these rates were 14 and 5 per cent, respectively. Although many of these offences are immigration related, some are status-neutral offences – such as crimes covered by the *Identity Documents Act 2010* – which are disproportionately applied against foreigners found in possession of forged identity cards when trying to enter or exit the country, secure employment or access services within the country. In 2011, 1412 defendants were found guilty of various offences of possession of forged identity documents, of whom the vast majority (1081) were given a custody term.[6] Although these figures are not disaggregated by nationality, the fact that these offences were originally enacted to tackle immigration fraud may suggest that immigration fraudsters are often captured by them (Aliverti 2012: 423).

Albeit in smaller numbers, status-neutral offences in counter-terrorism legislation are disproportionately used against foreigners and foreign-born nationals. 'The threat of terrorism', Ashworth and Zedner (2014: 227) note, 'is commonly perceived as a primarily foreign threat'. Non-Britons made up half of those arrested, charged and convicted for terrorism offences in 2012. Of them, Algerians were the largest national group followed by Pakistanis and Iraqis (Home Office 2013: table A.12abc). Sentences for these offences tend to be high, averaging 17 years in 2011 (Ashworth and Zedner 2014: 181).

One can argue that the substantive criminalization of foreigners for drug and forgery offences merely reflects offending rates among this group. Several academics (Wacquant 2006; De Giorgi 2010; Melossi 2012: 29) claim that the racial, social and economic marginalization of foreigners in European societies, which drives them into the underground economy, explains their high representation in European prisons for these crimes.[7] Indeed, some of them are implicated in the illegal economy in the dual role of perpetrators and victims. Although there are no precise figures, recent high-profile court cases[8] indicate that some defendants charged with drug offences – especially drug mules and those working on cannabis farms – and identity fraud are themselves victims of human trafficking (see also Hales and Gelsthorpe 2012). While irregular immigration status plays an important role in their marginalization, a growing number of EU nationals – from new accession countries such as Bulgaria and Romania, in particular – are increasingly found among the foreign population in European prisons (Melossi 2013: 423; Ugelvik 2014: 108).

The high level of representation of foreign nationals for certain categories of offence has also been explained by the targeted police enforcement of 'visible non-national ethnics'[9] (Wacquant 2006: 89) and the application of facially neutral bail and sentencing rules that adversely affect non-residents. In the same way that non-citizens are predominantly criminalized through specific status-neutral crimes – especially those who by dint of their irregular status are more likely to be involved in 'deviant' activities – status-neutral rules adversely affect foreigners facing a criminal proceeding, particularly those who are undocumented. In 2012, untried foreign national prisoners comprised 14 per cent of the total population of foreigners behind bars, compared to only 8 per cent of Britons (MoJ 2013a: table A1.18). While between 1999 and

2009 untried receptions among Britons fell by 28 per cent, they rose sharply by 136 per cent among foreign nationals (Bank 2011: 194). One of the main reasons for the high remand rates among unconvicted foreign national defendants is that foreigners with weak 'links to the community' are more likely to be considered flight risks by the courts and less likely to be bailed than British defendants.

The existence of ties to the community is also important at the sentencing stage, particularly as proxy for non-recidivism and the effectiveness of deterrence. As Hudson (1998: 234) explains:

> Community ties provide support for efforts to change from a criminal to a non-criminal lifestyle, and also are important as sources of informal social control. ... People with strong community ties are assessed as having much to lose by continuing criminality, and therefore not in need of punishment to supply a further deterrent.

Highly mobile foreigners are unsurprisingly judged as unsuitable for non-custodial sentences. Although immigration status is formally irrelevant for sentencing, in practice foreignness, lack of immigration status and eligibility for deportation are automatically seen by the judiciary as obstacles to release (Aliverti 2013b: 44).

'Non-citizen' criminal law

In addition to criminalization through status-neutral offences, foreign nationals reach the criminal courts in good numbers through the operation of status-based crimes. In Britain, following the creation of a myriad of immigration-related offences between 1999 and 2009, prosecution and conviction rates for these offences soared. Foreigners in breach of their immigration status reach the criminal justice system most typically because of irregularities with their identity documents. Non-nationals make up about half of those in prison serving a custodial sentence for 'fraud and forgery' offences. Immigration prosecutions cluster into three main offences: assisting unlawful immigration, seeking leave to enter or remain, or postponement of revocation by deception and being unable to produce an immigration document.[10] While this branch of the law targets non-citizens in breach of immigration rules, it extends to those who purposively or recklessly help immigration offenders – including British citizens.

An obvious instrumental logic underpins the operation of these offences. They are often used to provisionally seclude unruly migrants while preparing for their expulsion from the country when administrative removal is not possible. Although the majority of people who breach immigration rules and are detected at ports of entry or inside the country are routinely denied entry or administratively removed, a minority of immigration defaulters are prosecuted. The criteria guiding this decision are vague[11], so in practice caseworkers have

134 *Ana Aliverti*

wide discretion. One of the most important factors in determining to refer such a case to the police and the Crown Prosecution Service is whether the person can be removed. Because a removal is considered to be more cost effective than a prosecution, the immigration department prioritizes the former. The instrumentality and resulting inconsistencies in the use of criminal prosecutions against immigration defaulters were highlighted and objected to by the Independent Chief Inspector of Borders and Immigration in a recent inspection report, when he observed:

> Parliament has ... put in place criminal offences for these types of behaviour, with the possibility of custodial sentences, so the practice of opting for the use of removal rather than criminal investigation and prosecution should be supported by a robust analysis and evaluation process.
>
> (Vine 2012: 39)

For some time, several US academics (see, for example, Eagly 2010; Chacón 2012) have been alerting to the steep increase in prosecution rates for immigration crimes, particularly illegal entry and re-entry. From 1997 to 2009, immigration prosecutions soared more than tenfold (Sklansky 2012: 166), while plateauing since 2011 due to a decline in apprehensions on the southern US border. The exponential increase and patterns of prosecution led to speculation that the criminal justice system is predominantly called forth to perform the work of immigration law, namely immigration screening (Eagly 2010: 1349, 2013). In Europe, most countries criminalize immigration contraventions although the rate of enforcement of these offences remains relatively low and is in decline.

In combination, the operation of 'citizen' and 'non-citizen' criminal law contributes to the high proportion of non-citizens behind bars in countries across the Atlantic. In 2014, foreign-born inmates represented 25 per cent of the US federal prison population.[12] While there are important variations across jurisdictions, foreigners are consistently over-represented in the prison population of Western European countries, with a share of the prison population averaging 21 per cent (Aebi and Delgrande 2010: Table 3). Arguably, however, focusing on criminalization *strictu sensu* leads to a distorted picture of the extent of the punitive management of immigration. Indeed, due to their status, non-citizens in breach of the law are likely to be handled outside the criminal justice institutions.

Non-criminal punitive law

Criminal lawyers often describe punishment as the most intrusive form of state coercion. Because of the stigma associated with it and the severity of the resulting sanction, particularly if it entails internment, a criminal conviction is prefaced by a plethora of additional protections and safeguards. In recent years the creation of an array of civil preventive orders, which authorize the

Foreigners, punishment and the liberal state   135

imposition of coercive measures outside the criminal proceeding, has undermined the basic tenet of liberal criminal law (Ashworth and Zedner 2010). Immigration law sanctions a range of quasi-criminal measures, like administrative detention and removal. Although formally they stand outside the criminal law and are regulatory in nature, they resemble past and current forms of punishment and are frequently deployed to attain ends germane to punishment: deterrence, incapacitation and retribution (Bosworth 2011, 2012, 2013).

Since the ultimate penalty against foreigners in breach is territorial ejection, unsurprisingly prosecution and punishment are often adjudged ill suited to deal with them. In the UK, there is a longstanding practice of pursuing administrative action (removal), instead of prosecution, against foreigners suspected of having committed offences while in the country. This practice is largely underpinned by a pragmatic rationale, since removal is considered a less cumbersome and more (cost) effective means to rid the country of both petty offenders and terrorism suspects (Aliverti 2013a: 62; Ashworth and Zedner 2014: 244). Although this practice is highly inconsistent and varies according to the force in charge, in recent years the use of immigration-type measures to address crime-related problems has become increasingly institutionalized.

In September 2012, the Metropolitan Police and the Border Force launched Operation Nexus in London. The scheme has a clear crime prevention goal: 'to reduce the impact of criminal offending by foreign nationals'.[13] Interestingly, the police have justified the scheme on equality grounds. Since arresting British nationals is easier because more is known about them, so the argument goes, 'to level up the playing field between foreign nationals and domestic suspects we need to improve the information sharing currently in place in order to bring all law breakers to justice no matter where they come from'.[14] With the practice of systematically checking immigration status upon arrest through fingerprinting, immigration staff have been stationed at twenty-one police stations across the London metropolitan area. In principle, all custody police officers are responsible for checking the detainee's identity upon arrest through fingerprinting and if they suspect that the detainee is a foreign national they are required to undertake further checks and searches. However, in practice, checks on immigration and Association of Chief Police Officers criminal records databases are rare (National Audit Office [NAO] 2014: 22).

The main aim of the operation is to identify, at an early stage, foreigners whose presence in Britain is not conducive to the public good by dint of their criminality, and to remove them. Nexus seems to target 'high-harm' and petty criminality alike, although information on the precise remits of the operation is patchy and vague.[15] By early 2013, a quarter of the total number of people checked under Nexus (41,712) were foreign nationals, of whom half were non-EU citizens (House of Commons 2013: 19). Yet, little is known about how many of these people were removed from the country and for which crime type. Although the operation to date has primarily been limited to the London metropolitan area, where it is estimated that around 28 per cent of arrests have involved foreigners, and recently rolled out in the West-Midlands, Manchester and Scotland, there have been calls to expand it nationally (NAO 2014: 23).[16] Mindful of the potential abuses to which the scheme could lead, critics claim that Nexus virtually institutionalizes 'deportation on suspicion', as a substitute for the adversarial trial as the paramount procedure to establish criminal liability (Webber 2013). The additional enforcement route offered by immigration law to deal with unruly foreigners is by no means new. Yet Operation Nexus articulates and formalizes fairly longstanding, informal arrangements between immigration and crime enforcement while exploiting new technologies to trace the international criminal records of arrestees.

In the same way that counter-terrorism measures have disproportionately affected foreigners of certain nationalities and ethnic backgrounds, so too are status-based measures that stem from immigration law more directly implicated in the criminalization of foreigners suspected of terrorist activities (Ashworth and Zedner 2014: 242). In this view, immigration law with its vestiges of extra-constitutionality squarely fits the logic of exception underpinning counter-terrorism policy-making. Since the 9/11 attack on the US, a number of provisions in British counter-terrorism legislation have reinforced the association between foreignness and terrorism, the most obvious of which was the now abolished regime of indefinite detention of foreign terrorist subjects.[17] This law was abolished following a decision by a strong majority in the House of Lords which ruled that, given that both nationals and foreigners pose a threat to national security, it is disproportionate and discriminatory to impose the burden of detention without temporal limits only on the latter group.[18] After the 7/7 London bombings, concerns that home-grown, naturalized British citizens are behind terrorist plots led the government in 2006 to modify the law of nationality and exercise its powers of denaturalization more often against those involved in 'treasonable conduct'. Gibney observes that until 2006 the government rarely deployed its denaturalization powers. Yet from 2006 to 2011, thirteen British citizens were denaturalized, almost all of them due to links to Al-Qaeda-type terrorism (Gibney 2013: 651). More recently, the British Parliament gave leeway to the government to strip naturalized British citizens of their citizenship even if it makes them stateless.[19] As opposed to previous reforms, this new measure singles out naturalized citizens in a move criticized by many for reinforcing their citizenship status as 'second class' and contingent. The British Government introduced the new ground for citizenship deprivation in response to the Supreme Court's decision in *Al-Jedda* that held that the Secretary of State is not authorized to deprive a person of their British citizenship on the ground that it is conducive to the public good if the Secretary is satisfied that the order would make that person stateless.[20] While under international law states are only allowed to render their citizens stateless in highly exceptional circumstances, the British Government succeeded in convincing the parliament that the new ground would not jeopardize the state's obligations under the 1961 United Nations *Convention on the Reduction of Statelessness*. Hence, it managed to circumvent treaty restrictions without withdrawing from it.

Foreigners, punishment and the liberal state 137

Foreigners in breach of the law are liable to quasi-penal measures not only in lieu of punishment but also in addition to it.[21] Once they serve their sentence and are awaiting their removal, foreigners are liable to be detained either in special removal facilities or in prisons (see Bosworth, this volume).[22] In January 2011, over 1,600 foreign national prisoners were locked up under immigration powers, pending deportation, in Britain. Twenty-seven per cent of them had been detained for longer than 12 months (Vine 2012: 19).[23] After serving a custodial sentence, the odds of being deported are extremely high, increased further since the entry into force of mandatory deportation in August 2008.[24] In January 2012, 5,178 foreign national offenders serving a custodial sentence in England and Wales were being considered for deportation at the end of their sentence, comprising around half of the total foreign prisoner population, which includes detainees in the immigration estate. Although deportation figures are dominated by non-Europeans[25], the absolute number of European Economic Area and EU national offenders who are subject to removal from the UK and have been deported has steadily risen since 2008.[26] This upward trend may reflect the growing focus of current immigration politics and policies on EU nationals – particularly those from new accession countries.

The foregoing discussion points to the deleterious effect that foreignness has on those accused or convicted of a criminal offence, irrespective of the seriousness of the offence. Foreignness triggers removal even for the lesser offences for which nationals are let off or given penalty notices, simple cautions or other minimum intervention sentences. Criminal convictions are almost inexorably paired with deportation for non-citizens. Despite sitting outside the criminal law proper, the operation of immigration measures in lieu of or in conjunction with punishment results in the significant expansion of the state's punitive powers over non-citizens. Concomitantly, this quantitative and qualitative alteration of the state exercise of punitive powers has inescapable repercussions for our understanding of 'punitiveness' and how it should be counted and measured. More to the point, we should ask whether traditional quantitative measurements of punitiveness – above all, prison statistics – are suitable to inform our understanding of the extent and intensity of non-citizen justice. The point made by Franko Aas in relation to Norway seems to hold true outside Scandinavia: when it comes to non-citizens, '[c]riminal law is applied not only to punish, but also to deport, while deportation is used not only for immigration purposes, but also because an individual is seen as a law and order problem' (Aas 2014: 525). Whether deportation is civil or criminal is a moot point in the light of the additional, more painful consequences that await foreigners who are in breach of the law at the expiration of their punishment proper.[27]

Concluding remarks

This chapter sought to disentangle the variegated ways in which nationality and immigration status are implicated in criminalization. In highlighting the crucial role that formal citizenship status plays in criminal justice, this account does not ignore the existing gender, racial and class inequalities in the enforcement of criminal laws within the community. While the force of formal and substantial criminalization continues to fall disproportionately on the unemployed, young, racialized male, overt discrimination against this group in the form of rules that authorize their systematic disadvantage is nowadays rare in modern liberal states (Hudson 1998). Even if the resemblance between the governance of the vernacular poor and the proletariat coming from outside is obvious and hence it is tempting to draw parallels, it is important to keep sight of the relevance of nationality in the governance of the latter. Citizenship, in combination with other factors – particularly gender, race and socioeconomic status – operates to systematically disadvantage certain groups. Further, criminal justice discrimination against non-citizens traces older discriminatory vectors. In this vein, mass mobility has not disturbed the division of labour that the penal system has historically been called on to perform, which is to deal with the wrongdoing of the poor, but rather has reinforced it (Hudson 1998: 246; Stumpf 2012: 50).

This chapter explained the role of legal and bureaucratic categories in the production of social distance and the erosion of responsibility towards others. Nationality is the last category that allows legally sanctioned differential treatment. Citizenship status, as a legitimate ground for singling out a social group for differential treatment, is regarded as self-evident, taken for granted and as such in no need of being questioned or challenged. Marie-Benedicte Dembour (2003: 93) refers to the 'fiction of nationality', the main function of which is to conceal discrimination. In the specific context of human rights law, she argues that, rather than being treated as a legal creation, nationality is generally conceived of as an 'objective given'. Despite allowing legally sanctioned differential treatment based on an arbitrary condition over which the affected individual has no control, the reification of nationality makes it immune to challenge and shields it from ethical scrutiny. Challenging the legitimacy of nationality and immigration status as sorting devices does not necessarily entail questioning the state's prerogative to exercise controls over entry and residence. Instead, the claim is to disentangle and destabilize the existing inexorable link between formal membership and punishment (Zedner 2013). The dominant theories of punishment are strongly anchored on the premise that punishment plays a fundamental role in reasserting the ties that link the offender to her political community. When members are punished, their membership status is not withdrawn, but is temporarily suspended, and punishment has a crucial function in reasserting the value of being a member. The legitimation of punishment based on formal membership to a political community does not fare well and is ill suited to justify its infliction in contemporary pluralist societies (Hudson 2006). The unsuitability of the criminal law to accommodate those with weak membership claims makes recourse to it at times redundant and unnecessary, at others instrumental to the pursuit of immigration enforcement (Aliverti 2013a; 2014). In both cases, non-members

Foreigners, punishment and the liberal state 139

fall foul of the limits of universality of rights and as a consequence are systematically disadvantaged.

The most obvious, and questionable, ways in which citizenship is entangled with issues of justice is through instances of what Richard Ericson calls 'counter laws' or emergency penal legislation (Ericson 2007: 24; Hudson 2003: 35), specifically the provisions on indefinite detention and citizenship stripping in counter-terrorism laws. Yet, the everyday management of non-citizens is more mundane, and less glamorous and controversial. It occurs in the realms of the 'normal', rather than the exceptional. Despite the abundant suffering it generates, its invisibility and lack of garishness are key to its public palatability and acceptability (Barker 2013). This everyday, dispassionate infliction of violence as a result of immigration enforcement goes generally unnoticed.

For modern liberal states, such as Britain, the ethically contentious dimensions of the 'dirty' business of keeping people out of their shores are silenced – and the exercise of those controls legitimized – under the guise of the pursuit of efficient and sustainable migration management. The involvement of criminal justice institutions in this sphere has further contributed to erasing the thorny ethical aspects of migration enforcement by reducing unauthorized immigration to a matter of law-breaking and (individual) criminal responsibility, while exonerating those doing the blaming from the conditions that prompt inward mobility in the first place (Jamieson 1999: 136). At the same time, the creeping of immigration status and nationality into criminal justice decision-making has led to a blurring of individual blameworthiness. As consideration of foreignness and immigration status becomes paramount for decision-making, issues concerning the (criminal) liability of the suspect/defendant pale into insignificance against the substantive liability that ensues for breaching the boundaries of immigration status. Quietly and subtly, but sweepingly, foreignness permeates criminal justice decision-making. In doing so, it has a unifying effect and works to ultimately create a single, one-fits-all form of governance of those who, for a range of reasons, are not meant to be here.

Notes

1 Thanks to Sage for granting permission to reproduce previously published material in this chapter.
2 I am grateful to the participants of the symposium at Prato, Italy for their comments and suggestions. Thanks also to Lila García and Raja Shankar for their comments on earlier drafts.
3 In Britain, for instance, one-tenth of the population are foreign born while 7 per cent are non-British. Obviously, these figures do not cover undocumented foreigners and glosses over regional variations. Indeed, in 2012 foreign-born citizens made up 40 per cent of Londoners (Rienzo and Vargas-Silva 2011). The changing UK demography has been particularly evident in the past 20 years, during which period the foreign-born population almost doubled. Estimates for the coming decades forecast a similar trend.
4 Among the range of drug offences, foreigners are more likely to be convicted for illegal import and export of drugs and less likely to be themselves users than their

140 *Ana Aliverti*

British counterparts, who tend to be involved in possession and criminality linked to drug abuse (such as shoplifting or handling stolen goods) (HMIP 2009: 8).

5 House of Commons, Hansard 23 April 2013, column 786W. The MoJ makes it clear that 'if you are from outside the EEA and receive a custodial sentence for a drug offence (not including possession only), you may be liable for deportation. If your sentence is less than 12 months, you will still retain an in country right of appeal against this' (MoJ 2009: 8).

6 Source: MoJ, Justice Statistics Analytical Services, retrieved through Freedom of Information request 82636.

7 In 2012, the proportion of black and minority ethnic groups in prison who were foreign nationals was nearly three times as high as among British national prisoners (MoJ 2013b: 16).

8 For example, *R v O* [2008] EWCA Crim. 2835; *L v Children Commissioner* [2013] EWCA Crim 991.

9 The fact that, in 2012, 62 per cent of the foreign national prison population in England and Wales was from a minority ethnic background may support this hypothesis (Berman 2013: 10).

10 Respectively, ss 25(1) and 24A(1), *Immigration Act 1971*; and s 2(1), *Asylum and Immigration (Treatment of Claimants, etc.) Act 2004*.

11 Factors that might weigh on the decision include the seriousness of the offence; whether it is linked to organized criminality; evidence of repeated offending; and the possibility to use alternative sanctions, most importantly removal: UKBA. Standard Acceptable Criteria (SAC), Version 1.0, 28 April 2009 (unpublished document).

12 20 per cent of whom were born in Latin America. In 2012, foreign-born citizens amounted to 13 per cent of the total US population. See www.bop.gov/about/sta tistics/statistics_inmate_citizenship.jsp (accessed 21 May 2014).

13 In the words of Assistant Commissioner Mark Rowley. See the Metropolitan Police website: http://content.met.police.uk/News/Custody-teams-in-place-to-dea l-with-prisoners-from-other-countries/1400012971915/1257246741786 (accessed 15 May 2014).

14 Ibid.

15 See a rather piecemeal and outdated account of Nexus at: http://content.met. police.uk/News/Operation-Nexus-launches/1400012909227/1257246741786 (accessed 15 May 2014).

16 The obvious resemblance of Nexus to the US-based Secure Communities reminds us of the striking pace of policy transfer in this field: see Kohli *et al.* 2011.

17 Part IV, the *Anti-Terrorism, Crime and Security Act 2001* was replaced by a regime of civil preventive orders (control orders), which was subsequently rebranded as TPIMs.

18 *A and Others v Secretary of State of the Home Department* [2004] UKHL 56.

19 *Immigration Act 2014*, s 66.

20 *Secretary of State for the Home Department (Appellant) v Al-Jedda* [2013] UKSC 62.

21 In between both options, foreigners may be sent back to their country of origin before release through the Early Removal Scheme and the Facilitated Return Scheme.

22 In August 2012, there were 572 foreigners in prison under immigration act powers (FOI 24317 of 20 March 2012, by Gemma Lousley).

23 As Vine (2012: 18) shows in his report, one of the main reasons for post-sentence detention is the difficulties involved in obtaining travel documents.

24 Non-EU foreign nationals sentenced to more than 12 months imprisonment are automatically liable to be deported. In 2011, those so removed comprised 1825 out of 4500 foreign national offenders deported from the UK (House of Commons, *Hansard*, 7 March 2013, Col 1172W).

25 In 2011, the largest group of people deported came from Asia (55 per cent), followed by Africa (20 per cent), and the Americas (10 per cent). European nationals made 10 per cent of the total, while Middle Eastern nationals comprised 7 per cent (Blinder 2012: 7).

26 The number of EU nationals deported rose from 642 in 2008 to 1726 in 2012, while the number of convicted EEA foreign nationals subject to removal grew from 933 (2010) to 1559 (2012) (House of Commons, *Hansard*, 16 Apr 2013, col 303W and 12 Mar 2013, col 146W).

27 In addition, foreign prisoners are usually not eligible for the training and rehabilitation treatments offered to nationals.

References

Aas, K.F. (2013) 'The ordered and the bordered society: migration control, citizenship and the Northern penal state', in K.F. Aas and M. Bosworth (eds), *The borders of punishment: criminal justice, citizenship and social exclusion*, Oxford: Oxford University Press.

Aas, K.F. (2014) 'Bordered penality: precarious membership and abnormal justice', *Punishment & Society*, 16: 520–541.

Aas, K.F. and Bosworth, M. (eds) (2013) *The borders of punishment: criminal justice, citizenship and social exclusion*, Oxford: Oxford University Press.

Aebi, M. and Delgrande, N. (2010) *Council of Europe annual penal statistics 2008*, Strasbourg: Council of Europe.

Aliverti, A. (2012) 'Making people criminal: the role of the criminal law in immigration enforcement', *Theoretical Criminology*, 16: 417–434.

Aliverti, A. (2013a) *Crimes of mobility: criminal law and the regulation of immigration*, Abingdon: Routledge.

Aliverti, A. (2013b) 'Sentencing in immigration-related cases: the impact of deportability and immigration status', *Prison Service Journal*, (205) (special edition: *Migration, Nationality and Detention*): 39–44.

Anderson, B. (2013) *Us & them? The dangerous politics of immigration control*, Oxford: Oxford University Press.

Ashworth, A. and Zedner, L. (2010) 'Preventive orders: a problem of under-criminalization?', in R. Duff, L. Farmer, S. Marshall, M. Renzo and V. Tadros (eds), *The boundaries of the criminal law*, Oxford: Oxford University Press.

Ashworth, A. and Zedner, L. (2014) *Preventive justice*, Oxford: Oxford University Press.

Bank, J. (2011) 'Foreign national prisoners in the UK: explanations and implications', *The Howard Journal*, 50: 184–198.

Barker, V. (2013) 'Nordic exceptionalism revisited: explaining the paradox of a Janus-faced penal regime', *Theoretical Criminology*, 17: 5–25.

Bauman, Z. (1991) *Modernity and the holocaust*, Cambridge: Polity.

Bauman, Z. (1993) *Modernity and ambivalence*, Cambridge: Polity.

Bauman, Z. (2000) 'Social issues of law and order', *British Journal of Criminology*, 40: 205–221.

Bauman, Z. (2004) *Wasted lives: modernity and its outcasts*, Cambridge: Polity.

Benhabib, S. (1992) *Situating the self: gender, community and postmodernism in contemporary ethics*, Cambridge: Polity.

Berman, G. (2013) *Prison population statistics: briefing papers*, online, available: www.google.co.uk/url?sa=t&rct=j&q=&esrc=s&source=web&cd=2&ved=0CDkQFjAB&

142 *Ana Aliverti*

url=http%3A%2F%2Fwww.parliament.uk%2Fbriefing-papers%2Fsn04334.pdf&ei=
zR7gUaveOuqh0QWIqoCwDQ&usg=AFQjCNFc5woMqfEk6pJKE2rqLrXlLM5o
Yg&sig2=ubz07v2QRVxB2FeNUY1O9A&bvm=bv.48705608,d.d2k (accessed 11 July 2013).

Blinder, S. (2012) *Deportation, removals and voluntary departures from the UK*, Oxford: Migration Observatory, University of Oxford, online, available: www. migrationobservatory.ox.ac.uk/sites/files/migobs/Briefing-Deportations.pdf (accessed 26 June 2014).

Bosniak, L. (2008) *The citizen and the aliens: dilemmas of contemporary membership*, New Jersey: Princeton University Press.

Bosworth, M. (2011) 'Deportation, detention and foreign-national prisoners in England and Wales', *Citizenship Studies*, 15: 583–595.

Bosworth, M. (2012) 'Subjectivity and identity in detention: punishment and society in a global age', *Theoretical Criminology*, 16: 123–140.

Bosworth, M. (2013) 'Can immigration detention centres be legitimate? Understanding confinement in a global world', in K. Franko Aas and M. Bosworth (eds), *The borders of punishment: migration, citizenship, and social exclusion*, Oxford: Oxford University Press.

Bosworth, M. (2014) *Inside immigration detention*, Oxford: Oxford University Press.

Bosworth, M. and Kaufman, E. (2011) 'Foreigners in a carceral age: immigration and imprisonment in the United States', *Stanford Law & Policy Review*, 22: 429–454.

Bowling, B. (2013) 'Epilogue: the borders of punishment – towards a criminology of mobility', in K.F. Aas and M. Bosworth (eds), *The borders of punishment: migration, citizenship, and social control*, Oxford: Oxford University Press.

Castles, S. (2005) 'Hierarchical citizenship in a world of unequal nation-states', *Political Science & Politics*, 38: 689–692.

Chacón, J. (2012) 'Overcriminalizing immigration', *Journal of Criminal Law & Criminology*, 102: 613–652.

Cole, P. (2000) *Philosophies of exclusion: liberal political theory and immigration*, Edinburgh: Edinburgh University Press.

De Giorgi, A. (2010) 'Immigration control, post-Fordism, and less eligibility: a materialist critique of the criminalization of immigration across Europe', *Punishment & Society*, 12: 147–167.

Dembour, M. (2003) 'Human rights law and national sovereignty in collusion: the plight of quasi-nationals at Strasbourg', *Netherlands Quarterly of Human Rights*, 21: 63–98.

Duff, R. (2001) *Punishment, communication and community*, Oxford: Oxford University Press.

Dummett, A. and Nicol, A. (1990) *Subjects, citizens, aliens and others: nationality and immigration law*, London: Weidenfeld and Nicolson.

Eagly, I. (2010) 'Prosecuting immigration', *Northwestern University Law Review*, 104: 1281–1360.

Eagly, I. (2013) 'Criminal justice for noncitizens: an analysis of variation in local enforcement', *New York University Law Review*, 88: 101–191.

Ericson, R. (2007) *Crime in an insecure world*, Cambridge: Polity.

Fraser, N. (2008) 'Abnormal justice', *Critical Inquiry*, 34: 393–422.

Fraser, N. (2010) 'Who counts? Dilemmas of justice in a postWestphalian world', *Antipode*, 41: 281–297.

Gibney, M. (2013) '"A very transcendental power": denaturalisation and the liberalisation of citizenship in the United Kingdom', *Political Studies*, 61: 637–655.

Foreigners, punishment and the liberal state   143

Gilroy, P. (1982) 'Police and thieves', in J. Solomos, B. Findlay, S. Jones and P. Gilroy (eds), *The empire strikes back: race and racism in 70s Britain*, London: Hutchinson in association with the Centre for Contemporary Cultural Studies, University of Birmingham.

Hales, L. and Gelsthorpe, L. (2012) *The criminalisation of migrant women*, Cambridge: Institute of Criminology, University of Cambridge.

HMIP (2009) *Race relations in prisons: responding to adult women from black and minority ethnic backgrounds*, London: HM Inspectorate of Prisons.

Home Office (2013) *Operation of police powers under the Terrorism Act 2000 and subsequent legislation: arrests, outcomes and stop and searches, Great Britain, 2012 to 2013*, London: Home Office.

House of Commons (2013) *Fifteenth report: the work of the immigration directorates (April – September 2013)*, London: The Stationery Office Limited.

Hudson, B. (1998) 'Doing justice to difference', in A. Ashworth and M. Wasik (eds), *Fundamentals of sentencing theory: essays in honour of Andrew von Hirsch*, Oxford: Clarendon Press, Oxford University Press.

Hudson, B. (2003) *Justice in the risk society*, London: Sage.

Hudson, B. (2006) 'Punishing monsters, judging aliens: justice at the borders of community', *Australian & New Zealand Journal of Criminology*, 39: 232–247.

Istat (2012) *Statistiche report: i detenuti nelle carceri Italiane*, Rome: Ministero della Giustizia.

Jamieson, R. (1999) 'Genocide and the social production of immorality', *Theoretical Criminology*, 3: 131–146.

Kohli, A., Markowitz, P. and Chavez, L. (2011) 'Secure communities by the numbers: an analysis of demographics and due process', *Policy Brief October 2011*, Berkeley, CA: University of California.

McLeod, A. (2012) 'The U.S. criminal-immigration convergence and its possible undoing', *American Criminal Law Review*, 49: 105–178.

Melossi, D. (2012) 'The process of criminalization of migrants and the borders of "Fortress Europe"', in J. McCulloch and S. Pickering (eds), *Borders and crime: pre-crime, mobility and serious harm in an age of globalization*, Basingstoke: Palgrave.

Melossi, D. (2013) 'Punishment and migration between Europe and the USA: a transnational "less eligibility"?', in J. Simon and R. Sparks (eds), *The Sage handbook of punishment and society*, London: Sage.

Ministry of Justice (MoJ) (2009) *Public protection manual: foreign nationals*, London: Ministry of Justice and HM Prison Service, online, available: www.justice.gov.uk/downloads/offenders/public-protection-manual/1000489DChapter7ForeignNationalsPPM.pdf (accessed 26 June 2014).

Ministry of Justice (2010) *Offender management caseload statistics 2009*, London: MoJ.

Ministry of Justice (2013a) *Offender management caseload statistics 2012*, London: MoJ.

Ministry of Justice (2013b) *Statistics on race and the criminal justice system*, London: MoJ.

National Audit Office (2014) *Managing and removing foreign national offenders*, London: National Audit Office.

Prison Reform Trust (2012) *No way out*, London: Prison Reform Trust, online, available: www.prisonreformtrust.org.uk/Portals/0/Documents/NoWayOut.pdf (accessed 15 August 2013).

Rienzo, C. and Vargas-Silva, C. (2011) *Migrants in the UK: an overview*, Oxford: Migration Observatory, University of Oxford, online: www.migrationobservatory.ox.ac.uk/briefings/migrants-uk-overview (accessed 7 November 2014).

Sklansky, D. (2012) 'Crime, immigration, and ad hoc instrumentalism', *New Criminal Law Review*, 15: 157–223.

Stumpf, J. (2007) 'The crimmigration crisis: immigrants, crime, and sovereign state', *Lewis & Clark Law School Legal Research Paper Series*, 2: 1–44.

Stumpf, J. (2012) 'The justice of crimmigration law and the security of home', in B. Hudson and S. Ugelvik (eds), *Justice and security in the 21st century*, Abingdon: Routledge.

Ugelvik, T. (2014) 'The incarceration of foreigners in European prisons', in S. Pickering & J. Ham (eds), *Routledge handbook on crime and international migration*, Abingdon: Routledge.

Vázquez, Y. (2011) 'Perpetuating the marginalization of Latinos: a collateral consequence of the incorporation of immigration law into the criminal justice system', *Howard Law Journal*, 54: 639–674.

Vine, J. (2012) *An inspection of how the UK Border Agency and Border Force handle customs and immigration offences at ports*, London: Independent Chief Inspectorate of the UKBA, online, available: http://icinspector.independent.gov.uk/wp-content/up loads/2013/01/An-inspection-of-how-the-UK-Border-Agency-and-Border-Force-ha ndle-customs-and-immigration-offences-at-ports-FINAL-WEB.pdf (accessed 14 August 2013).

Wacquant, L. (2006) 'Penalization, depoliticization, racialization: on the over-incarceration of immigrants in the European Union', in S. Armstrong and L. McAra (eds), *Perspectives on punishment*, New York: Oxford University Press.

Webber, F. (2013) *Deportation on suspicion*, London: Institute of Race Relations, online, available: www.irr.org.uk/news/deportation-on-suspicion (accessed 28 May 2014).

Young, I. (1989) 'Polity and group difference: a critique of the ideal of universal citizenship', *Ethics*, 99: 250–274.

Young, I. (1990) *Justice and the politics of difference*, New Jersey: Princeton University Press.

Zedner, L. (2010) 'Security, the state, and the citizen: the changing architecture of crime control', *New Criminal Law Review*, 13: 379–403.

Zedner, L. (2013) 'Is the criminal law only for citizens? A problem at the borders of punishment', in K.F. Aas and M. Bosworth (eds), *The borders of punishment: criminal justice, citizenship and social exclusion*, Oxford: Oxford University Press.

7 Immigration detention, ambivalence and the colonial Other[1]

Mary Bosworth

Introduction

In common with most economically developed countries, the United Kingdom (UK) expends considerable effort on attempting to identify who among its new arrivals and those already resident has the right to enter or remain in the country. Those without this right are forced to leave. As elsewhere, Britain uses a number of strategies in its pursuit of border security and migration control. This chapter shall concentrate on just one of them: immigration detention.

It may seem strange, given the vociferous and categorical nature of most contemporary political and public discourse on migration, to frame an account of immigration detention through the notion of ambivalence. Yet, as this chapter will demonstrate, many of those within detention centres, as well as individuals working in the immigration sector, seem unclear about the purpose of, nature of and justification for such places. Such uncertainty includes factual questions (How does the system work?) and normative ones (Is it morally right to lock people up on the basis of their citizenship?). Detainees often contest their identity and treatment, while staff mull over the justifications for and efficacy of their tasks, wondering about the moral nature and form of their own role and identity. Most are united by a concern about the duration of detention and the confinement of long-term UK residents.

Ambivalence does not always protect people. Nor does it necessarily reduce the power of the state. Sometimes it amplifies inequalities. It can also compound the pains of detention. Without a clear narrative or justification, detainees (and some staff) struggle to make sense of their experiences. Their confusion is unnerving and painful. In any case, doubt is easily overridden or muted by other forces – particularly, as others have observed elsewhere, by bureaucracy (Bauman 1989; Cohen 2001). It exists in the shadow of and contributes to anti-immigrant discourse, policy and practices of securitization.

Nonetheless, and notwithstanding such caveats, the reservations articulated by staff and detainees reveal how, in the intimate surroundings of custodial institutions that are sites structured by face-to-face encounters, the logic of detention, however partially, may become destabilized. For, despite the liminal and stigmatized status of the institutions and those within them, relationships

146 *Mary Bosworth*

are forged and moments of recognition and empathy occur (Levinas 1961/ 2011). Ambivalence can be institutional and individual. It links into other affective concepts and feelings – particularly ambiguity, anxiety, frustration, anger, trust, despair and moderation. Above all, the words of staff and detainees reveal the salience of identity and an inverse of our usual expectations. Strangers do not raise questions; rather, it is those who are familiar who confound. Whereas immigration detention is based on the belief that certain people simply do not belong, exclusion, it turns out, is morally, as well as practically, difficult to enforce (for more details on the latter, see Gibney 2008, 2013; Aas 2013).

Ambivalent origins

Although the immigration detention system in the UK today owes a lot to the era of New Labour (1997–2010) (Bosworth 2008; Bosworth and Guild 2008), its origins date to the passage of the Immigration Appeals Act 1969 (Bosworth 2014).[2] This piece of legislation, the Member for Bolton, Gordon Cakes, made clear, sprang from concerns that the British Government was failing to treat fairly members of its Commonwealth, who at the time were recognized as culturally and legally British subjects:

> It is very important that we have a system of appeal, and that justice is seen to be done, because of our status as a nation … our prestige as a nation that believes in the rule of law and justice for all its citizens is still unchallenged throughout the world. Yet the very point where a Commonwealth citizen or alien sets foot on our shores has for 55 years been the point where the rules of justice have not applied, where he has had to be subject to an arbitrary decision by a civil servant with no right of appeal. That happens just when he has arrived at the place that he and his countrymen have been taught to regard as the mother of freedom and justice.
> (Mr Gordon Cakes, Bolton, West. HC Deb
> 22 January 1969, vol. 776, col 509)

Turning such people away at the airport, without hearing their appeal, Cakes argued, was unfair and un-British. They deserved the right to have their case heard. Yet for that to happen, the state had to accommodate them.

While an existing building at the airport could hold some arrivals briefly before they were placed on a return flight, it was not sufficient for the number of Commonwealth citizens who were given in-country right of appeal. Nor could it offer adequate accommodation for them while they awaited the decision-making of the immigration service. Forced to act, the government rapidly converted a building outside the airport into the Harmondsworth Immigration Detention Unit, on a site that has been occupied ever since for this purpose.[3]

Much has changed since Harmondsworth opened its doors. Most obviously, the system is considerably larger. These days there are 11 Immigration

Immigrant detention and the colonial Other 147

Removal Centres (IRCs, see Figure 7.1) – renamed thus in 2001 by the Labour government to more clearly signify their intent. An additional 1,000 supplementary beds are available in prison for individuals held under Immigration Act powers. Foreign citizens may also be held for up to five days in police custody, or in a short-term holding facility in ports in the UK and across the Channel in France, and for 24 hours in an immigration reporting office. They may also be detained in hospital or in a young offenders' institution. There is one so-called pre-departure accommodation unit for up to nine families. Together there are at least 4,000 bed spaces, in a system that has an annual turnover of 30,000.

In addition to creating the first immigration detention unit, the Immigration Appeals Act 1969 established the modern bureaucracy of immigration control. Over time, as in other areas of government, this system has grown exponentially, with a web of tribunals, judges and specialist solicitors. Underpinned and legitimated by a series of pieces of legislation on asylum, immigration

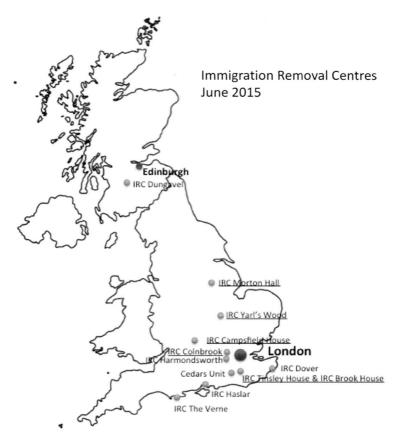

Figure 7.1 UK Immigration removal centres, June 2015

and citizenship (Wilsher 2012; Aliverti 2013), immigration detention is framed by a complex system of laws and policy that seem at times deliberately designed to obfuscate and render unfamiliar and unreachable those within (Bauman 1989).

Finally, and in opposition to some of the proximity-eroding effects of the bureaucracy of detention, there is also a national network of advocacy groups working with and for detainees in the UK. International agencies and non-government organizations assist some to resettle abroad. The whole system is monitored by HM Inspectorate of Prisons (HMIP), the Prison and Probation Ombudsman and the Independent Monitoring Board, who produce regular reports in which aspects of life inside the detention centres are laid bare.

As it was in 1970, Harmondsworth and six of the 11 centres are contracted out to a private custodial company, who run it on behalf of the Home Office. The prison service has responsibility for the remaining four centres with a similar arrangement. Within each centre a complement of Home Office staff oversee the contract and manage the immigration files of the detainees, passing information between them and their caseworker, who decides their fate.[4]

Most detainees and staff are men, with only one centre, Yarl's Wood, set aside for single adult women, although a handful of females can be found at Colnbrook and Dungavel.[5] Female staff, though outnumbered, can be found in all establishments. Detainees tend to congregate in groups from former British colonies, revealing the enduring nature of these ties. Increasingly, they are joined by individuals from current and recent war zones as well as from countries just beyond the margins of the European Union (EU). Many have had an asylum case rejected, while a small number are currently being considered for refugee status. Others are ex-prisoners, visa over-stayers, or entirely undocumented. Anyone facing removal or deportation can be detained, although the size of the estate pales beside the estimates of those living in the community who fit into this category. To some extent, detention has become a potential risk for anyone without citizenship, while remaining uncommon for most.

Uncertainty and ambivalence: making sense of detention

Although the government presents IRCs and border control more broadly as necessary for order and security in a world defined by mass mobility, individual testimonies from detainees and staff reveal a far messier reality. People hold simultaneously conflicting views about these institutions and those held within them. Many staff struggle to understand their job or the people in their care, searching for a clear narrative and explanation of a practice that is often difficult to understand or justify. Detainees, too, are usually unclear why just one aspect of their identity – their citizenship – trumps everything else. They find the nature of the custodial institution in which they are held not only hard to endure, but also difficult to comprehend. These are, in short, institutions about which those within them – detainees and staff alike – feel

Immigrant detention and the colonial Other 149

ambivalent, unsure of their ethical and legal grounding, uncertain about their justification or effect (Bosworth 2013).

The concept of ambivalence has a varied and complex genealogy. On the one hand, its roots can be found in the field of psychoanalysis. It was Sigmund Freud (1919) who first proposed that overcoming and integrating ambivalence towards others (particularly the mother) was central to the task of becoming a subject. When ambivalence is too great, and individuals cannot reconcile themselves, he said, they suffer psychological disorder and trauma. Even when it is managed, they experience a sense of loss, guilt or mourning. Ambivalence, in this account, is integral to the nature of human subjectivity.

Half a decade on, sociologist Robert Merton took up the idea of ambivalence to refer to 'opposing normative tendencies in the social definition of a role' (Merton 1976: 12). 'Unlike the psychological orientation', he wrote:

> the sociological one focuses on the ways in which ambivalence comes to be built into the structure of social statuses and roles. It directs us to examine the processes in the social structure that affect the probability of ambivalence turning up in particular kinds of role-relations. And finally it directs us to the social consequences of ambivalence for the workings of social structures.
>
> (Merton 1976: 5)

People feel uncertain and conflicted, he asserted, 'not because of their idiosyncratic history or their distinctive personality but because the ambivalence is inherent in the social positions they occupy' (Merton 1976: 8).

From a sociological perspective, in other words, ambivalence springs from social organization and structure. It is not merely part of our sense of self, but inherent in the fabric and social structures of the world in which we live. Some people, like migrants, Merton argued, experience such dissonance more than others due to their social-structural position, rather than their biography. Citing Chicago School sociologist Robert Park's (1928) essay 'The marginal man', Merton claimed that resident foreign nationals occupy an awkward liminal space in which they are personally and collectively tied to their origins while searching out new connections and opportunities. They are, as a group, thus particularly susceptible to sociological ambivalence (Merton 1963).

Thirty years later, in *Modernity and ambivalence*, Zygmunt Bauman (1991) revisited the relationship between migration, belonging and social structure. He did not mince words: 'There are friends and enemies. And there are strangers' (Bauman 1991: 51). In this binary, the stranger is 'the bane of modernity … an entity ineradicably ambivalent blurring a boundary line vital to the construction of a particular social order or a particular life-world' (61). In Bauman's view, neo-liberal states in particular are unable to tolerate ambivalence or ambiguity among their residents. Bids to regulate and incarcerate groups whose arrival and existence they cannot prevent, his argument

150 *Mary Bosworth*

suggests, spring from a desire, however impotent and doomed to fail, for order.

There are clear resonances between Bauman's ideas and the growing practice of border control. Critical scholars around the globe have made much of the closing of borders and the recasting of mobility as a security risk and pollutant (Aas 2011; Bigo 2008; Aas and Bosworth 2013). Such notions chime also with the practice of detention. Yet, it is possible to overstate the matter. As I have observed elsewhere (Bosworth 2014: 204), 'from within a multicultural society like the UK, with its long tradition of colonial and postcolonial rule and influence and of offering sanctuary to the politically dispossessed, Bauman's pessimistic insistence on the irrevocable mistrust of the stranger seems overstated and, in its emphasis on the view from nowhere, paternalistic (Ahmed 2000). Who, after all, decides who is the stranger? How do we recognize this figure among our various and varied friends and enemies?'

It is not just that Bauman obscures alternative possibilities, but also that, in his theoretical bent, he overlooks the lived experience of his claims. What is it like to be cast as a stranger? What is it like to live among them? From a researcher's perspective, how might we study uncertainty and ambivalence in the field? What are the methodological implications of these concepts? What is their effect on day-to-day life?

Such questions direct us to the talk surrounding detention, whether in parliamentary debates, media accounts, or, as in this chapter, in the words of staff and detainees. They also return us to matters of subjectivity. This time, rather than Freud, feminist accounts, with their interest in anxiety, trust, uncertainty, agency, guilt, mourning and the law, illuminate the affective, constructed and reconstructed nature of identity (Butler 1995, 1997; Hollway and Featherstone 1997; Parker 1997).

Who is detained and how does it feel to be locked up? What is it like to be a detention custody officer? How do women and men reconcile their fears, frustrations or confusion? Who are these people and how do we recognize them as such? (Bosworth and Slade 2014; Fraser 2007). In posing these kinds of questions, a concern with ambivalence could provide the basis for a critique of, or at least a challenge to, current practice.

Everyday life in detention: coping in an environment of uncertainty

IRCs are notoriously uncertain (Bosworth 2014; Griffiths 2013). In the UK, there is no statutory upper limit to the duration of detention, so, in principle, detainees can be held indefinitely (Stefanelli 2011). While policy and case law[6] should limit detention to those who are facing imminent departure, the reality is that nobody can know for sure for how long they will be confined.

Time is not the only uncertain aspect of detention. Identity is also contested. On the one hand, 'Border control targets those whose identity has been already fixed as a foreigner, rather than offenders, whose identity is linked to behaviour. The mere fact they are in detention is evidence enough of their foreign identity and deportability' (Bosworth 2014: 174). On the other hand, nationality is just one axis of most people's sense of self. In any case, most foreigners, even those whose immigration status could allow for detention, will not be confined. For those within detention, the arbitrary nature of their pathway to detention compounds their frustration and confusion.[7]

Although strictly speaking a purely legal category, citizenship is for many more fluid. Not only did the women and men in this research attempt to assert alternative forms of 'equivalent citizenship' as tax-payers, mothers, hard workers (Bosworth 2012), but they found it difficult to accept the overweening logic of a passport. 'My dad was British', Aufa[8] pointed out.

> He was here in 1958 and my mum, everybody got it. But when I applied, because I have criminal record in 1988 right, and they refuse, and they told me to apply again. But I never bothered .... I wasn't a traveller. Or maybe I go after three, four years once in Pakistan, yeah. And I don't really need visa. I wasn't thinking about is a British passport important.
>
> (Pakistan, Brook House)

Facing deportation, Aufa had only belatedly realized his precarity and the effect it would have on his intimate relationships. 'The kids aren't going to come with me. They're teenagers, they're 16, 13, 19. They don't want to know Pakistan. Wife don't want to go Pakistan. Dad's here, all like, all my first cousins, my uncles' (Pakistan, Brook House).

Those, like Aufa, who had resided in the UK since childhood felt British regardless of their legal status. While their nationality may have been otherwise, culturally and emotionally, they pointed out (and some staff agreed), they were embedded in the UK. Like those first arrivals in Harmondsworth, such people hailed overwhelmingly from the 'New Commonwealth': India, Pakistan, Bangladesh, Jamaica and Nigeria. 'I've got family, I've got kids', Ridoy pointed out. 'I've got parents living here. I've got friends. I grew up here. I went to school. I went to college' (Bangladesh, Morton Hall). His immigration problem, like Aufa's, was that he had committed a crime. In so doing, he activated the mandatory deportation rule set up in the UK Borders Act 2007,[9] introduced following media criticism of the government in 2006, when it became known that over a 10-year period around 1,000 foreign prisoners had failed to be considered for deportation as the rules required. This scandal, which cost then Home Secretary Charles Clarke his job, signalled a shift in the debate in the UK over detention, in which the 'bogus asylum seeker' became replaced by the 'dangerous' foreign national offender (Bosworth and Guild 2008; Kaufman 2013). Such concerns have yet to abate (NAO 2014) and have, as Emma Kaufman observes, radically shifted the meaning and effect of the prison – from punishment, deterrence and rehabilitation to exclusion and the identification of citizens (Kaufman 2013, 2015; Kaufman and Bosworth 2013).

152　*Mary Bosworth*

The differential treatment of a system that promises to reintegrate citizens while excluding foreigners feels painful and unfair. Matters are compounded for those who have lived in the UK for a long time, since, as Ridoy pointed out:

> I didn't come as a criminal from my country. I came as a child. If anything, your, your country and this country have made me the criminal, if that's how they want to label me. Because that's how they want to label me. I don't see any difference between me and my siblings. But my siblings are British, and, and I didn't make the passport. So I'm getting penalized for that reason.
>
> (Bangladesh, Morton Hall)

Detention custody officers were often, at least momentarily, troubled by accounts like these. It was not that everyone agreed that all long-term residents should stay. Ex-offenders like Ridoy and Aufa, in particular, sparked mixed views. On the one hand, staff felt like they had served their sentence. On the other hand, some were afraid of the dangers they might pose, or impatient to expel those who had broken the law. Detainees, too, objected to being held alongside those who had served a criminal sentence, perceiving them as a threat to their own security and stigmatizing by association.

Nor did many staff or all detainees argue that removal centres should be closed and borders opened. To the contrary, even those awaiting deportation usually accepted that states could dictate such matters. Not everyone resident in the UK, they asserted, had a right to remain.

Nonetheless, most people struggled, at least in part, to come to terms with what they were doing and experiencing. Staff, at all levels, were inconsistent in their accounts, frequently wondering who should determine such matters. Often, and in contrast to public discourse, they were sympathetic to former offenders. They preferred some nationalities to others. Some were sympathetic to asylum seekers. Others steadfastly refused to believe their stories.

Most predictably, detainees felt that their incarceration was unfair. Few detainees accepted that they were the kinds of people who should not be allowed to stay. The view that it was always someone else who deserved such an approach was common. Their crimes and personal life were rarely considered to be a sufficient reason for their expulsion, even though some admitted that their legal status allowed for it. They did not want or deserve it. Even so, they were not necessarily opposed to border control altogether. Instead, they set up a hierarchy of deserts, in which they were the ones badly treated. Such a viewpoint tended to rest on three types of claims: the British state, women and men claimed, unfairly overlooked (their) meaningful, long-term ties; the Home Office did a bad job of identifying risk and dangerousness in former offenders; and the British Government was blind to the dangers people would face at home.

Such matters, as the quotes above demonstrate, were not mutually exclusive. Long-term British residents who had been convicted of criminal acts

Immigrant detention and the colonial Other 153

slotted into at least two categories of identification. They could face a dangerous and difficult life in their homeland. On occasion their criminal offence related to their asylum case, as they had been convicted of document fraud.[10]

Those who were seeking asylum often faced an uphill battle. 'No-one wants to talk to us or believe us', Masun complained (Iraq, Tinsley House). By virtue of their location in detention, the asylum cases of these women and men had already been judged without merit. Under these circumstances, they found it difficult to lay claim to this identity position and its legal protections.[11]

Detainees did not only contest their identities, but also the nature of the centres in which they were held. In their complaints, they often drew parallels between their treatment and other practices and institutions. Some, like Ken, objected to the involvement of the private sector. 'It is all a business for them!' he expostulated bitterly. 'They don't care about people. This is modern slavery. They just lock you up to make business out of you' (Nigeria, Tinsley House). Boseda agreed, proposing a broader analogy, in which the similarities to slavery were not limited to financial gain but related to the manner in which detainees were treated. 'The worst of this is the humiliation, the horrible treatment, the inhuman treatment', he moaned. 'It is slavery, like they did with generations before, they are doing with us. Otherwise why would they keep in detention for five months someone who has committed no crime? This is enslavement of us' (Nigeria, Tinsley House).

More typically detainees (and staff) compared detention to prison. As I have written about elsewhere, there are a number of overlaps between IRCs and prisons, from their staff to the razor wire that surrounds them (Bosworth 2007, 2012, 2014). At the time the research was conducted, around 50 per cent of those in detention had served a prison sentence. People's views, however, were inconsistent.

For some, detention was just another form of imprisonment. 'This place is prison', Aatifa asserted angrily (Pakistan, Yarl's Wood). For others, detention was far better. 'When I came to detention centre [after prison]', Ike recalled:

it was a release. I feel free in here. You can do anything you want. No one tells you every second what to do. No one structures every minute of your day, saying eat now, get out now. The facilities are very good in here, food is good, and officers are very good.

The difference between the two institutions, he explained, lay in their staff:

In prison they are very closed-minded. There was only one officer that was very good. She anticipated your needs before you needed them and did her best to explain you things and do them for you. In here most officers are very nice. They treat you well. You are free in here. The only thing missing is being able to go outside, but I can talk to my family any time I want during the day.

(Jamaica, Tinsley House)

154   *Mary Bosworth*

For Ike, the distinction between prison and detention affected how he saw himself. Previously employed in a skilled, white-collar job, Ike had lost his indefinite leave to remain as a result of a criminal conviction. Prison had, in that sense, changed him. More broadly speaking, it had been an environment in which he could not be himself. Despite being the threshold to his deportation, however, Tinsley House, he asserted, did not have the same effect:

> I would recommend this place to people who are in trouble outside. I would tell them to come here and sort their head out; this is like being on benefits. The prison has changed me for life and I will never forget. Here it is 150 per cent better. The officers here are not rude to you and you don't give them trouble. Only 0.5 per cent might give them trouble in here if they know they are being deported and know that the officers will ask them to. When I drive past the prison I want to change the route and not go past there, but when I drive past here I have no trouble at all. I would not recommend prison to my enemy and I would recommend this to my friends.
>
> (Jamaica, Tinsley House)

Elsewhere, in the high-security establishment IRC Colnbrook, male detainees were far more critical. In a direct contradiction to Ike's account, Giv argued that detention custody officers failed to match up to their counterparts in prison. 'A prison officer has to, you know, pass some exams and everything to get that job', he observed. Detention custody officers did not seem to have been as well trained. 'This [place] should be same', he asserted:

> I say this is should be same as a prison, because first night when I came here, I been hold in reception for about six, seven hours. In end when I start complaining they, I said, 'Look, even a prison doesn't do that, you know, three hours maximum you stay in the reception and they take you to the wing. What you doing?' They said, 'No, actually this is run exactly the same as a prison, you know, regime.' I thought, 'No way!' Right. So if it's in that aspect is same to prison, this is what it should be as well, you know, hire somebody who got qualifications properly.
>
> (Iran, Colnbrook)

For Giv, an asylum seeker from Iran who had served a prison sentence for a violent crime, the problem with immigration detention was precisely that it was not a prison (see also Bosworth 2010).

While at first glance such testimonies are confusing, the comparison between detention centre and prison, whatever the verdict, reveals the same point: *in each case detainees were looking for a position from which to make a moral and ethical claim.* Whereas Ike found the staff in Tinsley House more respectful and empathetic, Giv felt that the absence of clear rights generated moral distance, creating a disrespectful and incompetent workforce. In both cases, the men aspired to inclusion despite their position within an inherently exclusionary institution. When considered in this light, the ongoing comparison with the prison makes sense, since for all but a few, penal institutions typify that paradoxical relationship between inclusion and exclusion, as prisoners will, eventually, be released.

It was not only detainees who pondered the relationship between IRCs and the prison. Staff did as well. Like detainees, they too were unpredictable in their views. Sometimes, prison was held up as a preferable form of confinement, a potential means of reform. In terms of the open-ended nature of detention, for example, many believed that prisons offered a better model. Reflecting a commonly held view, Scot was clear, 'They just need to change the law to get rid of indefinite detention. We don't hold any prisoners like that. It doesn't make sense' (SMT, Yarl's Wood). Solon from Brook House agreed: 'There should be a max, max of six months' (DCO, Brook House).

For other reasons staff sometimes expressed a wish that IRCs were more prison-like. Their salaries, they thought, would be higher. Their ability to control those in their care would be greater. Their jobs would be more secure, and their job status higher (Bosworth and Slade 2014).

At other times, however, staff members eschewed the relevance of the prison altogether. It was not just that most staff did not actually aspire to be prison guards, but also that they did not believe that detainees should be treated like prisoners. As Alisa asserted:

> We should give them what facilities they need ... I don't think personally that anyone detained should have to live in wings ... because they've only broke the law of paperwork, haven't they really? It's different if they're murderers or drug barons and things like that, then they deserve to be locked up and locked down, in my opinion. But not detention, no.
>
> (DCO, Tinsley House)

Her colleague Allen concurred. 'You've got to try and respect them while they're there', he remarked, 'Because they're not there for punishment .... If they've been to prison, they've done their punishment. They're there to sort their immigration case out' (DCO, Tinsley House).

Again, rather than adjudicating between these claims, in a futile attempt to establish the relative merits and weaknesses of these two forms of custody, such claims are more fruitfully considered as representative of the institutional uncertainty of IRCs. These are sites that, notwithstanding their razor wire and architectural design which apes that of the prison, are not entirely penal. Those within who have been convicted of a criminal offence are not serving a sentence. Without that clear logic, Solon made clear, the purpose and effect of detention are rendered opaque:

> I just think places like this are a waste of money ... I don't believe in detention centres as a whole. Believe in prisons. You know, we've always had them. But I don't really see the need for this sort of thing now.

Immigration is such a big problem. Got 8,000 people in centres [sic], there could be 15 million in England. Such a small proportion that it's almost a waste of money.

(DCO, Brook House)

Such a view was often compounded by a lack of clarity about the population. We have already seen how staff worried about the justice of removing long-term residents. They were also critical of the failure to deport ex-prisoners from the prison. Why send such people to detention, they wondered. Surely they should leave the country on the day on which their prison sentence ends (Kaufman and Bosworth 2013).

As was often the case, one senior officer explained, such issues could be connected. Arabella noted:

If they were British citizens, no matter what crime they had committed, whether it be murder, rape, child porn, most horrendous things, they get a sentence, say it was, you know, X. They serve their sentence, say, say they'd served two years, and, and they'd got a sentence, you know, whatever, or three years, and done one and a half years. They then do another one and a half years on licence, but they still get to go home. And unless they breach that licence they, they're, they're at home, aren't they, with their family. But these guys do the one and a half years, thank you very much, and then they [the Home Office] go, 'Right, well, you're gonna be deported so we're not gonna let you out on the street. We're sending you to detention. But because we haven't got everything that we need you might stay there for another four years.' So they've actually done longer in detention than what they did for the original crime.

(DCM, Morton Hall)

Such an outcome, Arabella claimed, was not only difficult for detainees, but also for staff. The men in Morton Hall, understandably enough, she felt, found their treatment upsetting. 'I try and see it from their point of view', she said. 'It is very frustrating. And I can see, and I understand the frustration' (DCM, Morton Hall). Her concern was not limited to the detainees, however. Rather, for Arabella the whole system was problematic and, in its inefficiencies and confusion, shaped her professional sense of self. First of all, she argued, custodial staff felt disempowered. This was a common complaint. 'There's very little we can do about it', Arabella explained.

And, and that, that in itself is, like, you're just continually getting their anger for something nobody can change. Nobody here can change. And that in itself is frustrating for us, and very frustrating for them, and we're just in a no-win situation.

(DCM, Morton Hall)

The problem, she thought, rested elsewhere, in the organizational structure of detention, and particularly in the hands of the immigration authority.

Unlike prisons, IRCs are governed locally and at a distance by a range of government and non-government actors and agencies. While day-to-day life is dictated by the custodial staff and the terms of the custodial contract, immigration matters are handled exclusively by the Home Office. Each removal centre houses a complement of immigration officers, whose job is to pass information between the detainees and their caseworkers, who determine when or whether they will be deported. Such figures, who wield ultimate power, rarely if ever meet those about whom they are making decisions (Bosworth and Bradford forthcoming).

This distance, while evidently effective as a means of eroding proximity and thus minimizing the kinds of claims that detainees might be able to make, was, in most people's view, extremely inefficient and hard to justify. From Arabella's perspective, for instance, the distance between these decision-makers and the subjects affected by their rulings made her job much more challenging: 'I just think there's so many things that could be changed that people are ignoring cos they don't have to deal with it' (DCM, Morton Hall). There were also ongoing errors:

> So, like, the UKBA [UK Border Agency] side, they, the most ridiculous things happen ... I mean, for example, we watch them issue removal directions to the wrong detainee. So there's a detainee going, 'Oh, my God, I'm going.' And then they're not. They go, 'This ain't me.' So they then go through all the frustration that they're being deported to Pakistan when they're from Bangladesh, panicking that they think, 'Oh, my God, what's happening?', and it isn't even him.
>
> (DCM, Morton Hall)

Such accusations, which were made in every establishment by staff and detainees alike, were compounded by other concerns about the Home Office and its inner workings. At the most basic level, officers did not understand the immigration process. 'I don't understand immigration', Rebecca admitted, 'and ... it's not my job to understand it' (DCM, Brook House). The problem was not only that she did not fully grasp how decisions were made – a common complaint (Bosworth and Kellezi 2012) – but that Rebecca was unsure about their moral standing. 'When you're sending an 80-year-old woman back to Zimbabwe', she observed:

> where she's sitting on the floor of her room, crying her eyes out. ... Crying her eyes out, saying, 'My son's been killed. My husband was killed, my daughter – I don't know where she is, what's happened to her. I watched a baby being cut out of somebody's stomach.' And they were sending her back to Zimbabwe to nobody. And you've got to escort her to the van that's going to take her to the airport. It just, you can't think

about it, you can't .... Yes it may have been a whole pack of lies, she may have been the biggest drugs dealer in the world, I don't know ... it's not for me to judge but ... it was heart breaking, to be perfectly honest with you.

(DCM, Brook House)

Although this is an extreme example, nearly all staff expressed reservations about the treatment of particular individuals. While the cases that generated sympathy often resonated with broader, racialized and gendered ideas, the variety of staff as well as the range of concerned accounts I heard would guard against too cynical an interpretation. Instead, their emotions, whether hesitation, confusion and guilt, or anger, frustration and indifference, revealed quite clearly that when it is close and personal, border control is difficult to enforce.

This is not a story of heroism, however. No officer interviewed ever reported refusing to follow orders. Despite their qualms, they fulfilled their tasks and secured the border. Moral concerns can, indeed, be silenced by task-focused bureaucracy and by an authoritarian and complex power structure (Bauman 1989; Hall 2012). Officers could deny and turn away from their feelings (Bauman and Donskis 2013), laying the blame at the door of the Home Office, the detainee, their superior officer.

In this respect, the limits of ambivalence are revealed, and, perhaps counter-intuitively, its critical potential as well. While complaints about the overall system, particularly the Home Office, were widespread and vehement, custodial staff were usually moved by only a handful of individual stories. In these examples, as well as the cases where officers took an opposing view, the power of denial and its relationship to recognition and misrecognition come into view. Whereas Bauman argues that ambivalence arises from unknowability and the stranger, in detention, *ambivalence springs from the recognition of shared humanity.* Such recognition generates uncertainty and, on occasion, shame. These unsettling and unpleasant emotions must be addressed or denied (Bosworth 2014; Cohen 2001).

The paradox posed by recognition is most clearly apparent in the staff testimonies about children. These days in the UK, children should only ever be detained briefly as part of family groups in the Cedars' pre-departure accommodation or in Tinsley House. When the research was underway, however, a small number of them continued to be housed in the women's establishment, Yarl's Wood. At that time, their numbers were in decline, as the coalition government observed one of the Liberal Democrats' pre-election promises. While the official view, a member of the senior management team made clear, was that children had no place in detention (Bosworth 2014: 200), officers were more conflicted.

'I liked having kids here', Lily ruefully admitted. 'I probably shouldn't say that, but it was nice for us. I liked messing about with them. We had a lot of fun. We would put up the bouncy castle in the gym and mess about. And you know, it was a nice change. Sometimes we get sick of just dealing with the females, so it was more fun' (DCO, Yarl's Wood). Children thus offered Lily an alternative role to her usual one. She did not have to control them as she did the adult women. Instead, she was allowed to play with them. By engaging in distinct activities with the children, Lily could be a different person. Their presence, in other words, altered her sense of self, reminding us of Levinas's observations on the integral nature of the 'Other' to our ethical frame (Levinas 1961/2011).

Given the overwhelming evidence about the deleterious impact of detention on children, we can see that Lily had expended considerable effort in over-looking (misrecognizing) the children themselves and their suffering, in reca-librating her sense of self. Not all of her colleagues were up to the task. 'Going down to reception at 2 o'clock in the morning', Sean recalled, 'and bringing a family with three children that have still got their school uniforms and satchels on their back, that took a bit of swallowing, that did, yeah' (DCO, Yarl's Wood). For this man, under these circumstances, the presence of children was unnerving. Unlike their parents, they had not firmly been 'Othered'. Their status as children trumped their nationality and so, in con-trast to Lily, who found affirmation in their presence, Sean felt uncomfortable and uneasy. Their youth and their school uniforms were clearly out of place. They were also, his testimony makes clear, in the wrong time. Children should be in bed at 2 am – and not being booked into a detention centre.

Denial: the cost of ambivalence

In reflecting on their job, individual staff could often be erratic. Rebecca, for instance, from Brook House, who otherwise seemed sympathetic and concerned, fluctuated between sympathy and dislike for the detainees. She differentiated starkly between them on the basis of their nationality, praising Jamaicans and Nigerians, while condemning Iraqis and Afghanis. Memorably, she also claimed that she could 'tell someone's nationality by the shape of their head' (DCM, Brook House).

A psychoanalytically informed approach to ambivalence might focus on the cost to staff of admitting and denying the humanity of the detainees. A materi-alist one would emphasize their economic precariousness, as poorly paid and insecure employees. In both counts, it is clear that staff have limited tools to navigate the moral and ethical challenges of enforcing the border.

In acknowledging their fears and emotions, these staff can feel vulnerable. Their job becomes difficult to justify and, in response, many turn away. 'This place', Solon noted:

> It just like erases your senses. Bit drastic, but I think that's how it is. I think it just sickens you up, this job. I think it's the same for prison officers. It'll just sicken you up. If you don't, you'll take it to heart too much, and then that's when it starts affecting you in your head. So you just deflect it off.
> (DCO, Brook House)

160 *Mary Bosworth*

Unlike prison officers, who can conjure notions of 'deserts' or 'rehabilitation' to justify or legitimate their career, those working in detention have no straightforward rationale for their job. They fundamentally lack a clear ethical framework to guide their actions and responses (Bauman 1993). In their search for solutions, the cause and nature of their ambivalence are revealed.

Some subscribe to a nationalist account of border control, a view that, all too often, is racialized (Bosworth and Kellezi 2014). According to an officer in Yarl's Wood healthcare unit, for example:

> the Jamaican ladies are quite difficult because – I'd imagine the officers probably find the same – culturally, they're very, they're quite loud, they're quite shouty. And, you know, they'll stand at that desk and they're going, 'Ha, ha, ha, ha, ha', and you're going, 'Stop shouting'. 'I'm not shouting.' And they don't think they are shouting [laughs] but actually you're like that behind, behind the counter. That can be quite difficult. But we, we always try and take everybody on an individual basis.
>
> (DCM, Yarl's Wood)

Officers are taught to mistrust the accounts of those in their care, revealing the distancing effect of discourses of securitization (Bigo, 2008). 'There is a very fine line between empathy and conditioning', Luke explained:

> We are not meant to be sympathetic because we didn't cause the problem. If you're empathetic then it's easy for them to ask for something. You're dwelling in their past and that's affecting you and you're not dealing with them. So, helping them is a problem.
>
> (DCO, Colnbrook)

Nonetheless, many of the staff presented themselves as 'caring' for people under difficult circumstances. 'It is difficult, seeing people being removed, [and] in some cases to places they are being taken to are not safe', Abayomi admitted. 'In some cases you really feel for them' (Chaplaincy, Tinsley House). Often the same individuals will take both approaches, depending on their view of a particular detainee. Everyone is compassionate sometimes. Morality, it seems, is context specific, not universal.

Most try to externalize the problem, blaming either the detainees or the Home Office for the problems they see. Usually, both are found wanting. Most importantly of all, Abayomi makes clear, staff steer clear of discussing or getting involved in what detainees are really concerned about: their immigration case. 'We do not advise on immigration issues', he said simply. 'We are not lawyers' (Chaplaincy, Tinsley House). Together, these attitudes and behaviours can create considerable normative uncertainty, as Rebecca made clear:

> We've got to go and use force on somebody, you're potentially forcing somebody into a situation where they're going to be taken back and

Immigrant detention and the colonial Other 161

tortured, killed, whatever. And I'm not suggesting that happens every time, but there have been occasions where you think, 'Is it right, what I'm doing?' Moral, you know?

(DCM, Brook House)

Conclusion

As this chapter has demonstrated, ambiguity and doubt have characterized the pursuit of immigration detention since it began (see also Bosworth 2014: chap. 1). While ambivalent and uncertain voices are often drowned out by their opponents, a number of concerns, confusions and critiques have always been present. Such matters deserve attention and raise the possibility for thinking and acting otherwise (Hemmings 2012).

It is important not to overstate the potential for change, under current political and legal structures. So, too, we should not deny that 'ambivalence' itself can, for seemingly benign reasons, facilitate detention. Uncertainty can also be painful. Yet, the hesitations and anxieties evident among detainees and staff alike are striking. Notwithstanding their cultural, ethnic or other forms of difference, these accounts reveal that people held in detention are often familiar, with recognizable aspirations, anxieties and plans. Despite their precarity, their lives matter (Butler 2004, 2009). They are not, in fact, strangers after all.

Notes

1 Thanks to Oxford University Press for granting permission to reproduce previously published material in this chapter. Mary also gratefully acknowledges funding from the European Research Council under her Starting Grant (313362) Subjectivity, Identity and Penal Power.

2 However, the power to detain foreigners as foreigners has existed for far longer still (Wilsher 2012; Bosworth 2014; Wray 2006).

3 These days, the original site is occupied by IRC Colnbrook, while IRC Harmondsworth is just next door.

4 This aspect, in which the key determining figure in the immigration management of detainees is offsite and never meets them, demonstrates the importance of proximity in building ethical relationships founded on empathy and recognition. The system, which has few supporters within the detention estate, is not, however, as Bauman might lead us to expect, rational or particularly efficient. Instead, caseworkers are notorious for losing files, failing to manage removals or accurately identify those behind bars. Their work has been the subject of official critique (HMIP and ICISBI 2012), although as yet we lack a sustained academic account of this aspect of border control (see Bosworth and Bradford forthcoming; see also Bosworth 2014).

5 Since March 2011, Yarl's Wood has included a small short-term unit for single men. It also usually has a small number of men in adult family groups.

6 In 1984, Hardial Singh appealed his post-sentence detention in Durham prison (*R. v. Governor of Durham Prison, ex-parte Hardial Singh*, [1984] 1 WLR 704). In his ruling, then Justice Woolf made the first legal statement about the indefinite nature of detention. 'While the power given to the Secretary of State to detain individuals is not subject to an express time limit', Woolf determined, 'it does have

162 *Mary Bosworth*

limitations. The detainee can only be detained if he is subject to a deportation order, or is awaiting his removal. Further this period of waiting is limited to what can be deemed reasonably necessary for the Secretary of State to act to remove the detainee. If he is not acting with reasonable speed, then the Secretary of State must cease the detention' (Woolf, J., at p. 706, *R v. Governor of Durham Prison ex. parte Hardial Singh* [1984] 1 WLR 704). Known as the 'Hardial Singh principles', this statement was the first attempt to determine the foundations of a time limit to detention in case law – a goal that has yet to be achieved in UK law.

7 Some were detained as they 'signed on' as an asylum seeker, others as a result of a workplace raid. Still others had been caught when immigration officers came to their door looking for someone else. Everyone seemed to know someone with similar legal status who had either never been detained or had been released.

8 A pseudonym. All names of participants have been changed.

9 The UK Borders Act made detention mandatory for former foreign national prisoners from outside the European Economic Area (EEA) sentenced to more than 12 months in prison, irrespective of when their removal was likely to be scheduled. The EEA includes all 27 Member States of the EU plus Norway, Iceland and Liechtenstein.

10 Although there is an accepted human right to seek asylum, Britain has criminalized arriving without a passport or using a false passport. Currently, a number of cases where the individual was convicted, served a prison sentence and subsequently was awarded refugee status have been returned to the Court of Appeal by the Criminal Cases Review Commission (Hoyle and Sato, forthcoming). Such people, unless they are awarded refugee status, may end up in detention, due to the mandatory deportation requirements of the UK Borders Act.

11 In fact, this individual was granted temporary admission to further his asylum claim.

References

Aas, K. F. (2011) '"Crimmigrant" bodies and bona fide travellers: surveillance, citizenship and global governance', *Theoretical Criminology*, 15: 331–346.

Aas, K. F. (2013) *Globalization and crime*, London: SAGE.

Aas, K. F. and Bosworth, M. (2013) *The borders of punishment: migration, citizenship and social exclusion*, Oxford: Oxford University Press.

Ahmed, S. (2000) *Strange encounters: embodied others in post-coloniality*, London: Routledge.

Aliverti, A. (2013) *Crimes of mobility: criminal law and the regulation of immigration*, Abingdon: Routledge

Bauman, Z. (1989) *Modernity and the Holocaust*, Cambridge: Polity Press.

Bauman, Z. (1991) *Modernity and ambivalence*, Cambridge: Polity Press.

Bauman, Z. (1993) *Postmodern ethics*, Cambridge: Polity Press.

Bauman, Z. and Donskis, L. (2013) *Moral blindness: the loss of sensitivity in liquid modernity*, Cambridge: Polity Press.

Bigo, D. (2008) 'Globalized (in)security: the field and the ban-opticon', in D. Bigo and A. Tsoukala (eds), *Terror, insecurity and liberty: illiberal practices of liberal regimes after 9/11*, London: Routledge.

Bosworth, M. (2007) 'Border crossings: immigration detention and the exclusive society', in M. Lee (ed.), *Human Trafficking*, Collumpton: Willan Publishing.

Bosworth, M. (2008) 'Border control and the limits of the sovereign state', *Social & Legal Studies*, 17: 199–215.

Immigrant detention and the colonial Other   163

Bosworth, M. (2010) 'Reinventing penal parsimony: an introduction', *Theoretical Criminology*, 14: 251–256.

Bosworth, M. (2012) 'Subjectivity and identity in detention: punishment and society in a global age', *Theoretical Criminology*, 16: 123–140.

Bosworth, M. (2013) 'Can immigration detention be legitimate?' in K. F. Aas and M. Bosworth (eds), *Migration and punishment: citizenship, crime control, and social exclusion*, Oxford: Oxford University Press.

Bosworth, M. (2014), *Inside immigration detention*, Oxford: Oxford University Press.

Bosworth, M., and Guild, M. (2008) 'Governing through migration control: security and citizenship in Britain', *The British Journal of Criminology*, 48: 703–719.

Bosworth, M. and Kellezi, B. (2012) *Quality of life in detention: results from the MQLD questionnaire data collected in IRC Yarl's Wood, IRC Tinsley House and IRC Brook House, August 2010–June 2011*, Oxford University, Centre for Criminology.

Bosworth, M. and Kellezi, B. (2014) 'Citizenship and belonging in a women's immigration detention centre', in C. Phillips and C. Webster (eds), *New directions in race, ethnicity and crime*, Abingdon: Routledge.

Bosworth, M. and Slade, G. (2014) 'In search of recognition: gender and staff–detainee relations in a British immigration detention centre', *Punishment & Society*, 16: 146–164.

Bosworth, M. and Bradford, B. (forthcoming), 'Case worker decision making and legitimacy in immigration control'.

Butler, J. (1995) *Bodies that matter: on the discursive limits of sex*, New York: Routledge.

Butler, J. (1997) *The psychic life of power: theories in subjection*, Stanford, CA: Stanford University Press.

Butler, J. (2004) *Precarious life: the powers of mourning and violence*, London: Verso.

Butler, J. (2009) *Frames of war: when is life grievable?*, New York: Verso.

Cohen, S. (2001) *States of denial: knowing about atrocities and suffering*, Cambridge: Polity Press.

Fraser, N. (2007) 'Transnationalizing the public sphere: on the legitimacy and efficacy of public opinion in a post-Westphalian world', *Theory, Culture and Society*, 24: 7–30.

Freud, S. (1919) *Totem and taboo: resemblances between the psychic lives of savages and neurotics*, London: G. Routledge & Sons.

Gibney, M. (2008) 'Asylum and the expansion of deportation in the United Kingdom', *Government and Opposition*, 43: 146–167.

Gibney, M. (2013) 'Deportation, crime, and the changing character of membership in the United Kingdom', in K. F. Aas and M. Bosworth (eds), *The borders of punishment: citizenship, migration and social exclusion*, Oxford: Oxford University Press.

Griffiths, M. (2013) 'Living with uncertainty: indefinite immigration detention', *Journal of Legal Anthropology*, 1: 263–286.

Hall, A. (2012) *Border watch: cultures of immigration, detention and control*, London: Pluto Press.

HC Deb 22 January 1969, vol. 776, col 509.

Hemmings, C. (2012) 'Affective solidarity: feminist reflexivity and political transformation', *Feminist Theory*, 13: 147–161.

HMIP and ICISBI (2012) *The effectiveness and impact of immigration detention casework: a joint thematic review by HM Inspectorate of Prisons and the Independent Chief Inspector of Borders and Immigration*, London: HMIP and ICIBI, online, available at: www.justice.gov.uk/downloads/publications/inspectorate-reports/hmip

164   *Mary Bosworth*

ris/thematic-reports-and-research-publications/immigration-detention-ca sework-2012.pdf (accessed 15 December 2014).

Hollway, W. and Featherstone, B. (eds) (1997) *Mothering and ambivalence*, London: Routledge.

Hoyle, C. and Sato, M. (forthcoming) 'Last chance for justice: the CCRC's response to the wrongful conviction of asylum seekers', unpublished paper.

Kaufman, E. (2013) 'Hubs and spokes: the transformation of the British prison', in K. F. Aas and M. Bosworth (eds), *The borders of punishment: migration, citizenship and social exclusion*, Oxford: Oxford University Press.

Kaufman, E. (2015) *Punish and expel: border control, nationalism and the new purpose of the prison*, Oxford: Oxford University Press.

Kaufman, E. and Bosworth, M. (2013) 'Prison and national identity: citizenship, punishment and the sovereign state', in D. Scott (ed.), *Why prison?*, Cambridge: Cambridge University Press.

Levinas, E. (1961/2011) *Totality and infinity: an essay on exteriority*, trans. A. Lingis, New York: Springer.

Merton, R. K. (1963) 'Sociology and ambivalence', in E. Tiryakian (ed.), *Sociological theory values and sociological change*, New York: The Free Press.

Merton, R. K. (1976) *Sociological ambivalence and other essays*, New York: The Free Press.

National Audit Office (NAO) (2014) *Managing and removing foreign offenders*, London: NAO, online, available: www.nao.org.uk/wp-content/uploads/2014/10/Ma naging-and-removing-foreign-national-offenders.pdf (accessed 15 December 2014).

Park, R. (1928) 'Human migration and the marginal man', *The American Journal of Sociology*, XXXIII: 881–893.

Parker, R. (1997) 'The production and purposes of maternal ambivalence', in W. Hollway and B. Featherstone (eds), *Mothering and ambivalence*, London: Routledge.

Stefanelli, J. N. (2011) 'Whose rule of law? An analysis of the UK's decision not to opt-in to the EU asylum procedures and reception conditions Directives', *International & Comparative Law Quarterly*, 60: 1055–1064.

Wilsher, D. (2012) *Immigration detention: law, history, politics*, Cambridge: Cambridge University Press.

Wray, H. (2006) 'The Aliens Act 1905 and the Immigration Dilemma', *Journal of Law and Society*, 33: 302–333.

Cases

R. v. Governor of Durham Prison, ex-parte Hardial Singh, [1984] 1 WLR 704.

8 Controlling Roma in Norway[1]
Governing through the administration of social distance

Nicolay B. Johansen

Introduction

In this chapter I sketch the control policies used to target the non-native, mostly Romanian Roma population in Norway and how these policies bring about undocumented levels of suffering. These policies have the more or less explicit goal of driving these groups out of the country, and in this chapter I investigate the attributes and underlying rationale of this strategy. My point of departure is that Roma are subjected to control policies that deviate from a narrow penal tradition, and despite being non-members of Norwegian society they are on the receiving end of an elaborate array of indirect control measures. It is my claim that these control strategies depend on the creation of more or less closed social fields that I call a 'funnel'. In using the metaphor of a 'funnel', my intention is to suggest something that is an alternative to the use of brute force. A funnel directs people to a certain destination, and an effective funnel functions as a channel, in this case without relying on police and/or policing methods. By identifying the policies as part of a totality, I do not deny that policing methods are important, but claim that there are other aspects of the administrative policies targeting these groups that are more important.

Like Ticktin, I examine the rationalities underlying policies (2011). These policies contain some features that are engendered by the administrative nature of the policy field. First, the field is fragmented, being divided into distinct policy spheres. Second, it is not officially recognized as a policy field, thus the different measures are not considered part of a totality. These traits are characteristic of all the political fields I call funnels (Johansen 2013b).

Furthermore, these policy characteristics are a cause of misery for Romas. If we look closely, the measures lead to a great deal of suffering and despair: hunger, fatigue, poor health and sleepless nights. Yet these conditions are more or less invisible to the authorities. The invisibility of the hardship suffered by the targets of control might very well be one condition enabling the application of this policy. Responsibility for the production of misery is fragmented, the policy fields are not acknowledged, health services are outsourced to non-government organizations (NGOs) and information loops are closed.

166 *Nicolay B. Johansen*

These attributes of the funnel produce a 'social distance' between policy-makers and the public, on the one hand, and the targeted group, on the other. Suffering is consequently rendered invisible, and the personnel administering the infliction of pain are largely isolated from responsibility, only exposed to fragments of the total impact on the life situations of the target group. Thus, funnel policies can bring about undocumented degrees of hardship.

My argument, then, is that the policies adopted with the purpose of controlling the Roma in Norway have a funnel character, which creates the conditions for harsh treatment through measures borrowed from administrative law and administrative organizations, which in turn produce social distance. I am not arguing that the policies are illegitimate; rather, the policies should be acknowledged as a totality, to make political discussion of the issue possible.

Funnel policies

The focus of this chapter is on the control strategies adopted in a neo-liberal welfare state – in this case, Norway. For most scholars, the Nordic countries are examples of the socio-democratic welfare state (see, for example, Pratt 2008a, 2008b). Indeed, compared to most states, these countries are well-functioning providers of welfare and nothing like (in)famous neo-liberal experiments, such as Pratt's native New Zealand. However, the Nordic states are also suffering from the impacts of globalization (Aas 2013). More importantly, however, neo-liberalism should not be considered as solely characteristic of right-wing political regimes. In Foucault's terms, it involves the deployment of indirect measures of control, which imitate markets. In Norway, the privatization of the state sector and the implementation of what has been termed the 'audit society' (Power 1997) have been carried out by the Left, and the political culture is permeated by the ideal of freedom (Johansen 2015).

Globalization substantially increases the pressure on nation-states by challenging borders and sovereignty (Brown 2010). Bosworth and Aas, among others, have pointed to the implications of globalization in regard to migration policies (Bosworth and Aas 2013), which have included the emergence of so-called crimmigration law (Stumpf 2006), leading to penal policy becoming a device in immigration politics, and vice versa.[2]

One part of my argument is that an understanding of the control of the Roma needs to take into account a number of separate administrative phenomena. Together, these policy spheres and their distinct administrative fields constitute a totality that is neither fully recognized nor considered as a whole. Elsewhere I have elaborated on the concept of funnel policies as a distinct form of handling marginal groups in Norway (Johansen 2013b). Funnels work in the following way: the targets of control are isolated in a life situation which is intended to be more untenable than the alternative. The concept of 'control situation' encapsulates how policy frames people's lives both directly and indirectly through the combined actions of a range of institutions, broadly understood (for example, institutions may be 'private' or imitate the market). The idea, then, is that it is necessary to look at the institutions that frame individuals, and the way in which they combine to constitute a 'life situation'. Thus, 'control situation' refers to the institutional set-up, while 'life situation' refers to the end result for the individual.

Funnels are constituted by all the institutions relevant to the control situation, which include the labour market, social services, health care/treatment programmes, non-governmental organizations (NGOs) and their services and so on. These are the cornerstones of the control situation, or the 'big technology' (Dean 2010). From the fragmented institutional approaches emerges a certain political sphere with certain mechanisms and distinctive qualities. Implementation of the mechanisms requires attention to detail and refinement, to ensure that the subjects cannot escape the control mechanism. I call this 'small technology'. The big and small technology combine to produce a situation that is intended to be worse than the desired alternative – leaving the country. We can see the results of this strategy in the area of health (Johansen 2013a, 2013b) – an issue to which I return later in the chapter. My primary concern at this point is to identify the distinctive nature of funnel policy.

There is a particular structure at the heart of funnels as administrative fields. By creating a life situation that is so unpleasant that the subject decides to leave, the government adopts a strategy that resembles what Foucault, and some of his followers, call governmentality (Rose *et al.* 2006). However, governing by indirect measures is no simple matter, especially when it comes to poor people. Below I detail a conflict between the state and non-native Roma in Norway, in which the state sought to deprive them of places to sleep. It is my contention that such an attempt only makes sense as part of a more comprehensive political paradigm. In short, this struggle for the night must be seen as one struggle resulting from funnel policies. I demonstrate that the Roma are controlled through assemblages of such administrative efforts and that the rationales identified with the funnel structures are pervasive. Rather than looking at these efforts as fragmented political areas, I therefore claim that they constitute separate fields of pressure. These fields are not territorial but social, resting on an administrative ability to isolate the subjects in similar, but distinct, situations.

My conceptualization of funnel policies borrows from Rose's understanding of governable spaces (Rose 1999). He refers to a growth of different policy areas termed 'abstract' and 'irreal' spaces of domination. Fields/spaces of domination are produced by assemblages of 'technologies'. A diverse set of institutional contributions, employing a variety of means, thus constitutes areas in which particular combinations of control devices are implemented. These fields are not 'unreal'; on the contrary, they are as concrete as any social field can be, but they have also come about through historically and socially contingent processes. Rose restates the claim that Foucault made famous, that power can only be understood in relation to specific phenomena.

168 *Nicolay B. Johansen*

And, in Rose's analysis, it is the 'powers of freedom' that are under scrutiny. I follow Rose, both in his advice to be concrete and in giving attention to the uses of freedom.

The Roma in Norway

The funnel policy that I discuss relates to the non-native Roma, but this policy cannot be understood properly without reference to the history of what is now called indigenous Roma and the state. 'Roma' is a term intended to include the ethnic groups who migrated to Europe from India in the fourteenth century. It is assumed that those we know as Roma first came to Norway in the nineteenth century (Engebrigtsen 2012). The term covers several ethnic groupings with different histories and non-identical languages, but most of those who call themselves Roma have not been properly integrated into Norwegian society. Although there are areas where some of the Roma population are settled, they are also known to be nomadic. There is no official number of ethnic Roma: Statistics Norway does not register ethnic status. However, it is commonly assumed that there are between 400 and 500 individuals (Lidén and Engebrigtsen 2012). The Roma were known to be travelling people in the nineteenth century, when the (first) Norwegian sociologist Eliert Sundt documented the lives of the people inhabiting this country. Indeed, he wrote a whole volume dedicated to the Roma (Sundt 1974/1852). Travelling people have always, so it seems, caused problems for states (Scott 1998). And the Roma population has always been in some sort of conflict with the Norwegian authorities. The Roma have insisted on preserving their cultural values and lifestyles, and the state has insisted that they should submit to the norms of the majority.

The Roma population lived in a kind of tense harmony with the majority population in the nineteenth century, when their labour, craftsmanship and merchandise were sought after in rural communities. But they were not integrated and were never publicly accepted or acknowledged as 'proper' Norwegians. An integration unit was established in 1897, administered by a Christian society (*Norsk misjon blant hjemløse*). 'The mission' used brutal methods to curb expressions of Roma lifestyles (Engebrigtsen 2012). The removal of children and the sterilization of women were not uncommon (Lidén and Engebrigtsen 2012). And when the horrors of the Nazi regime began to be known, Roma trying to enter Norway were not allowed in (Hvinden 2000), as was the case for Jews (Johansen 1984; Michelet 2014). From the 1960s, the state attempted a new approach, in line with the emerging welfare state (Lidén and Engebrigtsen 2012).

In 1970, a 'gypsy office' was set up (Hjemdal 1983). Roma were offered houses and welfare benefits. These policies are now considered scandalous, as the houses were abandoned and several welfare frauds have since been unveiled. Newspapers still often report stories of Roma children who do not attend school, are illiterate or not integrated with ethnic Norwegians. Even more frequently readers are informed about violent internal struggles between the leaders of the two Roma clans.

The Roma were acknowledged as a national minority in 1999, and received formal apologies from state officials in 2000 and 2004 (in accordance with the European Council's *Framework Convention for the Protection of National Minorities*). At the same time, a fund for compensation was also established (Pettersen 2005).

Thus, when the Romanian Roma began to enter Norway and became visible in public spaces, the Norwegian public and state already had a history with similar ethnic groups. This history meant that the public's attitudes on this issue have been characterized by a combination of sympathy and bad conscience, on the one hand, and repulsion and antipathy, on the other. But the non-native, mostly Romanian Roma do not relate to the indigenous Roma. This was made clear by an incident that occurred in a quarry: when new Roma had set up a camp, the local self-proclaimed king of the gypsies paid them a visit. But they did not acknowledge him, and he came away annoyed and speaking ill of the people in the camp.

Romanian Roma are European Union citizens and entitled to a three-month tourist visa, provided they are able to support themselves financially.[3] These conditions are rarely fulfilled, but seldom checked at entry points. Still, their stay in Norway is not necessarily illegal. It is hard to measure how many Roma have come to Norway since 2005 or how many are present at any particular moment. Their influx is sometimes referred to as a 'wave' and it is said that the country is 'swamped' (Johansen 2014b). But the absolute numbers are probably quite small; 1,000 would be a high estimate. These groups are 'unwanted' inasmuch as they are associated with begging, pickpocketing and the littering of public places. Some (right-wing) politicians have taken the line that they should be denied entry, but the focus of this chapter is the slightly more subtle means employed to make them leave. If they were also prevented from begging, they would inevitably have a stronger incentive to return to Romania. However, a prohibition on begging offended certain political sensibilities, so other, indirect strategies employing administrative law have been pursued instead.

Civil administration may serve as a humanitarian alternative to the direct use of force and penal measures, but it also functions as a 'middle man', creating a distance between policy-makers and political targets. What we find is an instance of what Bauman, in *Modernity and the Holocaust*, described in terms of institutionalized distance. Increasing social and physical distance has a tendency to clear actions of their moral dimensions, and thus, says Bauman, 'socially produced distance' facilitates the inhumane treatment of others (1989: chap. 7). Key to such distancing is the 'optical principle'. Bauman claims that some 'pre-social' bond originates from face-to-face meetings where the parties actually see each other. Moral proximity, then, arises when people interact in ways that promote visual meeting points. He uses the development of weapon systems as an example: they have systematically been developed to kill at a greater distance. However, distance can also result from the use of intermediaries and experts. One aspect of modernity that Bauman highlights is the demand for efficiency. When the goal of eliminating the Jews was adopted, the enterprise became a question of efficiency, Bauman claims. He shows how professionals, bureaucrats and scientists went about their businesses zealously, even if they did not feel hatred for Jews. How could this be?, he asks. Modernity replaces morality with technicalities and efficiency. Ordinary people undertake their jobs as usual, carrying on with their lives. Moral problems are thereby translated into practical problems, provided that the people suffering the consequences are out of sight. Brutality and murder are thus made possible because participants and bystanders do not see the consequences and do not feel responsible. Moral indifference emerges from the invisibility of the victims.[4]

Social distance takes several forms, in Bauman's account, but he does not examine the cultural dimension in the same detail. When Bauman uses the term 'the Other' he refers to another person, in the biblical meaning, as someone just like oneself (via the philosopher Levinas). In the social sciences, the Other is primarily used to denote those belonging to groups deviating from the majority, and Bauman implicitly switches between these meanings of 'the Other'. Otherness understood in the latter way is a cultural and/or legal category. Categories differ in regard to their attributes and moral status. Bauman's book *Modernity and the Holocaust* (1989) considers the mass murder of the category 'Jews'. Thus, in this reading Jews are sociologically similar to 'strangers', 'foreigners' and 'outsiders' (Simmel 1964; Schütz and Wagner 1970; Becker 1973), constructed as different and morally inferior (Goffman 1989). Bauman seems to imply that the significance (and membership) of categories (partly) evaporates when people meet face to face. In his view, if social distance is to be removed, the first requirement is meeting points where the parties can face each other.[5]

I examine the Norwegian policies on the Roma in the light of such distancing. In the following sections, I describe how the administrative policies on the Roma together constitute a social field designed to pressure them to leave. In the final section, I discuss how this administrative set-up produces social distance.

The struggle for the night

The Roma have gradually taken a central position in the Norwegian public sphere. First, they have become visible as beggars in city centres. Second, as beggars they have become one of the most hotly debated issues in the press.

Begging in public was decriminalized in 2006, ending a regime of control directed at drunkards, loiterers and Roma that lasted for more than 100 years. The Vagrancy Act (*lov om løsgjengeri, betleri og drukkenskap*, 31 May 1900) that was overturned illuminates the current topic in several ways. The Vagrancy Act was an integral part of the Norwegian 'penal complex' that was established in the years 1896 to 1902 (Johansen 2014a2014c). In this 'complex', many laws were passed that aimed in various ways to control the lower classes, the poor and the unruly. Penal measures were combined with administrative justice, producing a flexible legal system to deal with what was considered to be disorder. These laws were passed via the same political process that led to the penal law, and they were understood to be parts of a 'greater totality' (Hagerup 1911; Ulvund 2014). For our purposes, however, the most significant fact is that the law regulating loitering and begging was not a part of the Penal Code. Begging and loitering, as well as public drunkenness, were sanctioned by sentences to labour camps. These camps were considered to be a form of treatment, rather than punishment (Hauge 1996). Accordingly, the subjects of control were not offered the rights and protections that follow from being tried before a criminal court. Yet the sanctions that were meted out administratively were nonetheless considered more painful by those subjected to them, and indeed the sentences were longer than the equivalent punishment for similar violations of the Penal Code (Christie 1960).

The penal complex established in 1900 has not been a uniquely Norwegian or Nordic phenomenon. The details may differ around Europe and the western hemisphere, but the combination of penal and administrative laws grew out of the ideologies known as the 'third school' in the latter part of the nineteenth century (Garland 1985). The special feature of Nordic countries is perhaps primarily that they have developed a reputation for mild penal cultures (Cavadino and Dignan 2006; Lacey 2008; Pratt 2008a; Pratt 2008b), which has drawn attention to the policies pursued in this region. The significance of Nordic penal exceptionalism has been subject to debate (Ugelvik and Dullum 2012; Pratt and Eriksson 2013), and the jury is still out on whether the Nordic countries really are as exceptional as some claim. Barker has taken a broader look at Swedish policies regarding immigrants, together with convictions in criminal courts. Her conclusion is that Swedish policies regarding the segments of the population that are generally considered problematic are less humanitarian than they appear at first sight (Barker 2013).

I, too, suggest a broader perspective. It is quite possible that the criminal justice system, seen *in toto*, as a penal complex, would look less humanitarian were the focus on prisons. One aspect that would certainly give the impression of greater severity is the prevalence of sanctions imposed outside the funnel of penal justice (such as administrative fines and expulsion). However, I am concerned with the categorical Others – the non-citizens. The debate about Nordic exceptionalism might shed some light on the cases presented, but this chapter is not tackling the core issues of that debate: the policies regarding 'inner, moral disorder'. In the words of Aas and Bosworth, it is not about 'policing', but 'soldiering' (Aas and Bosworth 2013). Although punishment has become more of an issue in the handling of foreigners, especially those who cause trouble (Aas 2007; Aas 2013; Mohn 2013), the penal system itself does not cover policies pursued in countering unwanted behaviour and unwanted residency among foreigners in Norway. Most notably, deportation

172   Nicolay B. Johansen

is not considered a punishment. The decision to deport is the result of an administrative process managed by the immigration authorities. The fact that deportation has been used historically as punishment (Beattie 1986), and that it is perceived as such, does not alter the fact that legally it is not.

I have argued that the legal authority to deport should be included in what is understood as the penal complex, along with the Vagrancy Act, mentioned above (Johansen 2014a; Johansen 2014c). These measures complement each other when seen from a broader political perspective. Punishment paves the way for deportation, and deportation can replace punitive sanctions (Stumpf 2006; Bosworth and Aas 2013). Romanians are the foreigners who are most often deported (according to the annual reports of the immigration authorities), but there is only circumstantial evidence that these deportations involve Roma.

However, the Vagrancy Act has been abolished and a different legal complex has emerged in its place. In 2005, there were practically no beggars on the streets of Norwegian cities (Brattvåg 2007). Some drug addicts were seen, but begging was not considered a public nuisance. This was a key reason for the abolition of the Vagrancy Act (Ot.prp. nr. 113 [2004–2005]). Quite soon, however, a new type of beggar started to be seen on the streets, and it became clear that most of them were Roma from Romania. This triggered a debate about whether the abandonment of the prohibition on begging had been premature. There were loud calls for strict measures, which in political circles debates concentrated on how begging could be stopped.

In the spring of 2013, the Labour Party, which headed the ruling coalition, presented its strategy to combat begging (Johansen 2014b). This strategy had six main elements, the most striking feature of which was the absence of a prohibition on begging. Instead, the coalition gave local authorities the power to require those wanting to beg to register at a police station. The government also lowered the threshold for expelling foreigners without residence permits and took steps towards forbidding begging at certain times and in certain places. Thus, the way was opened for some limited forms of prohibition, more or less meeting the advocates of prohibition half-way. In addition, they came up with extra funds for Roma in Romania, funds for research, and funds for 'emergency projects'. The services provided by these emergency projects include 'local facilities', such as toilets and showers for Roma settling in an area where such facilities do not already exist.

In the following paragraphs I argue that another strategy is developing in the battle to combat begging, which in part contradicts prohibition. I present some details of the steps taken between 2011 and 2013 to stop Roma roaming the streets of Norwegian cities. The premises in this endeavour were that begging was identified with the Roma and was a problem of such magnitude that something had to be done. The following account is based on newspaper reports of conflicts between Roma and representatives of the Norwegian authorities. The references will not be meaningful for those who do not speak a Nordic language. I have therefore settled for a general reference to a more thoroughly worked piece that I wrote about this topic in Norwegian (Johansen 2014b).

During the summer of 2012, a series of conflicts arose over Roma camps within and just outside Oslo. Four incidents happened over the summer. One camp was set up in a central part of the city, in an area mainly inhabited by immigrants (Grønland). Politicians complained of the disgusting conditions in this camp, including faeces and garbage in open areas. Rumours circulated that Roma were catching and eating rats and pigeons. Two toilets were provided, despite claims that they would attract more beggars. Another camp was set up in a recreational area outside the city, in a forest (Sognsvann). Then a smaller camp was started in a park in a gentrified area (Sofienbergparken, Grunerløkka). A camp set up in an abandoned quarry in the north-eastern suburbs of Oslo (Årvoll) lasted a little longer. Yet all these camps were dismantled by the police, who first gave the residents orders to leave and then set a time limit for their orders to be carried out. Some of the Roma were frustrated by the persistent attention of the police and organized a small protest outside the Town Hall, and some prominent intellectuals and clergy advertised a sleep-in with the Roma in Sofienbergparken to show their support. But to no avail. Yet another camp at Sognsvann was cleared by the police in the early autumn.

Later, news emerged of another camp that was set up in the Sognsvann area during the autumn, and which served as a base for a small group of Roma who stayed over the winter. Another group spent the winter nights underneath a large intersection. The ground underneath this intersection was deliberately covered with large rocks to prevent the homeless from using it as a shelter: thus, anyone camping there endured very uncomfortable conditions, besides the noise from the traffic itself. Nonetheless, the Roma had somewhere to sleep, even in winter.

At the start of 2013, there was public anxiety that the new season would bring a substantially larger group of Roma beggars. Again, the sleeping places were cleared. And the rocky shelter underneath the intersection was made even more inaccessible for the homeless and others.

A support organization for Roma had let some of them sleep in a house in the city centre. This time the fire brigade came in and ordered them to leave, for which they gave two reasons. First, the premises were not regulated for housing purposes, so their occupation of them was a violation of the planning and buildings act. Second, the fire brigade deemed sleeping on these premises to be unsafe.

Next, a group of Roma moved into a famous abandoned building. The media quickly learnt of this occupation and the police cleared the place. A couple of days later the police were called to a nearby park where the Roma had erected some tents. The same ritual was repeated. Soon after this, it emerged that some Roma had occupied a less conspicuous municipal building on the other side of the city – an empty house owned by the municipal Department for Welfare (Omsorgsbygg) that had no running water and no electricity. Omsorgsbygg demanded that the house be vacated, saying that it was unfit and dangerous. Other camps were also initiated in the cat-and-mouse game that went on in 2012 and 2013. It is possible that the police left some of the Roma alone during this time, if only for a little while. Yet my account is based on newspaper reports, which one can assume led to greater pressure on the authorities to do something about the 'Roma camps'. Either way, the result was that the Roma were ejected. At the political level, this game ended with a law passed in the Town Hall that prohibited any form of camping or sleeping on public land in Oslo and surrounds. With this vote, the battle over the night came to a temporary end. The police were given the measures they needed to support the political determination to combat beggars.

It should also be mentioned that some NGOs responded to this legislation by erecting sleeping facilities adapted to the needs of the Roma, although capacity was soon exhausted. These NGOs applied for the funds made available through the package mentioned above, which was introduced at almost the same time as the 'prohibition on sleeping'. What we find here, then, is a conflict between strategies on Roma and those on begging. Politically, there is a tension between parties advocating a penal strategy and those calling for the development of a many-faceted field of pressure that exerts control through the establishment of a governable space. To some extent, these conflicting political perspectives reveal that funnel policies should be considered as a political and administrative reality. Insofar as a penal strategy is 'real' (or 'irreal', in Rose's terms), as 'governable space', the same must be said about the alternative – the funnel.

These attempts to make the Roma leave Norway reveal a markedly coherent and combined approach from a variety of independent institutions. Yet the consistency does not stem from an underlying eagerness to get rid of these people. It is hard to tell whether there was any communication between the organizations, with the police, fire brigade and property owners all joining in the enterprise. Perhaps they were all simply responding to the same political mood. No matter how, the end result was a strategy for making life unbearable for those targeted.

This chimes with the demand from various parties that hygienic facilities should not be provided. I have not attempted to describe a distinct governable space as regards the visiting Roma population; what I have sought to make evident are fragments of such a space. As a funnel policy, this strategy is incomplete, since the complete elimination of all possible sleeping places is doubtless an unattainable goal. Moreover, there are other parts of life that are left untouched (although their effective exclusion from labour 'helps'). A thorough-going version of this strategy would put the subjects of control in a situation that denies all the basic needs of the human body. It is characteristic of my approach that the policies produce social distance in two ways. First, the policies are not acknowledged as being part of a totality that exerts pressure on certain people. Second, they are not acknowledged as being part of a coordinated effort. Accordingly, no one is responsible for them.

Rationalities and funnels

I have demonstrated that the Roma in Norway are subjected to control mechanisms through which a broad variety of administrative organizations operate more or less in coordination and I have argued that the policies on the Roma have become something akin to a funnel. One question remains unresolved in this regard: whether it is reasonable to consider the field constituted by the different institutions as 'real', or 'irreal' space in Rose's terms, as a 'governable space'. When I suggest that this field needs to be politically recognized, does it make sense to claim that it is 'real'?

I have cited indirect evidence to support the proposition that it should be thought of as a political totality. The zealous attempts to prevent the Roma from finding sleeping places do not constitute a funnel that puts pressure on all aspects of their life situation. But the Roma are already effectively excluded from legitimate sources of income. The sleeping place strategy is part of the small technology, which contributes to the big technology that constitutes the field. The arguments heard in political circles that hygienic facilities should not be erected indicate that some people consider policy on the Roma to be a particular space for government. Thus, the MP Per Sandberg said on the broadcasting network NRK that, if hygienic facilities were to be erected, it would 'send a signal that they are welcome and that we are catering for their presence'. He then sidestepped the question of whether we should make conditions for them unbearable, stating that 'it is already unbearable' (Sandberg quoted in Sandvik and Sollund 2013). Sandberg is a right-wing politician, but numerous other (local) politicians of different stripes have expressed similar views. I contend that comments such as that quoted above reveal the underlying rationale of Norwegian policies on the Roma.

The core of the matter is deprivation of the means to support life. The most basic need for humans, as for any other living creature, is food. The German word for food is '*lebensmittel*'. Like '*livsmedel*' in Swedish, it is translated as 'means for living'. In modern life, money is the major, if not sole, means to support life. Deprivation of money is therefore deprivation of *lebensmittel*, so we might include shelter, clothing and medicine in the meaning of this word. The dominant policy as regards irregular migrants is to deprive them of the 'means to live' (Johansen 2013b). As funnel policies go, 'irreal space' is more complete, but the principles are the same.

By eliminating sources of sustenance, one produces incentives. Incentives may be weak or strong. Let us look at the situation in another governable space in Norway – 'regional politics' (there is broad consensus among Norwegian politicians to keep the entire countryside inhabited). To encourage people to live in the northern parts of Norway, a set of tax reductions have been put in place. People living in the counties of Troms and Finnmark (in the far north) pay less income tax and may have their contribution to the public funding of education reduced by 10 per cent each year (Aalbu 2004). Although these sums can add up to a substantial part of the economy of a household, it

176   *Nicolay B. Johansen*

manipulates small parts of the resources available for households; it is measured in percentages. The policy regarding Roma is to manipulate the source of sustenance – to take away fundamental necessities. Still, the deprivation of *lebensmittel* must be considered a negative incentive. The key point is that the decision to move to the desired place is left to the individual.

As in the case of spreading the population over all the territory of Norway, the state does not rule by direct decisions, deciding which persons shall move here or there. There are financial benefits for people who choose to live for any length of time in the north, and the levels of benefit are calculated to attract roughly the desired number of people. But the people who move decide to do so themselves. Incentives are made available, calculated to prompt a certain number of people to make the desired decision and act like 'constraints' in Durkheim's terms.

In principle, the same types of incentives are offered to Roma. In the case of citizens and district policies, the incentives may be said to be presented to the population as a whole. In the case of Roma, measures are aimed directly at them.[6] Yet the rationale is the same. Although the policy sketched above does not affect the entire life situation of the targeted group, it adds another deprivation to their notorious poverty. Thus, we can reformulate the policies as attempts to produce misery. The police are not always needed, as the Roma are deprived of the necessities of life and forced into destitution. But the choice to leave is still theirs.[7]

This mechanism is nothing new in the history of the poor. 'Less eligibility' has long been a guiding principle in gauging benefits and welfare activities (Morris and Rothman 1995). Still, less eligibility takes another form today in the funnels I have described. When prisoners were given conditions worse than those of everyday life, the aim was to ensure that no one considered life in prison or the workhouses preferable to freedom. In my examples, less eligibility is used strategically to produce a result, and subjects have to be forced to make a calculation. In the nineteenth century, the end point (the prison) was designed to avoid a pull effect. The funnel policy adjusts the starting position, to create a push effect.

The strategy involved in this funnel policy resembles various general trends in western government. As has been mentioned, the frame of reference here is the Foucauldian perspective on neo-liberalism. One striking element is that it borrows from, or resembles, strategies known as governmentality (Foucault 2004; Dean 2010). Governmentality is a rationality developed to manage a population of disciplined citizens (Foucault 1979; Rose *et al.* 2006). But this is not necessarily the case with the Roma. Governmentality consists of relatively soft measures: techniques classed as 'incentives' and 'programmes'. They are characterized as 'regimes of knowledge', and the population, generally speaking, responds to them. But this is because they are already disciplined: governmentality would not be a viable strategy if the population were not to a certain extent already 'docile' (Rose *et al.* 2006).[8] Visiting Roma are not part of the population, and one cannot assume that they are 'docile'. The authorities

Controlling Roma in Norway 177

attempt to govern this group by manipulating their surroundings, but, as I briefly discuss below, they do not produce knowledge about the people subjected to manipulation. Still, there is an inherent logic in their policies, indicating familiarity with governmentality. Thus, the rationale is based on a premise that is at odds with the characteristics of the population to be administered.

One may wonder about the origins of this strategy and rationality in regards to the Roma. One possible answer is that the funnels were developed when governments had utilized the tools of government that have been in use for the past 200 years, forgetting that these tools were developed for a population of citizens (Walters 2010). In addition, the ambiguities resulting from the troubled history of the Roma, in both Norway and Europe, may have led to a degree of cautiousness.

Othering, indifference and invisibility in funnel policies

I have asserted that the strategies utilized to deal with the Roma are incomplete as funnel policies. But, as I pointed out, the mechanisms that deny them legitimate means of supporting life are already in place. Space transcends the paradigm associated with the penal tradition. In governable spaces, administrative measures take centre stage instead. Although penal measures play an important part, they only play a part in constituting the control situations.

This causes some confusion at the political level. Public debates fail to take account of the realities, both as regards governable space and its implications for the people subjected to it. The fact that the space is not recognized as a proper field of politics hinders the public from considering its impact.

From this point of view, penal institutions lose their pivotal role as distributors of punishment. Pain is delivered by denying access to *lebensmittel* (including the opportunity to sleep). This denial is enforced by the police, administrative organizations and, to some extent, possibly even private organizations and NGOs (Redfield 2005; Walters 2010; Ticktin 2011; Lee 2013).

The perspective I offer makes a comparison of penal regimes less straightforward. To compare penal policies and the control of the Roma via governable spaces would require more detailed descriptions than we have seen so far in the discussion of Scandinavian exceptionalism in the literature. However, looking at social control through the lens offered by Rose and the governmentality tradition offers an opportunity to make different kinds of comparisons, between the use of penal and administrative measures, or between direct and indirect forms of power. My ambition here has been to establish the concept of funnels and governable spaces in relation to the control of the Roma. Along with this, I have also sketched the nature of this control in the Norwegian neo-liberal welfare state.

I now turn to consider some other aspects of funnel policies such as their production of social distance. The examples mentioned demonstrate that funnel policies decrease proximity and facilitate harsh treatment. Bauman pointed to the significance of social distance as a necessary condition for atrocities

178   *Nicolay B. Johansen*

(Bauman 1989). Social distance paves the way for inhumane treatment by depriving victims of moral value and/or by alienating the perpetrators from the consequences of their actions. While the policies regarding the Roma may be brutal in many respects, they are still of course a far cry from the atrocities with which Bauman grappled.[9] In the first place, I believe, policies regarding foreigners develop from the dilemmas facing nation-states under pressure from globalization. Second, the policies I examine differ in important ways from large-scale killing: while murders are directed at specific individuals, these policies indirectly condemn groups to destitution.

The separate measures taken to combat the Roma and begging appear devoid of moral value. Instead, a technical attitude dominates when such groups are considered. The unacknowledged nature of the control, and its administrative character, renders the funnels opaque, thus facilitating harsher treatment of those targeted. It effectively hides those subject to such punitive control measures, and therefore creates a situation characterized by indifference to their plight. A closer look at how the funnels are construed reveals that they, in stark contrast to society as a whole, conspicuously lack procedures for information gathering. Thus, the targeted groups are made even more invisible.

How effective are the control measures described above? Presumably, they produce compliance (voluntary exit from the territory) to some extent. But we must also assume that they produce poor health. Lack of sleep produces fatigue, which must have some impact on people's general health. We might assume, then, that poor health is more or less part of the plan. Additionally, bad living conditions must necessarily, in the long run at least, have some negative effect on the bodies of the subjects. It is therefore difficult to imagine that unhealthiness has no place in the strategies of funnel policies. My argument here goes further than this: I claim that the control strategy leaves visible marks on the group as a whole. The health of the group mirrors the control situation. Thus, health indicators could serve as a means to monitor the impact of the policies. But health is not recognized as a distinct policy field and so it is not measured. Thus, the non-acknowledgement of the funnel character of the policies regarding the Roma is a prerequisite for the harsh treatment to which they are subjected.

I want to mention two more aspects of the policy described above: how it is divided into isolated sectors and contractual relations; and how the logic of the funnel transfers responsibility from state agencies to the subjects of control.

The funnels produce situations in which organizations and their representatives do not see the impact of their contributions. The firefighters evicting Roma from empty buildings are 'just' avoiding danger of fire. The police officers removing sleepy Romas are 'just' keeping that specific spot orderly.[10] In this way, the policies adopted a task focus, not a focus on their human consequences.

Additionally, the opaqueness of the policy depends on it not being recognized as a policy area. Furthermore, isolated in situations where they are supposed to make choices, the subjects are made responsible for their own plight. The suffering seen by health workers and NGOs is regarded as a consequence of the actions of the Roma themselves, not as the product of coordinated policies.

Meanwhile, the people who actually inflict the deprivations that add up to an undocumented totality of hardship are protected from responsibility. Bystanders and social workers, even idealists, may come to think of this suffering as the Romas' own responsibility, not that of government politics.

It should be evident from the above discussion that funnel policies cause suffering. The question remains: would this type of policy be acceptable if it were put to the test of public discussion, in light of its totality and consequences?

Conclusion

I have argued that the control policies targeting non-native Roma in Norway amount to a distinct social field, a governable space that I have compared to a funnel. The funnel has a particular rationale. It uses deprivation and suffering as a means to a political end. Government organizations insulate themselves from information about the real consequences of these policies by employing administrative organizations whose aims align with the ambition of forcing the Roma to leave the country.

The policy is unrecognized as a political and administrative field. There is no direct denial but no acknowledgement either. Accordingly, no systematic attention is paid to its dynamics, nor are its results scrutinized. The funnel character of these policies is decisive for the level of harshness inflicted, but there is a conspicuous absence of information about the groups targeted by the funnel policy. And the fragmented structure of the policy makes the targets of control less visible to politicians and the public alike.

Notes

1 Thanks to Polity Press for granting permission to reproduce previously published material in this chapter.
2 The chapters provided by Aliverti, Bosworth and Barker in the current volume bring up these issues (see also Aliverti 2013).
3 Norway's relation to the EU is complicated. Norway is not a Member State, but is party to a complex set of conventions and legislation, a bilateral agreement with the EU, which includes Iceland, Switzerland and Lichtenstein, the so-called EEA agreement.
4 However, Bauman's account of the Holocaust is controversial – see Scharff-Smith's chapter.
5 The Norwegian sociologist Nils Christie has also addressed some of the same issues and reaches similar conclusions. But Christie's discussions may add clarity to the concept of social distance. In a work less familiar to the international audience, (his first) he interviewed Norwegian guards in a concentration camp (Christie 1952, see also Halvorsen 2014) and developed a stance quite similar to that of Bauman. His final words have been central to his entire academic career: 'All of us could have been perpetrators under the same conditions', he says, and therefore: 'the goal must be to prevent the same conditions from reappearing' (Christie 1952, my translation). Christie handles the physical and the categorical dimensions of

180 *Nicolay B. Johansen*

otherness in more detail: the starting point is the existence of a category of person deprived of humanity (prisoners). And it is not just physical proximity and visibility that remove the moral distance between perpetrators and victims, but also linguistic presence. In a telling story, he describes how one prisoner learned some Norwegian and when he had a chance used it to talk to one of the guards. By doing that he entered into the guard's imagination as a human being, says Christie. Christie's conclusion was that the guards that were convicted of excessive cruelty towardsprisoners were the ones that did not see them as fellow humans. Thus, in Christie's view, social distance is a product of the interplay between 'otherness' as a category, and physical proximity. Apparently Bauman was not familiar with Christie's work when he wrote *Modernity and the Holocaust*. But since then they have struck up an academic as well as a personal friendship.

6 This strategy is not so easily pursued, as it conflicts with discrimination law. Roma, like any other ethnic group, cannot be addressed directly through law. The practical solution is to regulate (forbid) attributes characteristic of the targeted group. Attempts to criminalize begging are supported by more or less covert utterances linking this activity to the Roma as a group. Political ingenuity could, we must suspect, also include a tacit reliance on the police force to 'understand' who should be targeted. Here lies another basic criminological issue, but it is outside my topic and I will not discuss it further.

7 A shift in measures was implemented in 2014, where the government upped the uses of deportation drastically.

8 Foucault himself rejects the idea that his taxonomy of power relations should be understood as steps in a historical development, but it is hard to deny that 'discipline' constitutes the logical foundation of his uses of 'governmentality'.

9 For this reason one should be careful when using Bauman's analytical tools.

10 However, they do express some ambivalence (Hauan 2014) in line with the interviewees in Bosworth's chapter.

References

Aalbu, H. (2004) *Effekter og effektivitet: Effekter av statlig innsats for regional utvikling og distriktspolitiske mål*, (government paper preparing a law on 'regional politics'), Oslo: NOU.

Aas, K.F. (2007) 'Analysing a world in motion: global flows meet "criminology of the other"', *Theoretical Criminology*, 11: 283–303.

Aas, K.F. (2013) *Globalization and crime*, Los Angeles, CA: Sage Publications.

Aas, K. F. and Bosworth, M. (2013) 'The criminology of mobility', in K.F. Aas and M. Bosworth (eds), *The borders of punishment: migration, citizenship and social exclusion*, Oxford: Oxford University Press.

Aliverti, A. (2013) *Crimes of mobility: criminal law and the regulation of immigration*, London: Routledge.

Barker, V. (2013) 'Nordic exceptionalism revisited: explaining the paradox of a Janus-faced penal regime', *Theoretical Criminology*, 17: 5–25.

Bauman, Z. (1989) *Modernity and the Holocaust*, Cambridge: Polity Press.

Beattie, J. M. (1986) *Crime and the courts in England 1660–1800*, Oxford: Clarendon Press.

Becker, H.S. (1973) *Outsiders: studies in the sociology of deviance*, New York, NY: Free Press.

Bosworth, M. and Aas, K.F. (2013) *The borders of punishment: migration, citizenship, and social exclusion*, Oxford: Oxford University Press.

Controlling Roma in Norway 181

Brattvåg, H. (2007) *Folk fra Romania som tigger i Oslo: en rapport fra Kirkens Bymisjons prosjekt Rett i koppen*, Oslo: The Church City Mission.

Brown, W. (2010) *Walled states, waning sovereignty*, New York: Zone Books.

Cavadino, M. and Dignan, J. (2006) *Penal systems: a comparative approach*, London: Sage.

Christie, N. (1952) *Fangevoktere i konsentrasjonsleire en sosiologisk undersøkelse*, Oslo: UiO/ISO.

Christie, N. (1960), *Tvangsarbeid og alkoholbruk* (Forced labour and alcohol consumption), Oslo: Universitetsforlaget.

Dean, M. (2010) *Governmentality: power and rule in modern society*, London: Sage.

Engebrigtsen, A. (2012) *Tiggerbander og kriminelle bakmenn eller fattige EU-borgere?: myter og realiteter om utenlandske tiggere i Oslo*, Oslo: NOVA.

Foucault, M. (1979) *Discipline and punish: the birth of the prison*, London: Peregrine Books.

Foucault, M. (2004) '*Society must be defended: lectures at the Collège de France 1975–76*', New York: Picador.

Garland, D. (1985) *Punishment and welfare: a history of penal strategies*, Aldershot: Gower.

Goffman, E. (1989) *Stigma notes on the management of spoiled identity*, Englewood Cliffs, NJ: Prentice-Hall.

Hagerup, F. (1911) *Strafferettens almindelige del* (Commentary on the penal code), Kristiania: Aschehoug.

Halvorsen, V. (2014) 'Nils Christie: conflict as property', in M. Dubber, *Foundational texts in modern criminal law*, Oxford: Oxford University Press.

Hauan, H.M. (2014) *Politiets møte med tilreisende roma*, IKRS, Blogpost, online, available: www.jus.uio.no/ikrs/tjenester/kunnskap/kriminalpolitikk/meninger/2014/p olitiets-mote-med-tilreisende-roma.html (accessed 15 December 2014).

Hauge, R. (1996) *Straffens begrunnelser* (Justifications of punishment), Oslo: Universitetsforlaget.

Hjemdal, O. K. (1983) *Evaluering av arbeidet med sigøynerne*, Oslo: Sosialdepartementet.

Hvinden, B. (2000) *Romanifolket og det norske samfunnet: følgene av hundre års politikk for en nasjonal minoritet*, Bergen: Fagbokforlaget.

Johansen, N. B. (2013a) 'Elendighetstrakten: Om å styre av de som ikke teller', in N.B. Johansen, T. Ugelvik and K.F. Aas, *Krimmigrasjon? Den nye kontrollen av de fremmede*, Oslo: Universitetsforlaget.

Johansen, N. B. (2013b) 'Governing the funnel of expulsion', in K.F. Aas and M. Bosworth (eds), *The borders of punishment: criminal justice, citizenship and social exclusion*, Oxford: Oxford University Press.

Johansen, N. B. (2014a) 'Det strafferettslige kompleks (The penal complex)', in S. Flaatten and G. Heivoll, *Straff, lov, historie*, Oslo: Pax forlag.

Johansen, N. B. (2014b) 'Lik rett til å sove (equal rights to sleep)', in L. Finstad and H.M. Lomell, *Motmæle*, Oslo: Pax forlag.

Johansen, N. B. (2014c) 'Forcing immigrants out: new constellations of penal and administrative justice', *Report from the 50th research seminar, Skarrildhus, Denmark*. M. Tønder (ed.). Aarhus:Scandinavian Research Council for Criminology.

Johansen, N. B. (2015) *Det Nyliberale Janusansikt* (The two faces of neo-liberalism), Oslo: Novus forlag.

Johansen, P.O. (1984) *Oss selv nærmest: Norge og jødene 1914–1943*, Oslo: Gyldendal.

Lacey, N. (2008) *The prisoners' dilemma: political economy and punishment in contemporary democracies*, Cambridge: Cambridge University Press.

182 *Nicolay B. Johansen*

Lee, M. (2013) 'Human trafficking and border control in the global south', in K.F. Aas and M. Bosworth (eds), *The borders of punishment: criminal justice, citizenship and social exclusion*, Oxford: Oxford University Press.

Lidén, H. and Engebrigtsen, A. (2012, 6 Sept.) *Norske rom* (Norwegian Roma), Oslo: Center for Studies of Holocaust and Religious Minorities, online, available: www.hlsenteret.no/kunnskapsbasen/livssyn/minoriteter/norske-rom/norske-rom- (accessed 15 December 2014).

Michelet, M.B. (2014) *Den største forbrytelsen: ofre og gjerningsmenn i det norske Holocaust*, Oslo: Gyldendal.

Mohn, S.B. (2013) 'Passet påskrevet: Straff og kontroll av utlendinger i norsk offisiell statistikk', in N.B. Johansen, T. Ugelvik and K.F. Aas (eds), *Krimmigrasjon? Den nye kontrollen av de fremmede*, Oslo: Universitetsforlaget.

Morris, N. and Rothman, D.J. (1995) *The Oxford history of the prison: the practice of punishment in Western society*, New York, NY: Oxford University Press.

Ot.prp. nr. 113 (2004–2005) *Om lov om oppheving av løsgjengerloven og om endringer i straffeloven mv.* (Government paper preparing new legislation, upheaval of prohibition on begging).

Pettersen, K.-S. (2005) *Tatere og misjonen: mangfold, makt og motstand*, Trondheim: Norges teknisk-naturvitenskapelige universitet.

Power, M. (1997) *The audit society: rituals of verification*, Oxford: Oxford University Press.

Pratt, J. (2008a) 'Scandinavian exceptionalism in an era of penal excess: Part I – the nature and roots of Scandinavian exceptionalism', *British Journal of Criminology*, 43: 119–137.

Pratt, J. (2008b) 'Scandinavian exceptionalism in an era of penal excess: Part II – does Scandinavian exceptionalism have a future?', *British Journal of Criminology*, 48: 275–292.

Pratt, J. and A. Eriksson (2013) *Contrasts in punishment: an explanation of Anglophone excess and Nordic exceptionalism*, London: Routledge.

Redfield, P. (2005) 'Doctors, borders, and life in crisis', *Cultural Anthropology*, 20: 328–361.

Rose, N. (1999) *Powers of freedom: reframing political thought*, Cambridge: Cambridge University Press.

Rose, N., Valverde, M. and O'Malley, P. (2006) 'Governmentality', *Annual Review of Law and Sociology*, (2): 83–104.

Sandvik, S. and Sollund, S. (2013) *Frp: Dusj til tiggerne sender et signal om at de er ønsket her*, online, available: www.nrk.no/okonomi/frp_-tiggertiltak-gir-feil-signaler-1.11016405 (accessed 16 December 2014).

Schütz, A. and Wagner, H.R. (1970) *On phenomenology and social relations: selected writings*, Chicago, IL: University of Chicago Press.

Scott, J.C. (1998) *Seeing like a state: how certain schemes to improve the human condition have failed*, New Haven, NJ: Yale University Press.

Simmel, G. (1964) 'The stranger', in K.H. Wolff (ed.), *The sociology of Georg Simmel*, New York: The Free Press.

Stumpf, J. (2006) 'The crimmigration crisis: immigrants, crime and sovereign power', *American University Law Review*, 56: 367–419.

Sundt, E. (1974) *Fante: eller landstrygerfolket i Norge*, Oslo: Gyldendal.

Ticktin, M.I. (2011) *Casualties of care: immigration and the politics of humanitarianism in France*, Berkeley: University of California Press.

Ugelvik, T. and Dullum, J. (eds) (2012) *Penal exceptionalism?: Nordic prison policy and practice*, London: Routledge.

Ulvund, F. (2014) '"Dele af ét System"? Forebygging gjennom behandling eller uskadeleggjering", in S. Flaatten and G. Heivoll (eds), *Straff, lov, historie: historiske perspektiver på straffeloven av 1902*, Oslo: Norli.

Walters, W. (2010) 'Foucault and frontiers: notes on the birth of the humanitarian border', in U. Bröckling, S. Krasmann and T. Lemke (eds), *Governmentality: current issues and future challenges*, New York: Routledge.

9   On Bauman's moral duty[1]

Population registries, REVA and eviction from the Nordic realm

Vanessa Barker[2]

Introduction

In late March 2013, on a bus route from the main city terminal in central Stockholm to the connecting Eckerö ferry line to the island of Åland, a bus driver began separating the passengers as they boarded the bus. The driver later explained that he was sorting the passengers by the amount of luggage they were carrying and directed some passengers onto a second bus. But, according to those present, the bus driver separated the passengers according to their skin colour and directed 'foreign-looking' and 'dark-skinned' passengers to ride on a separate bus from that of the Swedish-looking passengers. This unlikely event was quickly picked up by the national and social media and dubbed 'the apartheid bus', as the bus ride had been divided into two distinct racial categories – one white and one black. One passenger who had been ushered onto a separate bus had not only been subjected to segregation but also felt as if he were about to be deported:

> It felt like we were on our way to Arlanda Airport to be deported from Sweden', he continued: 'We felt insulted, offended and discriminated against', 'I never thought this could happen in our Sweden.
> (Chatila quoted in Svahn 2013)

This sensational event was quickly doused and disavowed by the ferry lines as the unauthorized actions of one bus driver, who was then sent on leave. While providing fodder to the national press and tabloids alike, for social scientists this event may be all too easy to dismiss as unrepresentative, insignificant, individual prejudice, a one-off. But if we turn away, we may not ask the right questions, questions inspired by Zygmunt Bauman's unflinching look at the social production of immorality. The question is not: Why should this event matter? (Indeed, isn't it trivial?). Rather, we must ask: Why did no-one stop it? Why did passengers go along with it? Why did a Swedish passenger readily assume he was about to be deported and from his own country? How is that possible? How is deportation part of his imagination? It should be unthinkable, but was not. What does it tell us about our society? What are the social conditions that precipitated this event? And finally, what can we learn from it, and how might we change it?

This chapter calls upon Bauman's theory of morality and social proximity to try to answer these unsettling questions. Following Bauman, it suggests that systems of classification, what he calls definition, provide the foundation for social distancing, that pivotal moment when those perceived as 'Other' are cast out of the realm of shared moral responsibility. This moment of social separation paves the way for the infliction of harm or violence on others; it enables the punishment of others. This chapter argues that ethnic classification schemes in Sweden, specifically the way in which population registries count foreignness, have grafted social distance onto the structure of society, creating false binaries between native Swedes and foreigners. The registries do not simply provide descriptive statistics about the population but also the 'infrastructure', or a cultural 'toolkit', for understanding and guiding social action (Bowker and Star 1999; Swidler 1986). The material effect of the registries was on display during the REVA (*Rättssäkert och effektivt verkställighetsarbete*, translated as 'the legal and effective execution of policy') campaign, a programme of internal migration control carried out on public transport. As the police and migration authorities tried to serve deportation orders to those without legal authorization to remain in the country, officers mobilized this misleading map of social relations and instead stopped any 'foreign-looking' commuter to ask for identification, despite his or her Swedish citizenship, legal residency and social belonging. For those without a legal right to remain, REVA enacted a form of public punishment, a degrading ceremony in which those deemed 'Other' were publicly shamed, exposed and expelled, and denied the dignity of being dealt with behind closed doors in a police station, court house, migration office or their private residence.

To illustrate and develop my argument that the registries at once embody and produce social distancing, this chapter first reviews Bauman's key concepts on classification and morality. This step is important because Bauman's concerns with rationalization and bureaucratization are usually foregrounded in the context of criminal justice and border control, and, although these factors are significant, I want to focus on definition and classification by highlighting an understudied area. Classification schemes are critical to understanding the negative effects of the population registries on REVA, the deportation campaign. Second, this chapter reviews and analyses some key dimensions of the population classification in Sweden which creates divisions between native Swedes and others, particularly foreigners. Third, it discusses how REVA has depended upon those same divisions to further reproduce social distancing and, as a consequence, has contributed to the social production of immorality. To evidence these claims, this chapter draws on multiple data sources, including in regard to recent and publicly contentious events, public policies and practices on migration control, and public discourse in the national media about REVA, to examine how punishing others is made possible in a society based on

186 *Vanessa Barker*

equality that maintains open and humane immigration policies. The existence in Sweden of a programme like REVA is thus highly unlikely and therefore a compelling case for the analysis of the various processes of social and legal exclusion that it entails.

Bauman on moral duty

With chilling detail, Zygmunt Bauman (1989) explains in *Modernity and the Holocaust* how central features of modern life converged to produce one of the most horrific events in human history. Rather than see this event as an antithesis to modernity or as spontaneous savagery, Bauman argues that the Holocaust must be seen as emerging from both common and unique features of modernity: rationalization, bureaucratization and nationalism. These features were part and parcel of the civilizing process but, instead of dissolving violence, this process concentrated violence in the hands of the state. As Bauman explains, left unchecked by a weakened civil society and spurred on by a scientific quest towards racial purity, this state killing machine sent over 6 million Jews to their death. In a slow procession of bureaucratic routine, the Nazis successfully classified, separated, distanced and finally annihilated their victims. Each step brought victims closer to death; each step brought the perpetrators farther from moral responsibility. As Jews were essentially 'evict[ed] from the realm of moral duty' (Fein in Bauman 1989: 191), Bauman shows how the destruction of social responsibility towards others, while not the single driving force, nevertheless enabled the mass killing to occur, and with some degree of indifference. Jews were cast outside the moral community, outside the 'universe of obligations' (Fein in Bauman 1989: 191).

From this riveting and sometimes controversial analysis, Bauman develops a theory of morality based on the concept of responsibility. To Bauman, responsibility evokes a duty to others, a duty to do something, to look out for, to care for others (Bauman 1989: 182). We have this responsibility towards others not because it is strictly an obligation, imposed on us, or a matter of self-interest or reciprocity, but because this is what it means to be human. He writes: 'Becoming responsible *is* the constitution of me as a subject' (Bauman 1989: 183). This is what it means to be a human subject, what it means to be with others. Following philosopher Levinas, Bauman quotes Dostoyevsky: 'We are all responsible for all and for all men before all, and I more than all the others' (Bauman 1989: 182). For Bauman, responsibility for the other is the foundation of morality, with 'roots that reach well beneath societal arrangements' (Bauman 1989: 183). The *universe of obligation*, in line with Fein, demarcates a critical boundary between humanity and dehumanization: on the inside, moral principles are binding and make sense, while on the outside they are rendered meaningless (27). Casting the other out of this realm is not only a matter of distaste, prejudice or animus; it indicates a feeling of nothingness. Where rage is full of emotion and close engagement with another, once that person is cast out, s/he does not exist, thereby depleting emotions, hot or cold, from those on the inside. His/her presence no longer generates anger or empathy. It is thus existential death even though the person still stands.

Bauman goes on to explain where this type of immorality comes from. It is not inherent or even a natural state of being. It has to be constructed from the social realm. The refusal to take responsibility for the other – the very definition of immorality – is produced by specific kinds of social processes, namely social distantiation and social separation, the loss of proximity towards others (Bauman 1989: 184). As we become socially separated from one another, we feel less and less responsible for the other. This is how dehumanization begins. Bauman writes: 'This was the method of making invisible the humanity of the victims' (Bauman 1989: 26). In later work, he refers to this process as 'moral blindness' or 'adiaphorization', to capture the loss of sensitivity to others (Bauman and Donskis 2013: 15). Contemporary social conditions, particularly the widespread use of technology and bureaucracy, facilitate social separation, further eroding the principle of proximity.

It is at this point that we can take Bauman's insights into the social production of immorality – that is, the loss of responsibility and moral duty towards others – and try to apply them in new ways to the practices of punishment, including new configurations of border control that separate, distance, punish and ultimately expel migrants. Forms of mobility control such as criminalization, detention and deportation are not only enmeshed with criminal justice systems but are also rapidly transforming these very same institutions, as a growing body of work in border criminologies has shown (Stumpf 2006; Aas and Bosworth 2013; Aliverti 2013).

The banishment of foreign nationals vis-à-vis deportation is made easier by their exclusion from the moral realm of responsibility. They are already on the outside or close to the edge prior to their 'removal'. This distanced position is in part because their original inclusion in the moral community of the Global North has never been guaranteed, despite the rhetoric of equality that is so central to democratic societies. Sovereign states, democracies included, reserve the right to determine the population of the polity and maintain differential treatment of non-nationals (Bosniak 2006). Migrants' inclusion in the moral realm of responsibility has been further compromised, if not broken, by various processes of social distancing, some more severe than others. Social separation, the moment when migrants are literally and figuratively separated from the community – they are imagined to be different and spatially configured as such – includes a range of public and private acts such as official state policies that not only restrict but also criminalize migration, the existence of and growing reliance on immigration detention centres, citizenship regimes based on group membership and national belonging, population registries and racial profiling by the police. Also included are a host of interpersonal interactions that signal and make real the separation, ranging from small slights and minor indignities to societal-wide indifference to violence, all recently directed at poorer European Union (EU) migrants who ask for money on the city streets – 'the beggars' – whose identity and perhaps even humanity have become eclipsed by this master status, which creates a growing distance between 'us' and 'them'. All of these types of social distancing, which may not necessarily be linear, additive or determinate, nevertheless underpin and make deportation possible. By the time the deportee has reached the border, s/he has already been long gone from the shared imagination and shared realm of moral responsibility.

Before proceeding, I want to make clear why I am drawing on Bauman's work on the Holocaust. Parallels in social distancing are not used to make unwarranted associations or foreshadow inevitable doom. Contemporary border control does not operate at the same scale or with the same degree of intentionality as the absolute annihilation of a particular people, despite the dangerous conditions that have led to an untold number of 'deaths at the global frontier' (Weber and Pickering 2011). Instead, I reference Bauman to highlight how the same social processes endemic to modern society – classification, rationalization, bureaucratization and nationalism – while mutated under genocide, are still central organizing features of everyday life. Bauman asks us to face the facts. Rather than cordon off the Holocaust to Jewish or German history, he asks us to see the double-sided nature of modern society that brought it about and which is still with us today.

Furthermore, Bauman asks us to think more carefully about morality, in ways that have been underappreciated within border control studies. Critical border research has pinpointed the social production of illegality, blatant violations of human rights and human security (Dauvergne 2008; Dembour and Kelly 2011) and may view border controls as immoral, but most studies have linked these developments to various economic, political or social factors rather than to morality itself. For example, recent accounts of mobility control tend to highlight neo-liberal imperatives, demonstrating how border controls function to create and exploit a vulnerable, precarious and essentially 'deportable' labour force, to use de Genova's influential formulation (see also Melossi 2003; De Giorgi 2010). Alternatively, they may highlight the ways in which border control embodies postcolonial racism, upholding ethnic and racial hierarchies, separating and insulating the Global North from the poorer and darker Global South – or 'global vagabonds' as Bauman aptly described it (Fekete and Webber 2010; Krasmann 2007; Weber and Bowling 2008; Bauman 2000). These accounts have inspired a new generation of scholars to examine and interrogate what once seemed like self-evident state prerogatives, who have amassed a substantial theoretical and empirical literature. But this work is to some degree incomplete. Thinking more deeply about morality, we might come to understand racism not as a sufficient factor in border control but one that is itself bound up with the production of immorality, a step along the way towards social separation that alleviates any sense of responsibility rather than a raw expression of antipathy or hostility.

Social distancing in action: defining, sorting and separating

According to Bauman's theory of morality, classification, or what he calls definition, is decisive for social separation: a pivotal moment that begins the process of dehumanization, the loss of sensitivity to others and eviction from the moral community, and which paves the way for the infliction of harm or violence on others, including deportation.

He explains:

> Definition sets the victimized group apart (all definitions mean splitting the totality into two parts – the marked and the unmarked), as a *different* category, so that whatever applies to it does *not* apply to all the rest. By the very act of being defined, the group has been targeted for *special* treatment, what is proper in relation to 'ordinary' people must not necessarily be proper in relation to it.
>
> (Bauman 1989: 191)

For Bauman, classification is a form of division and separation. It is the process itself, of pulling apart, fixing identities, comparing categories and ordering types, which can be highly problematic. Bauman explains how, during the Holocaust, the Nazis successfully redefined Jews into an abstract category, reclassifying them from people they knew, neighbours, friends, shopkeepers and bankers into a derogatory set of characteristics, an 'embodiment of everything to be resented, feared, or despised' (Bauman 1989: 41). This process was met with resistance, counterclaims and reclassification. For example, Bauman references attempts by Germans to save their friends by reclaiming them as decent and worthy, distinguishing them from the abstract Jew. In France, during the occupation, French Jews similarly defined themselves as distinct, different, apart from the Jews who immigrated from the east, desperately trying to delay their own demise and claim special treatment.

Criminology and sociology have long been concerned with how systems of social classification set people apart from one another in ways that define identity, social status, social relations and even life chances. The history of the welfare state is a history of separating the worthy from the unworthy (Gordon 1994; Skocpol 1995); the criminal justice system is a mass sorting machine of harms, blames and pain; the imposition of the death penalty turns on those who *deserve* to die (Sarat and Shoemaker 2011). In the 'new penology', criminal offenders are sorted by risk factors rather than by moral blameworthiness (Feeley and Simon 1992). In Sweden, on a now infamous bus route, passengers were sorted according to skin colour, calling to mind racial segregation of the Jim Crow South.

In the case of mobility control, a key classification system turns on definitions of legality and criminality. As Catherine Dauvergne's (2008) *Making people illegal* so deftly shows, immigration and international law actually create illegality itself by sorting some statuses into legal categories but excluding

190 *Vanessa Barker*

others. This process leaves some of the most vulnerable people with the least amount of legal protection simply because their situation does not fit the imposed category. Yet, as asked by scholars and activists, how can anyone be illegal? (on the selective nature of law, see Weber and Pickering 2011). Likewise, Ana Aliverti's (2013) well-received *Crimes of mobility* analyses how immigration controls in Britain create new categories of criminality, where immigration violations, which were once administrative concerns, are now subject to criminal law (for more on 'crimmigration', see Stumpf 2006). As these and other related studies make clear, classification schemes are not just a matter of administrative convenience or neutral background noise but rather are critical to determining one's life chances.

Population registries: classification and social distancing

By taking a close look at Bauman's concerns with classification and definition, I want to examine one of the earliest types of classification schemes that is historically linked to and made possible the legal control of mobility: population registries. In Europe, population registries were introduced as early as the sixteenth century, primarily as control mechanisms to measure and tax the population in support of war and state building. In Sweden, population registries began to take their modern form in the seventeenth century, just as the 'control of strangers' became a major subject of political debate (Sköld 2004: 8). In a massive administrative effort led by the state, in cooperation with the church, the first registries attempted to include all Swedes and provide detailed information about an individual's vital statistics: births, deaths, marriages and, most notably for this chapter, migrations (Sköld 2004; Hofsten 1988; Nilsdotter Jeub 1993). The history, aims and development of these registries, particularly the role of the Swedish Church and local parishes in administering them, are critical for understanding modern nation building.

Here, I highlight how population registries as a type of classification scheme provide the 'infrastructure', including a set of 'work practices and routines', that influence and shape our understandings of the social world (Bowker and Star 1999). They not only shape how we count the population but also how we *imagine* the population. This way of thinking about population registries is indebted to the work of Michel Foucault, Nikolas Rose and Ian Hacking, among others, who have shown how modern forms of governance are intimately connected to and dependent upon statistical knowledge about the population (for discussion, see Garland 1997). In a previous study (Barker 2013a), I focused on the idea of the 'people's home', or *folkhemmet*, as critical for understanding the processes of social exclusion in Sweden. This concept fuses two meanings of the word 'folk' (people) – one based on *demos*, the people, as free and equal; the other on *ethnos*, a people related by blood (see Trägårdh 2000; Schall 2012). When an ethnic conception of belonging and citizenship is ascendant or dominant, ethnic minorities and foreign nationals are more likely to be subject to social marginality and social control across core areas of social life, including housing, education, labour markets, criminal justice and border control. While *folkhemmet* continues to exert both positive and negative effects on national belonging in Sweden, I think we need to look more closely at the impacts of population registries on these processes of exclusion. Population registries have been considered some kind of historical and neutral metric of the population but, because of this apparent neutrality and bureaucratization, they may function in more insidious ways. In Sweden, population registries have built social distancing into the social fabric.

They tend to be celebrated by researchers in Sweden as they contain a unique, reliable and almost complete record of data on all individuals' vital statistics and life histories. The data itself is considered a treasure trove which allows for highly sophisticated and robust types of statistical analysis that without a doubt have contributed to a much richer understanding of changing patterns of marriage, fertility and mortality. Yet, the categories, particularly around issues of migration and foreignness, tend to be taken as given – as fixed categories and social facts. Yet we know from comparative and historical research that the experience and meaning of ethnicity, for example, is much more fluid than is commonly understood and often the result of an ongoing historical process or conflict over boundary making (Wimmer 2008; Wacquant 1997). Who and what counts as Other is historically contingent and socially fluid. At this point it is pertinent to take a step back and look at how the categories of the data can tell us to some degree about the nature and character of social relations within the society that produces them, particularly around issues of difference and ethnic diversity. How do societies count difference? What counts as difference? Why do they count ethnic diversity?

Based on an in-depth survey and comparative analysis of 141 countries that enumerate ethnicity that she conducted, Ann Morning (2008) argues that we cannot take for granted the answers to these types of questions and that it cannot be assumed that the approach taken to counting is the same across nations. Ethnic enumeration can indicate a range of state interests and is not merely a numeric reflection of the population, as such. It has been used in different societies for different purposes, for repressive and liberating goals alike, from legitimating oppression to claiming rights based on difference. As detailed by Morning, it has been used historically in colonial and apartheid regimes for overt social control and, by contrast, in democratic societies to assert national unity (for example, to support the beliefs that we are all the same, in French republicanism, or that we are all different, in the Canadian mosaic). Ethnic enumeration has also been used more recently as a legal tool to counter discrimination by keeping track of the numbers (Rallu *et al.* in Morning 2008: 243). The act of counting itself is an indicator, a visible index, of the status and meaning of ethnic diversity in a society. In Sweden, as discussed below, ethnic diversity is not counted at all. Instead, foreignness is used as a proxy for ethnic diversity, which is not the same thing at all.

By way of example, Morning explains how the approach taken by the United States (US) to counting race is a global anomaly and indicates that

192 *Vanessa Barker*

society's inability to overcome the long shadow of slavery. The US is one of only 13 countries that use 'race' on its census forms, 11 of which are 'either New World former slave societies ... and/or their territories' (Morning 2008: 248). A majority of the countries that count ethnicity ask about ethnic identity, nationality or a similar variant to try to capture some sense of self-identified cultural difference or shared understanding of common descent. What is more, the US is the only country that separates race from ethnicity by asking different sets of questions about each. By doing so, Morning argues, the census form may be upholding antiquated 'essentialist biological understandings of *race*, since it is presented as distinct from culturally delineated and socially produced *ethnicity*' (Morning 2008: 260).

In the Swedish context, population registries similarly reflect and shape the character of social relations in that society. From their establishment in the early seventeenth century, the population registries counted migration, requiring migration certificates for those who moved in and out of parishes, save for the nobility (Nilsdotter Jeub 1993). Later statistical reports, modernized in the early twentieth century, contained detailed information about in and out migration, recording migratory flows and countries of origin and destination (Statistical Yearbook of Sweden 1914). The registries indicate the state's efforts and interest to identify, classify and keep track of population flows, internal and external, insiders and outsiders. This type of classification scheme continues to inform the content of the population registries today and radiates outward as it influences how we understand and characterize social relations. Further, it is significant that Sweden relies on population registries instead of a national census. Censuses tend to be based on bottom-up self-reporting that protects the identities of respondents. Population registries are top-down, state-controlled reporting mechanisms that also protect the anonymity of individuals but can link individual identity to the data. State agents in the Swedish Tax Agency are ultimately responsible for the selection of categories and collection of statistics from other state agencies such as the Migration Board and Social Insurance Agency. Statistics Sweden, which produces the official statistics on Sweden, similarly collects and collates statistics from reporting agencies. Although census categories can be narrow and inadequate, as Morning shows, they still allow for some degree of self-reporting and self-classification and have been a site for political struggle and recognition in the US. Indeed, the categories have changed over time, with the introduction of biracial choice in the 2000 Census, for example.

What is also significant for understanding contemporary forms of social distancing in Sweden is how the nearly unbroken record of vital statistics on the population contains no information about ethnicity. Instead, it contains multiple degrees and subcategories of foreignness. Statistics Sweden collects information on five categories of foreignness:

(1) foreign citizens;
(2) foreign born;

(3) foreign born who are Swedish citizens;

(4) Swedish born with two foreign born parents; and

(5) foreign background (all foreign born plus Swedish born with two foreign born parents).

(Statistics Sweden 2014)

The degree of foreignness is a principle way of classifying anyone who is not a native Swede or indigenous minority such as the Sami (discussed below). Even for those who were born in Sweden, their foreign origin is the overriding category. For those who naturalize, and Sweden does have high naturalization rates, their foreign origins do not disappear with their new status (Swedish citizens) but rather create a new foreign category: 'foreign born who are Swedish citizens'. Recalling Bauman, this process continues to divide and mark the population; he writes, 'all definitions mean splitting the totality into two parts – the marked and the unmarked' (Bauman 1989: 191). In Sweden, this marking is more fluid than the Bauman comparison implies, but it is nevertheless a structuring marker. For those born in Sweden but with foreign-born parents, their situation similarly creates another type of foreign category – one that highlights origins and blood ties rather than social or civic membership. This group is often referred to as 'second-generation immigrants', emphasizing family origin rather than social membership. It is worth noting that citizenship in Sweden follows *jus sanguinis*, citizenship by blood ties, rather than *jus soli*, citizenship by birth on the territory, thus similarly emphasizing origins over civic belonging (Swedish Tax Agency 2014; Migrationsverket 2014; Barker 2013a). In terms of population statistics, four of the five foreign categories preface origins, which may imply a preference to categorize by common descent or more provocatively a biological understanding of difference. The use of foreignness is a choice and one that needs to be examined more closely, especially because it goes against international norms of enumerating by ethnicity.

This emphasis on origins is surprising given the long-standing taboos on race in Sweden, a taboo connected to the horrors of the Holocaust and the country's own racial purification schemes vis-à-vis the Eugenics Movement (Broberg and Hansen 1996). The preference to categorize by foreignness despite purported intentions to avoid racial classification only serves to magnify and define difference as rooted in origins. The classification of indigenous populations in Sweden, including the Sami, Jews, Roma (indigenous, non-EU migrants), Swedish Finns and Tornedal Finns, as 'national minorities' further illustrates this tendency. These groups are the only groups that are singled out as a special category of minorities, in need of language and cultural preservation, on the basis of having lived in Sweden for a long time (Ministry of Integration and Gender Equality 2007). This distinction highlights their origins and heritage, which may reinforce not only that they are different from mainstream society but also that this cultural difference is rooted in biology. Minority status is conceived here as something belonging exclusively to these indigenous groups and quite possibly as an intrinsic characteristic.

This point about origins is further illustrated by the surfacing of the Roma Registries: secret files kept by the police on all people with Roma heritage. Exposed by an investigative journalist, the police were unable to explain why they kept detailed data files and social maps on all Roma in southern Sweden, including young people, old people, ordinary people and pillars of society – who were all stunned to find their names on this list. In their response, the police said that they were keeping track of criminal family networks, an explanation that only generated more heat because they were effectively suggesting that Roma were all criminals, inherently so since the police also kept tabs on infants. The police could not provide an explanation for the existence of this registry and nor did they have a register for any other group.

The way that classification schemes are used in Sweden presents a peculiar view of the population. Rather than reflecting an ethnically diverse society, which Sweden is, the registry data presents a picture of a population divided into natives, foreigners and indigenous people, with some subject to more control than others. This emphasizes fixed origins rather than the varied cultural beliefs, practices and voluntary associations, and fluid nature that ethnicity conveys (Morning 2008; Weber 1978; Wimmer 2008).

This classification scheme, and the social distance produced by it, has consequences for how we might imagine the nation and the social relations that play out within it. The emphasis on foreignness and the use of foreignness to denote ethnic difference create false binaries and undercut the idea of national unity – unity that could be based on difference. In one of the most compelling moments of the 2014 election campaign in Sweden, then Prime Minister Fredrik Reinfeldt asked his fellow citizens to 'open your hearts' to the massive influx of Syrian refugees coming into the country. He explained: 'These are people who come into Swedish society to build it together with us. Together we are building a better Sweden' (Reinfeldt quoted in Crouch 2014). Despite his efforts to connect foreigners to the building of the nation, his call for generosity and openness was met with a resounding 'no' vote: the Sweden Democrats, the anti-immigrant nationalist party, gained 12.9 per cent of the vote. This was an unprecedented win for that party, more than doubling its election results in 2010 and making it the third largest party in the country.

Population classification schemes are thus not neutral categories that reflect social reality; they are part and parcel of making up that reality and as such have material effects on processes of inclusion and exclusion. Following Bauman, we can think of these classification schemes as creating a gap or hole in moral responsibility towards others, as social distance decreases shared responsibility. Without a strong sense of duty towards others, the infliction of harm through expulsion and punishment can go unchecked. REVA, discussed below, is indicative of such a diminished duty of care.

Project REVA: classification schemes, rationalization, degradation and expulsion

The apartheid bus incident compels us to ask: How is it possible that a Swedish citizen could imagine himself deportable from his own country? I argue that this was made possible because events on the ground at the time suggested as much. In the early spring of 2013, around the same time as the segregated bus departed central Stockholm, deportation orders were becoming far more common across Sweden. Despite its reputation of openness towards migration, particularly refugees, Sweden has increased its deportation orders by 47 per cent since 2010 (Polisen 2013). Not everyone who enters has the right to remain in the country. This increase in deportation can be seen as part of a European, if not global, shift towards more restricted and stratified mobility control (Aas 2011; Bosworth 2008), partly in response to conflicts over national belonging (Bosworth and Guild 2008), the future of welfare states (Barker 2013b) and economic restructuring (De Genova 2010; De Giorgi 2010). In Sweden, this increase was partially realized by a joint police and Migration Board operation called Project REVA, known as 'the legal and effective execution of policy'.

Project REVA was intended to serve and expedite the processing of deportation orders to those without legal authorization to stay in the country (Migrationsverket 2012; Polisen 2013). To implement this directive, the police stopped commuters on public transportation to ask for identification. REVA was controversial and as of 30 June 2014 was officially no longer in operation. This break may be short lived, however, because of a new EU-wide initiative, known by its Roman military name, Mos Maiorum, aimed at locating and deporting irregular migrants in EU Member States (Sverige Riksdag 2014; Statewatch 2014). What made the Swedish operation so contentious across the political spectrum was not only the sheer spectacle – police sweeps through mass transit – but also the number of false positives. The police allegedly stopped commuters on the basis of their appearance, skin colour and 'foreignness', as reported widely in the national and local news media. Yet nine out of ten stops involved legal residents or Swedish citizens, according to police statistics (Sundkvist 2013). Citizens, of course, are not subject to deportation. One must ask: How and why did the police get this so wrong?

I contend that REVA is a prime example of the distorting effects that population registries can have on contemporary social relations, particularly around issues of immigration and border control. REVA depended upon and reproduced categories of foreignness that were readily at hand in a country that has not fully incorporated ethnic difference into its national narrative. The police tended to stop 'foreign-looking' people because of the assumption that ethnic difference – here very much conflated with physiological traits or phenotype, in line with the registry's emphasis on origins and ancestry – signals foreignness. As discussed above, non-ethnic Swedes are categorized by degrees of foreignness (for example, foreign born, foreign background, foreign

196 *Vanessa Barker*

parents) rather than as Swedes or as a hyphenated nationality (such as Iranian-Swede, Romanian-Swede, Kurdish Swedes or Afro-Swedes). This particular construction, taken as a neutral categorization schema, has the unintended consequence of producing a false binary between Swedes and foreigners. Woven into the seams of the society, this dichotomy can be understood as part of a repertoire of 'habits, skills, and styles' that help us make sense of social reality and act accordingly (Swidler 1986: 273). It is how we make sense of the world around us. The schema also provides a resource to assist the police to make sense of and sort social interaction. It is not that the police are necessarily racist but that they are using a deeply embedded cultural tool to locate, stop, classify, separate and ultimately try to remove difference from the territory. By relying on this binary, the police made a categorical error by failing to distinguish Swedes from those without legal authorization to remain in the country. Thus, those targeted were all placed in the same broad category, which subsequently communicated (intentionally or not) that foreigners do not belong in the country. These false positives pose a serious problem for Swedish society, indicating a pressing need to deal with difference.

REVA and rationalization: masking morality and punishing foreigners

REVA was controversial in part because of the manner in which it was implemented – policing and targeting difference. It should also have been more controversial for its use of legal cover. Here I want to connect this aspect to Bauman's concern with rationalization and bureaucratization. Initiated by the Alliance, a coalition formed among the then governing centre-right parties, increased deportation orders were justified not as a security measure or xenophobic impulse, but as a more effective way to regulate immigration and uphold the rule of law. To appreciate this argument, we might consider the guiding logic of Swedish migration policy. Swedish migration policy is based on a managerial model that is in conflict with its humanitarian components (such as eliminating barriers for Syrian refugees and accepting high rates of asylum seekers). Sustainability, rationalization and regulation are central to its stated mission and operation (Ministry of Justice 2014). In a key policy document on migration, the Ministry of Justice explains:

> The Government's objective is to ensure a *sustainable* migration policy that safeguards the right to seek asylum and, within the framework of *regulated* immigration, facilitates mobility across borders, promotes demand-driven labour migration, harnesses and takes into account the effects of migration on development and deepens European and international cooperation.
>
> (Ministry of Justice 2014, emphasis added)

Migration is not a free-for-all in Sweden; on the contrary, it is highly regulated and that regulation is highly valued.

For instance, at the height of the public outcry over the police sweeps, the prime minister defended the policy of deportation, explaining on national television: 'Those who have been denied entry or received deportation orders should leave the county' (Reinfeldt quoted in The Local 2013). He continued: 'If you've been rejected in a country with the most generous asylum and migration rules in the entire developed world, I think you should respect the decision' (Reinfeldt quoted in The Local 2013). In these straightforward statements, border control is explicitly linked to upholding the rule of law – a decision has been made, which must be followed and is to be understood within the presumed context of a just and humanitarian policy. Within this tight and common-sense framework, there is no room for individual circumstances or questioning the morality of deportation itself. Moreover, the responsibility for removal is placed back on the migrant him or herself; if s/he fails to comply, then the state will have no recourse but to call in the police, and the migrant has brought this on him/herself (on responsibilization, see Johansen 2013). In a similar vein, the Minister of Justice Beatrice Ask defended the deportation policy: a statement issued by her press secretary, Per Claréus, explained: 'In Sweden, we [follow] regulated immigration. This means that people who live and work in Sweden must have permission to do so. Controls are and should be a natural part of everyday police work' (Claréus quoted in Karlsson 2013). Thus, we are to understand deportation as a natural outgrowth of effective management. This practical, bureaucratic language works to neutralize, to a certain extent, the moral dimensions of deportation.

REVA, the enforcement dimension of the government's policy, was presented as a form of bureaucratic rationalization. It was intended to create a more efficient and coordinated effort across the varying government agencies responsible for migration and border control (Migrationsverket 2012). In the project description, for example, procedures are prioritized over the substance of the policy: deportation per se is not discussed, but rather management concerns with standardization, segmentation and consistency across agencies and regions (Migrationsverket 2012). The overarching concern is to streamline and standardize activities across agencies, including the Migration Board, the Border Police, the police and the Prison Service. The name itself, REVA, is, as mentioned earlier, an acronym which roughly translates as the legal, efficient and effective execution of policy. The name of this major government initiative does not indicate what the policy is actually about – deportation – but instead highlights its legality and efficiency. Recently, as REVA has come under criticism and been subjected to the media spotlight, a border patrol agent at Arlanda Airport has expressed concerns about this efficiency dimension, detailing the pressure placed on agents to fulfil targets and meet performance goals, which echo the managerial language of the new penology but in the form of its Swedish variant – the New Public Management Model (Ristic in Sincic 2014; Feeley and Simon 1992). This agent explained that the pressures to perform a certain number of internal border controls may have led to

198   Vanessa Barker

agents taking short cuts, such as stopping passengers based on their appearance or engaging in ethnic profiling – a practice he rejected as a violation of the policy, and which was similarly countered by his superiors at the Border Police (Ristic in Sincic 2014). Internal migration controls have increased substantially in recent years, with over 40,000 performed in 2012. This represents an increase of 40 per cent in two years (Polisen 2013), with 1,200 deportation orders served in that period. While it is doubtful that REVA has actually improved efficiency, since only 3 per cent of the internal controls led to deportation orders, there is no doubt that it has dramatically increased the number of internal controls and in turn the level of social conflict around this practice. In response to greater demands for efficiency and managerialism, short cuts have been made that depend upon the binary of foreigner/citizen built into the population registries, offering a quick but blunted tool to sort and classify suspects, leading to a high degree of inaccuracy, and exclusion.

The rationalization underpinning REVA may have masked moral questions about deportation, but it may also have contributed to the social production of immorality, in Bauman's terms. By classifying, separating and sorting foreignness and irregularity, the Swedish Government declined to take responsibility for those residing on its territory and failed to take responsibility for its own citizens wrongly stopped by the police and subject to internal migration controls. In the words of the Green Youth party spokesperson, it is 'deeply tragic that society's common resources are used so systematically to single out a marginalized group' (Rasmusson 2013).

Doubts about the legality of REVA have been raised by a range of critics, including politicians, activists and citizens. The name itself provokes this uncertainty: REVA is an acronym for the legal execution of policy. The redundancy in its name calls attention to the government's need to preface its legality. Doubts about its legality will surely be on the agenda at the upcoming conference on ethnic profiling, organized by the Discrimination Ombudsman (DO) (DO 2014). The DO is the government agency responsible for ensuring compliance with the Discrimination Act in Sweden and has taken up this issue for further discussion and investigation. The European Parliament has also received questions about the legality of REVA. In response to these questions, Cecilia Malmström, former European Commissioner for Home Affairs (2010–2014), explained that REVA seemed to be compatible with EU law. She wrote: 'Based on the information submitted and contacts with the Swedish authorities, the Commission cannot conclude that the control measures referred to by the Honourable Member are contrary to Union law' (Malmström 2014). Notable here is the use of the double negative, with the combination of the words 'cannot conclude' and 'contrary', which could be seen to weaken the effect of her affirmation. She went on to explain that, under Article 6 (1) of the Returns Directive, Member States (of the EU) not only have a right to issue return orders but are also obliged to issue return decisions to irregularly staying third-country nationals (Malmström 2014). She also made it clear that police controls were a 'necessary and legitimate tool' to enforce these decisions

(Malmström 2014). While her response on behalf of the commission seems to offer support to the programme, she insisted that enforcement must be carried out in a non-discriminatory and humane way, following the EU Charter of Fundamental Rights (Malmström 2014). But perhaps what is more interesting is her unprompted suggestion that under Article 6 (4) of this charter, Member States are 'free to grant such persons a permit for humanitarian or other reasons' (Malmström 2014). Deportation, then, even when already ordered, is not the only legal option. Member States, including Sweden, have far more freedom to act than government pronouncements about regulation would suggest. Malmström's response returns us to the issue of the morality of deportation: Is it really the only option? And is it the best option?

Diminished duty of care: REVA and public punishment

In relation to the social production of immorality, Bauman explains how the loss of sensitivity towards others plays a key role in social exclusion. It is this indifference to others that allows for the infliction of harm, harm that might otherwise have been perceived to be offensive or subject to condemnation. REVA embodies this indifference to others, an indifference that allowed the police to make a spectacle, a public punishment, of those perceived to be 'Other' as they stopped 'foreign-looking' commuters, momentarily detained and questioned them, and in some cases took them away, all under the gaze of the public, every passer-by watching, wondering what crime had been committed. Treated as suspects by the police, the commuters who were stopped had their identity, citizenship, belonging, status and criminality questioned by state authorities and in full view of the public. Their alleged crime was their suspect presence on the territory. This moment succinctly captures how mobility, particularly the mobility of racialized Others, or *global vagabonds*, has become meshed with criminalization (Fekete 2001; Weber and Bowling 2008). In this moment, crime categories such as the suspect and the offence infringe upon, if not replace, a migration frame based on free movement and human rights (on securitization of migration, see Huysmans 2006). It is noteworthy that in Sweden the Border Patrol, *Gränspolisen*, is administered by the national police force and is not a separate authority, and during the REVA campaign it was explicitly linked to the Migration Board. Border control relies on the intermeshing of various agencies such that distinct lines of institutional identity and aims may become blurred or interwoven.

Because the REVA encounter takes place in the public square, I suggest that it should be understood as a form of public shaming, degradation, akin to retrograde forms of punishment. In his compelling account of comparative penal sanctioning in *Harsh justice*, James Whitman (2003) defines punishment as degradation. Punishment is degradation, he explains, involving humiliation and the lowering of social status. He writes, 'it is treatment of others that makes them feel *inferior, lessened, lowered*' (Whitman 2003: 20, emphasis in original). Although Whitman links degradation to a distinctly American style

200 *Vanessa Barker*

of punishment, I think we can see elements of degradation operating among other criminal justice systems to a greater or lesser degree and operating in border control regimes across the Global North. In his chapter, John Pratt outlines similar public shaming of sex offenders in New Zealand, involving degradation that is central to their control (Pratt, this volume). While the Nordic systems have eliminated many of the inhumane and degrading penal conditions (Pratt and Eriksson 2013), elements remain in the system (Barker 2013a; Scharff Smith 2012) and were certainly operational during implementation of the REVA initiative, as those who did not belong were punished for it. In Bauman's terms, they were already outside the duty of care, outside the shared realm of moral responsibility, split off by the population registries, defined as foreign elements with ties and origins elsewhere, and excluded from the national narrative. Insofar as they were denied social proximity and its moderating effect on punishment, public degradation was permitted in a system that nominally opposes such treatment.

REVA degraded those it stopped and subjected to identity checks, even if this was not its stated intention or objective. Mass police sweeps and high-volume internal controls were meant to be pragmatic and efficient. But this bureaucratic imperative carried with it humiliating impacts. Those who were stopped described the procedure as 'deeply offensive' and 'discriminatory', in the words of Katarina Berggren, Deputy Chair of the Police Board in Stockholm and Mayor of Botkyrka, a diverse ethnic enclave south of Stockholm, as she publicly opposed REVA and called attention to its negative effects on her community members (Berggren in Karlsson 2013). If REVA had been applied universally, used to stop every commuter, then its public shaming function might not have been so damning. But, as noted above, these internal migration checks were not applied in a uniform way. Nor were they conducted in a private setting, at the migrant's last known address, for example. The public spectacle was clearly stigmatizing, punishing those who were told they do not belong, raising doubts about their status and lowering their position in the social order.

In one of the renowned objections to REVA, poet and playwright Jonas Hassen Khemeri wrote a public letter to the then Justice Minister, Beatrice Ask, requesting that she come and live in 'my skin' for a day. Khemeri's letter challenged the minister to try to understand what it is like living in Sweden as a member of an ethnic minority community, subject to police surveillance, suspicion and degrading treatment. His open letter was published by the national press, widely circulated and subsequently translated in part and published in *The Times*. Khemeri's words and experience capture the central themes of my analysis, evoking the texture of social distancing in its everyday reality. By bringing the reader into his skin, his body, he asks us to see, if not try to experience, what it is like to be subjected to doubt, discrimination and exclusion.

He details the shames and slights of his childhood, leading up to the moment when, as a college student studying economics, he was thrown into a police van. He recounts being asked for ID and then quite suddenly placed in a police van, in full view of the public and prying eyes, held there without recourse to explanation, without recourse to his innocence, held there simply because of his appearance, because he looked a certain way. In his open letter, he says he wishes the minister had been there with him but he 'sat there alone', assumed to be guilty of some unnamed crime. In his conclusion, he succinctly captures the dilemma of difference: '[I]t's hard to argue one's innocence from the back seat of a police van. And it's impossible to be a part of society when everyone continually assumes that you are not' (Khemeri 2013).

Khemeri's letter clearly illustrates the key aspects of social distancing: the conflation of ethnic difference with foreignness, the collapsing of foreignness into suspicion, and suspicion leading to police controls, all in public view. He was alone, he says, but not really, since everyone was watching him, casting judgement, affirming prejudices. Police controls are not simply private indignities but are very real and public spectacles in which one party is humiliated at the hands of another in full view. They are public spectacles where no one takes responsibility for the other. Khemeri uses his own experience to try to close this distance: this is his life, not just a public policy or a police order. These are human experiences, not managerial targets. His letter asks the minister, and by extension politicians and the public, to take responsibility for these actions, to realize a shared moral duty to care for others, to protect rather than inflict harm on others. But his last line – 'it's impossible to be a part of society when everyone continually assumes that you are not' – casts doubt on the possibility of closure.

In thinking of deportation as a public degradation ceremony (Garfinkel 1956), in which the status of the migrant is lowered and debased, we might be better able to understand the constitutive nature of deportation as it remakes members and populations. As Anderson *et al.* (2011) explain, deportation, in its constitutive capacity, recreates citizenship and subjects, affirming who belongs and who does not, but more insidiously reconstitutes the deportee as a non-subject as the state officially cuts all ties and obligations to the migrant. The deportee thus reconfigured holds no claim on the state's responsibility; there is no duty of care. In the EU, deportation from one Member State effectively means deportation from all EU Member States, which further intensifies the publicness of this public denouncement, expanding the realm from which the deportee is essentially banished.

Hence, the public spectacle of REVA's false positives and undignified removals, both enabled by the splicing of the population by the registries, are not only about discrimination but also degradation, further blurring the boundaries between border control and punishment. This degrading element may be undermining the principle of human dignity that is central to European penal systems (van Zyl Smit and Snacken 2009), so that it is not fully operational when it comes to border control in European welfare states, despite compulsory training in human rights across the Union. The degradation of deportation asks us to rethink what we have come to know and take for granted about

202 *Vanessa Barker*

migration and punishment in the European context, in which both fields are now more intermeshed and mutated than was previously the case (Bosworth 2014; Kaufman 2013).

Is there a way out? Closing gaps, recovering a moral duty of care

If we follow Bauman's work to its logical end, we could conclude that any attempt at classification, definition or categorization is a precarious act of splitting and separating the population, 'the totality into two parts', often with violent results (Bauman 1989: 191). The population registries do split and splice the population in Sweden, and during the REVA campaign had degrading effects on those deemed to be 'Other', cast out of a shared moral realm. But I do not think that this diminished duty of care is inevitable; the 'apartheid bus', despite its cultural significance, was a singular event, not a fleet of segregated buses. Moreover, social movements in Sweden actively resisted REVA, with frequent public protests and moral outrage; these protestors were not passive participants in the humiliation of their fellow human beings. They expressed a deep sense of public offence and indignation at the mobilization of these static racial classifications. And at times they were able to shut down these operations.

What we can take from Bauman is not foreboding predictions about the future, but a deep concern and sense of urgency about closing the gaps in moral worth. Social distancing wears away at our duty of care and diminishes our moral responsibility to others. These distances are not a priori, but socially constructed, and as such are mutable, flexible and more fluid than we think. Population registries in Sweden are well over 100 years old but they have changed over time and continue to change to reflect the current social reality. We need to see the category 'foreign background' for what it is: not as a proxy for ethnicity, not as a technocratic or politically correct way to avoid race, but as a destructive force that produces a false reality, and one that tears the population into pieces that do not fit together. We need to engage in a kind of 'civil repair', as Jeffrey Alexander calls it, to make up for past harms that have occurred in the civil sphere (Alexander 2001: 378). Introducing a census that includes self-reporting, for example, would go a long way towards remaking the population in its own image. It could break up and break away from the classification schemes that build social distancing into the bricks and mortar of Swedish society. It could help us rethink pluralism and deal with diversity in a way that does not relegate difference to life outside a shared moral realm.

In terms of deportation, Bauman can help us to see how the lack of connection with others allows for the infliction of harm on others. On the back of such social distancing, contemporary deportation regimes are engaged in punishment, degradation and exclusion of those deemed Other, who are often poor, racialized migrants from the Global South, 'global vagabonds' who are not perceived as part of the national community (Barker 2013b; Gibney

2013). Despite the rise in regional, transnational and even global concepts of citizenship (Isin 2012; Soysal 1994), almost all rights, duties, obligations, privileges and even life chances are still very much bound to national citizenship regimes and legal residency in a nation-state. The major challenge is to realize our moral duty to all humans, not only members, which is precisely Bauman's point.

Notes

1 Thanks to Polity Press for granting permission to reproduce previously published material in this chapter.
2 I would like to express my sincere appreciation to Anna Eriksson for organizing this challenging project and for running such a smooth and stimulating workshop in Prato. I thank all of the symposium participants, Ana Aliverti, Harry Blagg, Mary Bosworth, Anders Bruhn, David Green, Nico Johansen Per-Åke Nylander, John Pratt, and Debra Smith, for their feedback, questions, patience and criticisms. And thanks to Magnus Hörnqvist and Lars Trägårdh for their comments on a revised draft.

References

Aas, K. (2011) '"Crimmigrant" bodies and bona fide travelers: surveillance, citizenship and global governance', *Theoretical Criminology*, 15: 331–346.
Aas, K. and Bosworth, M. (eds) (2013) *The borders of punishment: migration, citizenship and social exclusion*, Oxford: Oxford University Press.
Alexander, J. (2001) 'The long and winding road: civil repair of intimate justice', *Sociological Theory*, 19: 371–400.
Aliverti, A.J. (2013) *Crimes of mobility: criminal law and the regulation of immigration*, London: Routledge.
Anderson, B., Gibney, M. and Paoletti, E. (2011) 'Citizenship, deportation, and the boundaries of belonging', *Citizenship Studies*, 15: 547–563.
Barker, V. (2013a) 'Nordic exceptionalism revisited: explaining the paradox of a Janus-faced penal regime', *Theoretical Criminology*, 17: 5–25.
Barker, V. (2013b) 'Democracy and deportation: why membership matters most', in K.F. Aas and M. Bosworth (eds), *The borders of punishment: migration, citizenship and social exclusion*, Oxford: Oxford University Press.
Bauman, Z. (1989) *Modernity and the Holocaust*, Cambridge: Polity.
Bauman, Z. (2000) *Liquid modernity*, Cambridge: Polity.
Bauman, Z. and Donskis, L. (2013) *Moral blindness: the loss of sensitivity in liquid modernity*, Cambridge: Polity.
Bosniak, L. (2006) *The citizen and alien: dilemmas of contemporary membership*, Princeton, NJ: Princeton University Press.
Bosworth, M. (2008) 'Border control and the limits of the sovereign state', *Social Legal Studies*, 17: 199–215.
Bosworth, M. (2014) *Inside immigration detention*, Oxford: Oxford University Press.
Bosworth, M. and GuildM. (2008) 'Governing through migration control: security and citizenship in Britain', *British Journal of Criminology*, 48: 703–719.
Bowker, G.C. and Star, S.L. (1999) *Sorting things out: classification and its consequences*, Cambridge, Massachusetts: MIT Press.

204 *Vanessa Barker*

Broberg, G. and Hansen, N.R. (eds) (1996) *Eugenics and the welfare state: sterilization policy in Denmark, Sweden, Norway and Finland*, East Lansing: Michigan State University Press.

Crouch, D. (2014) 'Rift emerges before vote in Sweden as immigration tests a tradition of openness', *The New York Times*, 12 September, online, available: www.nytimes.com/2014/09/13/world/europe/rift-emerges-in-sweden-over-immigration.html?module=Search&mabReward=relbias%3Ar%2C{%221%22%3A%22RI%3A10%22} (accessed 7 November 2014).

Dauvergne, C. (2008) *Making people illegal: what globalization means for migration and law*, Cambridge: Cambridge University Press.

De Genova, N. (2010) 'The deportation regime: sovereignty, space and the freedom of movement', in N. de Genova and N. Peutz (eds), *The deportation regime: sovereignty, space and the freedom of movement*, Durham, NC: Duke University Press.

De Giorgi, A. (2010) 'Immigration control, post-Fordism, and less eligibility: a materialist critique of the criminalization of immigration across Europe', *Punishment & Society*, 12: 147–167.

Dembour, M.B. and Kelly, T. (2011) 'Introduction', in M.B. Dembour and T. Kelly (eds), *Are migrants rights for migrants? Critical reflections on the status of irregular migrants in Europe and the United States*, London: Routledge.

Discrimination Ombudsman (DO) (2014) *Conference on ethnic profiling 21 November 2014*, Stockholm:Diskrimineringsombudsmannen, online, available: http://news letter.paloma.se/webversion/default.aspx?cid=4081&mid=255915&emailkey=f388a 278-6d69-456b-8971-0bb35b5c88f9 (accessed 7 November 2014).

Feeley, M. and Simon, J. (1992) 'The new penology: notes on the emerging strategy of corrections and its implications', *Criminology*, 30: 449–474.

Fekete, L. (2001) 'The emergence of xeno-racism', *Race and Class*, 43: 23–40.

Fekete, L. and Webber, F. (2010) 'Foreign nationals, enemy penology and the criminal justice system', *Race & Class*, 51: 1–25.

Garfinkel, H. (1956) 'Conditions of a successful degradation ceremony', *American Journal of Sociology*, 61: 420–424.

Garland, D. (1997) '"Governmentality" and the problem of crime: Foucault, criminology, sociology', *Theoretical Criminology*, 1: 173–214.

Gibney, M. (2013) 'Deportation, crime, and the changing character of membership in the United Kingdom', in K.F. Aas and M. Bosworth (eds), *The borders of punishment: migration, citizenship and social exclusion*, Oxford: Oxford University Press.

Gordon, L. (1994) *Pitied but not entitled: single mothers and the history of welfare, 1890–1935*, New York: Free Press.

Hofsten, E. (1988) 'Wargentin and the origin of Swedish population statistics', *Journal of Official Statistics*, 4: 261–264.

Huysmans, J. (2006) *The politics of insecurity: fear, migration and asylum in the EU*, London and New York: Routledge.

Isin, E. (2012) *Citizens without frontiers*, New York: Bloomsbury.

Johansen, N. (2013) 'Governing the funnel of expulsion: Agamben, the dynamics of force, and minimalist biopolitics', in K.F. Aas and M. Bosworth (eds), *The borders of punishment: migration, citizenship and social exclusion*, Oxford: Oxford University Press.

Karlsson, P. (2013) 'Ny kritik mot Reva-projektet', *Aftonbladet*, 1 March, online, available: www.aftonbladet.se/nyheter/article16337183.ab (accessed 7 November 2014).

On Bauman's moral duty 205

Kaufman, E. (2013) 'Hubs and spokes: the transformation of the British prison', in K. F. Aas and M. Bosworth (eds), *The borders of punishment: migration, citizenship and social exclusion*, Oxford: Oxford University Press.

Khemeri, J.H. (2013) 'Sweden's closet racists', trans. R. Willson-Broyles, 20 April, *New York Times Sunday Review* online, available: www.nytimes.com/2013/04/21/opinion/sunday/swedens-closet-racists.html?pagewanted=all&module=Search&mabReward=relbias%3Ar%2C{%221%22%3A%22RI%3A10%22}&_r=0 (accessed 7 November 2014).

Krasmann, S. (2007) 'The enemy on the border: critique of a programme in favour of a preventive state', *Punishment & Society*, 9: 301–318.

Malmström, C. (2014) 'Answers given by Ms. Malmström on behalf of the Commission', *Parliamentary questions, European Parliament, 14 May 2013*, online, available: www.europarl.europa.eu/sides/getAllAnswers.do?reference=E-2013-002306&language=EN (accessed 7 November 2014).

Melossi, D. (2003) 'In a peaceful life: migration and the crime of modernity in Europe/Italy', *Punishment & Society*, 5: 371–397.

Migrationsverket (2012) 'Projekt medfinansierat av Europeiskaåtervändandefonden 2012, Projektnamn: REVA – Rättssäkert och effektivtverkställighetsarbete del 3; Implementering', online, available: www.migrationsverket.se/download/18.5e83388f141c129ba6312ab8/1381926423879/projekt_rf_2012.pdf (accessed 7 November 2014).

Migrationsverket (2014) 'Becoming a Swedish citizen', online, available: www.migrationsverket.se/English/Private-individuals/Becoming-a-Swedish-citizen.html (accessed 7 November 2014).

Ministry of Integration and Gender Equality (2007) *National minorities and minority languages: a summary of the government's minority policy*, Stockholm:Government Offices of Sweden, online, available: www.government.se/content/1/c6/08/56/35/3b0f796c.pdf (accessed 7 November 2014).

Ministry of Justice (2014) 'Migration policy: fact sheet Ju14.04e' August', Stockholm: Ministry of Justice, Government Offices of Sweden, online, available: www.government.se/sb/d/574/a/245596 (accessed 7 November 2014).

Morning, A. (2008) 'Ethnic classification in global perspective: a cross-national survey of the 2000census round', *Population Research and Policy Review*, 27: 239–272.

Nilsdotter Jeub, U. (1993) 'Parish records: 19th century ecclesiastical registers', Information from the Demographic Data Base, Umeå:Demografiska databasen.

Polisen (2013) 'Arbetet med REVA påbörjat', 19 February, online, available: http://polisen.se/Arkiv/Nyhetsarkiv/Stockholm/2012/Arbetet-med-REVA-paborjat-inom-gransppolisavdelningen-Stockholm (accessed 7 November 2014).

Pratt, J. and Eriksson, A. (2013) *Contrasts in punishment: an explanation of Anglophone excess and Nordic exceptionalism*, New York: Routledge.

Rasmusson, M. (2013) 'Jakten på papperslösa intensifieras i Stockholm', DN.Debatt, 1 January, online, available: www.dn.se/debatt/stockholmsdebatt/jakten-pa-pappersslosa-intensifieras-i-stockholm (accessed 7 November 2014).

Sarat, A. and Shoemaker, K. (eds) (2011) *Who deserves to die? Constructing the executable subject*, Amherst: University of Massachusetts Press.

Schall, C.E. (2012) '(Social) democracy in the blood? Ethnic and civic idioms of Swedish nationhood and the consolidation of social democratic power, 1928–1932', *Journal of Historical Sociology*, 25: 440–474.

Scharff Smith, P. (2012) 'A critical look at Scandinavian exceptionalism: welfare state theories and penal populism and prison conditions in Denmark and Scandinavia',

206 *Vanessa Barker*

in T. Ugelvik and J. Dullum (eds), *Penal exceptionalism? Nordic prison policy and practice*, London: Routledge.

Sincic, P. (2014) 'Gränspolis om Reva: Varken rättssäkert eller effektivt', *DagensArena*, 25 February, online, available: www.dagensarena.se/innehall/granspolis-om-reva-varken-rattssakert-eller-effektiv/ (accessed 7 November 2014).

Skocpol, T. (1995) *Protecting soldiers and mothers: political origins of social policy in the United States*, Cambridge, MA: Belknap Press of Harvard University Press.

Sköld, P. (2004) 'The birth of population statistics in Sweden', *The History of the Family*, 9: 5–21.

Soysal, J. (1994) *Limits of citizenship: migrants and postnational membership in Europe*, Cambridge: Cambridge University Press.

Statewatch (2014) 'Special report: joint operation "Moss Maiorum" starts', 13 January, online, available: www.statewatch.org/news/2014/oct/eu-operation-mos-maiorum.htm (accessed 7 November 2014).

Statistical Yearbook of Sweden (1914) *Statistisk årsbok för Sverige*, Stockholm:Statistics Sweden, online, available: www.scb.se/en_/Finding-statistics/Historical-statistics/Statistical-Yearbook-of-Sweden (accessed 7 November 2014).

Statistics Sweden (2014) *Summary of population statistics, 1960–2013*, Stockholm: Statistics Sweden, online, available: www.scb.se/en_/Finding-statistics/Statistics-by-subject-area/Population/Population-composition/Population-statistics/Aktuell-Pong/25795/Yearly-statistics–The-whole-country/26040 (accessed 7 November 2014).

Stumpf, J. (2006) 'The crimmigration crisis: immigrants, crime and sovereign power', *Bepress* Legal series: working paper 1635, Berkley, CA: Bepress Legal Repository, online, available: http://law.bepress.com/expresso/eps/1635 (accessed 7 November 2014).

Sundkvist, F. (2013) '9 av 10 i polisens id-jakt har rätt att vistas här', *Metro*, 25 February, online, available: www.metro.se/nyheter/9-av-10-i-polisens-id-jakt-har-ratt-att-vistas-har/EVHmby!PMA3fueKtO7g2 (accessed 7 November 2014).

Svahn, C. (2013) 'Vi kände oss förolämpade och diskriminerade', *DN. STHLM*, 23 March, online, available: www.dn.se/sthlm/vi-kande-oss-forolampade-och-diskriminerade (accessed 7 November 2014).

Sverige Riksdag (2014) 'Den polisiära EU-operationen Mos maiorum' Interpellation 2014/15:9, online, available: www.riksdagen.se/sv/Dokument-Lagar/Fragor-och-anmalningar/Interpellationer/Den-polisiara-EU-operationen-M_H2109/ (accessed 6 November 2014).

Swedish Tax Agency (2014) *Population registration in Sweden*, Stockholm: Skatteverket, online, available: www.skatteverket.se/privat/sjalvservice/blanketterbroschyrer/broschyrer/info/717b.4.39f16f103821c58f680008017.html (accessed 7 November 2014).

Swidler, A. (1986) 'Culture in action: symbols and strategies', *American Sociological Review*, 51: 273–286.

The Local (2013), 'Reinfeldt defends migrant deportation push', 18 March, online, available: www.thelocal.se/20130318/46788 (accessed 7 November 2014).

Trägårdh, L. (2000) 'History of the concept of the people', in *The international encyclopedia of the social & behavioral sciences*, Oxford: Elsevier Science.

van Zyl Smit, D. and Snacken, S. (2009) *Principles of European prison law and policy: penology and human rights*, Oxford: Oxford University Press.

Wacquant, L. (1997) 'For an analytic of racial domination', *Political Power and Social Theory*, 11: 221–234.

Weber, L. and Bowling, B. (2008) 'Valiant beggars and global vagabonds: select, eject, immobilize', *Theoretical Criminology*, 12: 355–375.

Weber, L. and Pickering, S. (2011) *Globalization and borders: death at the global frontier*, Basingstoke: Palgrave Macmillan.

Weber, M. (1978) *Economy and society*, Berkeley: University of California Press.

Whitman, J. (2003) *Harsh justice: criminal punishment and the widening divide between America and Europe*, New York: Oxford University Press.

Wimmer, A. (2008) 'Elementary strategies of ethnic boundary making', *Ethnic and Racial Studies*, 31: 1025–1055.

10 Immobilization in the age of mobility[1]

Sex offenders, security and the regulation of risk

John Pratt

The later scholarship of Zygmunt Bauman, in particular *Liquid modernity* (Bauman 2001), focuses on the dramatically changing social arrangements of modern societies in the late twentieth and early twenty-first centuries, and the way in which this has led to their moral boundaries being redrawn, realigned and recalibrated. Nonetheless, his insights into the social production of immorality set out in *Modernity and the Holocaust* (Bauman 1989) remain very important, even though these are now being played out in the context and circumstances of these early-twenty-first-century societies.

In that book (and with echoes of Norbert Elias), modern society is given credit for the way in which its civilized attributes have led to the suppression of irrational drives and the display of unhealthy human emotions. In addition, the legitimate use of violence (and, we might add, the power to punish) has been largely removed from everyday life and concentrated almost exclusively in the authority of the central state. Yet those same processes that have allowed modern society to attach the label 'civilized' to itself contain within them the means to produce conduct quite contrary to such innate moral inhibitions, conduct based on fear and fantasy rather than scientific rationalities, demanding that those who are different or unacceptable in some way or other be variously punished, shut out, excluded, neutralized and, ultimately, as in the Holocaust itself, exterminated – such was the menace to the well-being of the rest of society that they were thought to constitute.

This process of 'Othering' reached its apogee in that event. It involved not only those who were directly responsible for or involved in the killings but:

> a much wider number of people who never in the process face consciously either difficult moral choices or the need to stifle inner resistance of conscience. The struggle over moral issues never takes place, as the moral aspects of actions are not immediately obvious or are deliberately prevented from discovery and discussion. In other words, the moral character of action is either invisible or purposefully concealed.
>
> (Bauman 1989: 24)

As such, the authorization and routinization of violence by the state was allowed to become a normal feature of everyday life (very few could or wished to challenge its power), alongside the dehumanization of its victims in public discourse: the only legitimate way to describe them came to be in terms of some form of sub-human species or other. Meanwhile, the physical and/or psychic distances that were created between all those beyond the immediate areas of atrocity and the victims eased, assuaged, left untroubled altogether the moral concerns and inhibitions of the former, as if the latter were either invisible or worthless.

But let us now leave the social production of immorality in Nazi Germany and move to the contemporary social arrangements of the main English-speaking societies on which this chapter is based. We are not talking about the Holocaust anymore. Instead, the theme is the unbearable tension that now exists in modern societies between increased freedom of choice and high levels of anxiety and insecurity. On the one hand, post-1980s' social and economic reconstruction has brought into existence multilayered opportunities for self-enhancement, pleasure and material reward. However, as a result of these same developments many of the state regulations now thought to have held individuals back from such achievements have had to be swept aside. This has coincided with the disintegration of other features of modern society that had offered security and stability in the form of familiar, identity-generating landmarks – employment tenure, marriage, trade union membership, church attendance and so on, as is well documented by Beck (1992), Fukuyama (1995) and others. This transformation has been welcomed by many politicians, their advisers, much of the mass media and all those in the consumer industry whose living is dependent upon the great mass of these societies regularly seeking out and enjoying the rewards of deregulation. For them, it is as if the more we are freed from such restraints, limitations, ties and loyalties, the more *mobile* we are, the more we are likely to make the most of all the enticing opportunities now available to us: 'individuals who are untied to place, who can travel light and move fast, win all the competitions that matter and count' (Bauman 2001: 62).

On the other hand, such uncertainties, entirely necessary if entrepreneurs are to maximize their potential, are far from 'glorious' for many others. Without those previous landmarks that acted as defining points on the map of everyday life, and with the state far more reluctant to throw lifelines to citizens who encounter difficulties as they make their journeys through it, unwelcome and unsettling risks and dangers seem to encroach on every step taken. As a consequence, what might be called 'the age of mobility' has, ironically and inevitably, also been accompanied by high levels of *immobilization*. Some of this has been self-imposed in the form of the development of gated communities or their equivalents, the most ostentatious and impenetrable forms of self-protection that are available to those who can purchase such high levels of security. The barriers and boundaries that are provided by these means represent defiant gestures of exclusion aimed at the stuff of nightmares

210 *John Pratt*

now thought to prowl in public space around them. Such developments are also exemplars of the new morality inscribed around the self and its enhancement. The more that individuals are exhorted to, and believe it necessary to take care of themselves to this ultimate extent, then the more boundaries are constructed around private space. But the more private space is walled off and made impenetrable, the more the insecurities of public space are illuminated, and the more threatening those inhabiting it become.

A good many of these concerns are directed at a group of men – almost exclusively men – who have committed sex crimes, many of a particularly serious and heinous nature: and they have been punished for them, most usually with significant prison sentences. Until recently, that was thought to be enough of a reaction to them. They had reached the limit of how much punishment could and should be inflicted on them. Indeed, punishment in modern society in the post-war period was intended to divest itself of any semblance of excess, brutality and arbitrariness associated with Nazism. It was meant to expiate the crimes of these offenders and, thereafter, through mechanisms such as parole and probation, encourage them to rejoin society – of course, it did not work out like that on many occasions, but at least that was the formal intention.

And it remains the case that, in these democracies, the state does not authorize or routinely use violence on its own citizens in the production of and reaction to immorality, even against those who pose the greatest risks to the well-being of others. What we find in recent years instead, however, is the introduction of innovative or revitalized penal measures against these offenders that very clearly step outside the limits on punishment previously imposed by the values of the post-Holocaust civilized world, and with increasing regularity: for some, prison sentences may be continued at their end (albeit under a different guise); those not in prison may have their movements in public space greatly restricted or confined, sometimes for indefinite periods; and others still, who may not have committed any offence at all, but are thought to be close to doing so, may be subject to legal controls that can lead to imprisonment if breached, even though they may never have actually committed an offence. And as such initiatives have been introduced, so such offenders, or suspects, have been routinely dehumanized in public discourse – this aspect of the Othering process does not seem to have changed – to the point where this becomes a legitimate and acceptable way to speak of and think about them. In such ways, the longing for security in the age of mobility has led to demands that those who put this at risk must be immobilized themselves. This can be achieved by more extensive use of the prison, but immobilization extends beyond this into public space as well, leading to a transformation of some of the conditions, routines and expectations of everyday life itself – both for potential offenders and all their possible victims.

What is it, then, that has made such divisions and exclusions possible? What particular social processes have brought about these exceptions to the penal standards of the civilized world? Why is it that it has been sex offenders at the forefront of these measures? What are the particular risks that they pose to public safety that have generated these extensive mechanisms of exclusion? Let us begin to address these questions by first examining the public, political and media reaction to the release of a New Zealand sex offender in 2012 and the subsequent measures that were taken to permanently exclude him from society, notwithstanding that he had reached the end of his sentence.

Contemporary dehumanization: the 'Beast of Blenheim'

Stewart Murray Wilson, then aged 66, was released on parole from Whanganui Prison in September 2012, after serving 18.5 years of a 21-year prison sentence for sexual offences imposed in 1996. These offences dated back to 1971 and included rape, attempted rape, indecent assault, stupefying his victims, attempted stupefying, wilful ill-treatment of a child, assault on a female and bestiality. The offences were against members of his family, women and children who were living for a while in his home and women hitchhikers whom he sought out and 'befriended'. In addition to the sexual offences against the women, and the occasion when he 'compelled' one of them to have sex with a dog, '[his] daughter ate her food from a bowl she shared with the family cats, was unkempt and covered in urine from head to toe, wore light clothing during winter months, had no underwear, and was forced to watch violent and sexual acts' (Courtney 2 May 1997: A1; A9).

After four previous unsuccessful applications, Wilson was granted parole in 2012. However, this was simply a strategy that allowed him to be imprisoned for as long as legally possible, but then released two days before the end of that time on a 2.5-year licence, and kept under strict control and surveillance post-prison. With this purpose in mind, the Parole Board imposed 17 restrictions on him. These included a requirement to live in a state house on prison grounds; a requirement to wear a GPS tracking device (the first New Zealand offender ever to be fitted with one); and prohibitions on any female visitors unless permitted by his probation officer, contact of any kind with anyone under 16 without supervision, attending Alcoholics Anonymous meetings, keeping pets, using the internet, riding a scooter and attending church. Furthermore, he would only be allowed to leave the prison grounds in the company of at least two security staff. Despite these safeguards, the news of his 'release' generated an outcry from significant sections of the local community, including the town council. Meanwhile, the Minister of Justice stated that the government would be 'putting forward a law change that would allow the Corrections Department to keep him "behind bars"' (Ensor, *Dominion Post*, 29 August 2012a: A3).

However, these reactions were not tailored to fit Wilson, an elderly man at the end of a long prison term, carrying all the physical and mental burdens of that experience. Instead, they were a reaction to his *alter ego* of 'the Beast of Blenheim'. He had been given this name by a journalist at the time of his convictions (Blenheim was the town where he was then living) and from that

212   *John Pratt*

time on was dehumanized – routinely so, since this identity was reinforced by the New Zealand media each time he intermittently appeared in public discourse thereafter. Newspaper features have included headlines such as: 'Beast may ask for new trial' (Anon, *Evening Post*, 24 January 2000: 2); (after being denied parole) '"Beast" must serve 4 more years' (Broun 30 December 2008: A4); '"Beast" must remain behind bars' (Anon, *Dominion Post*, 19 December 2009: A17); and 'High Court says Board fair in denying parole to "Beast"' (Anon, *Dominion Post*, 24 May 2011: A7). However, for several months in 2012, after the rejection of another parole application but with the latest possible date for his release being confirmed for September that year, Wilson then became a more regular news item, although always as 'the Beast'. The decision of the Parole Board, declining his application, was released to the public: 'the personal factors uniquely applying to this offender point to the strong likelihood of further similar sexually deviant behaviour occurring as soon as he has the opportunity to engage in it' (Anon, *Dominion Post*, 18 April 2012a: A9). In the same issue of that newspaper, as if to warn readers of the dangers that he still posed to their safety, the journalist who coined the phrase 'the Beast of Blenheim' recalled what to her had been his less than human features: 'On the occasions I met him when he was awaiting trial, this unattractive, toothless man, with shaking pasty-white hands and long lank hair greeted me like a long-lost friend but continued to deny his guilt' (Anon, *Dominion Post*, 18 April 2012a: B5). In other words, his very appearance, in addition to the offences he had committed, transformed him into this non-human monster.

Thereafter, his risk of reoffending was reported as being 'lifetime persistent' (Clarkson, *Dominion Post*, 6 July 2012a: A8), in the words of a psychologist who gave evidence against him in the High Court (to which he had unsuccessfully appealed against the plans for GPS tracking while he was on parole). Journalists also searched out some of his victims, whose recollections emphasized how dangerous someone with his bestial propensities and qualities must still be. One woman ('Sisters fear of Beast's return', Anon, *The Press*, 12 July 2012b: A5) who had stayed at his house explained that

> I was sleeping in the lounge which was near the kitchen. In the middle of the night, he got up and went to the kitchen naked. I thought that was weird … the next night [he] started drugging me. … One night I found pills in my [meal]. They weren't even crushed up, I found them in my mashed potatoes.

The *Dominion Post* (Clarkson 14 July 2012b: A20) then reported that:

> He is one of New Zealand's most dangerous sex offenders – and he will soon be roaming the streets. … He was once described by a victim as the 'angel of the devil' … Wilson instilled so much fear in people that neighbours sold their houses to get away from him. … Even social workers were afraid of him. One described being so scared of him that

she tried to get a climbing rope as an escape measure if he ever trapped her in her office ... Wilson will be freed on September 1.

Confirmation of his release date and the restrictions that had been imposed on him were reported under the headline 'Handling the Beast' (Anon, *The Press*, 10 August 2012c: A16).

The four main New Zealand newspapers[2] then focussed – with a remarkable intensity[3] – on the reaction of the Whanganui community to the confirmation of his release. That he had never had any previous connections with this town, nor had any victims there, were the reasons given by the Department of Corrections for its decision to move him to its prison just a few days before the release (under New Zealand victims' rights legislation of 2002, sex offenders cannot be released to addresses located near their victims' homes, thus making Whanganui ideal in this respect). In interviews with journalists, his new neighbours – those living in any proximity to his prison house on the outskirts of the town – indicated that they were afraid of becoming the latest in a new batch of his victims. One report told how a resident

> was having screens and latches installed on his home's windows and doors ... "I have a three year old daughter, a newborn and a 20 year old partner ... that's three potential victims living pretty close ... [he's] not even here yet and already we're having sleepless nights" ... [this man] was among about 270 people who attended a public meeting with Corrections Department officials last night.
>
> (Grocott 2012a: A5)

Although Wilson had not been convicted of any sexual offences against children, he had become ineluctably associated with such crimes, as this report suggests. Journalists encouraged this association by comparing the circumstances of his release and his likelihood of reoffending with other released but then reconvicted paedophiles, thereby adding to his menace. It was as if the appetite of the Beast was both insatiable and indiscriminate – his very presence put the security of all at risk.

Corrections officials did nothing to play down such associations and anxieties (Grocott 2012b: A5). Instead, assurances were given that the department had contained his risk to the public as far as was possible. Such a qualification, though, only seemed to confirm and reinforce the legitimacy of local anxieties and strengthen the opposition to his release. The local council petitioned the High Court not to release him at all. This was predictably declined; the judge stated that there was no jurisdiction to intervene and that, anyway, '[Wilson] has to be released somewhere'. It was in response to this that the council tried to organize a 'community shunning' of him:

> Whanganui councillors are planning to ban [the] serial sex offender from all council controlled property in the city ... it follows an initiative by

214   *John Pratt*

[a councillor] who has prepared 'ready to go' trespass notices for local business owners who wish to ban the man dubbed the Beast of Blenheim from their property ... if the Council and community embrace both plans, it would effectively mean Wilson could not go anywhere in Whanganui other than to the house on prison grounds where he will be released next week.

(Forbes, *Dominion Post*, 27 August 2012: A3)

Despite the banality of the release – Wilson's movement from one part of the prison to another – it still generated a great deal of excitement among the media. Having created, nourished and sustained 'the Beast' themselves, it was as if it were the task of reporters to inform the public of the latest details, however trivial, of the movements and actions of the monster that imperilled them, however restricted these were. For example:

Sun and daffodils for Beast's first day free: the serial sex predator dubbed the Beast of Blenheim basked in the sunshine of his new backyard ... his first moments of freedom after 18 years behind bars came before dawn as he stepped, wearing a green jacket, from a white prison van and walked through a gate about 20 metres to his new home.

(Ensor, *Dominion Post*, 30 August 2012b: A3)

For some weeks afterwards Wilson remained at the centre of attention, notwithstanding that there remained little 'news' to report.

This, though, was no deterrent for some journalists. The *Dominion Post* (Ensor 29 September 2012c: A1, A3) carried three features on him in the same issue, for example. The first, 'Face to face with the Beast', was an interview that he gave to one of its journalists in which he stated that 'I'm not out to hurt anyone or harm anyone or do anything stupid. I'm not bitter, I'm not twisted and I just want to get on and continue my life with a bit more freedom' – an assurance that was undermined by an introduction to the article reminding its readers, once again, that 'in 1996, a toothless man with a receding hairline was jailed for some of New Zealand's most heinous sex crimes'. In other words, the label of 'the Beast' would not allow the new identity he was trying to claim – that of an old man newly released from prison, trying to peacefully live out what was left of his life – to establish itself in the minds of the newspaper's readers. The second, under the headline 'Neighbours feared sex offender so much they moved away' (Anon, *Dominion Post* 29 September 2012d: A3), reprinted the earlier report claiming that 'even social workers feared him', once again reaffirming his perpetual menace. Similarly, the third, an editorial, claimed that 'a very real risk [of reoffending] remains', quoting in support the now retired detective who had first investigated his crimes ('Denials mean very real "risk"', Anon, *Dominion Post* 29 September 2012e: A3).

Eventually, though, this episode in the life of the man who had been turned into a beast reached its inevitable conclusion: 'sexual predator Wilson has been recalled to prison after he allegedly phoned a woman he had already been warned not to contact' (Ensor, *Dominion Post*, 22 February 2013: A1). She was a relative of two of his victims but had sent him a Christmas present. Wilson had called to thank her. Even though she said she had welcomed the contact, 'police visited [her] the day after one of his calls and told her that Wilson had been grooming her' (Anon, *Dominion Post*, 12 March 2013b: A3). He had also mentioned, it was claimed, 'escaping to Australia' – what could only have been either a joke or a ridiculous flight of fantasy since he had no passport and hardly any money. Nonetheless, his conduct was described by the Department of Corrections as being 'not pro-social', thereby justifying his return to prison.

That Wilson should receive so much sensationalized media attention is hardly unique to New Zealand. Since the media's reconstruction and deregulation in the 1980s, the days are gone when its primary task is to act as a purveyor of public information or education. What *is* unique to New Zealand among countries within the Organisation for Economic Cooperation and Development, however, is that there is no longer any state broadcasting authority still performing this task, providing balance and a yardstick against which the veracity and authority of other commercial outlets can be judged. Similarly, there is no history of an authoritative national broadsheet press that could perform the same function. Thus unrestrained, the New Zealand media were not only able to dehumanize Wilson by creating his 'Beast of Blenheim' *alter ego* but were also able to routinely and vigorously reinforce this identity – to the point where his reality as an ageing ex-prisoner was lost altogether – with little by way of a challenge to it.[4]

Sex offenders as intolerable risks

Of course, sex and sex offenders have always been able to sell newspapers or promote television programmes – there is nothing new in this. However, what has given Wilson and others like him particular purchase – a purchase that now turns them into predatory, prowling monsters – is that they seem to endanger all that has come to be valued most in these societies in the aftermath of post-1980s restructuring. First, they endanger the human body, particularly the bodies of women. If the body has come to be at the forefront of all the enhancements and enticements brought about by post-1970s social change, then 'the traffic between the body and the rest of the world where so many dangers lie in ambush cannot be avoided' (Bauman 2000: 63). The pursuit of such pleasures necessarily means exposure to all the dangers that lie scattered around the social fabric and seemingly strike at random. And thus, from nowhere, 'the Beast of Blenheim' was going to be unleashed on the hitherto unremarkable town of Whanganui. What, again, were the reasons for him being located in this town? It was because he had had no previous connection with it and, anyway, 'he has to be released somewhere'. As Bauman (2001: 148) observes, 'the most dreadful disasters now strike at random,

216   *John Pratt*

picking their victims with a most bizarre logic ... there is no way to anticipate who is doomed and who will be saved'.

Second, they endanger children. As increasingly scarce commodities in modern society due to the falling birth rate, their emotional value is now much higher than in earlier periods that saw higher birth rates (Zelizer 1985). But there is a new moral value attached to children as well, in addition to that given them by their physical scarcity. Amidst all the erosion of certainty and security, it is as if they have been invested with a profound emotional significance. As Furedi (2001: 107) puts the matter:

> at a time when very few human relations can be taken for granted, the child appears as a unique emotional partner in a relationship ... unlike marriage or friendship, the bond that links a parent to a child cannot be broken; it is a bond that stands out as the exception to the rule that relationships cannot [now] be expected to last forever.

Indeed, it is as if children have become 'symbols of purity, of origin, of identity, of what preserves the border against transgression at all costs' (Hacking 2003: 40). About to be uncaged amidst the linkages that had been drawn by the media between him and reoffending paedophiles, 'the Beast' seemed to be on the verge of penetrating what has become this most precious but also most precarious of borders, one that also demands more vigilant and careful guarding.

Third, Wilson seemed to endanger the Whanganui community itself. A town of 40,000 people, its population is in slow decline in contrast to the accelerating growth, principally through Asian immigration[5], in the country at large. Whanganui's population is also rather older and poorer than is the norm for New Zealand as a whole. The age of mobility has left the town behind and it will probably never be able to catch up. But if this means that it has atrophied, it also means that it has largely held on to its homogeneity and has been spared much of the turbulent reconstruction of New Zealand society at large. Accordingly, and as a counterweight to the lack of mobility of its citizens, it was as if this community represented 'an island of homely and cosy tranquillity in a sea of turbulence and inhospitality' (Bauman 2001: 182). This became all the more important in the context of the town's social and economic circumstances: 'being the only shelter offers an added value, and that value goes on being added to as the stock exchange where other life values are traded grows ever more capricious and unpredictable' (Bauman 2001: 182). Its citizens might be missing out on the prizes on offer to those with greater mobility elsewhere, but at least they had been spared the accompanying anxiety and insecurity: until it was announced that the dangerous outsider Wilson was to become Whanganui's newest citizen. The decision to release him then became a reminder that central government not only seemed powerless to assist the town to catch up with New Zealand's more prosperous regions, but it also threatened to jeopardize all that Whanganui had been able to hang on to as some sort of consolation prize for being left behind. Hence, 'in this fragile, lower borderline of respectability, but still worth defending' (Girling *et al.* 1998: 488), emerged the embittered reaction to this news and the attempts to organize community-wide opposition to Wilson independently of the government and its criminal justice organizations.

In response to the local outrage and national scandal generated by Wilson's release, the government made its own spectacular reaction. It would not be standing aside as some sort of hapless bystander as regards any such threats to public safety in the future. Instead, under the provisions of the Public Safety (Public Protection Orders) Bill 2013, Wilson and others like him would simply have their prison sentences prolonged at their end. The intended legislation allows those prisoners judged to be at a 'high level of imminent risk of serious sexual or violent offending' – that is, likely to commit such an offence as soon as the opportunity arises – to be held in 'civil detention' (meaning that 'they would be kept within the confines of a prison') on completion of their sentence. The level of risk necessary to invoke these measures involves 'an urge to reoffend', an 'inability to control emotions', an 'absence of understanding of the impact of their offending', and/or 'poor interpersonal relationships' and/or 'social isolation'. Furthermore, the legislation is retrospective. In the future, sexual offenders such as Wilson who are thought to constitute such a risk will not be allowed to wriggle free from its grasp by claiming that their offences predated it and that they are therefore immune from the new powers of detention that the bill would give the courts.

In this way, the promise of the legislation was able to establish a fleeting moment of solidarity (Bauman 1995). These measures taken to ensure that 'the Beast' and similar monsters would be kept in prison, whatever the legal niceties to the contrary, brought together local citizens, a government and its organizations previously seen as remote and limited in their ability to act on such matters, and a national media feasting on the distress provoked by the demons it had helped to create. It was also a solidarity that came at seemingly low moral (and economic) cost: simply ensure that the physical and psychic distance between all those 'normal' citizens and dangerous Others such as Wilson for whom no-one was prepared to speak is extended far beyond the horizon and never allowed to be reduced.

The Beast as a multinational moral dilemma

Again, though, this new kind of moral dilemma – how to render immobile those who pose intolerable risks to the mobility of others – is not unique to New Zealand. Similar 'beasts', similar reactions, similar measures are to be found in Australia, the United States (US) and England and Wales. As in the case of Wilson, there is usually a response to one very controversial and exceptional case that then becomes a sensational news story which also projects, in contrast with the utter, inhuman evil of the offenders, hallowed accounts of victims and their families and their attempts to come to terms with the loss of innocence that victimization has inflicted on them; or, more generally, that would be

218   *John Pratt*

inflicted on them if they were to become victims. What to do with such monsters, and how to protect the rest of society from the intolerable risks that they pose, then becomes a political crusade with promises from politicians from all major parties of much stronger protection from such risks in the future. In the US, in particular, the memorializing of the victims of these offenders by naming legislation after them gives these laws an additional sanctimony and authority (Garland 2001). Indeed, the continued detention of sex offenders after a finite sentence began in the US with the Washington State *Sexually Violent Predator Law 1990*. By 2011, 20 states had forms of legislation that allow the perpetrators of a sexually violent crime to be detained indefinitely by way of civil commitment after their prison sentence has been served. The criteria needed to invoke this (in addition to the conviction itself) are that such offenders are judged to be suffering from a 'mental abnormality' or personality disorder and that they are likely to reoffend unless confined in a 'secure facility' (meaning that such a prisoner is, again, likely to be moved from one part of the prison to another at the end of their sentence).

The provisions were extended to federal prisoners, even those who had never been charged with or convicted of a sex crime, in the *Adam Walsh Child Protection and Safety Act 2006*. This law was needed, the Solicitor-General claimed, 'to run a criminal justice system that does not itself endanger the public' (presumably by not releasing those thought to be at future risk of committing such crimes). Accordingly, having completed their sentence for what might have been an entirely different category of offence, prisoners can be detained indefinitely because they *might* commit a sexual offence if released. To facilitate their detention, the burden of proof on the prosecution is of a lower standard than 'beyond reasonable doubt', while 'clear and convincing evidence' is needed by a person so accused that they are not 'a sexually dangerous person'.

In England, the Criminal Justice Act 2003 allows for sex offenders to be made the subject of an indefinite imprisonment for public protection order. Once again, after serving a finite sentence for their crime, they can then be detained until their risk to public safety is judged to have abated. In addition, a sexual offences prevention order (Sexual Offences Act 2003) can be invoked in relation to those convicted sex offenders thought to be participating in or about to participate in a 'trigger event' (for example, waiting outside a children's playground). Such an order can prohibit them from activities thought to put children at risk of being sexually victimized, without the need for an offence to bring this about. Failure to comply with the terms of the order, however, would be a criminal offence, leading to imprisonment. In Queensland, Australia, the Dangerous Prisoners (Sexual Offenders) Act 2003, which allows for detention to be prolonged at the end of a prison sentence, was prompted by the release of the paedophile Dennis Fergusson at the end of his prison term, amidst local outrage and vigilante activity aimed at driving him out of any place he tried to settle. The Attorney-General (Queensland, Legislative Assembly 2003, *Debates*, 3 June 2003: 2484) justified the legislation by stating that it was:

akin to the detention authorized under mental health laws, except that the protection provided to the public by this new law is founded not on the mental illness of a person but on a different though equally sound principle of public policy.

Further, 'priority must be given to protecting the public ... from the serious danger [posed by those with] a propensity for committing [violent sexual] offences again'. Accordingly, 'the Act ... is intended to protect the community from predatory sexual offenders. It is a protective law authorizing involuntary detention in the interests of public safety. Its proper characterization is a protective rather than a punitive enactment' (Keyzer 2011: 27).

In New South Wales (NSW), Australia, the Crimes (Serious Sex Offenders) Amendment Bill 2013, schedule 1, 'sets out a scheme for the continued detention or supervision of serious sex offenders who pose an unacceptable risk of committing serious sex offences if not kept under supervision'. The primary objective of the act is 'to ensure the safety and protection of the community'. The risk that a person will present to the community does not need to meet the criminal law standard of proof – beyond reasonable doubt. Instead, the civil standard – 'a high degree of probability' – determines whether a prisoner is likely to commit a further sexual offence. By the same token, getting out of prison on parole has also become more difficult for such offenders. Parole judgements now have very little to do with an offender's response to rehabilitation but are much more related to assessment of the risks they would pose if released:

> the [New Zealand] Parole Board's role in the criminal justice system is to undertake an assessment of the risk that long-term sentenced offenders might pose to the safety of the community if they were to be released before the end of their sentence.
>
> (New Zealand Parole Board 2014)

At the other end of the criminal justice spectrum, the New Zealand Bail Amendment Act 2012 was designed 'to improve public safety and ensure the overall integrity of the bail system' (New Zealand Parliament 2012, Bills Digest number 1974). That is to say, it was intended to ensure the integrity of bail by eliminating it as a possibility for those thought to be at risk of committing serious crime while on remand. As such, 'a reverse burden of proof' has been introduced for offenders charged with sexual crimes (as well as drug offences and murder). They 'must now prove to the court that they should be released on bail and must satisfy the court that they will not commit any offence involving violence while on bail'. In justification of similar changes in England and Wales, advice given to the Attorney-General by the Crown Law Office (2012) argued that 'the presumption of innocence is an overarching principle of criminal justice but it does not directly apply to the consideration of bail prior to trial, which is concerned with anticipated behaviour rather than punishment for past conduct'.

The rise of the security sanction

All such measures clearly contravene long-established principles of punishment and criminal law: some are retrospective, a further period of detention can follow what should be the end of a prison term, criminal sanctions can be imposed for breaches of orders preventing behaviour that is not itself criminal, burdens of proof have been lessened, and presumptions in favour of bail have been reversed. And in relation to the Wilson case, he was simply moved to another part of the prison rather than released, opportunities for 'normal' behaviour were denied him because of the restrictive parole conditions, after-care organizations enforced his exclusion from the community rather than integrated him within it, and so on. Up to the 1970s, any departures of this nature from the penal framework of the civilized world led to extensive reflections on their morality (see, for example, Bottoms 1977 for a review of the agonizing ethical discussions regarding the legitimacy of forms of indefinite detention in the UK at that time). Where it was concluded that such departures *were* justifiable, then it was also thought that any such measures should be used with great caution (Floud and Young 1981).

What is it, then, that now makes it possible for those previous barriers and restraints on punishment to be pushed aside by these new laws and practices? By the mid-twentieth century, the previously existing principles of law and punishment and the parameters of possibility within them had become deeply embedded in modernity's 'solidarity project' (Garland 1996): a set of social arrangements intended to bring about stability and inclusion through the engineering processes of a strong state. However, the departures from these penal laws, principles and practices that we now find, are entirely consistent with new principles of law and punishment that fit *the post-solidarity project* social arrangements. While mobility at ever increasing speed has become the pathway to individual success, those same individuals are likely to have much more atomized lives, stripped from previous secure moorings and necessarily far more alert to risks and dangers, and demanding that, at all costs, their own mobility be safeguarded. It is out of *these* social arrangements that we find the rise of the 'security sanction', organized around protecting public safety by immobilizing and/or excluding those who endanger it, rather than protecting the rights of individual offenders from overarching state power and its abuses, as had previously been the case. And such sanctions are targeted particularly at sex offenders – intolerable risks, as we have seen – although not exclusively so. There are a variety of similar measures in place aimed at others who pose risks of varying kinds to public safety and well-being, ranging from terrorists at one end of this spectrum, to young people noisily playing football in the street, for which they are labelled 'anti-social', at the other.

The New Zealand parliamentary debate on the public protection legislation was couched in terms of the need to defend and protect these supervening community rights. Various speakers acknowledged that this would breach the country's (anyway unenforceable) Bill of Rights Act, but 'people must ask themselves whether they would place someone who has a very high risk of imminent and serious sexual or violent offending in any community in New Zealand, let alone their own' (New Zealand, House of Representatives 2013, *Debates*, 17 September 2013: 13441). And it was mentioned that 'the bill appropriately balances the right of New Zealanders to be free from almost certain serious harm versus the liberty rights of offenders who have served their sentence ... ordinary, everyday New Zealanders want to know and ensure that their safety is actually paramount in this parliament' (New Zealand, House of Representatives 2013, *Debates*, 17 September: 13449). As Valverde (2011: 11) notes in relation to the rise of such security-based measures, 'the logic of liberal legality can coexist with coercive measures as long as these ... are justified not as the exercise of absolutist sovereign prerogative but rather as protective measures to further the health of the "population"'.

In these respects, the parliamentary debate was of a much more measured tenor than that of the media reports of the likely impact of such legislation (for example, Vance 2012: A2). The bill was not legitimated on the basis that it represented some sort of punishment extravaganza, more in keeping with totalitarian societies; instead, it was legitimated on the basis that it remained in keeping with the penal practices of the democracies. 'Civil detention' was not, after all, it was claimed, an additional punishment: 'the bill is not about punishment; it is actually about protecting the community. Protection of the community in this small number of cases is a valid consideration against which to balance the longstanding principle of justice that you do the crime, you serve the time and when you have served the time, you are released and you are a free person' (NZ *Hansard*, 17 September 2013: 13446). And as another speaker clarified:

> it is really important that we have got pathways for these detainees [sic] – pathways so they can work towards being released at some stage, if that is an option for them. Each individual will have a management plan that identifies goals that could contribute to their eventual release. An annual review will be performed on each of these public protection orders. The High Court will look at each case every five years.
>
> (NZ *Hansard*, 18 September 2013: 13484)

In theory at least, those so detained would not be altogether abandoned and permanently shut out of society: a pathway, rather prolonged and obscure, but a pathway all the same, would be provided to allow them at some indeterminate point to find their way back to living freely in the community.

For those with a liberal conscience who might still be troubled by the legislation (although the bill was passed by 109 votes to 12, with the Labour opposition supporting the governing National [Conservative] Party), reassurances were given that these measures would only be used very irregularly. They were intended only for 'the worst of the worst', those who by definition exist beyond the boundaries of tolerance and acceptance in New Zealand and

222 *John Pratt*

similar societies, those whose presence would otherwise put the health of the rest of the population at risk. And anyway, it was as if any breaches of criminal justice procedures in relation to those who had made themselves so utterly worthless and dangerous – or at least those who had been dehumanized to this extent – were not worth worrying about; rather than that, if the government ignored their threat, then it would be negligent in its duty to safeguard the rest of the community. The Justice Minister, introducing the legislation, stated that:

> it is part of [the government's] programme to build a safer New Zealand, to protect our communities, to prevent crime, and to put victims first … only a small number of people are likely to be subject to a public protection order, but they are the very worst of the worst and they should not be inflicted on our community.
>
> (NZ *Hansard*, 18 September 2013: 13481)

Indeed, rather than undermining western democracies because of the way in which these measures extend the limits of punishment principles beyond their established framework, the New Zealand bill was presented as a method of strengthening democracy, thereby justifying its necessity and reaffirming its legitimacy.

Immobilization: in public space as well as prison

Of course, the most obvious way to immobilize those who pose such intolerable risks is to imprison them. In Bauman's work, the US 'supermax' prison is the ultimate manifestation of this strategy (Bauman 2001). However, in terms of bringing about more prolonged imprisonment, some aspects of the security sanction, particularly those that make the biggest departures from previously existing parameters of punishment, are still intended to be used with caution, as in the case of the New Zealand public protection orders – although in the US 5,000 or so 'sexual predators' exist in some sort of hinterland between prison and community in 'civil detention'. There is also the strong possibility that the 'worst of the worst' proviso that such legislation is meant for becomes diluted, allowing it to become a convenient way to remove a wider group of difficult or troublesome Others (New Zealand's public protection orders and the equivalent NSW measures are already extended to violent criminals). Other aspects, though, particularly when these can simply build on or remodel already existing but seldom used measures, such as the indefinite prison sentence, have become much more extensive. The English public protection measures targeted primarily at 'dangerous and violent and sexual offenders' led to 6,000 indefinite prison sentences between 2003 and 2011 (around 14 per cent of the total prison population there). Although these provisions were abolished in 2012, extended sentences and mandatory life terms will now be available for those sexual and violent offenders judged to pose 'a substantial risk of causing harm through reoffending by committing a further specified offence' (Crown Prosecution Service 2014). In New Zealand, the numbers serving the indefinite sentence of preventive detention increased from 12 in 1985 to 250 in 2012, following the passage of the Sentencing Act 2002 which made this available to first-time offenders (it had always previously required an element of recidivism) and lowered the age of eligibility from 21 to 18.

Beyond the prison itself, however, further restrictions on the movements of sex offenders in public space come into play, as in Wilson's 'release'. Under the provisions of the English Sexual Offences Act 2003, sex offenders, or those who were merely *suspected* of being a *potential* sex offender, would be banned from visiting parks or school locations. The Sexual Risk and the Sexual Harm Prevention Orders, under the provisions of the Anti-social Behaviour, Crime and Policing Act 2014, allow much the same scope for restrictions, while allowing them to be put in place where there is risk of sexual harm instead of 'risk of *serious* sexual harm', as in the previous legislation. In NSW, the state government introduced legislation allowing the eviction of child sex offenders from public housing in 2009 (following the arrival of Dennis Fergusson). The Premier's justification was that 'our key priority has to be firstly the protection of children, secondly the protection of the community more broadly and ultimately I also have a responsibility for community harmony in New South Wales' (Macey 2009). In various states in the US, whether through local ordinances or as restrictions in parole licences or probation orders, sex offenders are not allowed to enter 'Child Safety Zones' which include 'parks, beaches, and harbours [and] can extend to swimming pools [and] bus stops'. In parts of California they are also banned from fishing and surfing. In Florida, they are not allowed within 300 feet 'of a park, school or playground'. Indeed, the restrictions are so far reaching there that some sex offenders have had to make their homes under a road bridge.[6] In New Mexico they are banned from public libraries. In Long Island there are proposals to ban them from emergency shelters in the event of storms or disasters. There is also the likelihood that each time one locality imposes its own restrictions on the movements of these offenders in public space, this gives momentum to its neighbours to either replicate or exceed them: 'once one community has enacted "child safety zones" they often spread quickly to nearby towns, as municipal governments fear becoming local havens for sex offenders' (Lovett 2012).

In some US towns and localities, it has also become the practice to erect 'No Paedophile' signs at their entrance. This serves a dual purpose. It provides a definitive guarantee of the moral purity of those who live behind it; and a symbolic barrier built on such unity and solidarity against unwelcome 'strangers' and others who would seek to corrupt this.

The diffusion of state power and surveillance

However, these new or revitalized powers of punishment and control have been accompanied by a diffusion of state power and authority, rather than any further centralization of it. These measures are indicators of a weakened central state, rather than a strong one (Ramsay 2012), which has been eroded by the same array of forces that brought 'the age of mobility' into existence. In the light of this, its organs of government are regarded as either powerless to provide security or ineffective in so doing. Such weakness, or the public's lack of confidence or respect for government authority, then give encouragement to local communities to seek their own forms of formal and informal protection from the monsters who have emerged in their midst. Thus in Whanganui the local council both petitioned the High Court and tried to galvanize local citizens into joining the 'community shunning', amid the apparent ineffectiveness of central government. In the US, most of the initiatives against sex offenders have been the product of local referendum or plebiscite proposals in the local state electoral processes, bypassing the state and its criminal justice bureaucracies altogether. But in response to such indicators of local agitation and dissatisfaction, the more the subsequent message to the general public from government that it is listening to the concerns of 'ordinary people' rather than out of touch experts or state officials and that it intends to spectacularly shift policy away from safeguarding the rights of individual offenders towards protecting the community at large, then so much the better for politicians seeking to win back public support and credibility (Pratt 2007). In other words, the state and its organs of government are now likely to follow public concerns that lead to dehumanization rather than actively shape and construct and impose these concerns on the public.

Even so, the level of anxiety now raised by sex offenders is such that state assurances that the risks they pose will be curtailed by post-prison detention and the like may still not be sufficient guarantees of security. There are demands that the state also share penal power with other organizations (teachers, doctors, social workers and so on) and non-state agencies to monitor offenders' release and whereabouts and to police the restrictions on their movements. To varying degrees, this has allowed the public a share in this information, as evident in the range of community notification procedures in the US. However, when such developments are still judged to be inadequate, citizens may take their own initiatives to warn others of the presence of sex offenders (displaying naming and shaming posters on community noticeboards, for example) or drive them out altogether with vigilante activities – a further indication of the weakness of the central state. Indeed, these forms of vigilantism have become familiar events in England, Australia and New Zealand in recent years (see, for example, Thomas 2005).

In addition, the nexus of arrangements that is needed to provide the necessary levels of security in public space or in the hinterland between public and private requires much more extensive forms of surveillance and vigilance than has been available previously. As regards individual offenders, the most serious sex offenders may be subject to GPS monitoring for up to 10 years, as has been permissible in New Zealand since 2004. More generally, though, electronic surveillance allows the movements of many thousands of others – sometimes on parole licence after prison, sometimes as an alternative to imprisonment itself and sometimes even prior to conviction as a condition of bail – to be tracked. CCTV additionally provides for coverage of limitless areas of public space, rather than of the movement of individual offenders within it. This technology has come to be understood and promoted as a natural and essential remedy for all those whose mobility presents incessant risk and insecurity. Furthermore, it generates unceasing demands for the exponential growth of the private security industry to patrol areas of everyday life that might be prone to intrusion from sex monsters, but which remain beyond the scope of state police until a crime has been committed: schools, parks, play areas, housing estates, and so on.

At the mid-twentieth-century high water mark of the solidarity project, such levels of intrusion were a cause for considerable anxiety in the western democracies, exemplified by the popularity of George Orwell's (1947) *Nineteen eighty-four*. The absence of anything like the level of surveillance that features in the novel in those societies became one of the distinguishing characteristics between them and the Eastern Bloc. Indeed, the revelations of the extent of such intrusion in former East Germany after the fall of the Berlin Wall, as in Anna Funder's (2003) *Stasiland*, led to outrage at such wilful violations of privacy and fundamental human rights, as well as fascination that a society could degenerate into such an information-gathering machine. However, from around the same time, in the Anglophone societies, all-pervasive surveillance began to be associated with security and assurance rather than fear and suspicion: those who had done nothing wrong had nothing to fear, was the regular justification for these developments: surveillance would simply make more visible and more knowable to the community those whose past and likely future rightfully merited restriction, if not complete expulsion. In one of the first indicators of this shift in public mood in England and Wales, the Home Office (1994: 9) pamphlet *CCTV: looking out for you* reassuringly proclaimed that 'there is no evidence that the public regard CCTV as a threat to civil liberties'. Bennett and Gelsthorpe (1996: 87) then noted that 'people were either willing to offset their concerns about CCTV for the additional safety that it brought to their lives or their concerns about civil liberties were simply not strong enough to influence their decision-making either way'. Thereafter, and almost completely unproblematically, 'a new security architecture which designs surveillance technologies and techniques into our physical and virtual surrounds and embeds surveillance practices into everyday life [was generated]' (Zedner 2009: 76).

Conclusion

There is no uniform pattern of development of these measures of security and risk management. In some respects there have been significant setbacks to their progress (see McSherry 2013), For example, judges have declared some of these initiatives unlawful (although, as David Green and Jonathan Simon

226 *John Pratt*

note in this book, the US courts have been very reluctant to intervene in matters of prison administration, and in other respects have been prepared to accept the constitutionality of both the sexual predator and three strikes laws). And the European Court of Human Rights has kept a vigilant watch on English initiatives, making it impossible, for example, to have the Australian and New Zealand post-prison detention measures there.[7] That said, the very existence of this court is currently providing strong political momentum for that country to leave the European Union altogether. That said, the more that these societies distance themselves from the solidarity project and the possibilities of punishment that existed within it, the more there are likely to be demands for measures such as these – in relation to both sex offenders and the range of other unwanted or undesirable groups that put mobility at risk. As Bauman (2000: 217) writes, 'immobilization is the fate which people haunted with the fear of their own immobilization would naturally ... demand to be visited upon those whom they fear'.

The social and economic restructuring that has taken place in these societies enforces new divisions between the feared and those who are fearful of them. As this has occurred, the moral boundaries of law and punishment have been moved beyond those that fitted within the parameters of the solidarity project to allow for the emergence of the security sanction. Such reconfigurations of the penal framework are designed not simply to punish but to prevent from any further offending those who constitute intolerable or unmanageable risks. It can be enforced by imprisoning them indefinitely, by further periods of detention of unspecified length at the end of their sentence or by restricting their movements in public space. This is the social production of immorality in these democratic societies in the early twenty-first century. These are the reactions of the democracies to the monsters that an avaricious media – greatly freed from the previous restraints that state controls placed upon it – has created and has a vested interest in maintaining.

Notes

1 Thanks to Polity Press for granting permission to reproduce previously published material in this chapter.
2 New Zealand has regional daily newspapers rather than one with a national circulation. The four main ones are the New Zealand Herald (Greater Auckland region), with a daily circulation of 147,369; the Dominion Post (Greater Wellington and the lower half of the North Island), with a daily circulation of 73,397; The Press (Christchurch and the top half of the South Island), with a daily circulation of 68,011; and the Otago Daily Times (Dunedin and the lower half of the South Island), with a daily circulation of 36,824. While the New Zealand Herald has the largest circulation, it can be argued that the Dominion Post is at least as influential, given that the parliament, government bureaucracies and broadcasting organizations are all located in Wellington. Whanganui itself is located in the lower half of the North Island.
3 On 12 August 2014, there was a town meeting organized by two local councillors and attended by 200 people, in response to the Parole Board's announcement on

Immobilization in the age of mobility   227

8 August that Wilson was going to be released and located in Whanganui. The meeting was reported on 13 August and, from then until the day of his release on 1 September, the Dominion Post published 22 feature articles and editorials on the matter, the New Zealand Herald nine articles, The Press six articles and the Otago Daily Times three articles.

4 Under the headline 'Beast Ok', the Dominion Post (Anon 5 February 2013a: A3) reported that a complaint to the Broadcasting Standards Authority about the reporting of Wilson as 'the Beast' was declined

5 The 2013 Census shows that 5.1 per cent of the population in the Manawatu–Whanganui region are of Asian origin/descent, compared to 11.8 per cent for New Zealand as a whole and 22 per cent for Auckland. Even so, this figure for Whanganui itself is likely to be an overstatement. This is because the largest city in the region, Palmerston North, has a population of 82,000, 7.8 per cent of whom are Asian (a good proportion of whom are likely to be students enrolled at Massey University in this city).

6 http://en.wikipedia.org/wiki/Julia_Tuttle_Causeway_sex_offender_colony.

7 In *M v. Germany* [2009] ECHR no 1939/04, the court determined that retrospective post-sentence detention was not permissible in EU countries.

References

Anon (2000) 'Beast may ask for new trial', *Evening Post*, 24 January, p. 2.

Anon (2009) '"Beast" must remain behind bars', *Dominion Post*, 19 December, p. 17.

Anon (2011) 'High Court says board fair in denying parole to "Beast"', *Dominion Post*, 24 May, p. 7.

Anon (2012a) 'Board sets out reasons for keeping "Beast" locked up', *Dominion Post*, 18 April, p. A9.

Anon (2012b) 'Sisters' fear of Beast's return', *The Press*, 12 July, p. A5.

Anon (2012c) 'Handling the "Beast"', *The Press*, 10 August, p. A16.

Anon (2012d) 'Neighbours feared sex offender so much they moved away', *Dominion Post*, 29 September, p. A3.

Anon (2012e) 'Denials means very real "risk" remains', *Dominion Post*, 29 September, p. A3.

Anon (2013a) 'Beast Ok', *Dominion Post*, 5 February, p. A3.

Anon (2013b) 'Recall of "Beast" "waste of money"', *Dominion Post*, 12 March, p. A3.

Bauman, Z. (1989) *Modernity and the Holocaust*, Cambridge: Polity Press.

Bauman, Z. (1995) *Life in fragments*, Cambridge: Polity Press.

Bauman, Z. (2000) 'Social issues of law and order', *British Journal of Criminology*, 40: 205–221.

Bauman, Z. (2001) *Liquid modernity*, Cambridge: Polity Press.

Bottoms, A.E. (1977) 'Reflections on the renaissance of dangerousness', *Howard Journal of Penology and Crime Prevention*, 16: 70–96.

Beck, U. (1992) *Risk society: towards a new modernity*, London: Sage.

Bennett, T. and Gelsthorpe, L. (1996) 'Public attitudes towards CCTV in public places', *Studies on Crime and Crime Prevention*, 5: 72–90.

Broun, B. (2008) '"Beast" must serve 4 more years', *Dominion Post*, 30 December, p. 4.

Clarkson, D. (2012a) 'Risk from "Beast" will persist all his life, says psychologist', *Dominion Post*, 6 July, p. A8.

Clarkson, D. (2012b) '"Beast" to get extended supervision on release', *Dominion Post*, 14 July, p. A20.

228   *John Pratt*

Courtney, B. (1997) 'The "Beast of Blenheim"', *Dominion Post*, 2 May, pp. 1, 9.

Crown Law Office (2012) *Bail Amendment Bill 2012*, Wellington, online, available: www.justice.govt.nz/policy/constitutional-law-and-human-rights/human-rights/bill-of-rights/bail-amendment-bill-2012#-1 (accessed 29 April 2014).

Crown Prosecution Service (2014) 'Sentencing dangerous offenders', Wellington, online, available: www.cps.gov.uk/legal/s_to_u/sentencing_and_dangerous_ offenders/ (accessed 29 April 2014).

Ensor, B. (2012a) 'District council bans Beast from city's recreational areas', *Dominion Post*, 29 August, p. A3.

Ensor, B. (2012b) 'Sun, daffodils for Beast's first free day', *Dominion Post*, 30 August, p. A3.

Ensor, B. (2012c) 'Face to face with the Beast', *Dominion Post*, 29 September, p. A1; A3.

Ensor, B. (2013) 'Wilson goes back to prison', *Dominion Post*, 22 February, p. A1.

Floud, J. and Young, W. (1981) *Dangerousness and criminal justice*, Cambridge: Cambridge University Press.

Forbes, M. (2012) 'Council ready to trespass the "Beast"', *Dominion Post*, 27 August, p. A3.

Fukuyama, F. (1995) *Trust: the social virtues and the creation of prosperity*, New York: Free Press.

Funder, A. (2003) *Stasiland*, London: Granta.

Furedi, F. (2001) *Paranoid parenting*, London: Cappella Publishing.

Garland, D. (1996) 'The limits of the sovereign state: strategies of crime control in contemporary society', *British Journal of Criminology*, 36: 445–471.

Garland, D. (2001) *The culture of control*, New York: Oxford University Press.

Girling, E., Loader, I. and Sparks, R. (1998) 'A telling tale: a case of vigilantism and its aftermath in an English town', *British Journal of Sociology*, 49: 474–490.

Grocott, M. (2012a) 'Family fear having "Beast" as neighbour', *Dominion Post*, 16 August, p. A5.

Grocott, M. (2012b) 'Corrections boss: "I'd be nervous too"', *Dominion Post*, 16 August, p. A5.

Hacking, I. (2003) 'Risk and dirt', in R.V. Ericson and A. Doyle (eds), *Risk and morality* (pp. 22–47), Toronto: University of Toronto Press.

Home Office (1994) *CCTV: looking out for you*, London: HMSO.

Keyzer, P. (2011) 'The international human rights parameters for the preventive detention of serious sex offenders', in B. McSherry and P. Keyzer (eds), *Dangerous people: policy, prediction, and practice*, London: Routledge.

Lovett, I. (2012) 'Public-place laws tighten rein on sex offenders but raise questions, too', *The New York Times*, 30 May, p. A.15.

Macey, J. (2009) 'NSW introduces law to evict paedophiles', ABC News PM, 23 September, online, available: http://www.abc.net.au/pm/content/2009/s2694568.htm (accessed 20 November 2014).

McSherry, B. (2013) *Managing fear: the law and ethics of preventive detention and risk assessment*, New York: Routledge.

New Zealand Parliament (2012) *Bills Digest* no. 1974.

New Zealand Parole Board (2014) 'About us', Wellington, online, available: www.paroleboard.govt.nz/about-us.html (accessed 25 April 2014).

Orwell, G. (1947) *Nineteen eighty-four*, New York: Harcourt, Brace.

Pratt, J. (2007) *Penal populism*, London: Routledge.

Ramsay, P. (2012) *The insecurity state: vulnerable autonomy and the right to security in the criminal law*, Oxford: Oxford University Press.

Thomas, T. (2005) *Sex crime: sex offending and society*, Cullompton: Willan Publishing.

Valverde, M. (2011) 'Questions of security: a framework for research', *Theoretical Criminology*, 15(1): 3–22.

Vance, A. (2012) 'Dangerous paedophiles to be caged indefinitely', *Dominion Post*, 11 May, p. A2.

Zedner, L. (2009) *Security*, New York: Routledge.

Zelizer, V.A. (1985) *Pricing the priceless child: the changing social value of children*, New York: Basic Books.

11 From terra nullius to terra liquidus?[1]

Liquid modernity and the Indigenous Other

Harry Blagg

Disconcertingly, at a time when the world's Indigenous peoples struggle to hold on to their plots of earth, besieged by the exterminating angels of neo-liberalism and globalization, some influential social theorists of the Global North have proclaimed the death of all that is solid and stress the degree to which place has ceased to be the basis for belonging in a world of transience, fluidity and mobility. In opposition to this trend, Antonio Escobar (2001) poses the question: 'Who speaks for place, who defends it?' This chapter advances a defence of Indigenous place and, following Escobar, reinstates the materiality of place as a significant location for identity, social meaning and political struggle for the 'Other' of settler colonialism. Zygmunt Bauman's work has been influential in shaping our understanding of late-modernity, or what he prefers to call 'liquid' modernity, due to its increasing tendency towards individualism, transnationalism, privatization and fluidity – a domain of shifting allegiances and identities, rootless nomadism and fractured identities (see, for example, Bauman 2001). Bauman's thinking in relation to the liquidity of modern societies has provided a focal point of reference for contemporary cultural criminology focused on social exclusion and inclusion and the fate of the 'flawed consumer' (see Young 1999). I argue that a comparative criminology reliant on Bauman's work risks, unwittingly, erasing the foundations of resistance for many colonized subjects, hence inhibiting the search for 'decolonizing' practices.

Criminologists situated in the Global South may express reservations about the epistemological basis of Bauman's liquidity thesis because, like much social theory of the Anglosphere, it universalizes the experience of the Global North to encompass the Global South. The terms North and South, in the context of postcolonial theories, are metaphorical spaces, rather than firm geographical terrains – the South being a metaphor for the world colonized by violent means and suffering acutely from forces of neo-liberal global capitalism and imperialism (de Sousa Santos 2008). Australia is typical of settler colonist societies wherein the northern hemisphere has transported itself to the geographic south and created a North/South divide between itself and the Indigenous owners. The story here has less to do with liquid modernity than the historical mission of Euro-modernity to liquidate its Indigenous Other.

Liquid modernity and the Indigenous Other   231

In recent years 'colonial hysteria' (Galeano 1997) about mixedness, boundaries and cultural miscegenation has migrated from the periphery to the metropolitan centre itself, creating what Paul Gilroy (2011) calls Europe's 'postcolonial moment' – reflected in the emergence of anti-immigrant movements, such as the United Kingdom Independence Party in England. While the criminology of the Global North has fixated on the 'punitive turn' as the underlying logic of shifts in criminal justice policy in recent years, critical thinking in the Global South has theorized around the 'postcolonial' turn (Blagg 2012). Anthony and Blagg (2013) refer to this re-emergence of interest in colonial power as constituting a 'postcolonial turn', which they view _not_ in terms of a world _after_ colonialism has ended (it has not), but in terms of the diversity of cultural, social and political contestation and crises brought into being by a multiplicity of colonial projects (see also Blagg 2008, 2012; Blagg and Anthony forthcoming). This is similar to the concept of 'coloniality' as constituting 'long-standing patterns of power that emerged as a result of colonialism ... that define culture, labour, intersubjective relations, and knowledge production well beyond the strict limits of colonial administrations' (Maldonado-Torres, 2007: 16)

Postcolonial critique has been concerned with articulating and privileging the subjugated knowledge of colonized peoples and identifying the ways in which colonial structures of domination are negotiated and subverted by the colonized (Bhaba 1994). Postcolonial relations, postcolonial critique maintains, inhabit the present and construct the future: working from within a postcolonial framework entails installing a critique of colonial structures of power at the heart of contemporary criminological debate. Discursive and structural turns in the South, in relation to the management of colonized Indigenous peoples, have always tended to involve an excess of institutional violence and repression – rather than 'hegemonic' strategies intended to win the consent of the ruled within welfare capitalism (see Guha 1997). It is certainly the case that penal policy in many parts of the South has become increasingly more punitive in the past 20 years, as reflected in the rates of mass imprisonment (discussed later). However, mass imprisonment in Australia, and many other settler societies, is almost wholly confined to the Indigenous population and can be viewed as a new phase in the management of a dispossessed people, with punitive populism representing a fresh opportunity to 'govern through crime' (Simon 2007). Distinguishing between historical periods on the basis of shifts from penal welfare to punishment (Garland 2001) may play for a western audience but it elides the abiding _continuity_ of punishment and repression for managing the uncivilized colonial Other (Blagg 2008).

Postcolonial theory also stresses the extent to which colonization takes place in the realms of culture, knowledge and imagination. Spivak (1996) talks, for example, of the 'epistemological violence' of colonization. In a similar vein, Boaventura de Sousa Santos (2014) employs the term 'epistemicide' to describe how western domination has systemically denied the knowledge systems and epistemologies indigenous to the Global South. He describes this process as a

232   *Harry Blagg*

form of 'cognitive injustice' – a massive failure to respect the knowledge, rights and interests of groups who live differently. If nations are 'imagined communities' (Anderson 1983), then decolonization involves a reimagining and remapping of place, time and space to include Indigenous maps of meanings and profoundly embedded forms of wisdom.

Adopting Bauman's liquidity thesis as an analytical tool risks diminishing Indigenous lives as 'wasted lives' (Bauman 2004). Bauman's schema, which divides the world between the individualized, deracinated consumer of the west and the 'wasted' rest, condemned to static immobility, is paralleled in the works of other distinguished critical thinkers in the Global North who have proclaimed that sociology is done with many of its traditional categories, particularly those that nurture and perpetuate the transcendental illusions of modernist social theory, of which Marxism remained the principle example (see, for example, Giddens 1995). The new focus on movements, flows and migrations is particularly well illustrated in the 'new mobilities' paradigm, mapped out by John Urry and colleagues at Lancaster University (UK), which privileges systematic human transportation, migration and the transcendence of boundaries as the defining features of life in late modernity (Cresswell 2006; Cresswell and Merriman 2011; Hannam *et al.* 2006; Urry 2004). The flow of people across time and space; the identities, cultures and politics of migration; Diaspora; and transnationalism have become core concerns for sociologists working in this space.

This emphasis on mobility should not be allowed to gloss over the continuing importance of struggles and contestations around belonging to place in the Global South. Even Manuel Castells, whose work on 'networked societies' (2010) charted the emergence and domination of the 'space of flows', which had enormous influence on the mobilities and globalization literature, expresses concern that the focus on movement should not eclipse the importance of place, particularly in the context of nurturing social solidarity:

> dominant activities in our society are organized around the logic of the space of flow while most, and the most powerful forms of autonomous construction of meaning, and social and political resistance to the powers that be are being constructed, currently, are around *places.*
>
> (Castells 1999: 297 emphasis added)

Bauman's work can be located within a sociological turn that no longer sees collectively based forms of embeddedness in an era fixated on individualized consumption, rather than production and community. Atkinson (2008) criticizes Bauman for excessive focus on 'disembedding individualization and the individualized society' (Atkinson 2008). In this chapter I also question the generalizability of Bauman's treatment of genocide in *Modernity and the Holocaust* to the Global South, where genocides have not required the mobilization of the bureaucratic apparatuses of the unitary state to be effective. Instead we see a constellation of alliances, representing internal and external interests – from settler farmers through to agri-business and extraction industries (after the 'accursed wealth' that enriches the North and impoverishes the South) – as well as colonial settlers themselves acting as shock troops in the formulation of the settler state formation, as it was often they who were in direct conflict with Indigenous landowners. This process thus established the fundamental fault line in settler colonies, between the 'mainstream' who benefited massively from colonization and its privileges, and the dispossessed Indigenous population.

In this chapter I want to achieve a number of interrelated goals. First, notwithstanding the constant threat of the neo-liberal consensus, and the fatalism of much sociological and criminological theory regarding the inevitability of global homogenization and standardization, I want to make a case for the defence of place. Indigenous place continues to nurture and sustain radically alternative visions of a sustainable good life. Bauman's assertion that the ones who 'cannot at will leave their place' are the 'ruled', while those able to 'be elsewhere' are the rulers (Bauman 2001: 120), neglects the extent to which the reoccupation and defence of traditional place by Indigenous peoples is generating new narratives of emancipation in many parts of the Global South and that this is occurring because of, not in spite of, embeddedness in place. A contemporary example of this can be found in Bolivia's 'Pluri-National Government', which has initiated wide-ranging measures to recognize the rights of what the 2009 Constitution calls 'nation and rural native indigenous people', consisting of 'every human collective that shares a cultural identity, language, historic tradition, institutions, territory and world view, whose existence predates the Spanish colonial invasion' ((Plurinational State of) Bolivia's Constitution of 2009, published in English 2014)).

Second, I want to demonstrate how a focus on place can assist criminologists working from a postcolonial position to explore the mass imprisonment of Indigenous people: arguing that they are rooted in the oppressive use of the white justice system to dispossess Indigenous people of land, involving the *enforced* mobility of Indigenous people off traditional country. The apparatuses of the criminal justice system (such as police lock ups and regional gaols) were employed directly as concentration points for Indigenous people dispossessed of traditional lands (Blagg and Anthony forthcoming). Land has been at the heart of Indigenous claims since occupation and invasion. The solution, therefore, lies in resolving historical Indigenous claims over sovereignty, rather than more incremental reform of the justice system based on the discredited western 'what works' paradigm. Land, or 'country' for Indigenous Australians, can provide a meeting space – often referred to as 'a middle ground', 'engagement space' or 'liminal space' – where new 'inter-cultural' narratives and languages can be formed that bridge entrenched differences between colonizer and colonized. Before discussing this in detail, I want to briefly describe the scale of the problem in relation to the mass imprisonment of Indigenous Australians in the white settler's justice system.

Over-representation?

To speak of over-representation is to infer that mass imprisonment is somehow aberrant, reflecting what one critical high-level Australian Government inquiry referred to as a 'broken' justice system (House of Representatives Standing Committee on Aboriginal and Torres Strait Islander Affairs 2011). Viewed through a postcolonial lens, however, the 'hyper-incarceration' (Cunneen *et al.* 2013) of Indigenous people is no aberration but the logical outcome of several centuries of policies, laws and practices designed to complete the dispossession of Indigenous people as bearers of sovereignty. It is, then, an outcome of deliberate intervention by the settler state. It makes no sense to speak, therefore, of some 'normal' level of involvement in an alien white settler justice system, which has been imposed from outside, without Indigenous consent, and despite the fact that Indigenous people were already subject, and obedient, to a set of existing laws: *their own*. Within the history of colonial power and resistance, the prison is but one institution of involuntary confinement among many; and not necessarily the most destructive when compared to the damage to the Aboriginal collective caused by other sites of institutional violence such as missions, residential schools and orphanages that were deliberately designed to destroy Aboriginal family life. 'Kill the Indian in the child' was the saying in Canada; 'Kill the Indian, save the man' in the United States, as a justification for child removal to so-called residential schools where Indigenous children were forcibly, often violently and abusively, 'assimilated' (Human Rights and Equal Opportunity Commission 1997). Because assimilation was seen as in the best interests of Indigenous children (and a reflection of our 'tolerance'), it could be carried out in an uncompromisingly brutal fashion, 'for their own good' (Haebich 1992).

A snapshot of arrest and imprisonment rates of Indigenous people in Australia reveals that rates of contact continue to soar across Australia. Between 2000 and 2013 the adult Indigenous imprisonment rate increased by 57 per cent, widening the gap as the non-Indigenous rate did not show significant change (Australian Government Productivity Commission 2014). Recent data (Australian Bureau of Statistics [ABS] 2014) indicates that the difference between Indigenous and non-Indigenous imprisonment has steadily increased since the early 2000s. Indigenous people constitute around 28 per cent of prisoners (sentenced and remand) in Australia generally, while they constitute roughly 2 per cent of the population. In 'frontier' states such as Western Australia (WA), the Northern Territory (NT) and Queensland they make up a significant proportion of the prisoner population. In WA, for example, where they are 3.6 per cent of the population, they represent 40 per cent of the adult prison population generally, over 50 per cent of the women's prison population and a staggering 78 per cent of the juvenile detention regime (ABS 2014; Australian Government 2014). For Indigenous people the age-standardized imprisonment rate was 18 times the non-indigenous age-standardized imprisonment rate (3013.4 prisoners per 100,000 Aboriginal and Torres Strait Islander adult population compared to 166.6 prisoners per 100,000 adult non-indigenous population) (ABS 2014). In the NT, which has shown the highest increase in the rate of imprisonment of Indigenous people in the past decade, Indigenous people make up 86 per cent of the prisoner population (ABS 2014) and approximately 30 per cent of the total NT population. The Indigenous age-standardized imprisonment rate was 15 times the non-indigenous age-standardized imprisonment rate (2,390.2 prisoners per 100,000 Indigenous adult population compared to 155.2 prisoners per 100,000 adult non-indigenous population) (ABS 2014). Queensland has experienced a surge in imprisonment rates in the past few years, even by Australian standards: Indigenous people comprise 32 per cent (2,243 prisoners) of the adult prisoner population. The age-standardized imprisonment rate for Indigenous people was 11 times the non-indigenous age-standardized imprisonment rate (1,557.9 prisoners per 100,000 compared to 143.1 prisoners per 100,000 adult non-indigenous population) (ABS 2014). Mainstream criminology, by which I mean those criminological theories and methods developed on the basis of western paradigms of knowledge (a mix of positivist science and/or European enlightenment philosophies), can (and does) wheel out a virtual arsenal of theories to 'explain' Indigenous 'over-representation' in terms that resonate with mainstream values and interests (generally pathologizing Indigenous cultural and family life and/or identifying various proximate causes such as alcohol abuse – see Weatherburn [2014] as an example). Employing postcolonial and decolonizing narratives, however, we can construct an alternative account which situates Indigenous mass imprisonment within a historical framework of conflict over land and the management of those dispossessed by settler occupation.

Lineages of the settler state

Settler colonialism differs from other brands of colonialism in that it embraces not simply the exploitation but the wholesale appropriation of land, as though it were always/already the property of the European, awaiting 'discovery'. This ontology of settlement is, according to Patrick Wolfe (2008), inherently *eliminatory* (though, he insists, not inevitably *genocidal*). Settlement requires the extinguishment of Indigenous ownership of land, not always the extinguishment of the people themselves: genocide remains one among a range of strategies including forced assimilation, dispossession, enforced mobility and concentration in places of confinement. Settler colonists attempted to uproot Indigenous occupants and *replace* them in the soil: transplanting the Global North into the Global South. This has given settler societies a particularly rich and thematically nuanced repertoire of self-exculpatory and self-aggrandizing narratives, including biblical-scale themes of redemption and renewal, promised lands flowing with milk and honey, and such like. Such narratives obscured the crimes of land theft and the necessary denial of Indigenous

236 *Harry Blagg*

sovereign law. As Lisa Ford suggests, the eradication of Indigenous law became the 'litmus test of settler statehood' (Ford 2010).

A simple focus on the role of the colonial *state* apparatus in appropriating land and dispossessing Indigenous populations, however, is one dimensional, leaving unaddressed a signal feature of settler occupation: its dynamic of 'dual power' between centre and periphery, with the periphery frequently the decisive agency in 'nation building', often in advance of formal law and the apparatuses of the state, which often had to 'catch up' with the *de facto* annexure of space and give it formal status. Colonial government often followed rather than led, responding (sometimes reluctantly) to demands from 'pioneers' for protection, law and order, and the accompanying paraphernalia of legitimacy (such as court houses, lock-ups and gibbets). This gave rise to the characteristic relationship between the settler Diaspora and the imperial centre: vociferous demands for support for their beleaguered outposts, combined with equally vociferous demands for the centre not to meddle in local affairs (particularly where this involved local solutions to the 'native problem' – see Memmi [1991]).

The rapidity of occupation created a space of law filled by forms of local rather than central government, strengthening the monopoly of local settlers over emerging jurisdictional practices designed principally to erode Indigenous sovereignty (Ford 2010: 6) and formulating, in the process, the intimate relationship between judicial authority and influential local leadership so characteristic of settler colonialism. This intimacy is reflected in the historical power of lay Justices of Peace (the local Chamber of Commerce enrobed) in rural Australia who, literally, held the power of life or death when serving on WA's Courts of Native Affairs (Auty 2000, 2005). It is fair to say that the Diaspora itself was massively influential in shaping settler colonial society, with 'whiteness' (its vulnerability, safety, interests) trumping other concerns, often creating situations that overthrew the class differences of the colonial centre by offering rights, entitlements and privileges rarely experienced by the lower classes in the metropolis (Grimshaw 2006).

There was also a symbiotic relationship between frontier violence and the rule of law. Violence created the space (both metaphorically and figuratively) for law to be implanted, and the implanted law retrospectively legitimated the fruits of the founding violence and its methods. Agamben (1998) demonstrates how the imperative to create order from chaos permits sovereign power to authorize what he terms a 'state of exception' and suspend law. Colonial violence, therefore, was not the negation of law but the establishment of the preconditions under which law could be implanted. Furthermore, the state of exception created zones where 'the monopoly of violence could still fall outside the hands of the state' (Evans 2005: 70). Settlers often took the initiative in localized massacres and genocides (Reynolds 2013). Formal independence from the 'mother country' has not led to a simple consolidation of power into a unified state. 'Dual power' remains in the tensions and conflicts between the federal and state governments: states' rights remaining a thinly veneered

Liquid modernity and the Indigenous Other 237

defence of institutionalized racist policies and practices on a local level across many settler societies. In some instances, the settler state has never been fully able to wrest the monopoly of violence from the settler periphery (contradicting Elias's (1982) civilization thesis); it remains in the hands of imperilled citizens (white people) responding to 'threats' from the natives. Accordingly (and contra Bauman's *Holocaust* thesis), critical scholarship on settler colonialism suggests that the administrative power of the formal state was not the decisive factor in genocidal actions by colonists. Genocide, according to Wolfe, was:

> *not dependent on the presence or absence of formal state institutions or functionaries.* Accordingly ... the occasions on or the extent to which settler colonialism conduces to genocide are not a matter of the presence or absence of the formal apparatus of the state.
>
> (Wolfe 2008: 11, emphasis added)

Bauman's (1991) thesis on the Holocaust stresses the extent to which large-scale slaughter required the structures and organization of the modern state, bureaucratized and 'rational' in form. Yet this model may not appear to fit forms of genocide in the Global South. Larry Ray (2007), in his critique of Bauman's Holocaust thesis, suggests that mass killing can also be a highly personal and intimate act, involving performativity, catharsis, bonding and carnival (see also Katz 2008). To borrow some terminology favoured by the community crime prevention literature, localized genocide was often a robustly 'bottom-up' affair, which promoted social cohesion and integration among participants, creating ties and bonds, strengthening communal values (particularly the local against the centre) and cultivating a sense of shared belonging. The native was the region of chaos on the other side of the advancing frontier, the dark screen against which western civilization could be projected. But the native was also an arena where whites could safely – and without restraint or consequences – indulge in an excess of sexual and other forms of violence. For Edward Said (2003), the 'Orient' was not simply a space of colonial exploitation; it was a space of adventure and romance, of pleasures denied in the civilized realm of the homeland, including the intimate pleasures of killing the Other.

Understanding such violence requires moving beyond a narrow focus on state apparatuses to access the capillaries and networks of power that sustain ethnic and racial inferiorization, including what Derek Hook (2011) refers to as the 'extra-discursive' moment. Picking up on the work of Franz Fanon, particularly in his study of the impact of racial inferiorization on the psyche of the black man, Hook affirms the importance of:

> Understanding ... colonialism not merely as a means of annexing land and territory, but of appropriating culture and history themselves, that is, a way of usurping the means and resources of identity. The colonisation of

238 *Harry Blagg*

a land, its people, its culture, is also, in short, a 'colonising of the mind' in Ngugia aw Thiong's ... famous phrase, which receives its echo in Mandela's ... characterisation of apartheid as 'moral genocide'.

(Hook 2011: 20)

Bauman's work, I would suggest, tends towards a reductionist view of the state, in its relatively unified and discrete Westphalian form. Settler colonialism created new forms of state formation whose power was dispersed across space rather than centralized. The 'frontier', far from being an obscure and distant side show in the creation of state power, can be viewed as a birthing space for new forms of racialized politics, new hierarchies of power and profoundly inscribed cultures and epistemologies that were to shape, and continue to shape, social relations in contemporary settler societies. Bauman's stress on centralization, impersonality, detachment and distance as the modus operandi for modern genocide does not fit with intensely personal and intimate frontier genocide, such as the 'frontier' massacres of Indigenous men, women and children in North America (Sand Creek, Wounded Knee), Australia (Mistake Creek, Forrest River, Coniston) and countless sites in South America.

The politics of silence: forgetting Indigenous suffering

In 1968, the anthropologist W. H. Stanner spoke of the 'great Australian silence' in relation to Indigenous people (Stanner, 1968). In 2014, it is still possible for an Australian PM to speak of Australia as an 'unsettled' or 'scarcely settled, Great South Land', rather than a country with an uninterrupted occupation for 40,000 years. Indigenous peoples cannot gain purchase on the narrative structures of late-modernity. They belong to Europe's discursive past, so we find it difficult to see their *ongoing* struggles for recognition of Indigenous claims (which, because they inevitably involve land, appear quaintly anachronistic, the stuff of historical and anthropological research, rather than criminology). The tendency to forget Indigenous suffering is apparent in the way Australia memorializes its past as a convict settlement. While sites such as the Port Arthur convict prison enjoy World Heritage status, the carceral history of Indigenous Australia has been deliberately obliterated. For example, Rottnest Island off the coast of Perth in WA, a holiday destination 'blessed with a casual atmosphere, picturesque scenery, dazzling marine life and some of the world's finest beaches and pristine bays',[2] was the site of a brutal regime. It was the only penal establishment in Australia specifically for Aboriginal people, many of whom were from the distant Kimberley region in the state's far north, transported several thousand kilometres from home for defending their lands against white invasion: between 1838 and 1931 some 369 Aboriginal prisoners died on Rottnest Island (five by hanging) (Green 1998). There are no monuments celebrating Rottnest as part of Australia's penal past; instead, the cells that warehoused

Indigenous suffering have been knocked together to form *bijou* studios for guests at what is now the Rottnest Lodge.

The white diaspora's dreaming

Place remains the site and the stake of conflict between Indigenous peoples in settler colonist societies. Numbering Indigenous people amongst 'nomads' functions to dismiss Indigenous claims regarding continuing possession of land and justifies white occupation: indeed, the 'doctrine' of *terra nullius* rested on the fallacy that Indigenous people were nomads without a settled legal order (Falk and Martin 2007). Bauman's (2001) suggestion that 'we' are all part of one Diaspora or other, then, becomes particularly contentious, given that Indigenous politics is shaped by conflict with the Diaspora and its occupation of Indigenous land. Indigenous people rarely form Diaspora and remain ontologically embedded in traditional place. The elevation of individuality and uprootedness to the status of a universal condition stymies intellectual exploration of the ontologies and epistemologies of the non-western world. Diaspora are globally dispersed groups whose collective experiences, structures of sentiment and feeling, attachments and values are scattered across place and time (see Cohen 2008). The Diaspora of the Global North, since the founding British (which still forms the apex of the settler population, with other Diaspora occupying a subaltern space, as I discuss later), exists in an ambivalent relationship to the land it has occupied; literally fixing a mythologized version of the land it left behind into the Indigenous world. This fundamental distinction, between what I call the white mainstream Diaspora and the Indigenous minority, is at odds with *both* modernist sociological theories, which have tended to focus on structural difference based on class, ethnicity and gender, *and* new mobilities paradigms focused on movement, space and flow.

However, there are now alternatives to both of these paradigms emerging from within the Global South which are creating new 'epistemologies of the South' (de Sousa Santos 2008; Comaroff and Comaroff 2011) and increasingly counter-posing these, essentially Eurocentric, constructions with alternative readings of history that underline the extent to which modernity and late modernity have developed hand in glove with colonialism (modernity's 'underside' [Walsh 2009] or 'shadow' [Blagg 2008]). From the perspective of the Global South, therefore, the most profound epistemological and ontological divide is that between the European Diaspora and its Indigenous Other (the latter category embraces those brought to the colonized worlds as slaves and chattels, such as Africans). The specific form of the settler state and its foundational drive and energy were derived from the need to dispossess and subordinate the Indigenous Other. Thus, sharing out the rich spoils of dispossession became (and remains) the glue binding together the high and the low stratum of the Diaspora (including, on a subordinate basis, those 'not quite white' and/or 'white but not quite' and excluding groups such as Black Africans and Asians).

240   Harry Blagg

For Indigenous critics this remains the fundamental fault line in settler societies. Goenpul woman and Indigenous scholar Aileen Moreton-Robinson presents this argument thus:

> Indigenous people ... position all non-Indigenous people as migrants and diasporic. Our ontological relationship to land, the ways that country is constitutive of us, and therefore the inalienable nature of our relationship to land, marks a radical, indeed incommensurable, difference between us and the non-Indigenous. This ontological relation to land constitutes a subject position ... which cannot be shared with the postcolonial subject whose sense of belonging in this place is tied to migrancy.
>
> (Moreton-Robinson 2003: 45)

In relation to land or 'country', Indigenous Australians' sensibilities of belonging are, as Moreton-Robinson explains, *incommensurate* with western notions of occupation and ownership. Indigenous people both possess and are, in turn, possessed by country. Deborah Bird Rose describes this eloquently:

> Country in Aboriginal English is not only a common noun but also a proper noun. People talk about country in the same way that they would talk about a person: they speak to country, sing to country, visit country, worry about country, feel sorry for country, and long for country.
>
> (Bird Rose 1996: 9)

Culture for the Diaspora is portable and disposable, as Bauman (1991) correctly observes; it can be erased and reframed, wiped clean, written over, packed up and transported. In multicultural Australia, the culture of the homeland can be ceremoniously unpacked and paraded at officially sanctioned events: such as 'national wog day', in Melina Marchetta's (1992) irreverent reflection on the family secrets of the Italian Diaspora in Sydney. Elizabeth Povinelli (2002) identifies that the liberal multicultural state's 'cunning of recognition' lies in the extent to which it accepts and values cultural difference only to the degree that such differences do not constitute a 'radical alterity'. The liberal multicultural imaginary operates to funnel cultural difference along certain hegemonically sanctioned pathways. Indigenous 'culture' (paintings, music, dance) is celebrated but its connection to the occupation and possession of land – therefore its expressions of sovereign power – is denied. However, as Indigenous culture 'sits in place' (Escobar 2001) these hegemonically sanctioned limitations are constantly being tested (and contested) by Indigenous agency. While it is an exaggeration to say that Indigenous peoples will not develop their land, in terms of attracting employment or developing infrastructure, they rarely buy in to the ideology of 'development' as an ideal, desirable and necessary part of modernity. As Lisa Walsh maintains: '[t]he very idea of development itself is a concept and word that does not exist in the cosmovisions, conceptual categories, and languages of indigenous communities' (Walsh 2007: 220).

Many settler states began to dismantle the overt structures of oppression that sought to forcibly assimilate Indigenous people into the mainstream in the 1960s and 1970s, and instead began a limited dialogue with Indigenous people. Writing of Canada, Greg Caulthord refers to this new approach as the 'politics of recognition' which offered Indigenous people a limited bundle of rights while stopping well short of demands for self-determination and freedom or unfettered access to land (Caulthord 2014). For Caulthord, land has become a 'site of resurgence' for First Nation peoples and reconnection with land a form of decolonization that breaks the dominant preoccupation with land as an economic resource. Land, to adopt a phrase of Louis Althusser (2014), is the site and the stake of contestation between Indigenous people and the settler state. Land is also, I want to suggest, a key site of contestation in relation to decolonizing the justice system.

New dispossessions, new contestations

The settler state has not ceased dispossessing Indigenous Australians of their land. In September 2014, the federal government announced it was withdrawing AU\$90 million from almost 200 remote communities in WA, most in the far north Kimberley region. This would strip remote communities of utilities and services. The State of Western Australia has refused to make up any shortfall. The state government had recently bulldozed the Oombulgurri community in the East Kimberley. The community was closed in 2011 after a coronial inquiry concluded that it was in a state of crisis. A report by Amnesty International (Solonec 2014) disagreed with claims that residents left voluntarily because the community was 'unviable' and found many Balanggarra people (residents of Oombulgurri) living homeless and destitute in the town of Kununurra who wanted to return to their homeland. Furthermore, other work by Amnesty International had clearly demonstrated that Indigenous people thrive on traditional homelands and have better health outcomes than those living in towns:

> The evidence is particularly strong and growing in relation to health outcomes. Homeland residents have participated in various health research projects over the last 20 years or so. These studies point very strongly to significant improvements in health outcomes for Aboriginal Peoples in remote areas if they live in homeland communities, compared with Aboriginal Peoples who live in major towns. Homelands are seen as places of respite. Many play a role in rehabilitation of addicts and offenders.
>
> (Amnesty International 2011: 12)

The distinction between *whites operating in space* and *Indigenous people operating from the value of place* should not be turned into a rigid binary. Young Indigenous people in particular have become adept players in the use

242 *Harry Blagg*

of technologies, and talk of 'walking in two worlds' as they flesh out syncretized cultural practices that fuse together elements of Indigenous and non-Indigenous worldviews, but not at the expense of their identities as Indigenous people, while many non-Indigenous people are discovering the importance of place as a focal point for new politics around the environment and anti-globalization. However, the basic premise seems to me to be correct. It struck me forcefully in some recent work I undertook with the Aboriginal Family Violence Prevention and Legal Service (FVPLS), an organization that provides assistance to Indigenous victims/survivors of family violence and sexual assault and works with families and communities affected by violence. Typically, such a legal service includes a mix of, usually white, lawyers and, usually Indigenous, community workers – and this is the case with FVPLS. The Indigenous workers at FVPLS tended to be what I will call *present in place*, while the legal professionals tended to deal with *space and flow*. This had genuine repercussions for how priorities and strategies were defined. For the lawyers, most of their activities and energies were focused on the court. Furthermore, they only tended to see Aboriginal women as 'clients' and Aboriginal men as 'perpetrators'. This influenced how they viewed 'success' in their work, largely in terms of 'metrics' and 'deliverables', as demonstrated in the numbers of restraining orders granted.

The Aboriginal workers at FVPLS were working in an entirely different way – from their position 'in place', they understood the reciprocal ties of obligation that mean that for many women exiting an abusive relationship is profoundly difficult, and they operated on theories about violence that privilege the destructiveness of colonial policy and the creation of a 'patriarchal white sovereignty' (Moreton-Robinson 2007), rather than deracialized and decontextualized notions of male power and patriarchy as underlying communal violence. While not disputing that offenders need to be made accountable (seeing this in terms of accountability under Indigenous rather than white man's law), they tended to see solutions in terms of community and family healing rather than the white man's legal system.

Place is also becoming what Caulthold calls a 'site of resurgence' and contestation, in the area of diversionary strategies for youth. In the Kimberley region of WA, Kimberley Aboriginal Law and Culture, an influential community-controlled body representing the interests of Kimberley Aboriginal people in relation to cultural issues, is engaged in developing alternatives based around 'community-owned' justice mechanisms on Aboriginal country, in particular the *Yiriman* Project, which provides an intensive cultural immersion and 'healing' experience on traditional lands for at-risk young people (Blagg 2012). In other parts of the Kimberley, Traditional Owners are attempting to create similar projects, leveraging off their, limited, ownership of land under Australia's Native Title regime, to create on-country projects that build a 'hybrid economy' somewhere in between the mainstream world of work and Indigenous cultural practices. These practices involve working with, rather than exploiting, the land by nurturing native fruits and medicines. Traditional

Owner groups, such as the *Yawuru* people in the Kimberley, aim to build partnerships with mainstream agencies that will see on-country engagement in the hybrid economy replacing involvement in the white justice system for many *Yawuru* people, who are routinely rotated through the prison system because they are dispossessed of country, the victims of failed white policies of social engineering or survivors of inter-generational trauma.

Concluding comments

This critique is not intended as a rejection of western criminology per se – far from it. From the perspective of the South there is nothing inherently 'wrong' with the theories of the Global North, other than their claims to universal status and neglect of alternative epistemologies and ontologies. The task, therefore, is not one of dismantling but of remaining open to the reality that 'another knowledge is possible' (de Sousa Santos 2008). In this chapter I have attempted to reinstate the uniqueness and radical alterity of Indigenous worldviews and their embeddedness in place, countering the trend towards viewing all contemporary life as disembedded and liquid. Bauman's theory of 'liquid modernity' does not represent a stable platform for creating a 'counter-worlding' that will reduce the tendency of the settler state to punish the Indigenous Other. Indigenous resurgence is taking place through an engagement with traditional country and laying claim to land as the bedrock of Indigenous identity. Furthermore, *Modernity and the Holocaust* constructs a model of the genocidal state that does not conform with the eliminatory practices of settler colonialism. Redress for Indigenous suffering must take into account the multiple, decentred sites of extreme violence against the Indigenous Other, including mass killings by settlers, pastoralists and police auxiliaries, which did not require the impersonal and bureaucratized mechanisms of the state. A relevant criminology of the Global South would, instead, be aware of Indigenous knowledge and address the unresolved question of Indigenous sovereignty.

Notes

1 Thanks to Polity Press for granting permission to reproduce previously published material in this chapter.
2 www.experienceperth.com/destinations/rottnest-island.

References

Agamben, G. (1998) *Homo sacer: sovereign power and bare life*, translated by Daniel Heller-Roazen, Stanford, CA: Stanford University Press.
Althusser, L. (2014) *On the reproduction of capitalism: ideology and ideological state apparatus*, trans G.M. Goshgarian, London: Verso.
Amnesty International (2011) *The land holds us: Aboriginal peoples' right to traditional homelands in the Northern Territory*, Sydney: Amnesty International, online,

244 *Harry Blagg*

available: www.amnesty.org.au/images/uploads/aus/AI-homelands-report.pdf (accessed 8 January 2015).

Anderson, P. (1983) *Imagined communities: reflections on the origins and spread of nationalism*, London: Verso.

Anthony, T. and Blagg, H. (2013) 'STOP in the name of who's law? Driving and the regulation of contested space in Central Australia', *Social and Legal Studies*, 22: 43–66.

Atkinson, W. (2008) 'Not all that was solid has melted into air (or liquid): a critique of Bauman on individualization and class in liquid modernity', *Sociological Review*, 56: 1–17.

Australian Bureau of Statistics (ABS) (2014) *Prisoners in Australia*, Canberra: Australian Government, online, available: www.abs.gov.au/ausstats/abs@.nsf/mf/4517.0 (accessed 8 January 2014).

Australian Government Productivity Commission (2014) *Overcoming Indigenous disadvantage: key indicators*, Canberra: Australian Government.

Auty, K. (2000) 'Western Australian courts on native affairs 1936–1954: one of "our" little secrets in the administration of "justice" for Aboriginal people', *University of New South Wales Law Journal*, 23: 148–172.

Auty, K. (2005) *Black glass: Western Australian courts of native affairs 1936–54*, Fremantle: Fremantle Press.

Bauman, Z. (1991) *Modernity and the Holocaust*, Cambridge: Polity

Bauman, Z. (2001) *Liquid modernity*, Cambridge: Polity.

Bauman, Z. (2004) *Wasted lives: modernity and its outcasts*, Cambridge: Polity.

Bhaba, H.K. (1994) *The location of culture*, London: Routledge.

Bird Rose, D. (1996) *Nourishing terrains: Australian Aboriginal views of landscape and wilderness*, Canberra: Australian Heritage Commission.

Blagg, H. (2008) *Crime, Aboriginality and the decolonisation of justice*, Sydney: Hawkins Press.

Blagg, H. (2012) 'Re-imagining youth justice: cultural contestation in the Kimberley region of Australia since the 1991Royal Commission into Aboriginal Deaths in Custody', *Theoretical Criminology*, 16: 481–498.

Blagg, H. and Anthony, T. (forthcoming) *Decolonising criminology*, London: Palgrave Macmillan.

(Plurinational State of) Bolivia's Constitution of 2009 (2014) translated by Max Planck, Institute constituteproject.org, Oxford: Oxford University Press.

Castells, M. (1999) 'Grassrooting the space of flows', *Urban Geography*, 4: 294–302.

Castells, M. (2010) *The rise of the network society* (2nd ed.), Cambridge, MA: Cambridge University Press.

Caulthord, G. (2014) *Red skin, white masks: rejecting the colonial politics of recognition*, Minneapolis: University Of Minnesota Press.

Cohen, R. (2008) *Diaspora studies: an introduction*, Oxford: Routledge.

Comaroff, J. and Comaroff, J. (2011) *Theory from the south: or, how Euro-America is evolving toward Africa*, Boulder, CO: Paradigm Press.

Cresswell, T. (2006) *On the move: mobility in the modern western world*, London: Routledge.

Cresswell, T. and Merriman, P. (eds) (2011) *Geographies of mobilities*, London: Routledge.

Cunneen, C., Baldry, E., Brown, D., Schwartz, M., Steel, A. and Brown, M. (2013) *Penal culture and hyperincarceration: the revival of the prison*, London: Ashgate.

Liquid modernity and the Indigenous Other   245

de Sousa Santos, B. (ed.) (2008) *Another knowledge is possible: beyond northern epistemologies*, London: Verso.

de Sousa Santos, B. (2014) *Epistemologies of the south: justice against epistemicide*, Boulder, CO: Paradigm Publishers.

Elias, N. (1982) *The civilizing process, vol. II: state formation and civilization*, Oxford: Blackwell.

Escobar, A. (2001) 'Culture sits in places: reflections on globalism and subaltern strategies of localization', *Political Geography*, 20: 139–174.

Evans, J. (2005) 'Colonialism and the rule of law: the case of South Australia', in B.S. Godfrey and G. Dunstall (eds), *Crime and empire 1840–1940: criminal justice in local and global context*, London: Willan Publishing.

Falk, P. and Martin, G. (2007) 'Misconstruing indigenous sovereignty: maintaining the fabric of Australian law', in A. Moreton-Robinson (ed.), *Sovereign subjects: indigenous sovereignty matters*, NSW, Australia: Allen and Unwin.

Ford, L. (2010) *Settler sovereignty: jurisdiction and indigenous people in America and Australia, 1788–1836, vol. 166*, Cambridge, MA: Harvard University Press.

Galeano, E. (1997) *Open veins of Latin America: five centuries of the pillage of a continent*, New York: Monthly Review Press.

Garland, D. (2001) *The culture of control*, Chicago, IL: University of Chicago Press.

Giddens, A. (1995) *Politics, sociology and social theory: encounters with classical and contemporary social thought*, Stanford, CA: Stanford University Press.

Gilroy, P. (2011) 'Shameful history: the social life of races and the postcolonial archive', *Moving Worlds: A Journal of Transcultural Writings, Postcolonial Europe*, 11: 19–34.

Green, N. (1998) *Far from home: Aboriginal prisoners of Rottnest Island 1838–1931*, Perth: University of Western Australia Press.

Grimshaw, G. (2006) *Creating a nation*, Perth: Imprint Network, Curtin University of Technology, Australian Research Institute.

Guha, R. (1997) *Dominance without hegemony: history and power in Colonial India*, Cambridge, MA: Harvard University Press.

Haebich, A. (1992) For their own good: Aborigines and government in the south west of Western Australia, 1900–1940, Perth: University of Western Australia Press.

HannamK., SchellerM. and UrryJ. (2006) 'Editorial: mobilities, immobilities and moorings', *Mobilities* 1: 11–22.

Hook, D. (2011) *A critical psychology of the postcolonial: Biko, Fanon, racism and psychoanalysis*, London and New York: Routledge.

House of Representatives Standing Committee on Aboriginal and Torres Strait Islander Affairs (2011) *Doing time: time for doing – Indigenous youth in the criminal justice system*, Canberra: The Parliament of the Commonwealth of Australia, AGPS.

Human Rights and Equal Opportunity Commission (1997) *'Bringing them home': report of the National Inquiry into the Separation of Aboriginal and Torres Strait Islander Children from Their Families*, Sydney: Human Rights and Equal Opportunity Commission.

Katz, T. (2008) *Seductions of crime: moral and sensual attractions in doing evil*, New York, NY: Basic Books.

Maldonado-Torres, N. (2007) 'On the coloniality of being: contributions to the development of a concept', *Cultural Studies*, 21: 240–270.

Marchetta, M. (1992) *Looking for Alibrandi*, Sydney: Penguin Australia.

246 Harry Blagg

Memmi, A. (1991) *The colonizer and the colonized*, Introduction by Jean-Paul Sartre; afterword by Susan Gilson Miller (translated by Howard Greenfeld), Boston, MA: Beacon Press.

Moreton-Robinson, A. (2003) 'I still call Australia home: Indigenous belonging and place in a white postcolonising society', in S. Ahmed, C. Cataneda, A.M. Fortier and M. Shellyey (eds), *Uproot-ings/regroupings: questions of postcoloniality, home and place*, London and New York: Berg.

Moreton-Robinson, A. (2007) 'Writing off Indigenous sovereignty: the discourse of security and patriarchal white sovereignty', in A. Moreton-Robinson (ed.), *Sovereign subjects: Indigenous sovereignty matters*, Crows Nest, NSW: Allen and Unwin.

Povinelli, E. (2002) *The cunning of recognition: Indigenous alterities and the making of Australian multiculturalism*, Durham, NC: Duke University Press.

Ray, L. (2007) 'From postmodernity to liquid modernity: what's in a metaphor?', in A. Elliott (ed.), *The contemporary Bauman*, London: Taylor & Francis Ltd, Routledge.

Reynolds, H. (2013) *Forgotten war*, Sydney: New South Publishing.

Said, E. (2003) *Orientalism*, London: Vintage.

Simon, J. (2007) *Governing through crime: how the war on crime transformed American democracy and created a culture of fear*, New York: Oxford University Press.

Solonec, T. (2014) 'The trauma of Oombulgurri's demolition will be repeated across Western Australia', *Guardian Australia*, 27 November.

Spivak, G.C. (1996) *The Spivak reader: selected works of Gayatri Chakravorty Spivak*, Landry, D. and Maclaen, G. (eds), London: Routledge.

Stanner, W.E.H. (1968) *After the dreaming: black and white Australians – an anthropologist's view*, Boyer Lecture Series, Australia:ABC.

Urry, J. (2004) 'The "system" of automobility', *Theory, Culture & Society*, 21: 25–39.

Walsh, C. (2007) 'Shifting the geopolitics of critical knowledge', *Cultural Studies*, 21: 224–239.

Walsh, C. (2009) 'Development as buen vivir: institutional arrangements and (de) colonial entanglement', *Development*, 53: 15–21.

Weatherburn, D. (2014) *Arresting incarceration: pathways out of Indigenous imprisonment*, Canberra: Australian Studies Press.

Wolfe, P. (2008) 'Settler colonialism and the elimination of the native', *Journal of Genocide Research*, (2006) 8: 387–409.

Young, J. (1999) *The exclusive society: social exclusion, crime and difference in late modernity*, London: Sage.

12 Symbiotic Othering[1]
Terrorism, emotion and morality

Debra A. Smith

To be labelled a 'terrorist' has become synonymous with being morally reprehensible, and therefore devoid of an essential aspect of humanness. A terrorist becomes a non-human, something to be eliminated rather than someone to listen to or negotiate with. Yet those labelled as terrorists commonly claim to be working from a position of high moral authority. They may see themselves as altruistic, representing the powerless, and sacrificing themselves for the betterment of their communities. For the so-called terrorist, the existing power structures of society are inherently unfair and therefore violate deeply held moral ideals such as justice, autonomy and equality. Moral imperatives become the framework for justifying violence against those identified as upholding the existing social conditions.

So how do we make sense of the highly moralistic judgements and language around terrorism as each opposing side claims a monopoly on moral understanding and behaviour? One way is to follow Bauman's advice to avoid searching for the legitimacy of moral claims in the actions of each group. For Bauman, the Holocaust exemplifies how actions have no intrinsic moral value, with social organization rendering all social action adiaphoric – neither good nor evil – measurable only against the amoral requirements of the bureaucratic or the technical (Bauman 2000 [1989]: 215). In his search for the source of morality, Bauman turns to Emmanuel Levinas to suggest that the most solid foundations lie in the experience of being in the world with others (Bauman 2000 [1989]: 182, 214). Ideally, this experience generates a sense of unconditional responsibility; however, in societies where terrorist groups emerge, the experience of being in the world with others has become the experience of being in the world with the 'Other'. Rather than generating responsibility, this experience has become intolerable, to the point that violence has come to be seen as a viable and acceptable way of dealing with coexistence.

When Bauman endeavoured to understand how it is possible that violence against fellow human beings can come to be seen as a perfectly logical, indeed rational, response to a perceived social problem, he came to the conclusion that the answer lay in a process of transformation in which responsibility to the other erodes as social distance increases. Social distance, he argues, is the 'technological and bureaucratic achievement of modern rational society'

(Bauman 2000 [1989]: 184). The idea of the 'technical', the 'bureaucratic' and the 'rational' seems to evoke a process devoid of emotion, as emotions are often conceived of as impulses – the very antithesis of rational thought and meaning. Indeed, it is the non-emotional, the technocratic and endlessly bureaucratic diffusion of responsibility that, for Bauman, creates the social distance necessary for the systematic and efficient mass elimination of human beings. In this sense, social distance equates with emotional detachment and social proximity with emotional contiguity. While this may indeed be true, the process of arriving at a point of cold, dispassionate distance remains a process imbued with emotion.

Being in the world with others generates emotions. Emotions are central to the way in which we understand and relate to each other and to the strengthening or undermining of social bonds. They affect the judgements we make about our past, our present and our future, and about those we see as either facilitating or blocking our chances for a rewarding life. They also help us to tap into the energy we need to act, and influence the way we think about (in)justice. However, it is the special relationship that emotions have to the development of beliefs that can either consolidate or erode relationships, creating proximity or distance between individuals, groups and societies, which is most pertinent to understanding the social production of morality.

This chapter draws from interviews conducted with violent political activists operating in Northern Ireland[2] during the period known as 'the Troubles' to look more closely at the social production of distance that may lead to a decline in responsibility to the Other and provide a platform for the construction of alternative moral positions that are used to justify violence. Emotions have a special relationship to morality, with feelings of anger, compassion, envy, fear, grief, shame and love, to name just a few, providing knowledge and informing our judgements about what is fair and just. What follows highlights the symbiotic nature of producing the Other, as the failure to entrench a degree of emotional continuity and connectedness between the state and a section of its citizenry lays the foundations for the development of alternative and conflicting concepts of morality.

The agents of terrorism typically view the targeted group as responsible for some kind of gross moral violation, whether that be occupation of disputed territory, despoliation of culture or religion, or the unconscionable treatment of others (Barbalet 2006: 47). They cast their own violent actions as a morally righteous response to these violations. Indeed, so-called terrorists draw a sharp distinction between their violent actions and those of criminals by pointing to the altruistic nature of their goals as they promote the agenda of the group to which they belong (Schwartz *et al.* 2009: 539). This suggests that, while social distance may increase between some, it may simultaneously decrease between others as tightly defined identity groups form in opposition to the status quo.

It may make us uncomfortable to think that violent political extremists do not just blindly obey the commands of a few who have abandoned morality completely or are entirely lacking in morality themselves. However, in order to understand (as opposed to condone) violent political extremism, it is necessary to understand that, regardless of the perspective of others, members of terrorist groups do perceive their actions to be moral within the context of their particular circumstances. This would come as no surprise to Bauman, who argued that, rather than being a product of society, '[m]orality is something society manipulates – exploits, re-directs, jams' (Bauman 2000 [1989]: 183). I would add that this manipulation is not necessarily conscious, or controlled or directed from 'above', but rather a by-product of the reciprocal emotional processes arising in response to perceptions of discrimination, exclusion or not being valued. Ironically, those in power are held responsible for withholding or making impossible this sense of belonging by those who see themselves as excluded from the benefits of society, while those excluded are held responsible by society for rejecting the possibilities and benefits of belonging.

The approach taken throughout this chapter reflects three important propositions about emotions. First, emotion is viewed as intertwined with reason, rather than diametrically opposed to it. The ubiquitous yet erroneous belief that emotion works only to distort rationality, and therefore reason, does nothing to further our understanding of why people do what they do, including engaging in violent political extremism or, indeed, setting aside central components of liberal democratic principles to justify torture. When asking why people do what they do, we tend to look for reasons for their behaviour; so the customary dichotomy between reason and emotion ensures that emotion is largely absent from serious inquiries into behaviour (Zhu and Thagard 2002: 32). While it is certainly possible for emotion to contribute to flawed decisions or behaviour by unduly influencing outcomes, it is equally true that reason is flawed when emotion is not present at all.

Second, in this chapter emotions are viewed as a source of knowledge. In other words, our emotions communicate or 'tell us things' about the world and therefore may contribute to the development of epistemological positions (Frijda and Mesquita 2000: 69). The experience of emotion blends with thoughts and cognitions in order to inform us about the nature of social reality. Feeling sad or happy can be construed as evidence that something is bad or good, and feeling scared can be interpreted as evidence of a threat. Similarly, hope or anger may contribute to the belief that a particular political position is preferable.

Finally, personal emotions are viewed as operating within broader emotional contexts. Emotions permeate social life to the point that we ascribe them to the character of institutions, nations or processes, thereby enabling us to speak about the greed of financial markets, the humiliation of Arab nations, or the arrogance of foreign policy (Hoggett 2009: 1). Emotions are embedded within the norms, values, institutions and social structures in which we all live. For Simmel (1950 [1908]), faithfulness and gratitude played a substantial role in binding us together via the social relations that enabled the creation of permanent institutions. Similarly, in the *Protestant ethic and the spirit of capitalism*, Weber (2003 [1904/5]) explores how anxiety, stemming from uncertainty as to

250 *Debra A. Smith*

whether one is predestined to be saved or damned, helped to define the emerging capitalist economic system.[3]

Even more broadly, social theorists have identified emotion with entire epochs. The kind of enduring configuration of emotion that gives expression to a period or generation was referred to by Williams (1977: 131) as 'structures of feeling'. For instance, Elias (1982: 292) has argued that a key characteristic of modernity is the reification of shame, while Bauman (2006) and Beck (1992) have associated late-modernity with both fear and anxiety. A theme that ties these understandings of emotion together is that individual emotional responses take place within a wider emotional environment in which 'structures of feeling' and 'abiding affects' are expressions of economic, social, political and institutional forces (Clarke *et al.* 2006: 11). One 'function of the political state is to legitimate some emotions and differentially encourage, contain and dissuade others' in order to maintain social control (Barbalet 2006: 32; also see Bensel 2008: xi). Possibly the most well-known expression of this concept was in Niccolò Machiavelli's *The Prince*, when, in response to the question of whether it is better for a prince to be loved or feared, he counselled:

> that one would like to be both ... but ... it is far better to be feared than loved if you cannot be both ... nonetheless ... [a prince should] make himself feared in such a way that, if he is not loved, at least he escapes being hated.
> (Machiavelli 1986 [1532]: 96–97)

So, keeping in mind that emotions are a part of reason, that they operate as a source of knowledge and that they are not contained to the individual, this chapter considers how emotions can develop that encourage people either to gravitate towards a sense of social proximity or, conversely, to recoil and retreat, creating social distance and a subsequent reduction of responsibility towards the Other. Along with the erosion of responsibility there is an ensuing freedom from the kinds of norms and rules of behaviour that forbid using people as a means of achieving political ends. This chapter looks more closely at four emotions that help create social proximity or, conversely, social distance. Following Flam (2005), it focuses on the role of loyalty, anger, shame and fear in generating or undermining social bonds. Making extensive use of the words of men who have been convicted of terrorism offences in Northern Ireland during the Troubles, it illustrates the complex relationship among emotions, social proximity and distance, and the construction of a morality that considers responsibility to the Other to be a selective process.

Loyalty

Loyalty is, among other things, an emotional connection that is felt towards other people, groups, institutions, places or causes (Connor 2007: 132). As such, it is inextricably tied to a sense of belonging and, in Bauman's terms, of social proximity. National loyalty refers to the connection felt towards a

Terrorism, emotion and morality   251

particular nation, but the idea of loyalty is applied to a variety of relationships, ranging from the personal and familial to sports teams; political institutions; religious doctrines; gender, race, ethnic and class groups; locations; and causes, among other possibilities (Connor 2007: 2, 73). Social institutions play a direct role in building national loyalty by providing physical, psychological and existential security through the controlled use of the law and military, the provision of education, housing and income paths, social recognition and representation (Berezin 2002: 38; Connor 2007: 79; Flam 2005: 31; Grodzins 1956: 5–6). A claim of legitimacy is not enough to ensure national loyalty and obedience to the state if an individual or a collective group does not experience the sense of security and opportunity that it is seen as being the obligation of the state to provide. This becomes even more problematic when the experiences of security and loyalty are seen to be provided or withheld depending upon an identity marker, whether that be ethnicity, religion, class, gender or an array of other indicators of difference connected with status (Kemper 2001: 66).

In this sense, the history of Northern Ireland provided a challenge to the British Government in developing loyalty among Irish Catholics. Northern Ireland became a separate legal entity as a result of being partitioned under the Government of Ireland Act 1920. While it is not the intent of this chapter to re-examine the history of Northern Ireland, it suffices to say that partitioning effectively divided the 32 counties of the island into two parts: an independent Irish Republic comprising 26 counties with a majority Catholic population; and a devolved government within the United Kingdom (UK) comprised of the other six counties (four of which were predominantly Protestant), which became known as Northern Ireland (Rose 1971). The Northern Ireland state perceived itself as a Protestant state and systematically established policies that marginalized Catholics (Moloney 2002: 42). As a result, the history of Northern Ireland is undeniably characterized by discriminatory policies and extensive enmity towards its Catholic population (Moloney 2002: 42–45). Catholics in Northern Ireland were born into a state that was already deeply divided and defined, in part, by social distance. They were 'Taigs' or 'Paddy', the 'Irish Frankenstein', or the subject of jokes meant to imply stupidity. And yet they were also expected to become a part of the state, to internalize its norms and obey its rules, including developing a sense of loyalty to the existing regime.

Even though the members of the Provisional Irish Republican Army (PIRA) interviewed were largely from the second or third generation born into an already established Northern Ireland state, they did not express a sense of national identity that demonstrated affective ties to Britain, or more broadly, the UK.[4] As one participant noted:

> I have never ever felt British, I have always felt Irish and my family has been involved in Irish culture, I played Gaelic football, and my sisters went to Irish dancing and stuff like that …. Well, it's not like my family ever told me specifically that I wasn't British, or that I had to reject

252   *Debra A. Smith*

Britishness, or that I made a decision, I just grew up being Irish, I wasn't hostile or anything, I just didn't have a sense of it being relevant. I lived in Ireland and I was Irish, easy!

(Padraig, PIRA)

When invited to discuss this further in relation to a growing political awareness, the participant went on to say:

I mean, as I say, I didn't feel part of the state. ... To go to Dublin for the day it was to go to the capital ... um, well, if someone had've said go to London we would have said, 'What do we want to go to London for?' I mean, it was complete detachment, innocent, you know, not a thought-out position, or a political statement. It just wasn't relevant to me in any way.

(Padraig, PIRA)

In a similar vein, the following exchange with the same PIRA member highlights how a childhood dispute was framed in terms of the broader issue of feeling alienated from the state based on being Catholic:

the Queen didn't mean anything, the royal family didn't mean anything. I remember having an argument again with a wee Protestant friend about who was the richest, the Queen or the Pope ... it's nothing but a kid's argument. But it sort of reinforces there was a difference there, a different outlook, all of that sort of stuff. No affinity to the state and no affinity to Britain. ... Bear in mind too, I mean Catholics were almost excluded totally from the likes of the police force, the higher ranks of the civil service, the visual representatives of the state and all at that time. During the '50s and '60s all the heavy industry of ship building, the metal foundries almost exclusively were Protestant workforces you know, so you just didn't feel a part of it. That's how I would have felt at the time, not so much in opposition, just not a part of it, not me.

(Padraig, PIRA)

Clearly a sense of loyalty to the ruling state was not developing for Padraig during his childhood. While there was not necessarily a sense of hostility, there was more an ambivalence towards 'Britishness' in terms of the self.[5] In Bauman's terms, the foundations for social proximity were not solid, and a sense of exclusion and ambivalence, rather than responsibility, had begun to take hold. Another PIRA participant expressed his sense of dislocation from British rule as a young man by saying:

you knew the City Hall didn't belong to you, you knew even the police didn't belong to you ... everything was foreign to ya, around ya, ya felt like you were in a wee ghetto.

(Ruari, PIRA)

However, this participant described an incident that occurred when he was a little older, in which the sense of not belonging becomes more frustrating and acrimonious because of the deliberate misuse of his name in favour of the more generic Catholic identifier of 'Paddy':

> the military come in and there's a honeymoon period and my ma is out there making 'em tea and the next thing is they're starting searching us. So you were going to school in the morning and you'd be stopped by the military and thrown against the wall and, 'Paddy' they'd call ya, and I'd say, 'my name's Ruari', 'alright Paddy' [they'd say]. Fuck!
>
> (Ruari, PIRA)

A PIRA member, who as a child had hoped to become a British Merchant Marine, talked about his sense of not being valued by the state:

> The state … was a state designed by the Unionist and British. They carved it up to suit the political needs of only one section of the community. Every single facet of life within those six counties was geared towards one section of the community and the community that I was brought up in, the Catholic, Nationalist, Republic, you can call it what you like, we were second-class citizens. I didn't realise that [at the time] and I say that openly and honestly …. Maybe I didn't have to understand fully, it was enough to feel it.
>
> (Eamon, PIRA)

Eamon's observation that it was enough to 'feel' rather than understand or know that he was not a valued member of the nation equates to what is commonly known as a 'gut feeling'. His evaluation may or may not be an objective one, but it does contribute to the development of his personal belief system and to the way he makes judgements about his sense of responsibility to those he views as treating not only him, but also his community, as second-class citizens. The failure to embed a sense of loyalty within the social structures of a society risks laying the foundations for widening social distance built on mistrust, in turn arising from hurt, anger or fear (Connor 2007: 43). Loyalty is, in part, an emotional connection which helps to construct a person's social identity, offering a sense of belonging and identification that erodes social distance and strengthens responsibility towards others (Connor 2007: 132). The reasons behind a sense of 'not belonging' are often complex and may or may not have their roots in obvious political failures of the state. However, a perception that the state is either rejecting or excluding you from the security and opportunity it is expected to provide can transform a sense of ambivalence into hostility. Furthermore, a perception of being under threat and the subsequent development of hostility works to create emotional distance between the two opposing groups while simultaneously increasing the emotional saliency within the group that perceives itself to be under threat (Castano *et al.* 2008:

254   *Debra A. Smith*

264). In the following quote, Padraig clearly demonstrates how responsibility is connected to social proximity:

> I mean, my world was a war zone and you had to be on a side and so my side was my community, my family, my friends. To me there was no way to be neutral, you were loyal to those people you knew, who went to the same school or football club, or whose house you went to or you saw at church on Sunday. I mean, I think that the rioting and all that took place during that August in 1969 was the beginning of my awareness that you were on one side or the other. Up until then I had mostly Protestant friends actually.
>
> (Padraig, PIRA)

Padraig's words reveal that he felt he needed to choose a side, or a group, to be loyal to, and that there was an underlying conflict which did not allow him to negotiate differing levels or layers of loyalty among competing options. For Padraig, being loyal to his community ostensibly meant that he could not be loyal to those he perceived as outside his group. In a sense, Padraig's words demonstrate how the emotional bonds to broader society can be eroded, while the emotional connections to a more exclusivist group can become stronger in the face of perceived threat – a theme that will be explored more fully later in the chapter. For now, however, it is important to note that, when a sense of loyalty is established, it helps to guide behaviour, framing a set of moral obligations and responsibilities. In cases where people feel a sense of loyalty to the state they generally feel an obligation not to attack it or its citizens. However, when multiple layers of loyalty seemingly cannot be engendered, and loyalty is almost exclusively associated with a particular group, the logic of this group correspondingly prescribes behaviour, and moral obligations and responsibilities are limited to within it, rather than extended more broadly (Castano *et al.* 2008: 262). Take, for example, the way this PIRA member justifies being able to commit acts of violence:

> I didn't feel any loyalty to the Brits, none at all. I mean, what did they do for us except make our lives more difficult? We were subjected to constant searches, to guns in our faces and barbed wire and checkpoints around our homes. I mean, how the hell can you feel anything but resentment of that? ... No, my loyalty was to my community, and I was going to protect it. If some of 'em [the British] had to die in order for them to get the message that we didn't want 'em here, then so be it.
>
> (Mick, PIRA)

So while loyalty is an emotion that binds people together, these bonds also have the potential to exclude others. Indeed, the differing individuals, groups, causes and institutions to which someone is loyal must inevitably be balanced by alternative possibilities to which the person could be loyal but is not

Terrorism, emotion and morality 255

(Hirschman 1970: 82). Still, it is possible to choose some loyalties over others without necessarily developing a deep sense of hostility; this is what most of us do every day. Nevertheless, particularly under conditions of perceived threat, the tendency for loyalties to develop that are more exclusivist and hostile to others is increased, forming the foundation for 'in-group' and 'out-group' dynamics, largely because loyalties are associated with identities and as such mark our memberships and belonging as well as associated social roles (Connor 2007: 49).

Anger

Anger is generally understood as a 'sanctioning emotion' in the sense that it arises as an objection to a slight or signals that a perceived injustice has occurred. Additionally, a growing body of literature points to how anger is predominantly appropriated as a 'top-down' emotion (Hochschild 1983; Kemper 1978). This is not to say, of course, that only people with power or status get angry. Rather, the display of anger is more likely to attract negative sanctions when shown by those with less power and status. As Holmes (2004: 127) notes, 'it is oppressed groups in particular who have been encouraged to repress their anger'. One of the most recognizable examples of this is the traditional dichotomy of demonstrative anger by men as opposed to anger suppression by women (Hochschild 1983: 127). However, this may also apply to the relationships between boss and employee (Hearn 1993), parent and child, colonial power and native, or any other social relationship in which there is an imbalance between the power or status of one party in relation to the other. Bottom-up anger occurs when those with less power perceive their status to have been unjustly reduced or withdrawn by the more powerful other, and the negative sanctions directed towards the display of 'bottom-up' anger are part of the strategy for maintaining the status quo (Cropanzano *et al.* 2011: 165; Holmes 2004: 127; Kemper 2001: 66). The containment of extreme anger is arguably a goal aimed at maintaining political and social order, but in controlling anger there is also a risk of suppressing essential dialogues about injustice, which inevitably involve an element of anger (Lyman 2004).

It is self-evident that those who joined PIRA felt anger at the situation in which they found themselves. Indeed, anger, hate and humiliation are arguably the emotions most commonly attributed to those engaging in violent political extremism (see, for example, Moghaddam, 2005). However, here the focus is on anger as it is embedded in social structures and as it relates to either strengthening social proximity or increasing social distance. The following examples illustrate the way in which PIRA members experience their anger socially rather than subjectively, although this is in no way intended to suggest that the subjective experience of anger is neither present nor unimportant. Rather, these quotes demonstrate how the subjective experience of anger is mediated by social forces:

256 *Debra A. Smith*

In prison you're not allowed to express anger in any form, that's part of the control mechanism. In a sense, living in Belfast with the Brits all around, and remember that there were 27,000 British troops, plus the RUC [Royal Ulster Constabulary], plus the UDR [Ulster Defence Regiment] on top of that, so you're talking about an armed contingent of about 40,000 for a population of less than a million and a half people. Well, it's the same sort of control mechanism. If you were a Catholic in Belfast then you weren't supposed to be angry. That didn't mean we weren't. It just meant that we was illegitimate because of it, and so if we chose to show it we were goin' to get in trouble.

(Cian, PIRA)

For Cian, choosing to express anger equates with moving outside the socially prescribed behaviour associated with his status and role as a Catholic in Belfast and into the area of negatively sanctioned or proscribed behaviour. Another member, when relating his experience of being one of only a few Catholics working in a majority Protestant workplace, talked about being invisible:

they would just talk as if you weren't there, they would just talk about things and talk about your community ... about attacks on the RUC and they could be outraged and self-righteous and, well it does, I mean, it makes you angry ... but it's all about the hierarchy. They can feel suffering we obviously can't, or they have the right to feel angry but we obviously don't. It's not like they even have to tell you, you just know because you matter so little they don't even have to worry that you hear them talking that stuff.

(Liam, PIRA)

What Liam is effectively expressing here is an implicit understanding, embedded in the structure of society, about which group has the socially sanctioned right to express anger. He is conscious that both the representatives of the Protestant community as well as himself are angry at the existing social conditions, but also that his position as a Catholic means that his anger is in defiance of the accepted social norms. When asked what he 'did' with his anger, Liam replied:

Well ya just kept quiet didn't ya. Anyway, there was other ways of getting it out like throwing a few stones on the way home or something like that.

(Liam, PIRA)

Rather than displaying an irrational and uncontrollable rage, these members of PIRA demonstrate both an understanding of, and an ability to control, their anger. Liam makes a rational decision to suppress his anger when its expression may compromise his employment. He also easily identifies an alternative avenue for acting out by which he does not put himself at high risk

Terrorism, emotion and morality 257

of negative social sanctions yet which provides him with the 'release' of defying those norms that violate his deeply held values of fairness.

The sense that expressions of anger are the prerogative of the powerful and that displays of anger attract negative social sanctions may lead to anger suppression, thereby maintaining a sense of social order. However, as Liam's and Cian's reflections demonstrate, this does not mean that anger is not present. The experience of anger can work emotionally to create social distance from the established political institutions and those that support or uphold them, although this is by no means automatic. People go out and angrily protest against government policies or practices regularly, particularly within western democracies where this is defended as a legitimate form of political expression, without disconnecting from society more broadly. However, what seems especially pertinent to creating social distance is the perception that you are not 'allowed' to express anger based on *your social position or identity*. For Liam and Cian, it was the fact that they were Catholics under the rule of the British in Northern Ireland that provided the context for feeling that they could not express their anger without attracting negative sanctions that were heftier than those for their Protestant counterparts.

The idea that expressions of anger are seen as legitimate or not based on particular identity markers, such as being Catholic, may or may not be objectively accurate. However, the perception that group membership contributes to determining whether it is legitimate to express anger is especially relevant to understanding why some people find their anger reinforcing an oppositional stance to broader society in which responsibility to others is diminished. The implicit assumption arrived at is that being angry means you are pushed away and seen as a threat rather than having your voice heard and taken into consideration. As such, the shared experience of supposedly illegitimate anger connected to identity can help to bind people within these more exclusivist identity groups, while simultaneously isolating them from the broader society.

Shame

The idea that shame is a dominant social emotion is most famously expounded in Elias's (1982) seminal work, *The civilizing process*, in which he observes how the increasing importance of manners since the seventeenth century coincided with escalating shame and embarrassment over bodily functions, such as defecation or sexual intercourse, previously performed in public but now strictly contained within the private realm. For Elias, shame over violating tightly held social conventions ensures that people are automatically socialized into upholding certain social rules, ensuring that shame acts to promote solidarity in social relations.

Flam concentrates on two aspects of shame in relation to social structure. First, drawing on Simmel, she identifies shame as an emotion experienced when we fail to live up to either our own or others' internalized societal standards

258   *Debra A. Smith*

(Flam 2005: 22). Second, following Kemper, Flam suggests that shame reifies systems of domination by upholding systems of classification that ensure that those with less power are obligated to think of themselves as inferior or naturally flawed in terms of intelligence, skills, appearance and morals, among other things (Flam 2005: 22). As one member reflected on his surroundings growing up:

> it's oppressive, obviously you feel that, well, a lot of people felt they were not worthy to get jobs, you know, you weren't worthy enough to feel that, you know, you weren't good enough to match up.
>
> (Coilm, PIRA)

Both aspects of shame that Flam refers to with regard to the upholding of social order appears to depend on the acceptance of social norms as broadly valid. Coilm's comments suggest that there was a sense of shame internalized within some people in the Catholic community such that they sensed that their lack of employment was a result of some internal flaw. However, in explaining the difference between the period of relative peace leading up to the Troubles and the civil unrest that characterized the period from the late 1960s until the Good Friday Agreement in 1998, Coilm pointed out that:

> there was a change happening for my generation that didn't happen for the previous generation ... and it meant then that people ... coming into the '50s and the '60s had this opportunity of third-level education. And with education you change the way you think about yourself. We watched what was happening with Martin Luther King over in the United States and we saw, just like the Blacks in the Civil Rights Movement, that we were equal and as worthy as anyone else and that it was a structural kind of discrimination that was to blame for our conditions. ... But you still don't get, no, you still don't get the opportunity for the jobs ... Catholics are twice as much, are twice as likely to be unemployed. You're expected not to get above yourself you know.
>
> (Coilm, PIRA)

Coilm explained that:

> it is in the state's interest to keep people feeling like they're not worthy, it's in-built, like socially ingrained.
>
> (Coilm, PIRA)[6]

Shame is an emotion that operates by the adoption and internalization of the point of view of others, thereby ensuring a type of conformism (Barbalet 2001: 103; Cooley 1964 [1922]; Scheff 1988). As long as the societal myth of natural inferiority is believed, it is unlikely that any challenge to the status quo will gain momentum. However, once one realizes that the other person's point of

Terrorism, emotion and morality   259

view is not valid, shame is stripped of its power to ensure conformity and, as Coilm describes, can unleash a counter-reaction:

> that's where the anger and the frustration came to the fore because people then began to challenge it and say 'this is no longer good enough'. ... They still think they can humiliate the Irish. ... There's a, there's a pride about being Irish and about the contributions the Irish people have made over the centuries, abroad and at home, and the resistance that they've put up, you know ... and well, pride comes from resistance.
>
> (Coilm, PIRA)

Coilm here highlights the distinction between shame and humiliation. Once the other's point of view is no longer considered credible, the same criticisms or circumstances are viewed as humiliation – an emotion that does not take on the viewpoint of the other. For Coilm, higher levels of education were associated with the ability to think more highly of oneself, thereby rejecting any sense of inferiority and the subsequent shame that emanates from this. Instead, by rejecting the validity of what he viewed as a social norm, he interpreted the conditions of the Catholics in Northern Ireland as an attempt to humiliate, provoking in him an angry and frustrated response.

In another exploration of shame, Ruari relates the story of watching his mother being humiliated by British soldiers when he was 13 years old:

> I remember the first time them coming into the house and um ... my ma was in bed, she was all half naked or in a wee thing, and she was all baring the shoulders and things and my sisters went in, there was five or six soldiers. [My sisters were] holding the blanket up so she could put her shawl on and they just ripped it off and said, 'You Irish fuckin' bitch'. My sisters, like that was their mother, I mean, I, they could'a said, [sighing], bastards. But I think, um, it's terrible that they called that to my mother, that there's all that name calling and they're all sitting there with my wee sisters. And my dad and I, what can we do huh. We have to sit there and do nothing, can't protect 'em or stand up for them like you should because we was being held downstairs and just had to listen to the whole thing. ... Even now, every time I say that the hairs go up on the back of my neck because I remember.
>
> (Ruari, PIRA)

When asked if the inability to help his mother and sisters in that situation left him with a sense of shame, he responded with:

> They [the British soldiers] were there to put us down ... aye, at the end of the day we didn't see it as our problem, we saw it as they're the problem.

260   *Debra A. Smith*

They're the ones who should be ashamed. They're in the country, they need to get out.

(Ruari, PIRA)

Ruari did not acknowledge that his experiences were connected with a personal sense of shame, though it is hinted at through his acknowledgement that he 'should' be able to help his sisters. Rather, his immediate response was to draw attention to the role of the British soldiers as the ones who abrogated the expected standards of social behaviour and who therefore should feel ashamed. When describing an incident that took place closer to the time Ruari joined PIRA, his rejection of the authority of the British is more strongly articulated and, rather than express shame in a similarly disempowering circumstance, he expresses anger at what he sees as an attempt to humiliate him:

[When] you grow up in that estate you get, aye aye, let's go and play some football, and you see soldiers and you just get used to it – you never accept it. It's like strip searching in prison, you know, it's repeated and routine, so you go through with it, but you're still naked in front of some hellish fuckin' guard. So what I'm trying to say is you still don't accept it but it's a routine you go through, being put up against a wall and searched and spoken to like you are shit. It's humiliating and that's what it is meant to be, and you know that's what it's meant to be. In a way you don't give 'em the pleasure of knowing you're humiliated, especially if there is some wee girl you like watching it all happen. Instead you give 'em some cheek or you resist, that's better. No, there was no way I was going to be fuckin' humiliated, I just felt more justified in fighting for the Republicans.

(Ruari, PIRA)

The idea that a relationship exists between humiliation and the propensity to commit acts of violence is well established (Cook and Alison 2007: 4; Fattah and Fierke 2009; Moghaddam 2006; Moïsi 2009: 56–89; Speckhard 2005). While shame may play a role in strengthening social proximity by ensuring that a particular standard of behaviour is upheld, this can only be realized when there is an acceptance of the validity of the social norms that one is expected to adopt. Shame tends to focus on the self and relies on the belief that it is in some way deserved (Klein 1991: 117). Humiliation, on the other hand, is distinguishable from shame to the degree that it focuses on the harm done by others and judges that harm as undeserved (Gilbert 1997: 133; Klein 1991). Humiliation is more likely to alienate individuals and groups from the rest of society than experiences of shame. As such, it increases social distance and undermines social proximity. As the above examples suggest, experiences of humiliation, or even the perception that either yourself or those with whom you identify are being humiliated, turn the focus away from the self and towards the behaviours and practices of others. For this reason, humiliation

Terrorism, emotion and morality 261

has become a powerful tool for radicalization, provoking estrangement from society, along with a judgement surrounding the immorality of others and motivation to bring about change.

Fear

When fear emanates from and has consequences for society it can be viewed as more than just a personal infliction. Thucydides (1982 [1866]: 44) and Machiavelli (1986 [1532]: 131) recognized the role of fear in political motivation, while Hobbes (1991 [1651]: 188) argued that fear is central to both the origin of civil society and its means of preservation. It has also become common to talk about 'the politics of fear', a term that refers to the ability to appropriate fear in order to achieve particular political or policy outcomes (Altheide 2006; Massumi 1993; Mythen and Walklate 2006; Robin 2004; Sparks 2003). The kind of fear referred to in these instances is more than just personal (such as a fear of heights or flying), because it arises in the context of struggles and conflicts within and between societies, and is particularly related to a sense of apprehension over harm that may be inflicted on collective wellbeing (Robin 2004: 2).

Drawing on Weber, Flam (2005: 23–25) argues that fear is an intrinsic feature in all unequal power relations because, whenever there is a situation of inequality, the more powerful group is in a position to influence the life chances of the less powerful. From this perspective, fear works to encourage social order through engendering a degree of compliance and conformity to social norms. For example, fear of punishment may encourage people not to break the law, or fear of being unemployed may encourage people to get to work on time and be productive. However, a key tactic within social movements is to magnify the fear of existing power structures in order to motivate collective groups of people to challenge them. Therefore, a union movement may emphasize workplace insecurity, as happened in response to the introduction of 'Work Choices' under the Howard government in Australia in 2005, in order to mobilize people in response. Similarly, the fear of social exclusion may contribute to minority groups mobilizing in order to gain equal status and rights.

This suggests that, while some degree of socially embedded fear can be useful in maintaining the status quo, there is a balance, particularly within liberal democratic states, in which the fear of repercussions can be countered by the fear of not changing the present situation, which is viewed as unfavourable. One former PIRA member expressed how fear operated to ensure conformity, when talking about his childhood in Belfast:

> Well all my Protestant friends were great but they'd use certain words, words that say things, like derogatory things at times, and at that age you're scared to be different I guess, so you stay silent, don't draw attention to yourself and wait 'til something else gets your attention.
>
> (Ruari, PIRA)

262   *Debra A. Smith*

Certainly experiencing a fear of being different, particularly when young, is in no way unique to a future member of a violent political organization. On the contrary, it is the normality of this experience that demonstrates how fear operates to uphold group bonds. Nevertheless, in this example it is apparent that Ruari's fear of being different is connected to his identity as a Catholic among his Protestant friends. Later in this interview, Ruari touches on the theme of fear again and once more connects it to his Catholic identity, this time in relation to his father's fear that he would have no prospects for decent work when he left school:

> [My] da said, 'ah, don't be doing the English and the maths, be doin' the woodwork, concentrate on the woodwork 'cos you're going to Canada', because, you know, we all felt the lack of opportunities for Catholics and the inequality, like my da says …. But my mum says, 'oh my son's not goin' to go nowhere', and my dad's like, 'he's not goin' to go through what we went through'.
>
> (Ruari, PIRA)

Within Northern Ireland, inter-subjective fear is also apparent in the way that people negotiate public space in a manner that reflects their identity as either Catholics or Protestants (Lysaght 2005). For example, another PIRA member reflected on his childhood:

> You had to know which was a Catholic area or a Protestant area because if you walked up the wrong street it could mean you weren't safe. I mean, you never wandered into the Shankill if you was a Catholic unless you had a death wish, just like they [Protestants] wouldn't feel safe coming to the Lower Falls. Even in the mixed areas you had to know which side of the road to walk [on] or which houses to avoid. … I don't really know how to explain it. It was just a normal part of growing up that you learnt stuff like which streets you could use and which ones to avoid or which bus stops to get off and which ones you wouldn't. … It's like a built-in radar.
>
> (Ciarán, PIRA)

The sort of diffuse fear over exclusion or employment prospects is different to more immediate fears over physical harm. But the fact that the fears discussed above are perceived as being connected to the participants' identities as Catholics provides an insight into the way in which fear is understood by these men who ultimately committed to acts of political violence. The following example shows how a vague sense of fear, unconnected to any political perception, develops into something intrinsically connected to identity:

> Well, umm, well, it's kinda hard to explain [what growing up in Belfast was like] but it's a bit like a sense that the air is thick, like everything is heavy and at the same time kind of jumpy and anxious.
>
> (Padraig, PIRA)

Terrorism, emotion and morality 263

But, when recalling the events of August 1969, when most of the houses in Bombay Street were burned to the ground by rioting Loyalists, Padraig explicitly connects the experience of fear to a threat to his community:

> the adults at the time sort of speaking in hushed tones about what was happening, with concern on their faces .... You know, you'd just feel these things as a child rather than know all the politics ... there was tension and worry and concern and stuff like that. So while we didn't really know much concrete stuff, we were aware just by the atmosphere of fear that something was wrong and was kinda threatening us and our community.
>
> (Padraig, PIRA)

In a similar vein, Liam explained how his parent's fear about the welfare of their teenage children was also imbued with a sense of panic related to the fact that they were Catholic:

> You know, my older brothers and sisters and I remember they used to go to a dance and all the rest. My parents were just waiting, just waiting for them to come home and if they weren't home there was a certain panic [that] would arise. I am sure that parents do that all the time but this was about being us, being Catholic and all, not about a car crash or stuff like that, but a fear that they had been lifted or shot by a stray bullet or stuff like that. Being young you sort of don't talk about it, you just get on with it, or you think you are getting on with it.
>
> (Liam, PIRA)

As they became older, the connection between fear, identity and oppression became more overt in the eyes of PIRA members. For example, the following recollections describe incidents that took place in the year or so prior to each particular participant joining PIRA. The first two examples refer to the policy of internment without trial, while the third refers to the experience of being raided:

> You couldn't be sure what would happen to you once internment began. You could just be goin' about ya business and you'd be lifted off the street and there was stories and all about what happened during the interrogations. I mean I heard of this fella, he was the brother of a friend of mine ya see, and I heard terrible stories about what they did to him in interrogations and his poor family, getting threatened and abused an' all, and in that August, 1971 it was, they were all Catholics that were getting lifted and it didn't matter if you were involved in anything or not you just had to live with the fear that you'd be lifted and end up in the Crum [Crumlin Road Gaol]. In the end I was lifted. I got released [...] I still remember the bloody dread of what might happen in Girdwood.
>
> (Seán, PIRA)

264   *Debra A. Smith*

7,000 Catholic families fled their homes, 7,000 *Catholic* families, not 7,000 *Protestant* families. Why do you think that was? [...] It was because the Catholics knew they were the ones who were in the firing line. The Protestants, they had active paramilitary groups at the time as well, but they didn't have to fear being lifted. That was something for the Nationalist and Republic communities to worry about, ya know.

(Ciarán, PIRA)

the soldiers kicked ya door in at 4 in the morning and that's just, that's shocking, it's just traumatizing, but they do it because that's the trained role they do ... that's shock, at 4 o'clock in the morning, it's your worst fear, and it kept you in fear you know, whether it happens again or whether it doesn't it's all the same because once you know it can happen then there's always the fear that it might. That's part of what it means being a Republican.

(Ruari, PIRA)

The combination of what would generally be viewed as an unacceptable level of everyday fear and the sense that this is experienced unequally within society according to a particular identity marker – in this case 'Catholic', 'Nationalist' or 'Republican' – reinforces a sense of social and moral distance between one section of society and the mainstream. It also imbues the mainstream with a strong sense of illegitimacy from the perspective of those who are afraid. Of course, this works in the opposite direction. We are more accustomed to talking about violent political extremists – such as those whose words and stories are set out above – as the instigators of fear, as 'terrorizing' the broader community with their acts of violence. From the perspective of the broader community it is the fear evoked by their violence that contributes to their illegitimacy as political actors. Either way, when fear becomes pervasive within the context of everyday life it can be appropriated as a tool of identity formation whereby the feared and the fearful become increasingly polarized, with social proximity eroding and social distance increasing.

Conclusion: emotions matter

Social, as opposed to physical, distance is partly an emotional construct. It reflects a failure to generate the kinds of emotions that affirm the saliency of communal bonds and responsibility to others. Even if only a small proportion of people choose to pursue their political agenda using violence, these few exist within a larger group that either accepts or is apathetic to violence perpetrated against the Other. Berezin (2002: 48–49) argues that the secure state is also the empathetic state – the one in which the 'community of feeling' is extended widely to embrace as many as possible, and where citizenship produces feelings of belonging.

The social status of subordinate groups makes it almost impossible for them to experience the 'conventionally prescribed emotions' (Jaggar 1989: 166). If this is an individual experience, it may lead to confusion, self-doubt or personal existential crisis. However, when these emotions are shared by others, particularly others who share some salient common identity, dissident emotions may become validating and a source of alternate communal bonds and alternate moral perspectives that simultaneously contribute not only to the construction of the Other, but also to the withholding of responsibility for their welfare which Bauman, following Levinas, sees as so critical to the source of moral behaviour towards others.

The examples provided above were not the result of a negative emotional experience or episode as much as a sense that the particular experiences they were having were routine and habitual, indeed familiar aspects of everyday life connected to their identity, as the following exchange with the interviewer reveals:

MÁIRTÍN: But, you know, we were resigned in so far as that was what we expected from the British, that was what we expected from the courts, we expected to be tortured when we went into Castlereagh and we expected to be brutalized when we went in the H blocks. [...]

DEBRA: How did that leave you feeling about your existing circumstances?

MÁIRTÍN: Umm, I mean, I guess contempt maybe. I'm not sure whether that's the right word though. I keep going back to the word injustice, and I know that isn't a feeling as such, but it does include a whole lot of feelings all at once. I mean, of course it is easy to feel contempt towards people who consistently cause injustices to not only you, but to your whole community. I mean if it was just to me of course I'd be angry, but when you realize it's systematic against your whole community, well that brings up more complicated feelings I think. The thing is, I think you feel as if you only have two choices. Either you accept the world around you or you don't. For me, I just felt as if I couldn't accept it. I just didn't feel at peace with the way things were, always having this sense that you are a second-class citizen in your own country. And by that I mean, not just that I felt that way, but that we all felt that way. And even worse, was that somehow you were expected not to. It's hard to explain, Debra, I mean when you ask about stuff that isn't just the obvious political stuff about representation or education or jobs. I find it difficult to explain what it actually feels like in terms of living with this sense of injustice churning away in ya guts day after day. Sometimes you can ignore it I guess, but if I really think about it I suspect that many of my decisions, many of the judgements I made were influenced by that everyday sense of injustice. That *feeling* of injustice, if you like.

An awareness or experience of discrimination, unfair treatment, lower status or threat can work to create emotional, and therefore social, distance

266   Debra A. Smith

between groups, while simultaneously increasing the emotional saliency within the group that identifies itself to be under threat (Castano *et al.* 2008: 264). The following reflections from Coilm reveal the degree to which a group of people can symbiotically construct the Other when their emotional reactions are so deeply in conflict with another section of society. In recalling the period following the death of his comrade Bobby Sands, Coilm recalled:

> And when it happened it was just this awful sense of loss, right. ... I just had a total and absolute numb day, you know. It was just like frozen in time, and the screws comin' up were all jittery. ... And you're saying to guys, 'Everybody just keep a lid on it, don't anybody be doing anything because it'll just make it worse'. ... A couple of guys had to be um, almost physically restrained from um disappearing a screw off the front of the wing, just under the cell. But you knew ... they were chirpy, and a few about the place were making remarks and yeah, celebrating it, you know. ... But when the screws behave like that it just brings you back to reality. You see the profound disrespect for us and for what we are feeling, for our loss, and it hardens you. It, I mean, it makes you draw closer together. It is like we are two different species almost. There is no connection, no human connection. It is just obvious that they was on a totally different planet.
>
> (Coilm, PIRA)

The vulgar and callous reaction by some of the prison guards to the death of such a revered comrade was demonstrable proof among the prisoners of a profound sense that these guards were the Other, 'a different species' to whom no responsibility could, or should, be extended. The extent to which a person feels part of a particular group rests partially on the way in which they see their own emotional reactions reflected in the reactions of others. Being unable to recognize your own emotional reality in the eyes of others is part of the social mechanisms that lead to the dehumanization of the Other. For the members of PIRA represented in this chapter, their emotional experiences amounted to a process of transformation in which responsibility to the Other eroded as social distance increased. However, this was not a process for which they alone were responsible. Indeed, while the responsibility towards the Other is a reciprocal responsibility, Spinoza[7] reminds us that emotions are constituted specifically in reference to perceptions of power. As a result, those with power arguably have a responsibility to recognize and acknowledge the emotions of those who have become dominated or excluded within the existing social and political order.

Notes

1 Thanks to Polity Press and Cornell University Press for granting permission to reproduce previously published material in this chapter.

Terrorism, emotion and morality 267

2 All of the names of the interview participants have been replaced with pseudonyms in order to maintain anonymity.
3 Similarly, in *Politics as vocation*, Weber (1946 [1918]: 78) argued that the three legitimate forms of domination (traditional, charismatic and legal) are determined by 'highly robust motives of fear and hope'.
4 The 2011 Northern Ireland Census revealed that 87 per cent of people who 'felt' British *and* Northern Irish had been brought up in Protestant denominations. A similar percentage of Catholics (86 per cent), however, regarded themselves as Irish and Northern Irish only (NISRA 2013).
5 Furthermore, a 2004 study commissioned by the Office of the First Minister and Deputy First Minister found that even at the age of three, Protestant children in Belfast were twice as likely to identify the Union Jack as 'their own flag' than Catholic children, while Catholic children were twice as likely to dislike the police (see Connolly and Healy 2004: 4).
6 Ed Moloney (2002: 45), in his book *A secret history of the IRA*, suggests that it was the introduction of The Eleven Plus exams by a well-meaning Labour Party swept into office after the Second World War that was one of the main catalysts for the Troubles. The opening up of social mobility within British society collided with unionist privilege in Northern Ireland, resulting in a more highly educated Catholic population with correspondingly higher economic, social and political expectations that were then stymied by discriminatory policies and practices.
7 Spinoza's account of emotion is expressed most fully in the *Ethics* (1985), particularly Part III.

References

Altheide, D.L. (2006) 'Terrorism and the politics of fear', *Critical Methodologies*, 6: 415–439.
Barbalet, J.M. (2001) *Emotion, social theory and social structure: a macrosociological approach*, Cambridge: Cambridge University Press.
Barbalet, J.M. (2006) 'Emotions in politics: from the ballot box to suicide terrorism', in S. Clarke, P. Hoggett and S. Thompson (eds), *Emotions, politics and society*, Hampshire and New York: Palgrave Macmillan.
Bauman, Z. (2000 [1989]) *Modernity and the Holocaust*, Ithaca, NY: Cornell University Press.
Bauman, Z. (2006) *Liquid fear*, Cambridge: Polity Press.
Beck, U. (1992) *Risk society, towards a new modernity*, London: Sage Publications.
Bensel, R.F. (2008) *Passion and preferences: William Jennings Bryan and the 1896 democratic national convention*, Cambridge and New York: Cambridge University Press.
Berezin, M. (2002) 'Secure states: towards a political sociology of emotions', in J.M. Barbalet (ed.), *Emotions and sociology*, Oxford: Blackwell Publishing and The Sociological Review.
Castano, E., Leidner, B., and Slawuta, P. (2008) 'Social identification processes, group dynamics and the behaviour of combatants', *International Review of the Red Cross*, 90: 259–271.
Cian (PIRA) [Anonomous interview with author 9/12/2009].
Ciarán (PIRA) [Anonomous interview with author 27/11/2009].
Clarke, S., Hoggett, P., and Thompson, S. (2006) 'The study of emotion: an introduction', in S. Clarke, P. Hoggett and S. Thompson (eds), *Emotion, politics and society*, Hampshire and New York: Palgrave Macmillan.

268   *Debra A. Smith*

Coilm (PIRA) [Anonomous interview with author 23/11/2009].

Connolly, P., and Healy, J. (2004) *Children and the conflict in Northern Ireland: the experiences and perspectives of 3–11 year olds*, Stormont, Belfast: OFMDFM Equality Directorate.

Connor, J. (2007) *The sociology of loyalty*, New York: Springer.

Cook, D., and Alison, O. (2007) *Understanding and addressing suicide attacks*, London: Praeger Security International.

Cooley, C.H. (1964 [1922]) *Human nature and the social order*, New York: Schocken Books.

Cropanzano, R., Stein, J.H., and Nadisic, T. (2011) *Social justice and the experience of emotions*, New York and Sussex: Routledge.

Eamon (PIRA) [Anonomous interview with athor 16/12/2009].

Elias, N. (1982) *The civilizing process* (Vol. 2), New York: Vintage.

Fattah, K., and Fierke, K. (2009) 'A clash of emotions: the politics of humiliation and political violence in the Middle East', *European Journal of International Relations*, 25: 67–93.

Flam, H. (2005), '"Emotions" map: a research agenda', in H. Flam and D. King (eds), *Emotions and social movements*, New York: Routledge.

Frijda, N., and Mesquita, B. (2000) 'Beliefs through emotions', in N. Frijda, A.S.R. Manstead and S. Bem (eds), *Emotions and beliefs: how feelings influence thoughts*, Cambridge: Cambridge University Press.

Gilbert, P. (1997) 'The evolution of social attractiveness and its role in shame, humiliation, guilt, and therapy', *Journal of Medical Psychology*, 70: 113–147.

Grodzins, M. (1956) *The loyal and the disloyal: social boundaries of patriotism and treason*, Chicago, IL: Chicago University Press.

Hearn, J. (1993) 'Emotive subjects: organizational men, organizational masculinities and the (de)construction of "emotions"', in S. Fineman (ed.), *Emotion in organizations*, London: Sage.

Hirschman, A. (1970) *Exit, voice, and loyalty: responses to decline in firms, organizations, and states*, Cambridge: Harvard University Press.

Hobbes, T. (1991[1651]) 'The citizen: philosophical rudiments concerning government and society', *Man and citizen (De Homine and De Cive)*, Indianapolis, IN: Hackett.

Hochschild, A.R. (1983) *The managed heart: the commercialization of human feeling*, Berkeley, CA: University of California Press.

Hoggett, P. (2009) *Politics, identity, and emotion*, Boulder, CO and London: Paradigm Publishers.

Holmes, M. (2004) 'The importance of being angry: anger in political life', *European Journal of Social Theory*, 7: 123–132.

Jaggar, A.M. (1989) 'Love and knowledge: emotion in feminist epistemology', *Inquiry: An Interdisciplinary Journal of Philosophy*, 32: 151–176.

Kemper, T. (1978) 'Towards a sociology of emotions: some problems and some solutions', *The American Sociologist*, 13: 30–41.

Kemper, T. (2001) 'A structural approach to social movement emotions', in J. Goodwin, J.M. Jasper and F. Polletta (eds), *Passionate politics: emotions and social movements*, Chicago, IL and London: The University of Chicago Press.

Klein, D.C. (1991) 'The humiliation dynamic: an overview', *The Journal of Primary Prevention*, 12: 93–122.

Liam (PIRA) [Anonomous interview with author 24/11/2009].

Lyman, P. (2004) 'The domestication of anger: the use and abuse of anger in politics', *European Journal of Social Theory*, 7: 133–147.

Lysaght, K.D. (2005) 'Catholics, Protestants and office workers from town: the experience and negotiation of fear in Northern Ireland', in K. Milton and M. Svasek (eds), *Mixed emotions: anthropological studies of feeling*, Oxford and New York: Berg.

Machiavelli, N. (1986 [1532]) *The prince*, Middlesex: Penguin Books.

Massumi, B. (ed.) (1993) *The politics of everyday fear*, Minneapolis and London: University of Minnesota Press.

Mick (PIRA) [Anonomous interview with author 1/12/2009].

Moghaddam, F. (2005) 'The staircase to terrorism: a psychological exploration', *American Psychologist*, 60: 161–169.

Moghaddam, F. (2006) *From the terrorist's point of view: what they experience and why they come to destroy*, Westport, CT and London: Praeger Security International.

Moïsi, D. (2009) *The geopolitics of emotion: how cultures of fear, humiliation, and hope are reshaping the world*, New York, London, Toronto, Sydney, Auckland: Doubleday.

Moloney, E. (2002) *A secret history of the IRA*, London: The Penguin Press.

Mythen, G., and Walklate, S. (2006) 'Communicating the terrorist risk: harnessing a culture of fear?', *Crime Media Culture*, 2: 123–142.

NISRA (2013) *Detailed characteristics for Northern Ireland on identity, religion and health*, Belfast: Northern Ireland Statistics and Research Agency, online, available: www.nisra.gov.uk/Census/2011_results_detailed_characteristics.html (accessed 14 January 2015).

Padraig (PIRA) [Anonomous interview with author 8/12/2009].

Robin, C. (2004) *Fear: the history of a political idea*, Oxford: Oxford University Press.

Rose, R. (1971) *Governing without consensus: an Irish perspective*, London: Faber and Faber Ltd.

Ruari (PIRA) [Anonomous interview with author 7/12/2009].

Scheff, T.J. (1988) 'Shame and conformity: the deference-emotion system', *American Sociological Review*, 53: 395–406.

Schwartz, S.J., Dunkel, C.S. and Waterman, A.S. (2009) 'Terrorism: an identity theory perspective', *Studies in Conflict and Terrorism*, 32: 537–559.

Seán (PIRA) [Anonomous interview with author 17/12/2009].

Simmel, G. (1950 [1908]) 'Faithfulness and gratitude', in K. Wolff (ed.), *The sociology of Georg Simmel*, New York: The Free Press.

Sparks, C. (2003) 'Liberalism, terrorism and the politics of fear', *Politics*, 23: 200–206.

Speckhard, A. (2005) 'Understanding suicide terrorism: countering human bombs and their senders', in J.S. Purcell and J.D. Weintraub (eds), *Topics in terrorism: towards a transatlantic consensus on the nature of the threat* (Vol. 2), Washington, WA: Atlantic Council.

Spinoza (1985), *Ethics* (E. Curley, trans.), *The collected writings of Spinoza, vol. 1*, Princeton, NJ: Princeton University Press.

Thucydides (1982 [1866]) *The Peloponnesian war* (R. Crawley, trans.), New York: Modern Library.

Weber, M. (1946 [1918]) 'Politics as vocation', in H.H. Gerth and C.C. Wright Mills (eds), *From Max Weber: essays in sociology*, New York: Oxford University Press.

Weber, M. (2003 [1904/5]) *The Protestant ethic and the spirit of capitalism*, New York: Dover Publications.

Williams, R. (1977) *Marxism and literature*, Oxford: Oxford University Press.

Zhu, J., and Thagard, P. (2002) 'Emotion and action', *Philosophical Psychology*, 15: 19–36.

Index

7/7 London bombings, 136

Aboriginal Family Violence Prevention and Legal Service, Victoria, Australia 242
Adam Walsh Child Protection and Safety Act 2006, US 218
'adiaphorization' 2, 53, 112, 119–120, 187, 247
Alexander, Michelle 55–6
altruism 60
ambivalence surrounding immigration detention: concept of 145–6, 149; examples of 159–161
anger, among PIRA members 255–7
Anti-Social Behaviour, Crime and Policing Act 2014, UK 223
assimilation 234
asylum seekers 148, 151, 152, 153, 196
audit society 107, 116–17, 166 *see also* bureaucracy

Bauman, Zygmunt, 11, 14, 16–17, 20, 21, 30, 51, 52–53, 79, 125, 126–127, 149–150, 169–170, 185, 186, 196, 208–209, 230, 232, 237–238, 247–248
Bayley, Adrian 84–5
'Beast of Blenheim' *see Wilson, Stewart Murray*
belonging 201, 240, 249, 251–253
Bill of Rights Act, NZ 220–1
border control: harms of 125, 127, 150, 187–8, 199; attitudes towards 152; in Sweden 197–8; unjust nature of 127
border research 188
Breivik, Anders Behring 86
Brown v Platt 32, 34–5, 42–6

bureaucracy: as an enabler of the Holocaust 14, 57, 186; as an enabler of the social production of immorality 52–3, 103; bureaucratization in relation to REVA 196, 197; as an enabler of distantiation 169–70; in relation to 'funnel' policies 165–6, 166–7; in Swedish migration management 196–8; Bauman's concept of, in relation to population registries in Sweden 185
Bush, George W., former US President 65

Cakes, Gordon, Member for Bolton, UK 146
CCTV 110, 225 *see also* surveillance
censuses 192
Cheney, US Vice-President Dick 60
citizenship: as a basis for discrimination 138–9; fluid nature of 151; as a basis for discrimination 125, 127–8, 138; loss of *see* denaturalization; *see also* non-citizens; nationality
classification: according to citizenship status 125; during the Holocaust 189; of foreignness within Swedish population registries 192–4, 195–6; according to citizenship status; racial 37; as an enabler of distantiation and the social production of immorality 138, 185, 189–90; in relation to REVA, 202; *see also* population registries in Sweden
colonialism 230–1, 235–8, 239
community justice 67–8
constitutional law 31
control: measures in prisons 111–12; policies in Norway 165, 173–4, 178; *see also* security; 'security sanctions'

Index   271

counter-terrorism 129, 132, 136; *see also* terrorism
Crimes (Serious Sexual Offenders) Amendment Bill 2013, Australia, 219
crimes *see* offences
Criminal Justice Act 2003, UK 218
Criminals Return into Society Sweden, 106
crimmigration 129–130, 166, 190

Dangerous Prisoners (Sexual Offenders) Act 2003, Australia 218
degradation 53–4, 199–200, 201–2 *see also* humiliation; punishment
denaturalization 37–8, 136
deportation: effects of 151, 201–2; in Norway 171–2; in relation to exclusion 187; in Sweden 196, 197, 198, 202–3; in the UK 133–4, 135, 136, 156; rates in Sweden 195; views of, among immigration detainees 152; *see also* denaturalization
Diaspora 239
dignity 44, 54
discrimination 138; against non-citizens 138; based on class 128; racial 21, 56, 127, 128, 184–5; *see also* citizenship, as a basis for discrimination
distantiation: as a product of 'funnel policies,' 177–8; as a product of classification 185; as part of US prison officer training 56–7; Bauman's account of 14, 52–3, 169–70, 247–8; during the Holocaust 209; in prisons 24–5; in relation to anger 257; in relation to emotions 250; in relation to fear 264; between prisoners and prison staff, 94; in relation to shame 260; in relation to views of human nature 59; rise in the US prison system 58; towards foreigners and migrants 187–8; towards prisoners 78, 79–83; see also Bauman, Zygmunt; exclusion; Othering; social production of immorality

Eichmann, Adolf 22
Elias, Norbert 257
emotions 248, 249–50; as common to a group, 265–6
emotions see also anger
ethnic enumeration: in the US 191–2; nature of 191; *see also* ethnicity
ethnicity 192; relationship to foreignness 192–3; relationship to race 191–2;

understandings of 191; *see also* ethnic enumeration; foreignness
EU Charter of Fundamental Rights 199
EU law 198–9
'evolving standards of decency': concept of 32; in case law 35–6; in relation to *Brown v. Plata* 44, 45; in relation to *Harmelin v. Michigan* 38, 39, 41, 42; in relation to *Trop v. Dulles* 37
exclusion: in relation to Swedish population registries, 190–1; of Catholics in Northern Ireland 252, 254; in relation to terrorism, 249; of the Roma in Norway 175; of foreigners and non-citizens, 187; of sex offenders, 220; of the Other, 209–10; *see also* Othering

fear, among PIRA members 261–4
fluid borders, 129, 130
folkhemmet, concept of, 190–1
foreign national prisoners 130, 131, 134, 137; in Britain, 131, 132–3; in Italy, 131; in the US, 131; numbers of, 134; *see also* foreigners; prisoners
foreigners: deportation of, 187–8; exclusion of, 187; classification of, 185; criminalization of, 131–9; impact of immigration status on, 125–9; *see also* ethnicity; foreignness
foreignness recorded in Swedish population registries, 192–4, 195–6
Foucault, Michel, 167, 176
Fraser, Nancy, 124–125
Freud, Sigmund, 149
'funnel' policies: definition of, 165–6, 175–7; targeted at Roma in Norway, 166–8, 174, 177–9; *see also* bureaucracy

gay marriage 60, 61
globalization 124, 166
governable space 167, 175
governmentality 167, 176–7

Harmelin v Michigan, 35–6, 38–42
Himmler, Heinrich, 21, 23
Holocaust, 14–16, 29, 52, 186; killings during, 17–20, 21; research into, 11, 12
Hook, Derek, 237–8
Hoss, Rudolf, 19
Hudson, Barbara, 124
human rights: in constitutional law, 32; law, 4, 31, 44, 47, 138; of prisoners, 97;

272 *Index*

protections, 37, 54; violations of, 30–1, 34–5, 36, 41, 45, 188, 225
humiliation, 259–61; *see also* degradation

ideology, 15
Immigration Appeals Act 1969, UK, 146, 147
immigration control, management of, in the UK, 148; *see also* immigration detention; migration checks
immigration detainees, in the UK: attitudes towards detention, 148–9; children, 158–9; experiences of detention, 152–5; in the UK, 148; makeup of, 148; treatment of, 152–9, 153; *see also* immigration control; immigration detention
immigration detention: in the UK, 145–61; comparison with prisons, 153–5; history of, in the UK, 146–8; purpose of, 145; *see also* immigration detainees; immigration detention staff
immigration detention staff, attitudes towards detention, 148, 152, 155–9
immigration law, 134–7, 147–8
Immigration Removal Centres, UK, 147; management of, 157
immobilization, 209–10, 220, 222–3
imprisonment: aims of, 88; mass, 31, 33–5, 47, 51, 52–3, 55, 70, 231; of Indigenous Australians, 238–9; rates in the US, 55; *see also* foreign national prisoners; indefinite detention; Indigenous people; Indigenous Australians; prisoners; prisons
indefinite detention, 217, 218, 218–219, 221; rates of, 222–3
Indigenous Australians, 230; colonization of, by settlers, 235–8; imprisonment of, 238–9
imprisonment rates for, 234–5; killings by settlers, 236; *see also* Indigenous people
Indigenous people: colonization of, 230–3; in Sweden, 193–4; mass imprisonment of, 233–5; overrepresentation of, in prisons, 234; *see also* Indigenous Australians
'Indigenous place,' 233, 239–40, 242
insecurity, 209–10, 224
international law, 136

Justice Fellowship, 66
justice reinvestment, 64
justice, theories of, 124–5

Karlton, Judge Lawrence, 42
Kennedy, Justice, 39–40, 41, 43–4
Khemeri, Jonas Hassen, 200–1
Kimberley Aboriginal Law and Culture, 242
Kristof, Nicholas, 55

labour camps in Norway, 171
Labour Party, Norway, 172
legal civilizing process, 4, 32, 42, 44, 47
legal residents, 128
less eligibility, 55, 176
'liquid modernity,' 7–8, 209, 230, 232, 243
loyalty, among PIRA members, 250–5

Machiavelli, Niccolo, 250
Madrid v. Gomez, 25–6
March, James, 12–13
Meagher, Jill, murder of, 84
Merton, Robert, 149
migration checks: in Sweden, 185, 195, 196, 198, 199–200; in the UK, 135
Milgram, Stanley, 11, 16–17
mobility, 124, 188, 199, 209, 216, 232
Monroe, Kristen, 60
morality: in Bauman's Holocaust theory, 14–16, 52, 127, 170, 186; in relation to border control, 188; in relation to terrorism, 247; in relation to classification, 185; in relation to immigration detention, 158; in relation to terrorism, 248–9; in relation to treatment of the Roma, 178; relevance of Bauman's account of, for imprisonment, 79; *see also* social production of immorality
Moreton-Robinson, Aileen, 240
Morning, Ann, 191–2
My Brother's Keeper initiative, 62–3

National Association for Humanizing the Correctional Service, Sweden, 104
National Reception Units, Sweden, 108–9
National Socialism, 22
nationalism, 186
nationality, 125, 138–9, 151; *see also* citizenship
neo-liberalism, 101, 102, 166; desire for order, 149; Foucault on, 176; impact on Indigenous people, 7–8; in Norway, 166, 177; in relation to mobility, 188; in relation to restorative justice, 67; in

Sweden, 101, 102, 103, 106–7, 119–20; prison management based on, 5–6
New Public Management, 116–17, 197
New Zealand Bail Amendment Act 2012, 219
non-citizens, 127–9; criminalization of, 131–9; discriminatory treatment of, 129; impact of Westphalian model of justice on, 125; in Norway, 171; *see also* citizenship; foreigners
Nordic exceptionalism, 78–9, 101, 171
Northern Ireland, history of, 251

Obama, President Barack, 62
offences: begging in Norway, 170, 171, 172; begging in the EU, 188; counter-terrorism, 132; drug, 39–42, 61, 131; fraud, 131–2; sexual, 210, 211; status-based, 129, 131, 133, 136
Ohlendorf, Otto, 21–2
Olsen, Johan, 12–13
Oombulgurri community, 241
Operation Nexus, Britain, 135–6
Othering: in relation to collective emotions, 266; during the Holocaust, 208–9; in prisons, 24–6; of sex offenders, 210; role of ideology in, 20–24; techniques of, 11, 17–20; in relation to liberalism, 126–7; in relation to training of prison officers, 56–7; influence of view of human nature on, 59; of excluded groups, 264–5; of foreigners in Sweden, 185, 187, 199, 202; of prisoners, 51, 78, 79–83, 119–20; of the Indigenous Other, 239; understood according to definitions of the Other, 170; *see also* Bauman, Zygmunt; distantiation; exclusion; social production of immorality

parole, 84–6, 211, 219
participatory justice, 68–9
Penal Code, Norway, 171
Personal Officer Reform, Sweden, 105, 112–13, 118
population registries in Sweden, 185, 190–4; *see also* classification
Portman, US Senator Rob, 60
postcolonialism, 230–2
'postcolonial turn,' 231
Prison Litigation Reform Act 1996, US, 43, 45
prison research, 13, 24

prison staff: attitudes towards among prisoners and the public, 86–7; special security, 109–10; training/qualifications of, 56–7, 87–8, 114, 115–116, 118; *see also* prisoners; prisons
prisoner re-entry movement, 63–4
prisoners: decisions made about, 92–3; illness among, 34; in Australia, 81; in Norway, 81; interactions with staff, 90–7; mental illness among, 34; mistreatment of, 42; orders given to, 92; racial overrepresentation, 33–4; searching of, 112; smoking among, 112; treatment of, 89–90; treatment programmes for, 85, 113–14; *see also* foreign national prisoners; prisons; prison staff
prisons: comparison between Australia and Norway, 82–98; comparison between Europe and the US, 46–7; escapes from, 83–4; high-security, 84, 111; in Australia, 82–6; in Europe, 32; in Sweden, 103–20; in the US, 25, 30–2; life inside, 77, 79–83; open, 83–4; overcrowding in, 34, 43; supermax, 25; Swedish, 25; *see also* foreign national prisoners; prisoners; prison staff
protection of society, 102–3, 215–19, 220–2; *see also* risk; security; 'security sanctions'
Provisional Irish Republican Army, 251–66
proximity, 60, 82, 90, 115, 187, 200, 250, 254
punishment: based on membership/status, 138; in relation to 'security sanctions,' 220; in the form of degradation, 199–200, 201–2, 210; nature of, 171, 177; via non-criminal law, 135; *see also* degradation; humiliation

rehabilitation: as an aim of imprisonment, 88; decline of, since the 1970s, 58; in Nordic exceptionalism, 5–6, 101, 102; in the Norwegian prison system, 81; in the Swedish prison system, 103–4, 105, 109, 113–115, 116; in the US prison system, 64–5
remand, 133
restorative justice, 66–7
REVA, 185–6, 195–203; criticism of, 198; policy justifications for, 196–7
Right on Crime group, 64–5
risk, 102, 106, 108–9; posed by offenders, 212–14, 215–22; society, 209

274   *Index*

Roma in Norway, 165–79; begging among, 170, 171; camps, 173–4; deprivation of means to live among, 175; history/background of, 168; Romanian, 169
Roma Registries, Sweden, 194
Rose, Nikolas, 167–8, 175

Second Chance Act 2007, 61
security 107–12 *see also* risk; 'security sanctions'
'security sanctions,' 220–2 *see also* security
Sentencing Act 2002, NZ, 223
September 11, 2001 attack on World Trade Centre, 136
Sexual Offences Act 2003, UK, 218
sexual offenders, 210, 220, 222–3, 224
Sexually Violent Predator Law 1990, US, 218
shame, among PIRA members, 257–61
Shell protection, 110–11
Smarter Sentencing Act, US, 62
social distance *see* distantiation
social production of immorality, 14–16, 19, 52, 127, 185, 186–7, 208, 248; in Sweden, 198; *see also* Bauman, Zygmunt; distantiation; morality; Othering

solitary confinement, 24, 25, 32
Statistics Sweden, 192–193
Stier, Walter, 14–15
surveillance, 224–5; *see also* CCTV
Swedish migration policy, 196–7

terrorism: association between foreigners and, 136; label of, 8, 247; in relation to morality, 247, 248–9; offences, 250; *see also* counter-terrorism
'total institutions,' 79–82
Travis, Jeremy, 63
Trop v Dulles, 35, 36–8

Universal Declaration of Human Rights, 37
US Constitution, 31–2, 37; Eighth Amendment, 36, 37, 39–42, 43–4

Vagrancy Act, Norway, 170–1, 172

Warren, Earl, Chief Justice, 35, 37, 38
welfare state, 103–5
Westphalian model, 124, 125, 129, 238
Whitman, James, 199–200
Wilson, James Q., 58–59
Wilson, Stewart Murray, 211–17; media portrayals of, 211–15